W9-CFB-860

EatingWell®
VEGETABLES
THE ESSENTIAL REFERENCE

HOUGHTON MIFFLIN HARCOURT
BOSTON • NEW YORK • 2016

Rocky River Public Library

EatingWell®

President, Women's Lifestyle Group: Thomas Witschi

Editor-in-Chief: Jessie Price

Creative Director: James Van Fleteren

Food Editor: Jim Romanoff

Managing Editor: Wendy S. Ruopp

Nutrition Editor: Brierley Wright, M.S., R.D.

Senior Food Editor: Carolyn Malcoun

Test Kitchen Manager: Stacy Fraser

Associate Food Editor: Breana Lai, M.P.H., R.D.

Recipe Developer & Tester: Carolyn Casner

Nutrition Consultant: Jill Cerreta, M.S., R.D.

Art Director: Marla Emmighausen

Research Editor: Anne Treadwell

Associate Nutrition Editor: Julia Westbrook

Editorial Assistant: Lucy M. Casale

EatingWell Vegetables

Project Editor: Lisa Kingsley, Waterbury Publications, Inc.

Contributing Editor: Tricia Bergman, Waterbury Publications, Inc.

Contributing Editor & Stylist: Annie Peterson, Waterbury Publications, Inc.

Contributing Copy Editor and Proofreader: Peg Smith, Gretchen Kauffman

Principal Photographers: Karla Conrad, Helen Norman

Contributing Photographers: Erica Allen, Peter Ardito, Maryellen Baker, Noel Barnhurst, Leigh Beisch, Ken Burris, Penny De Los Santos, Michael Graydon & Nikole Herriott, Carin Krasner, Bryan McCay, Wendi Nordeck, Felicia Perretti, Laurie Proffitt, Andrew Scrivani, Ellen Silverman, Joe Vaughn, Jim Westphalen

Cover Photo: Helen Norman

Design Director: Ken Carlson, Waterbury Publications, Inc.

Associate Design Director: Doug Samuelson, Waterbury Publications, Inc.

Production Assistant: Mindy Samuelson, Waterbury Publications, Inc.

Houghton Mifflin Harcourt

Publisher: Natalie Chapman

Editorial Director: Cindy Kitchel

Executive Editor: Anne Ficklen

Editorial Associate: Molly Aronica

Managing Editor: Marina Padakis Lowry

Art Director: Tai Blanche

Production Director: Tom Hyland

Copyright © 2016 by Meredith Corporation, Des Moines, Iowa.

All rights reserved.

For information about permission to reproduce selections from this book, write to trade.permissions@hmhco.com or to Permissions, Houghton Mifflin Harcourt Publishing Company, 3 Park Avenue, 19th Floor, New York, New York 10016.

www.hmhco.com

Library of Congress Cataloging-in-Publication Data is available

ISBN 978-0-544-71528-8 (hbk)

ISBN 978-0-544-71531-8 (ebk)

Book design by Waterbury Publications, Inc., Des Moines, Iowa.

Printed in China

SCP 10 9 8 7 6 5 4 3 2 1

*Heirloom Tomato Salad
with Fried Capers*
(see recipe, page 463)

CONTENTS

12 Artichokes
20 Arugula
28 Asparagus
38 Avocado
48 Beans, shell
58 Beans, snap
70 Beets
80 Bok choy
88 Broccoli
100 Broccoli rabe
110 Brussels sprouts
120 Cabbage
134 Carrots
148 Cauliflower
160 Celery
168 Celery root
178 Chard
188 Chicories
202 Collard greens
210 Corn
220 Cucumbers
232 Eggplant
244 Fennel
252 Garlic
262 Jerusalem artichokes
268 Jicama

274 Kale
286 Kohlrabi
292 Lettuces & Salad Greens
304 Mushrooms
318 Mustard greens
324 Okra
334 Onions
350 Parsnips
356 Peas
370 Peppers
382 Potatoes
396 Radishes
406 Spinach
414 Squash, summer
426 Squash, winter
440 Sweet potatoes
450 Tomatillos
460 Tomatoes
474 Turnips & Rutabagas
484 Watercress
492 Yuca
498 Resources
503 Index
515 Contributors

CRAZY FOR VEGETABLES!

When you walk through a farmers' market, do you stop and admire the piles of radishes, the bundles of greens and the assorted peppers? In early summer, do you count the days until the first local tomatoes are juicy and ripe? Have you ever wondered how peppery arugula dressed with nothing more than good olive oil, Parmesan and sea salt can taste so darned amazing? For us, the answer to all these questions is a resounding "yes!" At *EatingWell*, we are crucifer crusaders, salad maniacs, crazy for carrots, in love with beets. After all, there's no other food group besides vegetables that has such delicious diversity of taste, color and texture.

We've been on a vegetable kick at *EatingWell* since we began more than 20 years ago. We celebrate vegetables in feature stories, share new ways to cook them and splash them across the cover of the magazine. Why so much focus on vegetables? It's partly that we're all about healthy cooking. But it's also that in Vermont, where *EatingWell* got its start, we are surrounded by farms growing some of the most outstanding specimens you can imagine. Just down the road from our office, a small farm grows a mix of salad greens that we can buy the day they're harvested and never get the same blend twice. One day we'll find herbs and edible flowers among the greens;

SUNRISE OVER VERMONT
EatingWell's home is in the fertile Champlain Valley of Vermont. The scene here is looking back at the Green Mountains from the Essex, New York, farm owned by former governor George Pataki. The farm raises antibiotic-free grass-fed beef and vegetables.

Roasted Cauliflower Salad with Walnuts
(see recipe, page 158)

the next, peppery mustards and baby kales. Farmers across the state invest in hoop houses to prolong the growing season for cold-loving crops like kale and chard. Root storage for beauties like beets, parsnips and kohlrabi has become an art form. Wherever we turn, there's inspiration.

In the *EatingWell* Test Kitchen, the chatter is about what's new in the produce aisle, what's in our editors' weekly community supported agriculture (CSA) shares, strategies for shopping farmers' markets and new ideas for pickling and preserving. Of course, it's not all food chitchat. There's the serious part of what we do in our Test Kitchen—recipe creation and testing to make sure our recipes work for you, are healthful and truly delicious. After all, we're here because we love food. If it doesn't taste great, it doesn't get published!

This book brings together our most delicious vegetable recipes from over the years. As with any *EatingWell* collection, this assortment is so cool because the recipes come from an array of people—cookbook authors, chefs, recipe developers, bloggers and our own editors—each with different backgrounds and culinary expertise. For example, on page 236 Mediterranean expert Nancy Harmon Jenkins transports us to Sicily with her eggplant caponata laced with hot chile peppers, olives, parsley and basil. Then on page 158 *(see photo, opposite)* you can sample the cauliflower salad with walnuts that James Beard Award-winning chef Michael Solomonov serves at Zahav, his restaurant in Philadelphia. You'll find a take on lasagna baked in a spaghetti squash that was developed by associate food editor Breana Lai on page 436. And there are over 200 recipes in between.

YOUR MOM WAS RIGHT. YOU SHOULD EAT THEM!
What eating well means is balance, not strict dictates. We're happy to enjoy a slice of pie or a little bacon. Instead of worrying about restricting the so-called "bad stuff," we fill up our plates with the good stuff. For dinner, that often means a salad as well as a side of vegetables. After that, the remaining space just isn't that big. A little bit of protein and perhaps a whole grain round out the meal.

Sounds healthy, right? Well, this isn't the way most of us eat. Ninety percent of Americans don't eat enough vegetables, according to the USDA. And things seem to be getting worse—U.S. per capita consumption of vegetables has actually gone down 7 percent in the last five years, according to a 2015 study from the Produce for Better Health Foundation. The recommended amount for everyone age 9 and up is two to three servings a day. (For most vegetables, like green beans, a serving is 1 cup. For raw leafy vegetables, like salad greens, a serving is 2 cups.)

All the fuss over getting enough veggies in your day is partly about the nutrients—in particular, fiber, potassium, folate and vitamin A. Most Americans don't get enough of these nutrients. Each one plays an important role in your health: Potassium helps regulate blood pressure, folate helps create new red blood cells, fiber can help with cholesterol levels and weight management, and vitamin A is key to keeping eyes healthy.

Another big reason to eat more veggies—your weight. Because most veggies are low-cal relative to other foods, when you fill up on them you naturally crowd out higher-calorie, less-healthful foods. In one recent study, people who ate five 1- to 2-cup servings of vegetables a day lost more weight in three months than their counterparts who ate half that amount. Researchers also concluded that this way of eating could be sustained over time, as opposed to a quick weight-loss fix.

If we would collectively eat more vegetables to shed pounds and reverse obesity trends, we'd change a lot more than the size of our belts. Right now, one in four deaths in the U.S. is caused by heart disease and 27 million Americans have type 2 diabetes. Both diseases, along with stroke and certain types of cancer, are correlated with obesity. These are preventable causes of death. In other words, changes in diet and lifestyle (eating more vegetables!) can correct these problems.

In addition to improving health, eating a whole lot more vegetables and less of everything else can lighten our impact on the planet. According to the Environmental Working Group, producing a kilogram of beef creates about 13 times more carbon emissions than a kilogram of broccoli.

And there are other impacts besides carbon. A 2009 study that compared vegetarian diets to meat-eating diets shows that an omnivore diet requires 2.9 times more water, 2.5 times more energy, 13 times more fertilizer and 1.4 times more pesticides.

HOW THIS BOOK WORKS

Now that we're clear on all the reasons you should be as crazy for vegetables as we are, let's talk a little about how to use this book. This is a reference book as well as a cookbook. It's organized alphabetically and each chapter is devoted to a different vegetable or group of vegetables. Driven by culinary considerations, we made judgment calls about which are clustered together. For example, romanesco (sometimes also called broccoflower) falls in the same botanical family as both cauliflower and broccoli. We include it in the cauliflower chapter because it cooks similarly to cauliflower. (If you have trouble finding a vegetable, flip to the index.) We also use the word "vegetables" liberally and include plenty of fruits, such as avocado and tomatoes, that tend to be used like vegetables.

Each chapter begins with basic information about the vegetable, what to look for, how to store and prep it. For several that are especially rewarding to grow, such as lettuce and summer squash, we include basic gardening advice. Then we get to cooking. You'll find a couple of our favorite simplest techniques for busy nights (we all have them) when you just want to know, for example, what temp and for how long you need to roast mushrooms. These techniques often involve nothing more than a little oil, salt and pepper. In some cases we add a tiny adornment—an herb, a splash of soy sauce or vinegar. Embellish with these basics at will.

Beyond basic technique, you'll find the recipes, ordered from simplest to more involved. Recipes span sides, salads, appetizers, soups and main courses. Some are vegetarian (check the index on page 514 to find those). All are vegetable-forward, like the frittata on page 185. It's loaded with chard and seasoned with just a bit of chorizo for a savory, spicy hit.

What we've found over the years, and what compiling this book reminds us of, is that the more you cook with vegetables the more you want to keep exploring. Say stir-fried carrots are already a regular in your house. Next up, try that technique with broccoli stems. If you've learned how to make your own dill pickles (page 227), how about spicy Mexican-style pickled carrots (page 140)?

Loving vegetables is easy when you know how to prepare them well. When you dress a salad with a zingy vinaigrette or sprinkle roasted cauliflower with savory herbs, loading up your plate with the good stuff is a pleasure. We all know that we should eat our veggies. With this book in hand it's going to be a matter of want, not should.

Jessie Price

Editor-in-Chief, *EatingWell*

Artichokes

The outward appearance of the artichoke is arguably intimidating, but it is actually one of the most beautiful forms found in nature: a flower bud. Artichokes are the unopened buds of a type of thistle that thrives in warm, sunny, temperate climates. As an ornamental plant, artichokes can grow to a height of 6 feet. The buds bloom into large, vibrant purple flowers.

Artichokes are common throughout the Mediterranean and North Africa. In the United States, nearly all commercially grown artichokes come from the area around Castroville, California. Artichokes vary in size. "Baby" artichokes are fully mature but grew farther down on the stem, in shadier conditions than their larger counterparts. They do not contain a choke (see page 14).

Artichokes can be steamed, boiled, braised, roasted, grilled or stuffed and baked. Cooking renders the base of each fibrous leaf meltingly tender. When dipped in melted butter or a savory sauce, each one becomes a delicacy. The Mediterranean origins of artichokes make them good companions to other ingredients and flavors from that part of the world—lemon, garlic, tarragon, parsley, oregano, capers, olive oil, aïoli, Parmesan and pecorino cheeses and pine nuts. Artichokes are synonymous with spring and pair well with other vegetables—peas, asparagus, fennel, fava beans, mushrooms and new potatoes—that offer the delicate flavors and tender bites of that season.

The season for artichokes begins in March, peaks in midspring, wanes in summer and then returns in the fall for a second but less prolific season.

Best in spring

AT THE MARKET

➳ Choose artichokes that are firm and heavy, with tightly closed heads and no brown spots. There is no flavor difference between small and large artichokes, so choose the size that is best for the recipe you are preparing or for the way you plan to serve them. To test for freshness, press the leaves together. A squeaking sound indicates that the artichoke is fresh.

➳ Although some unusual and heirloom varieties are grown by small producers, nearly all of the artichokes at the market are the Green Globe variety.

IN YOUR KITCHEN

➳ Store artichokes up to 4 days in a plastic bag in the refrigerator. Rinse under cold running water right before using.

➳ Snip off the thorn of each leaf using kitchen shears. Trim the bottom of the stem, then cut off about 1 inch off the top of the artichoke. Use a spoon to scoop out the fuzzy "choke" that sits right over the heart.

➳ As you clean and trim each artichoke, place in a large bowl of cold water along with the juice and rind halves of a lemon to prevent the artichoke from turning brown.

COOKING BASICS

BAKE/BRAISE Cut off the stem end of each trimmed and prepared artichoke to make a flat bottom. Sauté garlic in olive oil in a large pot. Add 2 cups low-sodium chicken broth and 1 tablespoon lemon juice; bring to a simmer. Carefully stand artichokes upright in pan. Drizzle with olive oil and season with salt and pepper. Cover and bake in a 375°F oven until tender, about 50 minutes. Uncover and continue baking about 10 minutes more. Remove from braising liquid. Serve with braising liquid for dipping.

GRILL Place each trimmed and prepared artichoke in a large pot with water to cover and juice of 1 lemon. Cover and bring to a boil; cook until the stem is tender when pierced with a fork, 12 to 15 minutes. Let cool; cut in half lengthwise and remove the choke and the first few inner leaves. Brush with olive oil and sprinkle with salt and pepper. Grill over medium heat until tender and lightly charred, about 5 minutes per side. Serve with lemon wedges.

STEAM Place trimmed and prepared artichokes stem-end up in a steamer basket over 2 inches of water in a large, deep pot. Bring water to boil over high heat. Cover and steam until the stem is are tender when pierced with a fork, 25 to 30 minutes for medium artichokes.

NUTRITION

➳ **1 medium artichoke: Calories** 64, **Fat** 0g (sat 0g), **Cholesterol** 0mg, **Carbs** 14g, **Total sugars** 1g (added 0g), **Protein** 3g, **Fiber** 7g, **Sodium** 72mg, **Potassium** 343mg.

BONUS Artichokes contain a type of fiber called inulin, which encourages healthy gut bacteria that can help prevent colon cancer and keep you regular.

How to prep

1. Snip the thorn off each leaf using kitchen shears. Trim the bottom of the stem or cut it off using a sharp chef's knife.

2. Cut off about 1 inch from the top of the artichoke.

3. Remove the fuzzy "choke" with a spoon *(right)*.

ARTICHOKES WITH LEMON & DILL

ACTIVE: 20 MIN **TOTAL:** 50 MIN

TO MAKE AHEAD: Prepare through Step 3. Refrigerate up to 2 days. Bring to room temperature before serving.

These simply prepared artichokes can be served at room temperature or chilled. Serve as a first course or as a side dish with grilled chicken or fish.

4 large lemons, divided, plus more for garnish	¼ cup chopped fresh dill, plus more for garnish
8 large artichokes	1 teaspoon salt
2 cups water	¼ teaspoon ground pepper
6 cloves garlic, chopped	1½ tablespoons extra-virgin olive oil

1. Squeeze the juice from 2 lemons. Fill a large bowl of cold water and add the juice and rinds. Use a paring knife to trim the bottom ¼ inch off the artichoke stems. Snip the thorn off the leaves with kitchen shears. Cut off about 1 inch from the tops. With a melon baller or spoon, scoop out the fuzzy chokes. Place the trimmed artichokes in the lemon water to prevent discoloration.

2. Squeeze ⅓ cup juice from the remaining 2 lemons. Combine the juice with 2 cups water in a large nonreactive pot wide enough to hold the artichokes in a single layer. Drain the artichokes and lay them on their sides in the pot. Top with garlic, dill, salt and pepper. Bring to a boil. Reduce heat to low, cover and simmer, turning the artichokes once, until tender when pierced with a fork, 18 to 20 minutes.

3. With a slotted spoon, transfer the artichokes to a deep platter. Simmer the liquid remaining in the pan over medium-high heat until reduced to 1¼ cups, about 10 minutes; spoon over the artichokes. Let cool to room temperature.

4. To serve, drizzle the artichokes with oil and baste with sauce. Garnish with chopped dill and lemon wedges, if desired.

SERVES 8: 1 ARTICHOKE EACH

Calories 105, **Fat** 3g (sat 0g), **Cholesterol** 0mg, **Carbs** 18g, **Total sugars** 2g (added 0g), **Protein** 5g, **Fiber** 9g, **Sodium** 445mg, **Potassium** 620mg.
Nutrition bonus: Vitamin C (38% daily value), Folate (28% dv), Magnesium (25% dv).

Artichokes & Wine

A few food-and-wine pairings create chemical interactions that you might want to avoid—and artichokes and wine is one of them. Artichokes contain a chemical acid called cynarin that makes wine taste sweeter and sometimes flat. To counter this effect, serve them with light, crisp, bone-dry wines that have high acidity and are unoaked. Good choices include a dry Sauvignon Blanc, Chenin Blanc and Grüner Veltliner, a citrusy Austrian wine.

ARTICHOKES, CAULIFLOWER, POTATO & ESCAROLE SALAD

ACTIVE: 1¼ HRS **TOTAL:** 1½ HRS
TO MAKE AHEAD: Refrigerate roasted vegetables and vinaigrette in separate containers up to 1 day. Bring to room temperature before assembling the salad.

The time it takes to prep fresh artichokes is well worth it. Their flavor and texture far exceed canned artichokes.

≈

Fresh Breadcrumbs

Don't toss your dry bread! Trim off any tough crusts and tear or cut the bread into pieces. Process in a food processor until coarse or fine crumbs form. Use right away or freeze in an airtight container up to 6 months. Thaw before using. One slice of bread makes about ½ cup fresh coarse breadcrumbs.

≈

ANCHOVY-GARLIC VINAIGRETTE

- 8 anchovy fillets, patted dry and minced
- 1 tablespoon minced garlic
- ⅔ cup extra-virgin olive oil, divided
- ⅓ cup red-wine vinegar
  Ground pepper to taste

BREADCRUMB TOPPING

- 1½ cups coarse fresh breadcrumbs (*see Tip*)
- 2 tablespoons extra-virgin olive oil
- ¾ teaspoon ground pepper

SALAD

- 12 baby yellow potatoes
- 4 cups cauliflower florets
- 3 tablespoons extra-virgin olive oil, divided
- ½ teaspoon kosher salt
- 4 large artichokes *or* one 8-ounce can artichoke hearts, rinsed
- 1 cup sliced celery
- 8 cups coarsely chopped escarole
- 6 cups sliced Belgian endive, radicchio *and/or* frisée

1. To prepare vinaigrette: Combine anchovies and garlic in a small saucepan with ⅓ cup oil. Warm over medium-low heat until fragrant, 2 to 4 minutes. Remove from heat and whisk in the remaining ⅓ cup oil and vinegar. Season with pepper.

2. To prepare breadcrumbs: Preheat oven 350°F.

3. Combine breadcrumbs with oil and pepper in a large bowl. Spread on a rimmed baking sheet. Bake, stirring occasionally, until golden brown, 15 to 20 minutes. Transfer the breadcrumbs to a small bowl.

4. To prepare salad: Increase oven temperature to 400°F.

5. Toss potatoes and cauliflower with 2 tablespoons oil and salt in the large bowl. Spread on the baking sheet. Roast for 10 minutes.

6. Meanwhile, if using fresh artichokes, remove all the leaves until you get to the fuzzy white chokes. Scrape the chokes from the artichoke hearts with a small spoon. Trim the dark green layer away from the outside of the heart and stem. (If using canned artichokes, thoroughly pat dry.) Cut the hearts into

⅜-inch-thick slices and toss with the remaining 1 tablespoon oil in the large bowl. Add to the baking sheet with the potatoes and cauliflower. Continue roasting until tender, 10 to 15 minutes more. When cool enough to handle, cut potatoes in half or in quarters.

7. Transfer the potatoes, cauliflower and artichoke hearts to the large bowl. Add celery and half the vinaigrette; let marinate for 15 minutes, stirring occasionally.

8. Toss escarole and endive (or radicchio or frisée) in another large bowl with the remaining vinaigrette. Divide the greens among 6 salad plates. Top each portion with about 1 cup of the marinated vegetables and a sprinkling of the toasted breadcrumbs.

SERVES 6: 2¼ CUPS EACH

Calories 472, **Fat** 38g (sat 5g), **Cholesterol** 5mg, **Carbs** 28g, **Total sugars** 2g (added 0g), **Protein** 7g, **Fiber** 11g, **Sodium** 436mg, **Potassium** 926mg. **Nutrition bonus:** Vitamin C (80% daily value), Folate (53% dv), Vitamin A (31% dv), Potassium (26% dv).

Arugula

This peppery green goes by many names, including rocket (British); ruchetta, rughetta and rucola (Italian); and roquette (French). How it got to be called arugula in America is a bit of a mystery. It is likely a mispronunciation of one of the Italian names that got repeated often enough that it stuck.

In the early 1980s, when Americans were just getting familiar with arugula, it was sold in small packages as an herb. Now it comes in bunches and bags and is enthusiastically tossed on pizza, turned into pungent pesto, even eaten solo. Drizzled with a little olive oil, a squeeze of fresh lemon, bit of salt and pepper and a few shards of shaved Parmesan, a plate of arugula makes an extremely simple and very tasty salad.

The spicy bite of arugula balances many flavors, including the sweetness of figs, beets, dried fruits and pomegranate seeds; the sharpness of blue cheese and goat cheese; and the saltiness of olives, capers and prosciutto. Its pungency also pairs well with the acidity in vinegar, grapefruit, lemon and orange.

While arugula is most often eaten raw, it can be chopped and tossed with hot pasta, grains, potatoes, scrambled eggs, or stirred into soup. When warmed, its character changes slightly as it wilts and the snappy flavor slightly softens.

Arugula is a relative of both radish and watercress, which makes a fine substitute for arugula in most recipes. Although arugula is primarily a cool-weather crop at peak season in spring and again in fall when leaves are young and tender, it is available year-round. As temps warm and leaves get big, flavor gets spicier.

Best in spring

AT THE MARKET

❧ Arugula comes in bunches with stems attached as well as prewashed in bags. Generally, the leaves of loose-leaf arugula packaged in bags are smaller than those in bunches. Baby arugula is simply a small, less mature and often milder version of arugula. The term "wild arugula" doesn't necessarily mean it was foraged from a field—although arugula does grow in the wild. Arugula and wild arugula are actually different yet related plants. In general, wild arugula has a narrower leaf and more fierce flavor than arugula.

❧ Look for arugula that is bright green with no yellowing, bruising, slimy spots or wet leaves. A little bit of limpness in the stems is fine.

IN YOUR KITCHEN

❧ Like most tender greens, arugula is highly perishable and should be bought no more than a few days before you plan to eat it. If it is in a bunch, wrap the root ends in damp paper towels, then place the bunch root-ends down in a plastic bag. Refrigerate for 2 to 3 days.

❧ To clean and prep the greens, cut off any tough stems. Swish the leaves in several changes of cool water, then remove from the water and spin dry in a salad spinner or place between two layers of paper towels or clean kitchen towels and gently roll. Use immediately or place wrapped arugula in a plastic bag and refrigerate up to 2 days.

COOKING BASICS

PESTO With the motor running, drop 1 clove peeled garlic through the feed tube of a food processor; process until minced. Stop the machine and add 5 cups baby arugula (5 ounces), ½ cup finely shredded Asiago cheese, ¼ cup toasted pine nuts, ¼ cup olive oil and ¼ teaspoon salt. Pulse and then process, scraping down the sides as necessary, until the mixture is a smooth paste. Makes about 1 cup.

SALAD Whisk 2 tablespoons olive oil, 1 tablespoon fresh lemon juice, ¼ teaspoon salt and pepper to taste in a large bowl. Add 8 cups baby arugula (8 ounces) and toss to coat. Transfer to a serving platter and top with ¼ cup shaved Parmesan cheese, if desired. Serves 4.

NUTRITION

❧ **1 cup arugula: Calories** 4, **Fat** 0g (sat 0g), **Cholesterol** 0mg, **Carbs** 0g, **Total sugars** 0g (added 0g), **Protein** 1g, **Fiber** 0g, **Sodium** 6mg, **Potassium** 74mg.

BONUS Arugula contains erucin, a compound that may guard against breast cancer by preventing cancer cells from dividing and multiplying. Erucin may also protect against prostate and lung cancers.

Grow Your Own

Arugula is extremely simple to grow. You don't even need a patch of land— it grows beautifully in a windowbox or container. Sow the tiny seeds in loose, well-drained soil in full sun or part shade as soon as the ground can be worked in the spring. Plant seeds ¼ inch deep and about 1 inch apart in rows. (Or scatter the seeds in a larger area.) Keep moist and replant every 2 to 3 weeks for a continuous supply. When seedlings are about 1 inch tall, thin plants to about 2 to 3 inches apart. Arugula is usually ready for harvest 30 to 40 days after planting. To harvest, cut about one-third of the outer leaves at a time from the base. The plant will continue to produce leaves. When the plant is about 12 inches tall—just before it develops flowers—pull up the whole plant by the roots. At this stage, the large leaves have the most robust flavor.

Arugula Pesto
(see Cooking Basics, opposite)

PEAR & ARUGULA SALAD WITH CANDIED WALNUTS

ACTIVE: 15 MIN **TOTAL:** 40 MIN
TO MAKE AHEAD: Prepare walnuts (Steps 1-2) and let cool completely; store airtight up to 1 day. **EQUIPMENT:** Parchment paper

The walnut oil used in the simple Dijon vinaigrette for this salad gives the dressing a subtle nutty flavor. If you don't have walnut oil, extra-virgin olive oil makes a fine substitute.

CANDIED WALNUTS

- 1 cup walnut halves
- 4 teaspoons water
- 2 tablespoons light brown sugar
- ½ teaspoon ground cinnamon
- ¼ teaspoon salt

SALAD

- 1 large clove garlic, minced
- ¼ teaspoon salt
- 2 tablespoons walnut oil
- 1 tablespoon Dijon mustard
- 1 tablespoon white-wine vinegar
- ¼ teaspoon ground pepper
- 8 cups baby arugula (8 ounces)
- 2 firm ripe red pears, sliced

1. To prepare walnuts: Preheat oven to 400°F. Line a small baking pan with parchment paper; coat with cooking spray.

2. Toss walnuts with water in a bowl. Sprinkle with brown sugar, cinnamon and salt; toss to coat. Transfer to the prepared pan. Bake until the sugar is melted and the nuts are just starting to brown, 6 to 8 minutes. Cool in the pan until the sugar hardens, about 10 minutes.

3. To prepare salad: Mash garlic and salt into a paste in a mortar and pestle or with the side of a knife on a cutting board. Transfer to a large bowl and whisk in oil, mustard, vinegar and pepper. Add arugula, pears and the walnuts; toss to coat.

SERVES 6: 1⅓ CUPS EACH

Calories 209, **Fat** 16g (sat 1g), **Cholesterol** 0mg, **Carbs** 17g, **Total sugars** 11g (added 4g), **Protein** 4g, **Fiber** 4g, **Sodium** 236mg, **Potassium** 251mg.

Candied Walnuts

The candied walnuts in this salad are also a crunchy, flavorful topping for pumpkin pie and oatmeal. If you make a big batch, be sure to use a larger baking pan so they have room to be in a single layer. For a touch of heat, add a pinch of ground chipotle or cayenne to the walnuts before baking.

(see *Tip*)

Agrumato Lemon Oil

This pizza gets a zesty drizzle of agrumato lemon oil, which is created when olives are pressed together with lemons. The resulting extra-virgin olive oil has an exceptionally bright lemony flavor. It's worth seeking out at gourmet markets or well-stocked natural-foods stores. If you can't find it, substitute 1 tablespoon extra-virgin olive oil and 1 teaspoon lemon zest.

WILD MUSHROOM PIZZA WITH ARUGULA & PECORINO

ACTIVE: 25 MINUTES **TOTAL:** 50 MINUTES

Lemon oil and arugula add just enough citrus and peppery bite to accent this pizza without overwhelming the meaty mushrooms. To that end, Sardinian or Tuscan Pecorino, both milder than Pecorino Romano, are called for, but other mellow grating cheeses, such as Parmigiano-Reggiano, will work as well.

3 tablespoons extra-virgin olive oil, divided
4 cups trimmed and sliced mixed fresh wild mushrooms, such as hen of the woods (maitake) and chanterelles
1 pound pizza dough, preferably whole-wheat
2 cloves garlic, very thinly sliced
4 ounces fresh mozzarella, thinly sliced and torn into ½-inch pieces
3 cups loosely packed arugula
1 tablespoon agrumato lemon oil (*see Tip*)
¼ teaspoon kosher salt
3 tablespoons shaved Pecorino Sardo *or* Toscano cheese

1. Place a pizza stone or large rimless baking sheet on the bottom rack and preheat oven to the highest temperature, preferably 500°F, for 30 minutes.

2. Meanwhile, heat 2 tablespoons olive oil in a large skillet over medium heat. Cook mushrooms, stirring occasionally, until beginning to brown, about 5 minutes. Remove from heat and set aside.

3. Roll dough on a floured surface into a 14-inch circle. Transfer to a floured pizza peel (or rimless baking sheet). Scatter garlic over the dough, then sprinkle with mozzarella and half of the mushrooms (reserve the remaining mushrooms for Step 5). Drizzle the remaining 1 tablespoon olive oil over pizza.

4. Slide the pizza onto the preheated pizza stone or baking sheet. Bake until browned, 10 to 15 minutes. Transfer to a cutting board and cut into 4 pieces.

5. Toss arugula with agrumato lemon oil and salt. Top the pizza with the arugula, the reserved mushrooms and cheese. Serve immediately.

SERVES 4: ¼ PIZZA EACH

Calories 494, Fat 28g (sat 6g), **Cholesterol** 26mg, **Carbs** 51g, **Total sugars** 4g (added 1g), Protein 17g, **Fiber** 4g, **Sodium** 621mg, **Potassium** 307mg.
Nutrition bonus: Calcium (21% daily value).

Asparagus

Every spring, slender, succulent spears of asparagus push through the soil and rise straight up from the ground like green missiles. The stalks, with fresh flavor and crisp texture that epitomizes the season, are actually the shoots of what would grow into a giant fernlike plant if they weren't harvested.

Asparagus comes in green and purple varieties. The purple variety turns dark green when cooked, as heat destroys the purple pigment. White asparagus—more common in Europe—is not a different variety, but simply asparagus grown without light. It has milder flavor and more tender texture than regular asparagus.

Asparagus can be eaten raw or cooked. It is so simple to prepare, and its fresh, green taste requires very little embellishment—usually nothing more than a little olive oil, salt and pepper. It is nice with green (immature) garlic, Dijon mustard, lemon, tarragon, dill and sorrel. A classic French preparation drapes it in hollandaise sauce. Another features blanched and chilled asparagus drizzled with vinaigrette and served with a grated hard-boiled egg on top.

Asparagus mixes well with other spring vegetables such as peas, lettuces, artichokes, fava beans, turnips and new potatoes.

Asparagus is in season from March to June. It takes a few years for a patch to get established, but once it does, the spears grow at lightning speed. A single spear can grow up to 7 inches in a 24-hour period. It also requires a bit of real estate. The time and space required to grow asparagus may be why the vegetable has historically had a reputation of being something of a luxury.

Best in midspring to early summer

AT THE MARKET

➣ Asparagus spears range from pencil-thin to thumb-thick and the size of the spear has no bearing on tenderness, but color does. The brighter the green, the more tender the spear. Both purple and white varieties tend to be slightly more tender than the common green variety.

➣ Look for firm, straight, crisp (not limp) brightly colored spears. Whatever the size of the spears, the tips of asparagus should be tightly closed and dry, with no bruises or slimy spots. The skin should be smooth.

IN YOUR KITCHEN

➣ Asparagus is best when used immediately after you bring it home. It can be stored for a day or two if the bottoms of the spears are trimmed and placed upright in a large jar with a little bit of water in the bottom. Cover the tops loosely with damp paper towels, plastic wrap or a plastic bag, then refrigerate.

➣ The bottoms of asparagus spears can be woody and fibrous. The spears naturally bend at the spot that should be removed. You can simply snap it off or cut it off with a sharp knife. If desired, remove the tough outer layers from the lower part of large spears with a vegetable peeler. Rinse the stalks in cool water before using.

COOKING BASICS

GRILL Oil a folded paper towel and, holding it with tongs, rub it over the grill rack. Toss 1 pound trimmed asparagus with 1 tablespoon olive oil. Season to taste with salt and pepper. Place asparagus on the grill perpendicular to the grates. Grill over medium-high heat, turning occasionally, until lightly charred, 5 to 7 minutes. Serves 2.

ROAST Toss 1 pound trimmed asparagus with 1 tablespoon olive oil on a rimmed baking sheet or in a large roasting pan. Spread in a single layer and season to taste with salt and pepper. Roast in a 450°F oven until tender, 15 to 25 minutes. If desired, drizzle with ½ to 1 teaspoon balsamic vinegar. Serve hot or at room temperature. Serves 2.

SAUTÉ Cut 1 pound trimmed asparagus diagonally into 1-inch pieces. Heat 1½ teaspoons sesame oil in a large nonstick skillet over medium heat. Add asparagus and stir-fry until it begins to soften, 1½ to 2 minutes. Add 1½ teaspoons reduced-sodium soy sauce and stir-fry for 1 minute. Add 1 teaspoon sugar and stir-fry for another 30 seconds. Remove from heat. Serves 2.

STEAM Bring 1 inch of water to a boil in a large pot fitted with a steamer basket. Add 1 pound trimmed asparagus, cover and steam until tender-crisp, 3 to 5 minutes. Toss with 2 teaspoons butter and season to taste with salt and pepper. Serve with lemon wedges. Serves 2.

NUTRITION

➣ **1 cup cooked asparagus: Calories** 40, **Fat** 0g (sat 0g), **Cholesterol** 0mg, **Carbs** 24g, **Total sugars** 2g (added 0g), **Protein** 4g, **Fiber** 4g, **Sodium** 26mg, **Potassium** 404mg.

BONUS If you're trying to lower your blood pressure, asparagus could help. These stalks contain asparaptine, which prevents blood vessels from constricting, improving blood flow throughout your body.

Tie in bundles before steaming for a dressed-up look.

≈

Miso

Miso is fermented soybean paste made by inoculating a mixture of soybeans, salt and grains (usually barley or rice) with koji, a beneficial mold. Miso is undeniably salty, so a little goes a long way. White or sweet miso (Shiromiso), made with soy and rice, is yellow and milder in flavor; use for soup, salad dressings and sauces for fish or chicken. Look for it near tofu at well-stocked supermarkets.

≈

PANKO-CRUSTED ASPARAGUS SPEARS

ACTIVE: 25 MIN **TOTAL:** 50 MIN

Warm from the oven, these crunchy spears make a tasty side dish or cocktail nibble. Before being coated in panko breadcrumbs, they are rolled in a flavorful sesame-miso sauce that doubles as a dipping sauce. Although we typically use whole-wheat panko-style breadcrumbs, for this recipe we recommend using white Japanese-style panko breadcrumbs for the best texture and flavor.

    Cooking spray, preferably canola oil
⅓ cup low-fat mayonnaise
 2 scallions, trimmed and finely chopped
 2 tablespoons white miso (*see Tip*)
 1 teaspoon chile-garlic sauce
½ teaspoon toasted sesame oil
 1 bunch asparagus (about 1 pound), trimmed
¾ cup Japanese-style panko
¼ cup sesame seeds

1. Preheat oven to 450°F. Line a rimmed baking sheet with parchment or foil; coat with cooking spray.

2. Combine mayonnaise, scallions, miso, chile-garlic sauce and oil in a small bowl.

3. Place asparagus in a shallow dish and toss with half the miso mixture (about ¼ cup), making sure the asparagus is well coated.

4. Combine panko and sesame seeds in another shallow dish. Working with one spear at a time, roll in the panko mixture and place on the prepared baking sheet, leaving a bit of room between each spear. Coat the prepared spears with cooking spray.

5. Roast the asparagus until the coating is browned and crispy and the asparagus is tender, 20 to 25 minutes. Serve with the remaining miso mixture as a dipping sauce.

SERVES 4

Calories 154, **Fat** 8g (sat 1g), **Cholesterol** 5mg, **Carbs** 19g, **Total sugars** 3g (added 1g), **Protein** 4g, **Fiber** 3g, **Sodium** 537mg, **Potassium** 186mg.

ASPARAGUS & BABY KALE CAESAR SALAD

ACTIVE: 20 MIN **TOTAL:** 20 MIN

Caesar salad gets a nutrition and flavor boost with the addition of crisp asparagus and dark, leafy baby kale. Use arugula or mixed greens if you can't find baby kale at your market.

¼ cup extra-virgin olive oil
1 large egg yolk (*see Tip*)
2 tablespoons lemon juice
1 small clove garlic, peeled
¼-½ teaspoon anchovy paste *or* ½-1 minced anchovy fillet
¼ teaspoon salt
¼ teaspoon ground pepper
¼ cup grated Parmesan cheese
1 bunch asparagus (about 1 pound), trimmed and very thinly sliced
1 5-ounce package baby kale
Cracked black pepper to taste

1. Combine oil, egg yolk, lemon juice, garlic, anchovy to taste, salt and ground pepper in a food processor (preferably a mini food processor). Process until creamy. Add cheese and pulse to combine.

2. Toss asparagus and kale in a large bowl. Add the dressing and toss to coat. Season with a generous grinding of pepper.

SERVES 4: 2 CUPS EACH

Calories 206, **Fat** 17g (sat 3g), **Cholesterol** 51mg, **Carbs** 9g, **Total sugars** 2g (added 0g), **Protein** 7g, **Fiber** 3g, **Sodium** 275mg, **Potassium** 435mg.
Nutrition bonus: Vitamin A (94% daily value), Vitamin C (90% dv), Folate (44% dv).

Egg Safety

When a recipe calls for raw eggs, you can minimize the risk of foodborne illness by using pasteurized-in-the-shell eggs. Look for them in the refrigerator case near other whole eggs.

Aged Goat Cheese

Goat cheese, also known as chèvre (French for "goat"), is earthy-tasting and slightly tart. Aged goat cheese has a nutty, sharp flavor and is drier and firmer than fresh goat cheese. Look for it in a well-stocked cheese section at large supermarkets and specialty cheese shops. We don't recommend using fresh, creamy goat cheese as a substitute—Manchego cheese is a better choice.

ASPARAGUS-GOAT CHEESE SOUFFLÉS

ACTIVE: 30 MIN **TOTAL:** 50 MIN
EQUIPMENT: Six 10-ounce ramekins

Puffy and warm, these savory soufflés are the essence of spring. Serve them alongside a big salad with a tangy vinaigrette for a light supper or a special brunch.

Cooking spray, preferably canola oil

1 bunch asparagus (about 1 pound)
2 tablespoons butter
3 tablespoons all-purpose flour
1½ cups nonfat milk, heated
½ teaspoon coarse salt, divided
¼ teaspoon ground pepper

Pinch of ground nutmeg
4 large egg yolks
1½ teaspoons truffle oil (optional)
1 cup crumbled *or* diced aged goat cheese (*see Tip*) or Manchego cheese
8 large egg whites, at room temperature

1. Position rack on lowest level of oven; preheat to 375°F. Coat six 10-ounce ramekins with cooking spray; place on a large rimmed baking sheet.

2. Steam asparagus as directed on page 30. Drain; refresh under cold water. Blot dry with a clean kitchen towel, then cut into ½-inch slices.

3. Melt butter in a medium saucepan over medium-low heat; whisk in flour and cook, whisking often, for 2 minutes. Turn off heat and slowly whisk in hot milk. Return heat to medium-low and continue whisking until thickened, 3 to 4 minutes. Whisk in ¼ teaspoon salt, pepper and nutmeg. Remove from heat and whisk in egg yolks, one at a time, and truffle oil, if using. Transfer the mixture to a large bowl. Stir in the asparagus and cheese.

4. Beat 8 egg whites in a large bowl with an electric mixer, slowly increasing the speed, until they begin to foam. Add the remaining ¼ teaspoon salt and continue to beat until the whites hold their shape; do not overbeat. Using a rubber spatula, gently stir one-third of the whites into the egg yolk mixture. Gently fold in the remaining egg whites just until blended. Divide the mixture among the prepared ramekins, filling them almost to the top.

5. Bake the soufflés on the bottom rack until puffy and golden and an instant-read thermometer inserted into the center registers 145°F, 20 to 25 minutes.

SERVES 6

Calories 206, **Fat** 13g (sat 7g), **Cholesterol** 150mg, **Carbs** 8g, **Total sugars** 4g (added 0g), **Protein** 14g, **Fiber** 1g, **Sodium** 373mg, **Potassium** 297mg.
Nutrition bonus: Vitamin A (22% daily value), Folate (21% dv).

Avocado

Botanically speaking, avocado is a fruit—a pendulous berry that grows on a tree and has a large seed, or pit, in the center. But, with the exception of some recipes for chocolate pudding and smoothies that call for avocado to add richness and creamy texture, it is generally viewed as a vegetable and given the savory treatment—at its simplest, a squeeze of fresh lime and a little salt.

Although avocado is native to Mexico and Central America, it has now firmly taken root in both Florida and California. Depending on the variety, avocados are distinctive in flavor, texture and size. The fruit can weigh from 8 ounces to 5 pounds. Much of the determining factor of flavor and texture is the oil content, which can range from 3 to 30 percent. Hass avocados, the pebbly-skinned and most widely available variety, are high in oil. Other varieties of this type include the large and creamy Reed, Fuerte, Bacon and Zutano. The oil content of these avocados ranges from 18 to 30 percent, giving them a dense, buttery texture and nutty flavor. (In India, avocado is called "butterfruit.") Florida avocados, which are larger and have smooth, bright green skin, range from 3 to 5 percent. With a juicy texture and fresh, grassy flavor, they are not the first choice for guacamole, but are good for slicing or dicing.

Avocado pairs well with flavors that cut through and complement its richness. Bright citrus and acidic fruits, such as mango, pineapple and tomato, are good choices. The heat of chiles and spicy radishes complements its sweet rich flavor, and so do certain herbs—cilantro, dill and basil, among them—as well as salty meats, such as prosciutto and bacon.

Hass avocados are available year-round, with best quality between midsummer and early fall. Florida avocados are in season from early summer to midwinter.

Best in midsummer to early fall

AT THE MARKET

⤐ By far, Hass avocados from California, Mexico and Chile have pervaded the commercial market more than any other variety. The Hass has a very rich flavor and holds up well when shipped—a crucial quality for a highly bruisable fruit that often travels hundreds of miles to its destination. While Florida avocados do make their way out of the state, they are not nearly as widely distributed as Hass avocados.

⤐ Choose very firm, blemish-free avocados. The harder the avocado, the fresher it is. It will transport more easily from the store to your house without getting damaged or bruised than a more ripe avocado will.

IN YOUR KITCHEN

⤐ Place avocados in a brown paper bag and allow to ripen at room temperature. (To speed ripening, place an apple or banana in the bag with the avocados. Both fruits release ethylene gas, which hastens the ripening of the avocado.) A perfectly ripe avocado yields slightly when gently pressed with your thumb. It's best to use ripe avocados immediately, but they can be stored in the refrigerator up to 1 week.

⤐ To prepare, cut the avocado in half around the circumference with a sharp chef's knife. Gently twist the halves to separate them. With the pit half face-up on a working surface, use a quick downward motion to penetrate the pit with the knife blade. Gently twist to pull the pit out of the avocado half.

COOKING BASIC

DRESSING Combine ½ ripe avocado, ¾ cup packed fresh cilantro, ½ cup nonfat plain yogurt, 2 chopped scallions, 1 garlic clove (quartered), 1 tablespoon fresh lime juice and ½ teaspoon each sugar and salt in a blender. Blend until smooth. Makes about 1 cup.

SALAD Soak ¼ cup thinly sliced red onion in ice water for 15 minutes. Cut 2 pitted firm ripe avocados in half crosswise into slices. Peel, core and slice a medium pineapple. Halve lengthwise into quarters, remove the core and cut each quarter crosswise into slices. Whisk 3 tablespoons olive oil, 1 tablespoon lime juice and ½ teaspoon salt in a small bowl. Drain onion; pat dry. Arrange half of the avocado, pineapple and onion on a serving plate. Sprinkle with ¼ teaspoon salt and drizzle with half the dressing; repeat the layers. Serves 8.

NUTRITION

⤐ **½ medium Hass avocado: Calories** 114, **Fat** 10g (sat 1g), **Cholesterol** 0mg, **Carbs** 6g, **Total sugars** 0g (added 0g), **Protein** 1g, **Fiber** 5g, **Sodium** 6mg, **Potassium** 345mg.

BONUS Avocados boast plant sterols, the same ingredient that's added to some margarines designed to help lower cholesterol. Sterols block how much cholesterol you absorb from a meal and tell your liver to produce less of it too.

How to prep

1. Cut in half around circumference of avocado. Twist halves to separate.

2. With a quick downward motion, cut into pit with a chef's knife *(above)*. Twist to pull out of the avocado half.

*Pineapple &
Avocado Salad*
(see Cooking Basics,
opposite)

JASON MRAZ'S GUACAMOLE

ACTIVE: 20 MIN **TOTAL:** 20 MIN
TO MAKE AHEAD: Press a piece of plastic wrap directly on the surface to prevent browning and refrigerate up to 6 hours.

Hass or Reed avocados, the kind grown at musician Jason Mraz's California ranch, are best for guacamole. Start with ripe avocados and it's hard to go wrong. Adjust the heat, tang or other flavorings to suit your tastes.

  4 ripe avocados, halved and pitted
  ½ cup chopped fresh cilantro
  ⅓ cup finely chopped red onion
  ¼ cup lime *or* lemon juice
  1 tablespoon extra-virgin olive oil
  ½ teaspoon fine sea salt
     Ground pepper to taste
     Hot sauce, finely diced fresh jalapeños, cayenne pepper *and/or* chipotle
      powder to taste

Mash avocados in a medium bowl. Add cilantro, onion, lime (or lemon) juice, oil, salt and pepper and stir to combine. Season with hot sauce, jalapeños, cayenne and/or chipotle, if desired.

MAKES: 3 CUPS (¼-CUP SERVING)

Calories 121, **Fat** 11g (sat 2g), **Cholesterol** 0mg, **Carbs** 7g, **Total sugars** 1g (added 0g), **Protein** 1g, **Fiber** 5g, **Sodium** 52mg, **Potassium** 341mg.

CHIPOTLE-CHEDDAR BROILED AVOCADO HALVES

ACTIVE: 30 MIN **TOTAL:** 30 MIN

These zesty avocados topped with melty Cheddar cheese are great with grilled chicken or steak.

  2 ripe but firm avocados, halved and pitted, skin left on
¼ cup shredded extra-sharp Cheddar cheese
  1 small chipotle chile in adobo (*see Tip*), minced (about 1 teaspoon), or to taste
  1 tablespoon lime juice, plus 4 wedges for serving
     Pinch of salt

1. Preheat broiler to high.

2. Place avocado halves on a baking sheet.

3. Thoroughly combine cheese, chipotle, lime juice and salt in a small bowl. Evenly divide the cheese mixture among the avocado halves. Broil 3 to 4 inches from the heat source until the cheese is bubbling and beginning to brown, 3 to 5 minutes. Serve warm with lime wedges.

SERVES 4: ½ AVOCADO EACH

Calories 191, **Fat** 17g (sat 4g), **Cholesterol** 7mg, **Carbs** 9g, **Total sugars** 1g (added 0g), **Protein** 4g, **Fiber** 7g, **Sodium** 99mg, **Potassium** 499mg.
Nutrition bonus: Folate (21% daily value).

Smoky Chipotles

In whatever form they are used, chipotle peppers add a touch of smoke and heat to foods. Chipotles are dried, smoked jalapeño peppers.

Ground chipotle chile powder is usually found with other specialty spices in large supermarkets. Chipotles are also sold packed in flavorful spicy adobo sauce. Look for the small cans with Mexican foods at large supermarkets. Once opened, they'll keep up to 2 weeks in the refrigerator or 6 months in the freezer.

PINK GRAPEFRUIT & AVOCADO SALAD

ACTIVE: 30 MIN **TOTAL:** 30 MIN

This is a special-occasion salad that combines grapefruit segments with creamy avocado, pungent red onion, crunchy pomegranate seeds and aromatic, herby basil. Look for grapefruit with firm, shiny skins that are heavy for their size, which means they will have lots of juice.

½ cup halved and very thinly sliced red onion
1 large lemon
1 tablespoon extra-virgin olive oil
½ teaspoon kosher salt
¼ teaspoon ground pepper
3 small red *or* pink grapefruit
1 large ripe avocado
⅓ cup fresh pomegranate seeds (*see Tip, page 198*)
4 large fresh basil leaves
8 small leaves Boston lettuce

1. Place onion in a small bowl of cold water to soak. Set aside.

2. Finely grate 1 teaspoon zest and squeeze 2 tablespoons juice from lemon. Whisk the zest and juice, oil, salt and pepper in a large bowl.

3. Peel grapefruit with a sharp knife, removing all peel and white pith. Working over the large bowl, cut the segments from the surrounding membranes and let them drop into the bowl. Squeeze the peels and membranes over the bowl to extract all the juice before discarding them. Halve, peel and pit avocado. Cut lengthwise into ¼-inch-thick slices, then cut the slices in half. Gently stir the avocado and pomegranate seeds into the grapefruit mixture.

4. Finely slice basil and drain the onion; gently stir into the grapefruit mixture. Arrange lettuce leaves on 4 salad plates, top with the grapefruit mixture and serve immediately.

SERVES 4

Calories 184, **Fat** 11g (sat 2g), **Cholesterol** 0mg, **Carbs** 22g, **Total sugars** 14g (added 0g), **Protein** 3g, **Fiber** 6g, **Sodium** 146mg, **Potassium** 594mg.
Nutrition bonus: Vitamin C (107% daily value), Vitamin A (51% dv), Folate (22% dv).

► Lima Beans

▲ Fava Beans

► Butter Beans

▲ Scarlet Runner Beans

Shell Beans

▲ **Black-Eyed Peas**

▲ *Edamame*

Evidence suggests that humans cultivated beans 7,000 years ago in what is now Central America. Shell beans are grown not for the pod but for the seeds inside. In late summer to early fall, you can find them fresh but most are dried. (Fava beans—a staple of Italian cooking—are the exceptions; they are in season in the spring.) Common types include black-eyed peas, butter beans, cannellini beans, cranberry beans (also called borlotti beans), edamame, fava beans and lima beans.

Beans that will be sold in dried form are harvested when 90 percent of the leaves have fallen off and both pods and seeds are dry. Fresh shell beans are harvested at the middle of their development, when the seeds are still plump and moist and the pods pliable. While dried and rehydrated beans are convenient and can be stored over the long term *(see Tip, page 52)*, fresh beans have a creamier texture and a sweeter, more buttery flavor. For that reason—and since this book is generally about enjoying vegetables in their just-picked state—we focus on fresh shell beans in this chapter.

The cuisines of Latin America, Italy, France and the southern United States make particularly good use of shell beans. Fresh shell beans are lovely as a side dish or main dish and are often braised in an aromatic liquid. Various forms of cured pork (bacon, smoked ham hock, prosciutto, pancetta), garlic, fresh herbs, tomatoes, chiles and greens complement most varieties beautifully.

Fava beans are planted as soon as the soil can be worked and are harvested mid- to late-spring. Other varieties are planted later. They need warmer soil and a growing season with temperatures in the 70s and 80s.

Best in spring (favas); other varieties in late summer to early fall

AT THE MARKET

❧ Fresh shell beans are not usually sold at supermarkets. Look at farmers' markets and natural-foods stores. Choose plump and bumpy pods that feel heavy. Bumpy pods are easier to rip open. Avoid pods that are dried out.

IN YOUR KITCHEN

❧ Fresh shell beans are vulnerable to mold—especially if there is moisture visible on the pods—and should be eaten as soon as possible after purchase. Store fresh shell beans still in the pods in a paper bag in the refrigerator for 2 to 3 days. Although the beans will stay freshest if they are not shelled until right before cooking, you can shell them ahead of time and store in a tightly sealed container up to 3 days in the refrigerator.

❧ To shell beans, snap off the end of each pod and pull off the string. Run your thumb the length of the pod to remove the beans. Note: Only fava beans have a waxy coating that requires blanching *(see Steps 3 and 4, right)*. One pound of unshelled beans yields between 1½ and 2 cups shelled beans.

COOKING BASICS

BOIL Sauté 1 small diced onion in olive oil in a saucepan until tender and golden. Add 2 cloves thinly sliced garlic and cook until fragrant, about 1 minute. Add 1 bay leaf, a couple of sage leaves, 1 tablespoon fresh marjoram or 1 sprig rosemary and stir until fragrant. Add 3 cups fresh shelled beans and water to cover by 1 inch. Bring to a boil and simmer gently, until the beans have a creamy consistency, about 30 minutes. Season to taste with salt and pepper. Drizzle with extra-virgin olive oil. Serves 3.

MICROWAVE Combine 2 cups shelled beans and 2 tablespoons water in a microwave-safe dish. Cover and cook on High until they have a creamy consistency, 4 to 8 minutes, depending on the size of the beans. Test at 1-minute intervals. Serves 2.

NUTRITION

❧ **1 cup cooked fava beans: Calories** 187, **Fat** 1g (sat 0g), **Cholesterol** 0mg, **Carbs** 33g, **Total sugars** 3g (added 0g), **Protein** 13g, **Fiber** 9g, **Sodium** 8mg, **Potassium** 456mg.

BONUS Shell beans are one of the best foods for weight control. Chalk it up to their satiating combination of slowly digested protein and fiber. Compared to other similar-calorie foods such as bread and potatoes, they've been found to be 31 percent more filling.

How to shell fava beans

1. Snap off the end of the bean and pull the string off of the pod.

2. Pop the beans out of the pod by running your thumb down the length of the pod.

3. Drop fava beans into boiling water for 30 seconds, then transfer immediately to ice water.

4. Remove the "cap" at the top of each bean and slip it out of its waxy coating *(right)*.

See Tip

To Cook Dry Beans

Rinse 1 pound of dry beans and place in a large bowl. Cover with 2 inches of cold water and soak at least 8 hours or overnight. (Or put the beans in a pot and cover with 2 inches of water; bring to a boil; boil for 2 minutes. Remove from heat and let stand, covered, for 1 hour.) Drain and transfer to a large pot and cover with 3 inches cold water. Bring to a boil, skimming off any foam. Reduce heat and simmer, stirring occasionally, until the beans are tender, 30 minutes to 2 hours. When beans are almost tender, add 1 teaspoon salt per pound of beans. Refrigerate beans in cooking liquid up to 1 week or freeze up to 3 months. For recipe substitutions, use about 1½ cups cooked beans in place of one 15-ounce can.

SUPER-GREEN EDAMAME SALAD

ACTIVE: 20 MIN **TOTAL:** 20 MIN
TO MAKE AHEAD: Refrigerate up to 1 day.

In the pod, edamame—green soybeans—make a delicious snack steamed and seasoned with toasted sesame oil and salt. Here, their nutty flavor enlivens a creamy bright green dressing made with avocado and spinach. If you can't find pink beans, substitute pinto beans or light red kidney beans.

4½ cups fresh shelled edamame *or* two 12-ounce packages frozen shelled edamame, thawed

1½ cups cooked pink beans *or* pinto beans (*see Tip*) *or* one 15-ounce can pink beans *or* pinto beans, rinsed

1 medium yellow bell pepper, finely diced

½ cup chopped fresh chives, plus more for garnish

2 cups packed baby spinach

1 ripe avocado

⅓ cup apple juice

¼ cup extra-virgin olive oil *or* avocado oil

3 tablespoons lemon juice

2 teaspoons reduced-sodium tamari *or* soy sauce

¾ teaspoon salt

¼ teaspoon ground pepper

1. Bring a large pot of water to a boil. Add fresh shelled edamame and cook for 3 minutes. Drain and immediately plunge into a bowl of ice water to stop the cooking process; drain well. (If using frozen edamame, you can skip this step because the beans are blanched before being frozen.)

2. Combine edamame, pink beans (or pinto beans), bell pepper and chives in a large bowl.

3. Combine spinach, avocado, apple juice, oil, lemon juice, tamari (or soy sauce), salt and pepper in a blender. Puree until smooth and creamy. Add the dressing to the bean mixture and stir to coat. Garnish with more chives, if desired. Serve at room temperature or cold.

SERVES 10: ABOUT ¾ CUP EACH

Calories 195, **Fat** 12g (sat 1g), **Cholesterol** 0mg, **Carbs** 15g, **Total sugars** 3g (added 0g), **Protein** 9g, **Fiber** 5g, **Sodium** 269mg, **Potassium** 560mg.
Nutrition bonus: Folate (61% daily value), Vitamin C (59% dv).

BLACK-EYED PEAS & OKRA

ACTIVE: 15 MIN **TOTAL:** 50 MIN

Also called cowpeas, these two-toned legumes are popular in Southern cooking and are often braised with ham hocks to create a stew-like dish of beans in flavorful "pot liquor." Here, they're featured in a classic Southern side dish that's perfect for potlucks. Adding the okra toward the end of cooking guarantees a tender—not mushy—texture.

- 1 tablespoon extra-virgin olive oil
- 1 medium onion, coarsely chopped
- 1 large clove garlic, finely chopped
- 3 cups low-sodium chicken broth
- 2 small bay leaves, preferably fresh
- 2 cups shelled black-eyed peas, fresh *or* frozen (thawed)
- 1 pound fresh okra, stem ends trimmed, cut into 1-inch pieces
- ½ teaspoon salt
- ½ teaspoon ground pepper
- ¼ teaspoon cayenne pepper, or to taste

Heat oil in a large saucepan over medium heat. Add onion and cook, stirring, until soft and translucent, 3 to 5 minutes. Add garlic and cook until fragrant, about 1 minute. Add broth and bay leaves; bring to a boil. Stir in black-eyed peas. Reduce heat and simmer, stirring occasionally, for 20 minutes. Add okra, salt, pepper and cayenne. Simmer until tender, about 15 minutes more.

SERVES 6: ABOUT ¾ CUP EACH

Calories 154, **Fat** 4g (sat 1g), **Cholesterol** 0mg, **Carbs** 24g, **Total sugars** 2g (added 0g), **Protein** 9g, **Fiber** 6g, **Sodium** 249mg, **Potassium** 362mg.
Nutrition bonus: Vitamin C (32% daily value).

Lima Bean Scene

There are two main varieties of lima beans—Fordhook and baby lima (which are not immature Fordhooks). Baby limas have a more tender texture and milder flavor than the larger and plumper Fordhooks. Creamy, aptly named butter beans are actually lima beans that are cooked and eaten when mature, not green, as most lima beans are.

LIMA BEANS WITH CHORIZO

ACTIVE: 40 MIN **TOTAL:** 1 HR 10 MIN
TO MAKE AHEAD: Refrigerate up to 2 days. Bring to room temperature or reheat on medium-low heat before serving.

A bit of chorizo sausage gives these beans a sassy hit of smoke and spice. Serve them as is (on small plates) or heaped onto slices of garlic-rubbed toast. Spanish-style chorizo is a dry, cured sausage—different from fresh Mexican-style chorizo, which comes in either a casing or in bulk and must be cooked before eating.

- 3 tablespoons extra-virgin olive oil, divided
- 2 medium carrots, minced
- 1 large red onion, minced
- 1½ tablespoons minced fresh thyme
- ¼ teaspoon crushed red pepper
- 3 ounces reduced-fat Spanish-style chorizo, finely diced
- 5¼ cups fresh shelled lima beans *or* three 10-ounce packages frozen baby lima beans, thawed (*see Tip*)
- 1 cup dry white wine
- ½ cup reduced-sodium chicken broth
- 3 cloves garlic, minced
- 1 tablespoon sherry vinegar
- ½ teaspoon kosher salt

Heat 1 tablespoon oil in a large saucepan over medium heat. Add carrots, onion, thyme and crushed red pepper and cook, stirring, until beginning to brown, 6 to 8 minutes. Stir in chorizo and cook, stirring occasionally, until heated through, about 5 minutes more. Add lima beans, wine, broth and garlic and cook for 5 minutes, scraping up any browned bits. Cover and cook over medium-low heat for 20 minutes. Remove from the heat and stir in the remaining 2 tablespoons oil, vinegar and salt. Let stand for at least 10 minutes before serving.

SERVES 12: ABOUT ½ CUP EACH

Calories 150, **Fat** 5g (sat 1g), **Cholesterol** 0mg, **Carbs** 17g, **Total sugars** 2g (added 0g), **Protein** 7g, **Fiber** 5g, **Sodium** 143mg, **Potassium** 370mg.
Nutrition bonus: Vitamin A (37% daily value).

PENNE ALLA PRIMAVERA

ACTIVE: 50 MIN **TOTAL:** 50 MIN
TO MAKE AHEAD: Refrigerate up to 6 hours; serve cold or at room temperature.

This penne tossed with spring vegetables is a perfect example of Mario Batali's rustic approach to great Italian food. (Recipe adapted from Molto Gusto *by Mario Batali and Mark Ladner; Ecco/HarperCollins Publishers, 2010.)*

¼ cup extra-virgin olive oil plus 2 tablespoons, divided

3 cloves garlic, thinly sliced

2 medium carrots, halved lengthwise and sliced ¼ inch thick

4 ounces morels, halved if large, *or* cremini mushrooms, thinly sliced

8 ounces asparagus, trimmed and sliced diagonally ¼ inch thick, tips reserved separately

1 cup shelled peas, fresh *or* frozen (thawed)

1 cup shelled fava beans *or* lima beans, fresh *or* frozen (thawed) (*see Tip*)

4 scallions, white parts only, thinly sliced

¾ teaspoon Maldon *or* other flaky sea salt

¼ teaspoon coarsely ground pepper, or more to taste

3 tablespoons kosher salt

1 pound penne pasta, preferably whole-wheat

⅓ cup coarsely chopped flat-leaf parsley

⅓ cup coarsely chopped fresh basil

⅓ cup coarsely chopped fresh mint

½ cup freshly grated Parmigiano-Reggiano cheese

Bean Swap

Fava beans have a very short season. If you can't find them, lima beans are a fine substitute.

1. Heat ¼ cup oil in a large pot over medium-high heat. Add garlic and cook until barely golden, about 30 seconds. Add carrots, reduce heat to medium and cook until beginning to soften, 3 to 4 minutes. Add mushrooms; cook until beginning to soften, 2 to 3 minutes. Add asparagus stalks; cook for 2 minutes. Add asparagus tips, peas, beans and scallions. Season with sea salt and pepper. Cook until vegetables are just tender, about 2 minutes.

2. Meanwhile, bring 6 quarts of water to a boil. Add kosher salt and pasta; cook until just tender, 10 to 12 minutes. Drain, reserving ½ cup cooking water.

3. Add the pasta and ¼ cup reserved cooking water to vegetables, tossing over medium heat. Cover, reduce heat to low and steam for 2 minutes. Stir in the remaining 2 tablespoons olive oil and a splash more reserved cooking water if necessary. Stir in parsley, basil and mint. Serve with Parmigiano.

SERVES 8: ABOUT 1¼ CUPS EACH

Calories 410, **Fat** 13g (sat 3g), **Cholesterol** 4mg, **Carbs** 60g, **Total sugars** 5g (added 0g), **Protein** 17g, **Fiber** 14g, **Sodium** 534mg, **Potassium** 536mg.
Nutrition bonus: Vitamin A (72% daily value), Folate (40% dv), Iron (35% dv), Magnesium (34% dv).

Snap Beans

Green beans, yellow wax beans and purple beans are all snap beans. (They are also referred to as "string beans," but the tough strings that run the length of the pod have been bred out of most American varieties.) Snap beans are a bit like people. They all have the same basic form, but some are short, some are long, some are slender, some are rounder and some are broader and flatter. They come in a variety of colors, and some are speckled and freckled. Whatever their appearance, snap beans all have the same fresh taste and crunchy texture.

Yellow wax beans are a bit more tender and have a milder flavor than green and purple beans. Purple beans have vibrant color when raw but turn green when cooked. Broad, flat Romano beans are snap beans, as are French filet beans or haricots verts—a type of green bean that is smaller than regular green beans. What all snap beans have in common is that they are harvested while the seeds inside are immature and the pod is tender and edible.

Cooked snap beans need only a little butter and salt, but they do take to certain enhancements, including other vegetables, such as tomatoes, onions and corn; crisp-cooked bacon or toasted walnuts or almonds; lemon; sesame oil and toasted sesame seeds; and herbs such as tarragon, dill and chives.

Just about the time the temperatures start to climb, it's time to pick the first crop of snap beans. Depending on where you live, the harvest continues from midsummer to early fall.

Best in summer

AT THE MARKET

Snap beans should snap. Avoid limp or flabby beans that do not break with a crisp sound. The one exception to this rule is French beans, or haricots verts. They don't have as crisp a texture as regular green beans and have a more bendable quality. In either case, avoid any snap beans that have brownish scars.

IN YOUR KITCHEN

Wrap snap beans in dry paper towels or place in a brown paper bag. Place in a plastic bag and refrigerate up to 4 days. French beans should be eaten immediately.

Cut off the stem ends. The most efficient way to do this is to line them up on a cutting board and do several at once. If they are curvy, cut or snip them individually; rinse in cool water. Small beans are most aesthetically pleasing left whole; larger beans can be cut in desired widths.

COOKING BASICS

BOIL Cook 1 pound snap beans in a large pot of boiling water until tender-crisp, 5 to 6 minutes. Drain and toss with 1 tablespoon olive oil or butter. Season with salt and pepper. Serves 4.

MICROWAVE Place 1 pound snap beans in a large microwave-safe casserole with 2 tablespoons water. Cover and cook on High until tender-crisp, stirring once, 4 to 5 minutes. Drain and toss with 1 tablespoon olive oil or butter. Season with salt and pepper. Serves 4.

ROAST Toss 1 pound snap beans with 1 tablespoon olive oil on a large rimmed baking sheet. Season with salt and pepper. Roast in a 450°F oven, stirring once, until tender and browned in spots, 25 to 35 minutes. Serves 4.

SAUTÉ Heat 1 tablespoon olive oil in a large skillet over medium-high heat. Add 1 minced shallot and cook, stirring, for 1 minute. Add 1 pound snap beans and cook, stirring often, until browned in spots, 2 to 3 minutes. Add ½ cup water. Cover; reduce heat to medium and cook, stirring occasionally, about 3 minutes for tender-crisp. Season with salt and pepper. Serves 4.

STEAM Bring 1 inch of water to boil in a saucepan fitted with a steamer basket. Add 1 pound snap beans. Cover; cook until tender-crisp, 5 to 7 minutes. Toss with 1 tablespoon olive oil or butter. Season with salt and pepper. Serves 4.

NUTRITION

1 cup of green beans: Calories 44, **Fat** 0g (sat 0g), **Cholesterol** 0mg, **Carbs** 10g, **Total sugars** 5g (added 0g), **Protein** 2g, **Fiber** 4g, **Sodium** 1mg, **Potassium** 182mg.

BONUS Silicon is critical for strong bones, yet few foods provide meaningful amounts of this mineral. Enter snap beans. They're a top source. You can also get silicon from bananas, carrots, bran cereal, whole-wheat bread and brown rice.

Grow Your Own

Snap beans fall into one of two categories—pole beans or bush beans. The categories have no bearing on flavor or appearance of the bean but refer only to the plant's growing habit. Pole bean plants can grow as tall as 6 feet and must be trained up a pole, trellis or teepee for support, while bush beans grow just 1 or 2 feet tall. Sow seeds directly in the ground in a sunny spot after danger of frost has passed. Soil should be well drained and have composted manure added before planting. Plant seeds every 4 inches in rows 2 feet apart for bush types. Plant seeds every 8 inches in rows 3 feet apart for pole types. Water regularly; mulch. When seedlings are a few inches tall, thin plants to one every 4 to 8 inches. Harvest most snap beans when pods are 6 to 8 inches long, 45 to 55 days after planting. To keep plants producing, harvest regularly.

In midsummer, the first slender, crunchy green beans appear, draped elegantly from plants with fan-like leaves and corkscrew tendrils that cling to the trellis or teepee for support.

GREEN BEAN & TOMMY-TOE SALAD

ACTIVE: 30 MIN **TOTAL:** 40 MIN

At first glance you may think that vinegar or lemon juice has been inadvertently omitted from the ingredient list. Not so. The juice of tiny ripe cherry tomatoes, called "tommy toes" in parts of the mountain South, is acidic enough and also contributes subtle sweetness—the perfect counterpoint to fresh beans.

  3 tablespoons extra-virgin olive oil
  1 large clove garlic, cut in half
  8 ounces green beans, trimmed, cut into 1-inch pieces (about 2 cups)
  ½ small sweet white onion, diced (½ inch)
  ½ teaspoon salt
  1 pint cherry tomatoes, halved

1. Place oil and garlic in a small bowl. Set aside.

2. Put green beans in a medium saucepan and add enough water to cover. Bring to a boil. Cover, reduce heat to maintain a simmer and cook until the beans are tender, 15 to 20 minutes.

3. Drain the beans and transfer to a serving bowl. Discard the garlic and add the garlic-infused oil to the beans. Add onion and salt; gently toss to coat. Let stand for 5 minutes.

4. Add tomatoes to the beans and gently stir to combine. Serve immediately.

SERVES 4: ABOUT ¾ CUP EACH

Calories 129, **Fat** 11g (sat 2g), **Cholesterol** 0mg, **Carbs** 8g, **Total sugars** 4g (added 0g), **Protein** 2g, **Fiber** 3g, **Sodium** 298mg, **Potassium** 309mg.
Nutrition bonus: Vitamin C (30% daily value), Vitamin A (20% dv).

THREE SISTERS SUCCOTASH

ACTIVE: 25 MIN **TOTAL:** 1 HR

Corn, squash and beans, known as the three sisters, were traditionally grown together by Native Americans. And the companions are as delicious married in the pot as they are harmonious in the garden. Succotash, from the Narragansett word msiquatash, *referred to a winter stew made from corn and beans but now also describes various vegetable blends, such as this summer garden mix. If you find lovely pattypan squashes, you could use those instead of regular zucchini or summer squash.*

12 ounces green beans, trimmed, cut into ¾-inch pieces (about 3 cups)

¾ teaspoon salt, divided

2 large ears fresh corn, husked

2 tablespoons extra-virgin olive oil

1 tablespoon butter

2 small summer squash *or* zucchini, cut into ½-inch pieces

¼ teaspoon ground pepper

2 scallions, finely chopped

1. Place beans in a large saucepan; add water to cover. Add ½ teaspoon salt. Bring to a boil. Cover, reduce heat to maintain a simmer and cook until the beans are tender, 20 to 30 minutes.

2. Meanwhile, cut corn kernels from the cobs: Hold an ear by its stem end in a deep bowl. Use a small sharp knife to cut off the kernels, letting them fall into the bowl. Then scrape down the cob with a small spoon, scraping the "milk" and remaining corn pulp into the bowl. (Discard the cobs.)

3. When the beans are done, drain, reserving the cooking liquid.

4. Heat oil and butter in a large, heavy skillet over medium heat. Add the corn and "milk." Stir to coat well, then add squash (or zucchini), the beans and 2 tablespoons of the bean-cooking liquid. Cook, stirring occasionally, until the corn and squash are tender, 8 to 12 minutes. Add more bean-cooking liquid if necessary to keep the mixture from sticking to the pan. Season with the remaining ¼ teaspoon salt and pepper. Sprinkle with scallions and serve immediately.

SERVES 6: ABOUT ⅔ CUP EACH

Calories 126, **Fat** 7g (sat 2g), **Cholesterol** 5mg, **Carbs** 15g, **Total sugars** 6g (added 0g), **Protein** 3g, **Fiber** 3g, **Sodium** 303mg, **Potassium** 367mg.
Nutrition bonus: Vitamin C (30% daily value).

SPICY STIR-FRIED STRING BEANS

ACTIVE: 25 MIN **TOTAL:** 25 MIN

Green beans hold up well to high heat, taking on a lightly charred exterior while retaining a pleasing tender-crisp interior. If you don't have a wok, a skillet works just as well.

¾ cup water
2 tablespoons reduced-sodium soy sauce
1 teaspoon cornstarch
1-2 teaspoons Asian hot sauce, such as sriracha
1 tablespoon canola oil
1 pound green *and/or* yellow wax beans, trimmed
4 teaspoons minced fresh ginger
3 large cloves garlic, minced
1 tablespoon toasted sesame seeds

1. Whisk water, soy sauce, cornstarch and hot sauce to taste in a small bowl.

2. Heat oil in a wok or large skillet over medium-high heat. Add beans, ginger and garlic; cook, stirring, until fragrant, about 1 minute. Add the sauce mixture; cook, stirring frequently, until the beans are tender-crisp, 4 to 6 minutes. Sprinkle with sesame seeds.

SERVES 4: ABOUT 1 CUP EACH

Calories 92, **Fat** 5g (sat 0g), **Cholesterol** 0mg, **Carbs** 11g, **Total sugars** 4g (added 0g), **Protein** 3g, **Fiber** 3g, **Sodium** 291mg, **Potassium** 282mg.
Nutrition bonus: Vitamin C (24% daily value).

NOT-YOUR-GRANDMA'S GREEN BEAN CASSEROLE

ACTIVE: 50 MIN **TOTAL:** 1 HR

Typical green bean casseroles bathe ingredients in canned soup and top them with canned onion rings or cheese. Our healthier version saves about 160 calories compared to a traditional recipe.

2½ pounds green beans, trimmed and cut into 1- to 2-inch pieces (about 8 cups)

3 tablespoons extra-virgin olive oil, divided

1 medium onion, thinly sliced

3 tablespoons all-purpose flour

¾ teaspoon salt

¼ teaspoon white *or* black pepper

2½ cups low-fat milk

1½ cups fresh whole-wheat breadcrumbs

1. Position racks in upper and lower third of oven; preheat to 425°F.

2. Toss green beans in a large bowl with 1 tablespoon oil until well coated. Divide between 2 rimmed baking sheets and spread in an even layer. Roast, stirring once and rotating the pans top to bottom about halfway through, until tender and beginning to brown, 20 to 25 minutes.

3. Meanwhile, heat 1 tablespoon oil in a large saucepan over medium heat. Add onion and cook, stirring frequently, until very soft and golden brown, 5 to 8 minutes. Add flour, salt and pepper; cook, stirring, for 1 minute more. Add milk and continue to stir, scraping up any browned bits, until the sauce bubbles and thickens enough to coat the back of a spoon, about 4 minutes. Remove from heat. (*See Tip.*)

4. When the green beans are done, remove from the oven. Preheat the broiler.

5. Transfer half the beans to a 2-quart broiler-safe baking dish. Spread half the sauce over them. Add the remaining beans and top with the remaining sauce. Combine breadcrumbs and the remaining 1 tablespoon oil in a small bowl; sprinkle over casserole.

6. Broil, watching closely, until the casserole is bubbling and beginning to brown on top, 1 to 5 minutes. Let stand for 10 minutes before serving.

SERVES 8: ABOUT 1 CUP EACH

Calories 187, **Fat** 7g (sat 1g), **Cholesterol** 4mg, **Carbs** 25g, **Total sugars** 10g (added 1g), **Protein** 8g, **Fiber** 5g, **Sodium** 337mg, **Potassium** 484mg.
Nutrition bonus: Vitamin C (31% daily value), Vitamin A (23% dv).

Vary It Up

To add extra flavor to the cream sauce, at the end of Step 3 stir in 1 tablespoon chopped fresh herb, such as thyme, sage or parsley. Or make it cheesy by topping with ½ cup shredded or crumbled cheese, such as Gruyère, Swiss, Cheddar or blue cheese, instead of breadcrumbs.

Bringing Eggs to
Room Temperature

Bring eggs to room
temperature by either
setting them out on the
counter for 15 minutes or
submerging them (in the
shell) in a bowl of lukewarm
(not hot) water for 5 minutes.

SUNNY-SIDE BEANS

ACTIVE: 35 MIN **TOTAL:** 1 HR
EQUIPMENT: Four 10-ounce ovenproof bowls or an 8-inch-square baking dish

In this lovely presentation, eggs are baked over a bed of saucy beans in ovenproof bowls or ramekins. (The runny yolk mingles deliciously with the melted butter.) The dish uses a combo of green or yellow wax beans in the pod plus a cup of the beans shelled out —known as "shelly beans"—or baby lima beans or crowder peas. Crowder peas are any variety of field pea, such as a black-eyed pea.

1½ **cups water**
12 **ounces green beans** *or* **yellow wax beans, trimmed, cut into 1-inch pieces (about 3 cups)**
1 **cup fresh shelled beans, fresh crowder peas** *or* **frozen baby lima beans**

¼ **cup minced onion**
2 **tablespoons butter**
½ **teaspoon salt**
4 **large eggs, at room temperature (see** *Tip***)**
Ground pepper to taste

1. Bring water to a boil in a large saucepan. Add green beans and shelled beans (or peas or lima beans). Reduce the heat to maintain a lively simmer and cook, uncovered, stirring occasionally, until tender, 15 to 20 minutes. (The beans will not be completely submerged in the liquid.) Stir in onion, butter and salt. Remove from heat, cover and let stand until the butter is melted.

2. Meanwhile, preheat oven to 350°F. Fill four 10-ounce ovenproof bowls (or an 8-inch-square baking dish) with hot water to warm them while the oven preheats.

3. Empty the bowls (or dish) and dry. If using bowls, place them on a baking sheet. Evenly divide the bean mixture and butter sauce among the bowls (or spread in the baking dish). Using a large spoon, make a ½-inch-deep well in the beans for each egg. Break an egg into each well.

4. Bake until the egg whites are just set, 15 to 20 minutes. Check after 15 minutes; if necessary, continue to bake, checking every minute or two, until the whites are set but the yolks are still runny. Remove from the oven and let stand 5 minutes; the eggs will continue to cook a little bit. Serve with a generous grinding of pepper on top.

SERVES 4: 1 EGG & ABOUT 1 CUP BEANS EACH

Calories 196, **Fat** 11g (sat 5g), **Cholesterol** 201mg, **Carbs** 15g, **Total sugars** 4g (added 0g), **Protein** 11g, **Fiber** 5g, **Sodium** 383mg, **Potassium** 435mg.
Nutrition bonus: Vitamin A & Vitamin C (22% daily value).

Beets

More than any other vegetable, beets taste of the soil in which they're grown. Sweet and earthy, with a mineral essence, beets have experienced a renaissance in recent years unrivaled by any other vegetable except perhaps kale.

There was a time when this humble root was considered a winter storage food that few were particularly enthused about eating. Beets were canned, boiled or pickled, and that was the end of it. But creative chefs began using beets in all kinds of interesting ways, and the reputation of the root has changed dramatically. Beets contain more natural sugar than starch—the highest amount of any vegetable—so roasting in the oven or grilling intensifies the sugar.

Beets are a vegetable with two distinct parts—both the roots and the leafy green tops are eaten. The latter can be prepared much like chard—a close relative—chopped raw in a salad, lightly sautéed in garlic and olive oil or quick-braised in liquid, such as chicken broth.

The sweetness of beets makes them natural companions to acidic and sharp flavors, such as lemon juice; assertive herbs, such as tarragon and cilantro; pleasantly bitter greens; blue cheese and goat cheese. The sweetness also means they taste delicious pickled. Grate raw and use in a relish or cut into julienne and toss into a salad. Try pickled beets as an accompaniment to hash made with leftover roasted meats and white or sweet potatoes.

Beets are a cool-weather crop, which means there is a harvest in the spring and then, if replanted in mid- to late summer, another harvest in the fall.

Best in spring and fall

AT THE MARKET

∙ Choose firm, bright-color beets that have unblemished skin with no cuts. It's best when the taproot—the long, thin root at the bottom of the beet—is still attached. If the greens are attached, they should look fresh. They can be a bit droopy, but avoid any with cuts or discoloration.

∙ Beets range dramatically in size, from tiny radish-size baby beets to young beets (1½ inches in diameter) to medium (2 inches in diameter) to large (more than 2½ inches in diameter). Medium beets are generally the best choice.

IN YOUR KITCHEN

∙ Cut off attached greens before storing, leaving 1 inch of the stem attached. Place unwashed beets in a plastic bag and store in the refrigerator up to 2 weeks. Store the greens separately in a plastic bag but use within a day or two.

∙ Scrub the beets gently with a vegetable brush.

COOKING BASICS

BOIL Place trimmed beets in a saucepan with water to cover. Add 2 tablespoons lemon juice. Bring to a boil. Reduce heat and simmer until tender, 45 minutes to 1 hour. Rinse beets under cool running water until they can be handled. Rub skins off.

BRAISE Melt 1 tablespoon butter in a large skillet over medium heat. Lay 1 pound scrubbed baby beets with greens attached in skillet. Cook until greens are wilted, 1 to 2 minutes. Add 1 cup chicken broth. Cover; reduce heat and simmer, undisturbed, until beets are tender, about 6 to 8 minutes. Season with salt and pepper. Serves 2.

ROAST Trim and peel 1½ pounds beets; cut into 1-inch wedges. Toss with 4 teaspoons olive oil, 2 tablespoons chopped fresh herbs, 1 teaspoon grated lemon peel, ½ teaspoon salt and pepper to taste. Spread on a baking sheet. Roast in the bottom third of a 450°F oven, turning once, until tender and browned, 20 to 25 minutes. Serves 4.

SAUTÉ Coarsely chop 8 ounces beet greens; thinly slice stems. Heat 1 tablespoon olive oil in a skillet over medium heat. Add 1 clove thinly sliced garlic; cook 1 minute. Add the beet greens and stems. Cook until softened, about 2 minutes. Season with ¼ teaspoon salt. Serves 2.

STEAM Peel trimmed beets and cut into ½- to 1-inch-thick cubes, wedges or slices. Place in a steamer basket over 1 inch of boiling water in a large pot. Cover and steam until tender, 10 to 15 minutes.

NUTRITION

∙ **1 cup of cooked sliced beets: Calories** 74, **Fat** 0g (sat 0g), **Cholesterol** 0mg, **Carbs** 17g, **Total sugars** 14g (added 0g), **Protein** 3g, **Fiber** 3g, **Sodium** 130mg, **Potassium** 518mg.

BONUS These root vegetables supply nitrate, which has been shown to enhance exercise performance. Eating just over a cup of beets an hour before a run has been shown to help people run five percent faster.

Grow Your Own

Beets are easy to grow. Plant in spring as soon as the soil dries and can be worked. Beets like loamy soil, lots of sun and consistent moisture. They need room to grow, so plant 1 inch deep and 3 to 4 inches apart, or plant closer together ½ inch deep and thin seedlings when they are 2 inches tall. Most varieties are ready for harvest 8 to 10 weeks after planting. Plant again in late summer for a fall crop.

▲ _Red 'Merlin'_
Jewel-tone red beets are the most familiar type of this earthy root vegetable. 'Merlin' has an especially high sugar content.

▲ _Chioggia_
This Italian heirloom variety has mild flavor and a pattern of concentric circles of red and white stripes that fades when cooked.

▲ _Golden 'Boldor'_
Sweet and juicy golden beets have a milder flavor and thinner skin than red beets. The 'Boldor' variety is prized for its consistently round roots.

PICKLED BEETS

ACTIVE: 40 MIN **TOTAL:** 40 MIN (PLUS 1 DAY MARINATING TIME)
TO MAKE AHEAD: Refrigerate up to 1 month. **EQUIPMENT:** 6 pint-size (2-cup) canning jars or similar-size tempered-glass or heatproof-plastic containers with lids

Tangy pickled beets are a favorite year-round. Try them as a garnish for Greek salad or as part of a relish tray at your next summer barbecue.

3½ pounds beets, peeled and cut into ⅛- to ¼-inch-thick slices
    (about 11 cups)
 1 tablespoon pickling spice
 3 cups distilled white vinegar *or* cider vinegar
 3 cups water
 2 tablespoons plus 2 teaspoons sea salt
 2 tablespoons sugar

1. Place a large bowl of ice water next to the stove. Bring a large pot of water to a boil. Add about a third of the beet slices, cover, return to a boil and cook for 5 minutes. Use a slotted spoon to transfer the beets to the ice water to cool. Repeat with the two remaining batches of beets.

2. Drain the cooled beets and divide among 6 pint-size (2-cup) canning jars or similar-size tempered-glass or heatproof-plastic containers with lids. Add ½ teaspoon of pickling spice to each jar.

3. Combine vinegar, 3 cups water, salt and sugar in a large saucepan. Bring to a boil and stir until the salt and sugar dissolve. Boil for 2 minutes. Remove from the heat.

4. Carefully fill jars (or containers) with the brine to within ½ inch of the rim, covering the beets completely. (Discard any leftover brine.)

5. Place the lids on the jars (or containers). Refrigerate at least 24 hours before serving. Store in the refrigerator up to 1 month.

MAKES: 6 PINT JARS (ABOUT 12 CUPS; ¼-CUP SERVING)

Calories 14, **Fat** 0g (sat 0g), **Cholesterol** 0mg, **Carbs** 3g, **Total sugars** 2g (added 0g), **Protein** 1g, **Fiber** 1g, **Sodium** 49mg, **Potassium** 108mg.

Bleeding Beets

Red beets can leave their mark. The intense hue of the juice gets on everything it touches—cutting board, sink, your hands, other foods. To avoid red-stained hands, wear plastic gloves when cutting red beets. To avoid an all-pink dish, you can also use golden or Chioggia beets in any recipe that calls for beets to mingle with other ingredients.

ROASTED BEET SALAD

ACTIVE: 40 MIN **TOTAL:** 3¼ HRS
TO MAKE AHEAD: Prepare through Step 4 and refrigerate up to 1 day; finish Step 5 and refrigerate up to 1 day more.

Tabbouleh—the Middle Eastern bulgur-wheat salad—was chef Michael Solomonov's inspiration for the look of this salad. For a pretty variation, try golden beets instead of red. If you can't find beets with greens attached, use 1 pound of beets and 8 ounces of chard leaves.

1½ pounds baby beets with greens attached	1 cup distilled white vinegar
1 head garlic	¼ cup sugar
4 tablespoons extra-virgin olive oil, divided	½ cup finely chopped toasted walnuts
¾ teaspoon kosher salt, divided	¼ cup finely chopped red onion
	¼ cup chopped fresh dill

1. Preheat oven to 325°F.

2. Rinse beets well. Cut off the greens, then cut the leaves off the stalks. Set the leaves and stalks aside. Remove excess papery skin from garlic head without separating the cloves, then cut the head in half horizontally.

3. Toss the beets, garlic, 2 tablespoons oil and ½ teaspoon salt in a small baking pan, such as a loaf pan. Cover with foil. Roast until tender, 1 to 1¼ hours. Let cool slightly.

4. Whisk vinegar and sugar in a medium bowl. Squeeze the garlic cloves out of their skins into the bowl. Peel and dice the beets; add to the bowl. Let marinate at room temperature at least 2 hours or refrigerate up to 1 day.

5. Finely chop the beet stems and very thinly slice the greens; place in a large bowl. Scoop the beets from the pickling liquid with a slotted spoon and add to the bowl. Drizzle the beet mixture with ¼ cup of the pickling liquid. Add walnuts, onion, dill, the remaining 2 tablespoons oil and ¼ teaspoon salt and gently toss to combine.

SERVES 8: ABOUT ⅔ CUP EACH

Calories 135, **Fat** 10g (sat 1g), **Cholesterol** 0mg, **Carbs** 11g, **Total sugars** 8g (added 3g), **Protein** 2g, **Fiber** 2g, **Sodium** 150mg, **Potassium** 235mg.

BORSCHT WITH BEEF

ACTIVE: 40 MIN **TOTAL:** 1¾ HRS
TO MAKE AHEAD: Refrigerate up to 3 days; garnish just before serving.

Even people who think they don't like beets love this vibrant vegetable-packed soup. The legendary dish served at New York's Russian Tea Room was the inspiration for this version.

4 teaspoons canola oil, divided
8 ounces sirloin *or* flank steak, trimmed, cut into ½-inch cubes
8 ounces mushrooms, sliced
4 medium beets (about 1 pound), peeled and shredded
1½ cups shredded cabbage
1 cup shredded carrots
1 cup finely chopped onion
1 cup finely chopped celery
½ cup red wine
6 cups reduced-sodium beef broth
1 cup no-salt-added tomato sauce
1 tablespoon Worcestershire sauce
¼ cup chopped fresh dill, plus more for garnish
½ cup reduced-fat sour cream

1. Heat 2 teaspoons oil in a large pot over medium-high heat. Add steak and cook, stirring frequently, until beginning to brown, 2 to 4 minutes. Transfer to a bowl.

2. Add 1 teaspoon oil to the pot and heat over medium-high. Add mushrooms and cook, stirring, until beginning to brown, 3 to 5 minutes. Transfer to the bowl.

3. Add the remaining 1 teaspoon oil to the pot. Add beets, cabbage, carrots, onion and celery. Cook, stirring frequently, until beginning to soften, about 10 minutes. Add wine and cook, stirring and scraping up any browned bits. Stir in the reserved mushrooms, broth, tomato sauce and Worcestershire sauce. Cover and bring to a boil. Reduce heat to maintain a simmer and cook, covered, until the vegetables are very tender, about 30 minutes.

4. Add the reserved beef. Simmer, covered, until heated through, 1 to 2 minutes. Stir in ¼ cup dill. Top each portion with 1 tablespoon sour cream and garnish with more dill, if desired.

SERVES 8: ABOUT 1⅓ CUPS EACH

Calories 151, **Fat** 6g (sat 2g), **Cholesterol** 24mg, **Carbs** 13g, **Total sugars** 8g (added 0g), **Protein** 10g, **Fiber** 3g, **Sodium** 436mg, **Potassium** 677mg.
Nutrition bonus: Vitamin A (52% daily value), Vitamin C (21% dv).

Bok Choy

In Cantonese, "bok" means "white" and "choy" means "vegetable"—but that's only part of the story. The many varieties of bok choy vary in color, taste and size. Some have more rounded leaves; some are curly or frilly. Some have light green stems. There are both dwarf and standard varieties—and you may see the name of this Asian vegetable spelled as bok choy, bok choi, pak choy or pak choi. And while the nomenclature may be a bit confusing, it is all essentially the same vegetable—a refreshing combination of crisp, succulent, white spoon-shape stems topped by juicy, dark green leaves that have a touch of sweetness.

Bok choy is a member of the brassica or cruciferous family of vegetables that includes cabbages, broccoli, kale, collards, mustard greens, cauliflower and Brussels sprouts. It is considered a nonheading cabbage because it grows in a cluster of stems and is sometimes referred to as "Chinese cabbage" (as is napa cabbage).

Bok choy is widely used in Chinese cooking, frequently in soups, salads, stir-fries and fillings for spring rolls, pot stickers, steamed buns and dumplings. Its mild flavor shines when stir-fried in sesame oil with a little garlic and/or ginger and a splash of soy sauce or a sprinkle of salt. Although it can be braised or stewed, it is best when exposed to a short blast of high heat—roasted, steamed, stir-fried or stirred into hot soup right before serving. Overcooking destroys its fresh flavor and texture.

Bok choy grows best in full sun in cool temperatures. It's at peak season from midwinter to early spring—just when the cravings kick in for something light and fresh and green.

Best in midwinter to early spring

AT THE MARKET

❧ Choose bok choy with firm, moist, unblemished stems and bright green leaves. Avoid wilted or bruised leaves that have yellowing or browning, holes or tears.

❧ The term "baby bok choy" refers to both dwarf varieties and to immature versions of standard varieties. Baby bok choy has a slightly milder flavor, more tender texture and a higher ratio of green leaves to stem than does mature bok choy.

IN YOUR KITCHEN

❧ Store bok choy in the refrigerator in a sealable plastic bag up to 1 week. Wash right before using.

❧ For baby or dwarf bok choy, cut a very thin slice from the bottom of the cluster of stems. Halve lengthwise, then plunge halves repeatedly, leaf-side-down, into cool water until the base of the stalks is clean and free of sand and grit. Change water if necessary.

❧ For mature bok choy, trim a slice off the end of the base of stems. Remove and discard any bruised or blemished leaves. Separate the stalks in a similar fashion to celery. Rinse each stalk thoroughly, checking the base of the stems, which are the most prone to retain sand and grit.

COOKING BASICS

GRILL Drizzle 4 halved, trimmed baby bok choy (about 1 pound) with 1 tablespoon toasted sesame oil and gently toss to coat. Season lightly with coarse salt and pepper. Grill over medium heat for 4 minutes; turn and grill until lightly charred, 4 to 5 minutes more. Serves 4.

STEAM Place 4 halved, trimmed baby bok choy (about 1 pound) in a steamer basket over simmering water. Cover and steam until stem ends are just tender when pierced, about 6 minutes. Drizzle with 1 tablespoon melted butter and 1 teaspoon minced fresh chives. Season to taste with salt and pepper. Serves 4.

STIR-FRY Thinly slice 2 pounds of trimmed bok choy. Heat 1 tablespoon each canola oil and toasted sesame oil in a large pot over medium-high heat. Add 3 cloves of minced garlic and cook, stirring constantly, until fragrant, about 30 seconds. Add the bok choy and cook, stirring, until wilted, about 5 minutes. Season with ¼ teaspoon salt and sprinkle with 1 tablespoon toasted sesame seeds. Serves 3.

NUTRITION

❧ **1 cup cooked bok choy: Calories** 20, **Fat** 0g (sat 0g), **Cholesterol** 0mg, **Carbs** 3g, **Total sugars** 1g (added 0g), **Protein** 3g, **Fiber** 2g, **Sodium** 58mg, **Potassium** 631mg.

BONUS This cruciferous cousin of broccoli is loaded with nutrients that help keep your skeleton strong, such as calcium, vitamin K and potassium. Swap in 2 cups of raw bok choy for lettuce in your salad and you'll rack up as much calcium as you'd get from half a glass of milk.

▲ **Canton Bok Choy**
Also called dwarf bok
choy, these crisp and juicy
heads are a diminutive
variety of the vegetable.
"Dwarf" and "baby" bok
choy are interchangeable.

▲ **Bok Choy**
The mature heads of
this vegetable feature
crisp, succulent stalks
topped by leafy greens
that can be rounded,
curly or frilly.

▶ **Choy Sum**
The name for this
Chinese green means
"vegetable heart," a
reference to the tender
central flowering stalk
of any of the plants in
the "choy" family.

▲ **Shanghai Bok Choy**
The most common variety
of "baby" bok choy, these
shapely heads are perfect for
halving and grilling, roasting
or steaming.

Mirin

Mirin is a low-alcohol rice wine essential to Japanese cooking. An equal portion of sherry or white wine with a pinch of sugar may be substituted. Mirin is available at Asian specialty markets and in the Asian section of some larger supermarkets.

ROASTED BABY BOK CHOY

ACTIVE: 15 MIN **TOTAL:** 15 MIN

A short stint in a hot oven, combined with a drizzle of lemony dressing, brings bok choy to the table in no time at all.

1¼ pounds baby bok choy (about 4 heads), trimmed, leaves separated
4 teaspoons canola oil
1 clove garlic, minced
¼ teaspoon kosher salt
½ teaspoon freshly grated lemon zest
1 tablespoon lemon juice
1½ teaspoons chopped fresh tarragon *or* ¾ teaspoon dried
1 teaspoon mirin (*see Tip*)
   Ground pepper to taste

1. Position rack in bottom third of oven; preheat to 450°F.

2. Toss bok choy, oil, garlic and salt in a roasting pan. Roast on lowest rack, stirring twice, until wilted and tender-crisp, about 6 minutes. Whisk lemon zest and juice, tarragon, mirin and pepper in a small bowl. Drizzle over the roasted bok choy.

SERVES 4: ABOUT ¾ CUP EACH

Calories 63, **Fat** 5g (sat 0g), **Cholesterol** 0mg, **Carbs** 4g, **Total sugars** 2g (added 0g), Protein 2g, **Fiber** 1g, **Sodium** 117mg, **Potassium** 527mg.
Nutrition bonus: Vitamin A (118% daily value), Vitamin C (64% dv).

VELVET CHICKEN WITH BABY BOK CHOY

ACTIVE: 45 MIN **TOTAL:** 55 MIN

This recipe uses a classic Chinese cooking technique that keeps the meat juicy and succulent, as the chicken stays creamy white.

Julienne Ginger

To finely julienne ginger, cut peeled fresh ginger into paper-thin slices, make a stack of 3 slices at a time, then cut into fine matchsticks (about ⅛ inch wide).

- 1 pound boneless, skinless chicken breasts, trimmed and cut into ¼-inch-thick bite-size slices
- 1 large egg white, lightly beaten
- 1 tablespoon cornstarch plus ½ teaspoon, divided
- 2 teaspoons Shao Hsing rice wine *(see Tip, page 482)* or dry sherry plus 2 tablespoons, divided
- ½ teaspoon salt, divided
- 3 tablespoons peanut oil *or* canola oil, divided
- ⅓ cup reduced-sodium chicken broth
- 2 teaspoons reduced-sodium soy sauce
- ¼ teaspoon ground white pepper
- 6 cups water
- ⅔ cup chopped scallions, divided
- 1 tablespoon finely julienned *or* minced fresh ginger *(see Tip)*
- ¼ teaspoon crushed red pepper
- 8 cups trimmed and halved baby bok choy (about 12 ounces)

1. Combine chicken, egg white, 1 tablespoon cornstarch, 2 teaspoons rice wine (or sherry) and ¼ teaspoon salt in a medium bowl. Stir until the cornstarch is totally dissolved. Stir in 1 tablespoon oil. Refrigerate, uncovered, for 30 minutes.

2. Meanwhile, combine broth, soy sauce, white pepper and the remaining ½ teaspoon cornstarch and 2 tablespoons rice wine (or sherry) in a small bowl.

3. Bring water to a boil in a large saucepan. Add 1 tablespoon oil. Reduce heat to low. Add chicken; gently stir to keep from clumping. Cook until opaque but not cooked through, about 1 minute. Drain and shake to remove excess water.

4. Heat a wok over high heat until a bead of water vaporizes within 2 seconds. Swirl in remaining 1 tablespoon oil. Add ⅓ cup scallions, ginger and crushed red pepper; stir-fry until fragrant, about 10 seconds. Add bok choy and remaining ¼ teaspoon salt; stir-fry until almost crisp-tender, 1 to 2 minutes. Add chicken. Stir broth mixture, swirl into wok and stir-fry until chicken is cooked through and coated with sauce, 30 seconds to 1 minute. Serve sprinkled with the remaining ⅓ cup scallions.

SERVES 4: ABOUT 1½ CUPS EACH

Calories 251, **Fat** 13g (sat 2g), **Cholesterol** 63mg, **Carbs** 6g, **Total sugars** 1g (added 0g), **Protein** 26g, **Fiber** 1g, **Sodium** 537mg, **Potassium** 600mg.
Nutrition bonus: Vitamin A (75% daily value), Vitamin C (42% dv).

TUNA & BOK CHOY PACKETS

ACTIVE: 15 MIN **TOTAL:** 30 MIN

Serve this moist and flavorful fish with a spoonful of brown rice to soak up the delicious juices that accumulate in the packet during cooking.

¼ **cup horseradish mustard**

¼ **cup finely chopped parsley, divided**

2 **tablespoons water**

¼ **teaspoon ground pepper**

8 **cups chopped bok choy**

1 **tablespoon extra-virgin olive oil**

1-1¼ **pounds tuna, wild salmon, mahi-mahi *or* cod, skinned if desired, cut into 4 portions**

1. Preheat oven to 475°F.

2. Combine mustard, 3 tablespoons parsley, water and pepper in a small bowl. Toss bok choy, oil and 2 tablespoons of the mustard sauce in a large bowl.

3. Cut four 20-inch sheets of foil. Arrange 2 cups of the chopped bok choy in the center of each sheet, top with a portion of fish and 1 tablespoon of the remaining sauce. Bring the short ends of foil together, fold over and pinch to seal. Pinch the side seams together to seal the packets, then place on a large baking sheet.

4. Bake the packets until the fish is opaque in the center, about 15 minutes (depending on thickness). When opening a packet to check for doneness, be careful of the steam. Serve, sprinkled with the remaining 1 tablespoon parsley.

SERVES 4: 3-4 OZ. FISH & ABOUT ⅓ CUP BOK CHOY EACH

Calories 201, **Fat** 7g (sat 1g), **Cholesterol** 46mg, **Carbs** 5g, **Total sugars** 2g (added 0g), **Protein** 30g, **Fiber** 2g, **Sodium** 258mg, **Potassium** 1,008mg.
Nutrition bonus: Vitamin A (114% daily value), Vitamin C (63% dv), Potassium (29% dv).

Cooking "en Papillote"

Cooking foods in foil packets is a variation on cooking "en papillote," or "in parchment"—a French technique of steaming foods in a hot oven in packets made from parchment paper. As a cooking method, it requires little to no fat. The food comes out moist and succulent—and the flavors mingle together beautifully.

It also makes for easy cleanup. You can use foil—or, if you'd like to try cooking "en papillote" the easy way— look for parchment cooking bags that require only a few folds to seal.

Broccoli

The "tiny trees" of the vegetable world start out as a dense head of unopened flower buds that is harvested from the center of a cabbage-like plant. The florets are surrounded by large waxy gray-green leaves that are also edible and can be used like collards or other dark leafy greens.

Although the blue-green Calabrese variety is the most familiar form, this brassica is part of a larger family that includes cabbage, cauliflower, Brussels sprouts and, of course, other varieties of broccoli, including Chinese broccoli and Broccolini. The name, broccoli, is in fact derived from the Italian word for "cabbage sprout."

Broccoli is delicious dressed with any combination of butter, olive oil, fresh herbs, garlic, lemon, crushed red pepper, olives, capers or anchovies—or lightly steamed and tossed with olive oil, golden raisins and toasted pine nuts.

Not surprisingly, Chinese broccoli pairs well with Asian flavors. Toss with peanut sauce, sesame dressing or a gingery Japanese dipping sauce.

Broccolini—a name trademarked by one of its growers—is a hybrid of broccoli and Chinese broccoli. Try it prepared like asparagus—roasted and dressed in vinaigrette or draped with a bit of hollandaise. It also takes well to sweet/salty/smoky flavors, such as ham and honey mustard. It is lovely hot, cold or at room temperature.

Broccoli is available all year but does best in cool weather and is at peak from mid-fall to mid-spring.

Best in midfall to midspring

AT THE MARKET

Broccoli is sold both as a crown (the top of the head only) or with several inches of stalk attached. Choose brightly colored broccoli with no yellow or brown spots, with tightly closed flower buds. Check the cut ends of the stalks. They should be fresh and moist, not cracked or dried out.

Choose slender stalks of Broccolini and Chinese broccoli. Avoid those with leaves that are wilted, yellowing or with holes or tears.

IN YOUR KITCHEN

Store broccoli, Broccolini and Chinese broccoli in a loosely closed plastic bag in the refrigerator up to 3 days.

To prepare standard broccoli: Cut off the stalk and trim the leaves. Break or cut into florets. Rinse thoroughly in a colander under cool running water. Although the florets are the prized portion of the head of the common Calabrese type, the stalks are delicious too. Peel them with a vegetable peeler or paring knife, if desired, to remove the tough, fibrous exterior, until they are a luminous pale green. Slice into coins or cut into cubes.

To prepare Broccolini and Chinese broccoli: Trim off the ends of the stalks. Rinse under cool running water.

COOKING BASICS

MICROWAVE Place trimmed spears from 1 head broccoli (or 3½ cups broccoli florets) in a large microwave-safe bowl with 2 tablespoons water. Cover and cook on High, stirring once, until crisp tender, 5 to 8 minutes. Serves 4.

ROAST Toss 4 cups broccoli florets with 1 tablespoon olive oil, ¼ teaspoon salt and freshly ground pepper. Roast on a large rimmed baking sheet in a 450°F oven until the broccoli is browned, 10 to 12 minutes. Serve with lemon wedges. Serves 4.

SAUTÉ Heat 1 tablespoon canola oil in a large skillet over medium-high heat. Add 2 tablespoons minced garlic and cook until fragrant, about 30 seconds to 1 minute. Add 6 cups broccoli florets and cook, stirring, until the broccoli is bright green, 2 minutes. Drizzle 3 tablespoons water over broccoli. Reduce heat to medium; cover and cook until just tender, about 3 minutes. Season with ¼ teaspoon salt. Serves 4.

STEAM Trim ½ inch off stalks of 1 head of broccoli (or 3½ cups broccoli florets). Remove tough outer layer of stalks with a vegetable peeler. Cut each stalk in half lengthwise. Bring 1 inch water to a boil in a large pot fitted with a steamer basket. Cover and steam the broccoli until tender, 5 to 7 minutes. Serves 4.

NUTRITION

1 cup of chopped raw broccoli: Calories 31, **Fat** 0g (sat 0g), **Cholesterol** 0mg, **Carbs** 6g, **Total sugars** 2g (added 0g), **Protein** 3g, **Fiber** 2g, **Sodium** 30mg, **Potassium** 288mg.

BONUS Broccoli owes its robust cancer-preventing abilities to glucosinolates, compounds that may sweep cancer-causing substances out of your body before they can harm cells. To reap the most glucosinolate action from your broccoli, cook it as little as possible as heat can quickly destroy these sensitive compounds.

◄ *Chinese Broccoli*
Also called gai lan, these slender stalks have dark green leaves and a slightly bitter flavor reminiscent of broccoli rabe—which makes a good substitute.

▼ *Broccoli*
This blue-green broccoli is the most common variety found in supermarkets—clusters of tightly formed buds on top of thick, meaty stalks.

▲ *Broccolini*
A hybrid of broccoli and Chinese broccoli, these bright green stalks topped with loose bouquets of buds have a crisp, smooth texture and a more delicate flavor than broccoli. Broccoletti is another sprouting broccoli, which has many shoots rather than one large head.

Toasting Nuts

Toasting nuts deepens the flavor and gives them a crisp, delightful crunch. To toast nuts, spread in a single layer in a small baking pan and bake in a 350°F oven until golden and fragrant, 5 to 7 minutes, stirring the nuts or shaking the pan once. Transfer to a small bowl or plate to cool. (When toasting hazelnuts, rub the nuts with a clean kitchen towel as soon as they come out of the oven to remove as much of the papery skin as possible.)

BROCCOLI & TORTELLINI SALAD WITH ARUGULA PESTO

ACTIVE: 30 MIN **TOTAL:** 30 MIN
TO MAKE AHEAD: Refrigerate up to 4 hours.

A quick arugula pesto dresses this simple broccoli and tortellini salad. Serve with fresh sliced tomatoes drizzled with olive oil.

- 1 medium clove garlic
- 5 cups baby arugula
- ½ cup shredded Pecorino *or* Parmesan cheese
- ¼ cup extra-virgin olive oil
- ¼ cup plus 2 tablespoons toasted pine nuts, divided (*see Tip*)
- 2 teaspoons freshly grated lemon zest
- ¼ teaspoon salt
- 2 9- to 10-ounce packages fresh cheese tortellini, preferably whole-wheat
- 5 cups small broccoli florets

1. Put a large pot of water on to boil.

2. With the motor running, drop garlic through the feed tube of a food processor; process until minced. Turn it off and add arugula, cheese, oil, ¼ cup pine nuts, lemon zest and salt. Process, scraping down the sides as necessary, until the mixture is fairly smooth; leave the pesto in the food processor while you cook the tortellini.

3. Cook tortellini in the boiling water until just tender, 6 to 8 minutes or according to package directions. Place broccoli in a colander and set it in the sink. Reserve ½ cup of the pasta-cooking liquid, then pour the tortellini and the rest of the cooking liquid over the broccoli in the colander. (Pouring the hot pasta and cooking liquid over the broccoli "flash-cooks" it, leaving it bright green and tender-crisp.)

4. Add the reserved ½ cup cooking liquid to the pesto in the food processor; pulse to combine. Transfer the tortellini and broccoli to a large bowl. Toss with the pesto. Serve sprinkled with the remaining 2 tablespoons pine nuts.

MAKES: 6 SERVINGS, ABOUT 1⅓ CUPS EACH

Calories 445, **Fat** 23g (sat 5g), **Cholesterol** 35mg, **Carbs** 45g, **Total sugars** 2g (added 0g), **Protein** 16g, **Fiber** 5g, **Sodium** 605mg, **Potassium** 314mg.
Nutrition bonus: Vitamin C (98% daily value), Vitamin A (45% dv).

MEDITERRANEAN ROASTED BROCCOLI & TOMATOES

ACTIVE: 10 MIN **TOTAL:** 20 MIN

Roasting brings out the subtle sweetness of broccoli and melts grape tomatoes into succulent morsels.

- 12 ounces broccoli crowns, trimmed and cut into bite-size florets (about 4 cups)
- 1 cup grape tomatoes
- 1 tablespoon extra-virgin olive oil
- 2 cloves garlic, minced
- ¼ teaspoon salt
- ½ teaspoon freshly grated lemon zest
- 1 tablespoon lemon juice
- 10 pitted black olives, sliced
- 1 teaspoon dried oregano
- 2 teaspoons capers, rinsed (optional)

1. Preheat oven to 450°F.

2. Toss broccoli, tomatoes, oil, garlic and salt in a large bowl until evenly coated. Spread in an even layer on a large rimmed baking sheet. Roast until the broccoli begins to brown, 10 to 13 minutes.

3. Meanwhile, combine lemon zest and juice, olives, oregano and capers (if using) in a large bowl. Add the roasted vegetables; stir to combine. Serve warm.

SERVES 4: ABOUT 1 CUP EACH

Calories 79, **Fat** 5g (sat 1g), **Cholesterol** 0mg, **Carbs** 8g, **Total sugars** 1g (added 0g), **Protein** 3g, **Fiber** 4g, **Sodium** 251mg, **Potassium** 379mg.
Nutrition bonus: Vitamin C (145% daily value), Vitamin A (58% dv).

BROCCOLI-CHEDDAR-CHICKEN CHOWDER

ACTIVE: 45 MIN **TOTAL:** 45 MIN
TO MAKE AHEAD: Refrigerate up to 3 days, slowly reheat over medium-low or microwave on Medium power.

In this delicious chowder, heavy cream is replaced with milk and flour-thickened chicken broth and we keep sodium amounts reasonable with lower-sodium broth. By making your own you save up to 300 calories, 20 grams of saturated fat and 500 milligrams of sodium per serving compared to many store-bought or restaurant chowders.

3 tablespoons extra-virgin olive oil

1 cup diced onion

1 cup diced celery

½ cup all-purpose flour

1 teaspoon dry mustard

¼ teaspoon salt

¼ teaspoon ground pepper

4 cups reduced-sodium chicken broth

1 cup whole milk

3 cups chopped broccoli florets

2 cups diced Yukon Gold potatoes

1 pound boneless skinless chicken breasts, cut into bite-size pieces

1 cup shredded Cheddar cheese, plus more for garnish

Finely diced red onion for garnish

1. Heat oil in a large pot over medium heat. Add onion and celery; cook, stirring frequently, until softened and beginning to brown, 3 to 6 minutes. Sprinkle flour, dry mustard, salt and pepper over the vegetables and cook, stirring, for 1 minute more. Add broth and milk; bring to a gentle boil, stirring constantly.

2. Stir in broccoli and potatoes and bring just to a simmer. Simmer, uncovered, stirring occasionally, until the potatoes are tender, 12 to 15 minutes.

3. Add chicken and 1 cup Cheddar and cook, stirring frequently, until cooked through, 4 to 6 minutes. Serve topped with a little more Cheddar and red onion, if desired.

SERVES 6: ABOUT 1½ CUPS EACH

Calories 352, **Fat** 17g (sat 6g), **Cholesterol** 66mg, **Carbs** 23g, **Total sugars** 4g (added 0g), **Protein** 27g, **Fiber** 3g, **Sodium** 664mg, **Potassium** 724mg.
Nutrition bonus: Vitamin C (64% daily value), Vitamin A (28% dv), Calcium (23% dv), Potassium (21% dv).

Peeling Ginger

There are two ways to peel ginger. Use a small sharp paring knife to remove the brown skin or scrape the gnarly root with a teaspoon.

STIR-FRIED CHINESE BROCCOLI

ACTIVE: 20 MIN **TOTAL:** 20 MIN
EQUIPMENT: 14-inch flat-bottomed carbon-steel wok

Like broccoli rabe, Chinese broccoli has a bitter bite. Adding a little sugar will balance the flavor without creating a sweet dish.

12 ounces Chinese broccoli *or* broccoli rabe
¾ teaspoon sugar
½ teaspoon salt
2 tablespoons peanut oil, divided
3 slices fresh ginger (¼ inch thick), peeled and smashed
¼ teaspoon crushed red pepper
2 tablespoons Shao Hsing rice wine *(see Tip, page 482) or* dry sherry

1. Trim ¼ inch off broccoli stalks. If the stalks are thicker than ½ inch, cut in half lengthwise. Keeping them separate, cut the stalks and leaves into 2-inch-long pieces. Combine sugar and salt in a small bowl.

2. Heat a 14-inch flat-bottomed wok or large heavy skillet (not nonstick) over high heat until a bead of water vaporizes within 1 to 2 seconds of contact. Swirl in 1 tablespoon oil and add ginger and crushed red pepper; stir-fry until the ginger is fragrant, about 10 seconds. Add the broccoli stalks and stir-fry until bright green, 1 to 1½ minutes. Swirl in the remaining 1 tablespoon oil and add the broccoli leaves; sprinkle with the sugar mixture and stir-fry until the leaves are bright green and just limp, about 1 minute. Swirl in rice wine (or sherry); stir-fry until the stalks are just crisp-tender, 1 to 1½ minutes. Remove the ginger before serving.

SERVES 4: ABOUT ½ CUP EACH

Calories 92, **Fat** 7g (sat 1g), **Cholesterol** 0mg, **Carbs** 4g, **Total sugars** 1g (added 1g),
Protein 3g, **Fiber** 2g, **Sodium** 319mg, **Potassium** 173mg.
Nutrition bonus: Vitamin A (46% daily value), Vitamin C (29% dv).

Broccoli Rabe

In the early decades of the 20th century, an Italian immigrant saw these slender green stalks growing wild in the fields of California and it made him think of home. He began breeding the plant in the 1930s and developed a variety with juicy stalks and an abundance of leaves and flowers that would appeal to Americans. This new variety was enthusiastically embraced in Italy as well, where it is most commonly known as rapini or broccoli di rape.

Broccoli rabe—also spelled broccoli raab—is often lumped with the broccolis but is more closely related to the turnip. (Although Chinese broccoli and Broccolini make good substitutes.) It has an assertive, nutty flavor, with a hint of mustardy bitterness. It is prized in Chinese and Italian cuisines, which value bitterness as a balancing flavor.

The sharp flavor of broccoli rabe enlivens sometimes bland foods, such as pasta, potatoes, chickpeas, cannellini beans, mild cheeses and bread. And because it is so bold, it also stands up admirably to chiles, lots of garlic, ginger, pungent olives and spicy Italian sausage.

It can be cooked similarly to broccoli, but it goes from pleasantly crisp-tender to mushy much faster. A quick sauté in olive oil with garlic, a little salt and crushed red pepper—and a squeeze of fresh lemon right before serving—is a simple and popular cooking method.

Like most brassicas, broccoli rabe is a cool-weather crop. Although it's available year-round, it is best from late fall to early spring—and actually at peak during the dead of winter.

Best in late fall to early spring

AT THE MARKET

➤ Buy broccoli rabe when it's young and slender. Although there is a fair amount of variance in its naturally bitter flavor from bunch to bunch, the bitterness intensifies the older it is and the longer it sits in storage.

➤ Choose firm, deep-green stems with tightly packed flower heads and fresh-looking leaves. Select stalks that have very few open yellow flowers.

IN YOUR KITCHEN

➤ Broccoli rabe can only be stored for a short time. To keep stalks in the center from spoiling, remove the rubber band or twist tie. Lightly wrap in a moist paper towel and place in a plastic bag. Store in refrigerator up to 3 days.

➤ Broccoli rabe usually needs only trimming at the bottoms of the stems. Rinse under cool running water and pat dry.

➤ Although it's not a necessity and can be erratic in its effectiveness, you can try to reduce the bitterness of broccoli rabe by blanching and shocking it. Drop in boiling water for 20 seconds, then immediately plunge in ice water. For a more tender texture and milder flavor, leave it in the boiling water 2 to 4 minutes, then plunge in ice water. Pat dry and proceed with recipe.

COOKING BASICS

BOIL Cook 1 pound trimmed broccoli rabe in a large pot of boiling water until tender when pierced with a fork, 3 to 5 minutes; drain well. Toss with 1 tablespoon olive oil and season with ¼ teaspoon each salt and pepper. Serve with lemon wedges. Serves 4.

BROIL On a broiler pan or large rimmed baking sheet, toss 1 pound trimmed broccoli rabe with 1 tablespoon olive oil. Season with salt and pepper; toss again to coat. Broil for 2 minutes. Turn, then broil until stalks are tender-crisp and leaves start to turn brown and crispy, about 2 minutes more. Sprinkle with 2 tablespoons toasted sliced almonds. Serves 4.

GRILL Cook 1 pound trimmed broccoli rabe in a large pot of boiling water until bright green and barely tender, 1 to 2 minutes; drain and rinse with cold water. Drain again. Combine 2 tablespoons olive oil, 2 teaspoons red-wine vinegar, 1 teaspoon garlic powder, ½ teaspoon chopped fresh rosemary, ¼ teaspoon salt and freshly ground pepper in a large bowl. Grill broccoli rabe over medium-high until leaves are just beginning to char, 1 to 2 minutes per side. Toss with dressing. Serves 4.

SAUTÉ Heat 1 tablespoon sesame oil in a large skillet over medium heat. Add 1 tablespoon minced shallot and cook, stirring, until shallot is softened, 1 to 2 minutes. Add 1 pound chopped broccoli rabe; toss to coat. Cook, stirring occasionally, for 2 minutes more. Stir in 1 tablespoon reduced-sodium soy sauce, 1 tablespoon lemon juice and ¼ teaspoon ground white pepper. Serves 4.

STEAM Bring 1 inch water to a boil in a large pot fitted with a steamer basket. Place 1 pound broccoli rabe in steamer basket. Cover and steam broccoli rabe until tender, 5 to 7 minutes. Toss with 1 tablespoon olive oil and season with ¼ teaspoon salt and pepper to taste. Serve with lemon wedges. Serves 4.

NUTRITION

➤ **½ cup of chopped cooked broccoli rabe: Calories** 28, **Fat** 0g (sat 0g), **Cholesterol** 0mg, **Carbs** 3g, **Total sugars** 1g (added 0g), **Protein** 3g, **Fiber** 2g, **Sodium** 48mg, **Potassium** 292mg.

BONUS This bitter crucifer is rich in kaempferol, a phytochemical that thwarts cancer by cutting off the blood supply to tumors and preventing cancerous cells from metastasizing.

Grilled Broccoli Rabe
(see Cooking Basics, opposite)

BROCCOLI RABE WITH OLIVES & GARLIC

ACTIVE: 20 MIN **TOTAL:** 35 MIN

Broccoli rabe is a staple of winter markets and tables throughout the Italian south. It can be part of an antipasto selection or a contorno—that is, a vegetable to accompany a main course of fish or meat. And it can be served on its own, with nothing but toasted bread with olive oil to scoop it up. Or sprinkle with sautéed breadcrumbs. (Photo: page 107.)

  2 bunches broccoli rabe (about 2 pounds)
¼ cup extra-virgin olive oil
  1 clove garlic, crushed and coarsely chopped
½ small dried hot red chile pepper
½ teaspoon salt
¼ cup very small black olives (Niçoise-type), pitted

1. Discard any coarse, yellowing or wilted broccoli rabe leaves. Cut away tough stems, leaving the flowers and stalks and the tender young side leaves. Thoroughly wash, leaving some water still clinging to the leaves.

2. Heat oil over medium heat in a deep pot large enough to hold all the broccoli rabe. Add garlic and chile pepper; cook, stirring, just until the garlic starts to soften, 1 to 2 minutes. Add the broccoli rabe to the pot by the handful, letting it wilt a bit before adding more. Cover and cook, stirring occasionally, until it is tender and just a few spoonfuls of liquid remain in the pan, 15 to 20 minutes. (There should be plenty of water for cooking clinging to the leaves, but check the pan from time to time and have a little boiling water ready to add if necessary.) When the broccoli rabe is tender, stir it well to mix it with its sauce and season with salt. Stir in olives and serve immediately.

SERVES 6: SCANT 1 CUP EACH

Calories 122, **Fat** 11g (sat 2g), **Cholesterol** 0mg, **Carbs** 4g, **Total sugars** 1g (added 0g), **Protein** 3g, **Fiber** 3g, **Sodium** 306mg, **Potassium** 218mg.
Nutrition bonus: Vitamin A (55% daily value), Vitamin C (44% dv), Folate (22% dv).

VIETNAMESE-FLAVORED BROCCOLI RABE

ACTIVE: 20 MINUTES **TOTAL:** 20 MINUTES

A simple dressing of fish sauce, lime juice and hot pepper gives broccoli rabe a Vietnamese twist. Try it with grilled pork and rice.

  1 bunch broccoli rabe (about 1 pound), trimmed and chopped
  1 tablespoon fish sauce (*see Tip*)
1½ teaspoons lime juice
  1 teaspoon sugar
  1 clove garlic, minced
⅛-¼ teaspoon crushed red pepper
  1 tablespoon canola oil

1. Cook broccoli rabe in a large pot of boiling water until bright green and barely tender, 1 to 2 minutes. Drain in a colander and gently press out as much water as possible.

2. Combine fish sauce, lime juice, sugar, garlic and crushed red pepper to taste in a small bowl; stir until the sugar is dissolved.

3. Heat oil in a large pot or large skillet over medium-high heat. Add the broccoli rabe and cook, stirring, until just tender, 2 to 3 minutes. Stir in the fish sauce mixture and cook, stirring, 1 minute more.

SERVES 4: ABOUT ⅔ CUP EACH

Calories 67, **Fat** 4g (sat 0g), **Cholesterol** 0mg, **Carbs** 5g, **Total sugars** 2g (added 1g), **Protein** 4g, **Fiber** 3g, **Sodium** 335mg, **Potassium** 229mg.
Nutrition bonus: Vitamin A (60% daily value), Vitamin C (40% dv), Folate (24% dv)

Fish Sauce

Fish sauce is a pungent Southeast Asian condiment made from salted, fermented fish. Find it in the Asian-food section of well-stocked supermarkets and at Asian specialty markets. We use Thai Kitchen fish sauce, which is lower in sodium than other brands (1,190 mg per tablespoon), in our recipe testing and nutritional analyses.

"Broccoli rabe" means "little sprouts" in Italian, which certainly describes the slender stalks topped by bouquets of tender, juicy buds.

Broccoli Rabe with
Olives & Garlic
(page 104)

—≈—

Perfect Pasta

There are so many shapes of pasta because there are so many types of sauce. Pasta is paired with sauce depending on its texture, weight and body. Thin pasta like spaghetti goes well with thinner, smoother sauces that coat the long strands, while larger tubular pasta, such as rigatoni or penne, works well with thicker or more textured sauces that get caught up in the hollow middles of the pasta pieces. The orecchiette ("little ears" in Italian) in this recipe nicely holds the chunky sauce in its scoop shape.

—≈—

ORECCHIETTE WITH BROCCOLI RABE

ACTIVE: 30 MIN **TOTAL:** 30 MIN

In this iconic pasta dish of Puglia, Italy, anchovies are mashed into olive oil to add amazing depth to the garlicky sauce. Assertive broccoli rabe has the featured role, though, so even anchovy avoiders needn't be afraid.

  2 **teaspoons salt**
12 **ounces orecchiette pasta (about 3½ cups) (see *Tip*)**
  2 **pounds broccoli rabe (about 2 bunches)**
  ¼ **cup extra-virgin olive oil**
  3 **cloves garlic, chopped**
  ½ **teaspoon crushed red pepper**
  8 **anchovy fillets, chopped**
  1 **pint cherry tomatoes, halved**
      Freshly grated Parmesan cheese (optional)

1. Bring 2 quarts of water to a boil in a large pot. Stir in salt, add pasta and cook according to package instructions until just tender. Drain, reserving ½ cup of the water.

2. Meanwhile, thoroughly wash broccoli rabe and trim off tough ends. Chop into 2-inch lengths. Leave some of the water clinging to the leaves and stems; this will help create a sauce.

3. Heat oil in a large skillet over medium heat until it starts to shimmer. Add garlic, crushed red pepper and anchovies, mashing the fillets until they dissolve. Add the broccoli rabe (you may have to do this in batches, stirring each batch a little until it wilts enough to add more). Cook, stirring, until almost tender, 6 to 10 minutes. Add tomatoes and toss until they begin to soften, about 2 minutes. Add the pasta and toss to coat. If it's too dry, add a little of the reserved pasta water. Serve immediately, garnished with Parmesan if desired.

SERVES 6: 1½ CUPS EACH

Calories 359, **Fat** 12g (sat 2g), **Cholesterol** 5mg, **Carbs** 50g, **Total sugars** 3g (added 0g), **Protein** 15g, **Fiber** 7g, **Sodium** 388mg, **Potassium** 484mg.
Nutrition bonus: Vitamin A (89% daily value), Vitamin C (63% dv), Folate (59% dv), Iron (29% dv).

Brussels Sprouts

If any vegetable has suffered an undeserved bad reputation, it is Brussels sprouts—mostly because the preferred cooking method used to be to boil them beyond recognition. But once it was discovered that they could be roasted to caramelized goodness—with a crisp exterior and tender, buttery interior—or shredded raw into light and crunchy salads, Brussels sprouts became a revelation.

On the plant, Brussels sprouts look like an alien creature that landed in the garden. A profusion of tiny cabbage-like heads—the buds of the plant—hugs a thick stalk that can get up to 2½ feet tall, crowned by a spray of blue-green leaves. Each stalk produces between 50 and 100 sprouts. And although they are not tiny cabbages, Brussels sprouts are part of the brassica family, as is cabbage.

Brussels sprouts are one of the last crops to be harvested from the garden, making them a truly fresh treat at the Thanksgiving table.

Brussels sprouts can be boiled (gently, please), steamed, roasted, grilled, braised and sautéed. Good flavor companions include onions, garlic and shallots; walnuts; caraway and fennel seeds; a mustardy vinaigrette; brown butter; bacon and other smoky, salty meats; nutty, pungent cheeses, such as Swiss or Gruyère; and herbs like sage and dill.

Try breaking the heads apart into individual leaves and quickly stir-frying—or scattering the leaves over the top of a pizza with Italian sausage or caramelized onions and blue cheese.

Brussels sprouts thrive in cool weather. They are at peak season from fall to early winter—and, in fact, taste even sweeter and milder after the first frost.

Best in fall to early winter

AT THE MARKET

Choose firm, bright green, tightly furled sprouts. Avoid sprouts that have brown spots or yellowing or are beginning to open. Try to get sprouts of approximately the same size so they cook evenly. Small sprouts have a sweeter, milder flavor than large ones. Although you might occasionally find sprouts still attached to the stalks, beware as the stalk sucks moisture out of the sprouts as they sit. If you want to buy them on the stalk, make sure they were picked recently, and cut them from the stalk when you get home.

IN YOUR KITCHEN

Store Brussels sprouts in a plastic bag in the refrigerator up to 1 week.

Trim a very thin slice off stem end of each sprout. Remove any brown or yellow leaves. Rinse in a colander under cool running water. Leave sprouts whole or cut in half, quarter or shred.

COOKING BASICS

BRAISE Heat 1 tablespoon olive oil in a large skillet over medium-high heat. Add 1 pound Brussels sprouts and cook, stirring often, until sprouts are browned in spots, 2 to 4 minutes. Stir in 1 cup reduced-sodium chicken broth, ¼ teaspoon salt and pepper to taste. Cover and reduce heat to medium-low. Cook until Brussels sprouts are tender, 10 to 15 minutes. Serves 4.

ROAST Toss 2 pounds halved Brussels sprouts with 2 tablespoons olive oil, ½ teaspoon salt and pepper to taste. Spread on a large rimmed baking sheet and roast in a 450°F oven, stirring once, until sprouts are tender, 18 to 20 minutes. Serves 8.

STEAM Place 1 pound quartered Brussels sprouts in a steamer basket over 1 inch boiling water. Cover and steam until tender, 7 to 8 minutes. Whisk 2 tablespoons walnut oil, 1 tablespoon finely chopped chives, 1 tablespoon cider vinegar, 1 teaspoon whole-grain mustard, ¼ teaspoon salt and pepper to taste in a medium bowl. Add sprouts to dressing; toss to coat. Serves 4.

NUTRITION

½ cup of cooked Brussels sprouts: **Calories** 28, **Fat** 0g (sat 0g), **Cholesterol** 0mg, **Carbs** 6g, **Total sugars** 1g (added 0g), **Protein** 2g, **Fiber** 2g, **Sodium** 16mg, **Potassium** 247mg.

BONUS With four times the cancer-combating glucosinolates of broccoli, these little gems boast more of these compounds than any other crucifer. Chopping them, as for a slaw, works to release even more of these cancer-fighters.

Grow Your Own

Brussels sprouts require little more than sunshine, regular water and ample space. Start seeds indoors in early spring, 90 days before the last frost. In spring, transplant 24 to 36 inches apart. Harvest when sprouts are 1 to 1½ inches in diameter, picking sprouts from the base of the plant upward.

How to prep

1. Cut a thin slice off of the stem ends.

2. Remove any brown or yellow leaves.

3. Leave sprouts whole, cut in half *(right)*, quarter or shred.

SHAVED BRUSSELS SPROUTS SALAD WITH LEMON-CHILE VINAIGRETTE & TOASTED HAZELNUTS

ACTIVE: 30 MIN **TOTAL:** 30 MIN

Using the slicing blade of a food processor on Brussels sprouts creates a big, fluffy pile of crunchy sprout ribbons. Here, they're dressed with a lemony vinaigrette spiked with crushed red pepper and sweetened with a bit of honey.

- 1 teaspoon finely grated lemon zest
- 2 tablespoons lemon juice
- 1 tablespoon honey
- ½ teaspoon crushed red pepper
- ½ teaspoon salt
- ¼ teaspoon ground pepper
- ¼ cup extra-virgin olive oil
- 1¼ pounds Brussels sprouts, stem ends trimmed and outer leaves removed
- 1 cup very thinly sliced red onion
- ½ cup chopped hazelnuts, toasted *(see Tip, page 92)*

1. Combine lemon zest, lemon juice, honey, crushed red pepper, salt and pepper in a large bowl. Whisking continuously, slowly drizzle in oil until all of it is incorporated and the mixture is thickened.

2. Shred Brussels sprouts in a food processor fitted with the slicing disk. Transfer to the bowl. Add onion and hazelnuts and gently toss to combine.

SERVES 6: 1⅓ CUPS EACH

Calories 201, **Fat** 15g (sat 2g), **Cholesterol** 0mg, **Carbs** 14g, **Total sugars** 6g (added 3g), **Protein** 5g, **Fiber** 5g, **Sodium** 216mg, **Potassium** 436mg.
Nutrition bonus: Vitamin C (128% daily value).

ROASTED VEGETABLE ANTIPASTO

ACTIVE: 45 MIN **TOTAL:** 1 HR

A pungent vinaigrette makes the flavor of these roasted vegetables pop. If you can't find small carrots, halve larger ones crosswise, then quarter lengthwise. Serve as a side or appetizer.

12 medium Brussels sprouts
 4 teaspoons extra-virgin olive oil plus 2 tablespoons, divided
 1 large fennel bulb, halved, cored and cut into ¼-inch wedges
12 very small, thin carrots (8 ounces)
 1 large beet, preferably golden, sliced into ¼-inch rounds
 1 teaspoon kosher salt, divided
 1 large clove garlic, minced
 2 tablespoons lemon juice
 1 teaspoon capers, chopped
 1 anchovy fillet, minced (optional)

1. Position racks in upper and lower thirds of oven; preheat to 425°F.

2. Trim and halve Brussels sprouts; toss with 1 teaspoon oil in a medium bowl. Spread in a single layer on half of a large rimmed baking sheet. Toss fennel in the bowl with another 1 teaspoon oil; spread on the other half of the pan. Toss carrots in the bowl with another 1 teaspoon oil and spread on half of a second rimmed baking sheet. Toss beet slices with another 1 teaspoon oil; spread on the other half of the pan. Sprinkle the vegetables with ½ teaspoon salt.

3. Roast the vegetables, stirring once halfway through and rotating the baking sheets top to bottom and front to back, until soft and beginning to caramelize, 25 to 30 minutes. Arrange on a serving platter.

4. Meanwhile, mash garlic and the remaining ½ teaspoon salt in a small bowl with the back of a spoon until a paste forms. Add lemon juice, capers and anchovy (if using). Whisk in the remaining 2 tablespoons oil; drizzle over the vegetables.

SERVES 6: ABOUT ¾ CUP EACH

Calories 117, **Fat** 8g (sat 1g), **Cholesterol** 0mg, **Carbs** 10g, **Total sugars** 3g (added 0g), **Protein** 2g, **Fiber** 4g, **Sodium** 260mg, **Potassium** 426mg.
Nutrition bonus: Vitamin A (126% daily value), Vitamin C (57% dv).

Bacon Sense

A little bit of bacon goes a long way to add a load of flavor to dishes such as this one, which calls for only 4 slices in a total of 10 servings. Another option is to buy center-cut bacon, which is cut from the center of the pork belly and has a higher lean-to-fat ratio.

SAUTÉED BRUSSELS SPROUTS WITH BACON & ONIONS

ACTIVE: 35 MIN **TOTAL:** 35 MIN
TO MAKE AHEAD: Prepare through Step 1, rinse with cold water; store airtight in the refrigerator up to 1 day. Finish with Steps 2-3, 15 to 20 minutes before serving.

The sprouts in this recipe are briefly boiled to get a jump-start on the cooking process—then finished in a skillet with onions, herbs and bacon. (Recipe adapted from The Art of Simple Food *by Alice Waters.)*

2½ pounds Brussels sprouts, trimmed
 4 slices bacon, cut into 1-inch pieces
 1 tablespoon extra-virgin olive oil
 1 large onion, diced
 4 sprigs thyme *or* savory plus 2 teaspoons leaves, divided
 1 teaspoon salt
   Ground pepper to taste
 2 teaspoons lemon juice (optional)

1. Bring a large pot of water to a boil. If sprouts are very small, cut in half; otherwise cut into quarters. Cook the sprouts until barely tender, 3 to 5 minutes. Drain.

2. Meanwhile, cook bacon in a large heavy skillet over medium heat, stirring, until brown but not crisp, 3 to 6 minutes. Remove with a slotted spoon to drain on a paper towel. Pour out all but about 1 tablespoon bacon fat from the pan.

3. Add oil to the pan and heat over medium heat. Add onion and cook, stirring often, until soft but not browned, reducing the heat if necessary, about 4 minutes. Stir in thyme (or savory) sprigs, salt and pepper. Increase heat to medium-high, add the Brussels sprouts, and cook, tossing or stirring occasionally, until tender and warmed through, about 3 minutes. Remove the herb sprigs. Add the bacon, thyme (or savory) leaves and lemon juice, if using, and toss.

SERVES 10: ABOUT ¾ CUP EACH.

Calories 77, **Fat** 3g (sat 1g), **Cholesterol** 3mg, **Carbs** 10g, **Total sugars** 3g (added 0g), **Protein** 4g, **Fiber** 4g, **Sodium** 303mg, **Potassium** 430mg.
Nutrition bonus: Vitamin C (130% daily value).

GARLIC ROASTED SALMON & BRUSSELS SPROUTS

ACTIVE: 25 MIN **TOTAL:** 45 MIN

For this dinner in a roasting pan, we start with Brussels sprouts and garlic, then add salmon, a little wine and fresh oregano.

14 large cloves garlic, divided
¼ cup extra-virgin olive oil
2 tablespoons finely chopped fresh oregano, divided
1 teaspoon salt, divided
¾ teaspoon ground pepper, divided
6 cups Brussels sprouts, trimmed and sliced (about 1¼ pounds)
¾ cup white wine, preferably Chardonnay
2 pounds wild-caught salmon fillet *(see Tip, page 368)*, skinned, cut into
   6 portions
   Lemon wedges

1. Preheat oven to 450°F.

2. Mince 2 garlic cloves and combine in a small bowl with oil, 1 tablespoon oregano, ½ teaspoon salt and ¼ teaspoon pepper. Halve the remaining garlic and toss with Brussels sprouts and 3 tablespoons of the seasoned oil in a large roasting pan. Roast, stirring once, for 15 minutes.

3. Add wine to the remaining oil mixture. Remove the pan from oven, stir the vegetables and place salmon on top. Drizzle with the wine mixture. Sprinkle with the remaining 1 tablespoon oregano and ½ teaspoon each salt and pepper. Bake until the salmon is just cooked through, 5 to 10 minutes more. Serve with lemon wedges.

SERVES 6

Calories 334, **Fat** 15g (sat 3g), **Cholesterol** 71mg, **Carbs** 10g, **Total sugars** 2g (added 0g), **Protein** 33g, **Fiber** 3g, **Sodium** 485mg, **Potassium** 921mg.
Nutrition bonus: Vitamin B$_{12}$ & Vitamin C (107% daily value), Potassium (26% dv), Vitamin A (20% dv).

Cabbage

The sturdiest of vegetables, cabbage is also among the most versatile. Raw in slaw or cooked countless ways, its leaves are strong enough to stuff yet also make fabulous fillings in Chinese dumplings, Polish pierogi and German bierocks. Although there are more than 400 varieties of this cruciferous vegetable, a few have become more widely used than others.

Green cabbage, the most familiar, is a crucial element of colcannon, a homey Irish dish of buttery mashed potatoes combined with finely chopped cabbage. Other than salt and water, it is the sole ingredient in sauerkraut. Both choucroute garni—the hearty Alsatian dish of sausages, smoked meats and potatoes—and a grilled bratwurst at the ballpark would sorely lack without tart, crunchy kraut.

Red cabbage, often enhanced with sweet flavors, is braised with apples, onions, vinegar and brown sugar as a classic side to pork chops and roast pork.

Nubby, crinkly-leaved Savoy cabbage is tender even when raw, making it ideal for slaw. The frilly, pastel-green leaves of napa cabbage are lovely shredded raw for salads or quickly stir-fried. Napa is the base for kimchi, the spicy Korean condiment.

Despite its sturdy nature, cabbage does not hold up to prolonged exposure to heat. Overcooked, it takes on a sulfurous taste and emits an unpleasant aroma. Properly cooked, it turns a delightful silky texture with a bit of bite to it.

Cabbage is a cool-weather crop. Although there is a harvest in spring, the peak season for cabbage is late fall through winter.

Best in late fall through winter

AT THE MARKET

🐦 Choose cabbage that feels heavy for its size and that has bright color—whether red/purple or some shade of green. Avoid cabbage that has brown spots or other discoloration, wilted leaves or holes or tears in the leaves.

🐦 Savoy and napa cabbage will feel lighter than the denser heads of red and green cabbage. Avoid napa cabbage that has leaves with dry-looking tips.

IN YOUR KITCHEN

🐦 Store red, green and Savoy cabbage in a plastic bag in the refrigerator up to 10 days. Store napa cabbage in a plastic bag in the refrigerator up to 5 days. If cabbage is cut, the edge may dry out and brown. Cut a slice off to remove any discolored area and use the rest.

🐦 To prepare red, green and Savoy cabbage, remove any wilted outer leaves. Cut head into quarters. Remove the very thick core from each quarter.

🐦 To prepare napa cabbage, remove any wilted outer leaves from cabbage head. It can be halved, quartered, or sliced crosswise. Or separate stems from core, depending on intended use. (Napa cabbage does have a core, but because of its mild flavor and delicate texture, it does not need to be removed.)

COOKING BASICS

BRAISE Heat 2 teaspoons canola oil in a large pot over medium heat. Add 2 thinly sliced onions and cook, stirring, until the onions start to turn golden, about 8 minutes. Add 1 quartered, cored and sliced red cabbage and cook, stirring occasionally, until it wilts, 5 minutes. Stir in ⅔ cup reduced-sodium chicken broth and 1 teaspoon each caraway seeds and sugar; bring to a simmer. Cover and cook over low heat until very tender, 15 to 20 minutes. Add ¼ cup white vinegar. Increase heat to high and cook, stirring, until most of the liquid has evaporated, 8 to 10 minutes. Season to taste with salt and pepper. Serves 8.

COLESLAW Combine 3 tablespoons each reduced-fat mayonnaise and nonfat plain yogurt, 1 tablespoon Dijon mustard, 2 teaspoons cider vinegar, 1 teaspoon sugar, ½ teaspoon caraway seeds or celery seeds, and salt and pepper to taste. Add 2 cups each shredded red and green cabbage and 1 cup grated carrots. Toss well. Serves 6.

SAUTÉ Heat a large skillet over high heat until a bead of water vaporizes within 1 to 2 seconds of contact. Swirl 1 tablespoon canola oil in the pan. Add 2 teaspoons each minced garlic and minced ginger and stir-fry for 10 seconds. Add 6 cups thinly sliced napa cabbage and stir-fry until it just begins to wilt, about 1 minute. Add 2 tablespoons reduced-sodium soy sauce and cook, stirring, until the cabbage is tender-crisp, 1 to 2 minutes. Stir in 1½ teaspoons sesame oil. Serve immediately. Serves 4.

NUTRITION

🐦 **1 cup of chopped raw green cabbage:** Calories 22 **Fat** 0g (sat 0g), **Cholesterol** 0mg, **Carbs** 5g, **Total sugars** 3g (added 0g), **Protein** 1g, **Fiber** 2g, **Sodium** 16mg, **Potassium** 151mg.

BONUS All types of cabbage contain the anti-cancer compound sulforaphane; however, red cabbage boasts the most. When compared to green cabbage, red cabbage serves up 13 times as much of this cancer quasher.

► **Savoy Cabbage**
This loose-leaf cabbage has a sweeter taste and more delicate texture than either red or green cabbage.

▲ **Red Cabbage**
This brightly colored cabbage has a stronger but sweeter flavor than green cabbage—and more vitamins and nutrients.

▼ **Green Cabbage**
Also called Dutch white, this most familiar kind of cabbage grows in firm, dense heads. The squeaky, slightly rubbery leaves have peppery flavor raw but sweeten with cooking.

▲ **Napa Cabbage**
Also called Chinese cabbage, it has stout, barrel-shape heads not nearly as dense as red or green cabbage. It has a mild flavor and tender texture.

ROASTED CABBAGE WITH CHIVE-MUSTARD VINAIGRETTE

ACTIVE: 10 MIN **TOTAL:** 30 MIN

Roasting cabbage at a high temperature is a revelation in both flavor and texture: It brings out the sweet cabbage flavor and turns the leaves silky soft, not at all soggy or watery. Serve the wedges drizzled with the chive-mustard vinaigrette as a side dish for roast poultry, meat and fish or alone with crusty bread.

CABBAGE

- ½ medium green cabbage (1-1½ pounds), outer leaves removed
- 1 tablespoon extra-virgin olive oil
- ¼ teaspoon salt
- ¼ teaspoon ground pepper

VINAIGRETTE

- 2 teaspoons Dijon mustard
- 2 teaspoons white balsamic *or* white-wine vinegar
- 1 teaspoon lemon juice
- ¼ teaspoon ground pepper
- ⅛ teaspoon salt
- 3 tablespoons minced fresh chives
- 2 tablespoons extra-virgin olive oil

1. Preheat oven to 450°F. Coat a large baking sheet with cooking spray.

2. To prepare cabbage: Cut cabbage half into four wedges and cut out any thick core, leaving the wedges as intact as possible. Drizzle the cut sides with 1 tablespoon oil and sprinkle with ¼ teaspoon each salt and pepper. Place the wedges flat-side down on the prepared baking sheet.

3. Roast the cabbage for 12 minutes. Carefully flip over (it's OK if it falls apart a little) and roast until browned on both sides, about 8 minutes more.

4. To prepare vinaigrette: Combine mustard, vinegar, lemon juice, pepper and ⅛ teaspoon salt in a small bowl. Add chives and oil; stir until well combined.

5. Transfer the cabbage to a serving plate (or plates) and drizzle with the vinaigrette while still hot. Serve hot or at room temperature.

SERVES 4: 1 WEDGE EACH

Calories 125, **Fat** 11g (sat 2g), **Cholesterol** 0mg, **Carbs** 7g, **Total sugars** 4g (added 0g), **Protein** 2g, **Fiber** 3g, **Sodium** 271mg, **Potassium** 205mg.
Nutrition bonus: Vitamin C (72% daily value).

SIMPLE SAUERKRAUT

ACTIVE: 30 MIN **TOTAL:** 3-6 WEEKS
TO MAKE AHEAD: Refrigerate the fermented sauerkraut up to 6 months.
EQUIPMENT: 5- to 6-qt. glass, ceramic or stone container or crock with lid and resealable plastic bags

For the best sauerkraut, choose firm fresh heads of cabbage and use canning, pickling or kosher salt (not iodized salt). To be sure your cabbage-to-salt ratio is right for fermentation, start with as close to 5 pounds of untrimmed cabbage as you can. Pack the cabbage mixture into the container as tightly as possible (eliminating any air pockets). Keep it submerged in the brine at all times.

5 pounds green cabbage
3 tablespoons noniodized salt, such as canning, pickling *or* kosher, divided
   Salt brine, as needed and for water weights (1 teaspoon noniodized salt, dissolved, per 1 cup water)

1. Rinse the cabbages under cool water and remove the tough outer leaves. Cut the cabbages into quarters and cut out the core. Using a large, sharp knife, a food processor with a slicing blade or a mandoline, very thinly slice the cabbage. Place about one-third of the cabbage in a large clean bowl and sprinkle with 1 tablespoon salt; using clean hands, vigorously knead the salt into the cabbage until the cabbage starts to release a little liquid. Repeat with the remaining two-thirds of the cabbage and the remaining 2 tablespoons salt, vigorously kneading the salt into the cabbage after each addition.

2. Once all the cabbage is in the bowl, using both hands, massage the cabbage mixture vigorously, using your fingers to squeeze and bruise the cabbage, releasing as much of its liquid as possible, about 10 minutes.

3. Transfer the mixture and its liquid to a 5- to 6-quart glass, ceramic or stone container. Using your clean fists or a clean kitchen tool, pack the cabbage into the container with as much force as possible, removing all air pockets. Let stand, uncovered, for 2 hours. Pack the cabbage down once again. It should be completely covered in liquid. If not, add enough additional salt brine to cover.

4. Fill a sealable plastic bag (or bags) about two-thirds full with salt brine (instead of plain water in case they leak during fermentation). Place bag (or bags) directly on the surface of the cabbage mixture, using the bag(s) as water weights to keep the cabbage fully submerged at all times. Use enough water weights to cover the whole surface. Cover the container with a clean dish towel and place the lid on top. Place in a cool (60°F to 64°F), dark place. The cooler the temperature, the slower the fermentation. If your only option is a warmer spot, the fermentation will be quicker.

5. Check the sauerkraut every few days. Remove any scum or bits of white/light gray mold from the surface with a clean spoon and wipe off the plastic bag as necessary. (White/gray mold is not harmful. If you see any black mold, discard the sauerkraut. Pink-color "slime" on the surface is a yeast that, while not harmful, spoils the flavor and texture.) Pack the sauerkraut back down and replace the water weights. If the sauerkraut is not fully submerged, add additional salt brine. Replace the dish towel and lid.

6. After 2 to 3 weeks, use a clean fork to take out a sample to taste. If you like the flavor and have seen bubbles on the surface (a sign of fermentation), it's ready to be refrigerated. If you want more flavor, re-cover and continue fermenting until it develops a flavor that you like. When you like the taste, transfer the sauerkraut and liquid to smaller airtight containers. Refrigerate up to 6 months.

MAKES: ABOUT 10 CUPS (¼-CUP SERVING)

Calories 14, **Fat** 0g (sat 0g), **Cholesterol** 0mg, **Carbs** 3g, **Total sugars** 2g (added 0g), **Protein** 1g, **Fiber** 1g, **Sodium** 290mg, **Potassium** 96mg.
Nutrition bonus: Vitamin C (35% daily value).

CHINESE CHICKEN SALAD WITH CITRUS-MISO DRESSING

ACTIVE: 45 MIN **TOTAL:** 45 MIN

This salad has terrific crunch, thanks to sugar snap peas and napa cabbage.

GOMASIO
- ¾ cup sesame seeds
- ¾ teaspoon sea salt

DRESSING
- ⅓ cup freshly squeezed clementine *or* orange juice (about 3 clementines)
- 3 tablespoons rice vinegar
- 2 tablespoons white miso paste (*see Tip, page 32*)
- 1 tablespoon honey
- 1 tablespoon toasted sesame oil
- 2 teaspoons sambal oelek

SALAD
- 6 cups thinly sliced napa cabbage
- 2 cups sugar snap peas, thinly sliced diagonally
- 4 clementines *or* mandarins, peeled and sectioned
- 2 cups shredded cooked chicken breast
- ½ cup coarsely chopped fresh mint
- ¼ cup sliced scallions, white and green parts

1. To prepare gomasio: Toast sesame seeds in a medium-size dry skillet over medium heat, stirring constantly, until golden brown, 4 to 5 minutes. Add salt and cook, stirring constantly, for about 1 minute more. Transfer to a plate or bowl and let cool completely.

2. Transfer mixture to a spice grinder and pulse a few times to grind coarsely; there should be a few whole seeds remaining (or use a mortar and pestle).

3. To prepare dressing: Whisk juice, vinegar, miso, honey, sesame oil and sambal oelek in a small bowl.

4. To prepare salad: Combine cabbage, peas, clementines, chicken, mint and scallions in a large bowl. Drizzle with the dressing and toss gently to combine.

5. Divide among 4 large salad plates or shallow bowls. Sprinkle each serving with 1 teaspoon of the gomasio (*see Tip*).

SERVES 4: 2½ CUPS EACH

Calories 271, **Fat** 8g (sat 2g), **Cholesterol** 60mg, **Carbs** 25g, **Total sugars** 15g (added 4g), **Protein** 27g, **Fiber** 6g, **Sodium** 462mg, **Potassium** 767mg.
Nutrition bonus: Vitamin C (143% daily value), Vitamin A (40% dv), Folate (30% dv), Iron & Potassium (22% dv).

Low-Salt Seasoning

Gomasio [goh-MAH-shee-oh] is a Japanese seasoning made with toasted sesame seeds coarsely ground with a small amount of sea salt. It has a wonderful nutty flavor that sparks up plain roasted or grilled vegetables, sautéed greens, salads and grilled fish. Store leftover gomasio in an airtight glass container in the refrigerator up to 3 weeks.

BAVARIAN LEEK & CABBAGE SOUP

ACTIVE: 50 MIN **TOTAL:** 1 HR 10 MIN
TO MAKE AHEAD: Refrigerate up to 3 days.

German cuisine is full of hearty soups. Although this soup is traditionally made with ham hocks, it's wonderful with smoked bratwurst as well.

3 tablespoons extra-virgin olive oil

2 medium leeks, white and light green parts, halved and thinly sliced *(see page 336)*

1 cup coarsely chopped carrot

1 cup diced celery

2 tablespoons chopped fresh thyme

6 cups low-sodium chicken broth *or* Slow-Cooker Chicken Stock *(see Tip)*

1 12-ounce bottle lager

8 cups thinly sliced green *or* Savoy cabbage

3 cups diced red potatoes

2 bay leaves

4 cups chopped greens, such as chard *or* kale

12 ounces smoked bratwurst *or* kielbasa, cut into ½-inch rounds

¾ teaspoon salt
   Ground pepper to taste

½ cup reduced-fat sour cream
   Chopped fresh parsley for garnish

Heat oil in a large pot over medium heat. Add leeks, carrot, celery and thyme. Cover and cook, stirring occasionally, for 10 minutes. Add broth (or stock), lager, cabbage, potatoes and bay leaves; cover and bring to a boil. Uncover, reduce heat and simmer for 10 minutes. Stir in greens and sausage and cook, stirring occasionally, until the potatoes are tender, 10 to 15 minutes more. Season with salt and pepper. Discard bay leaves. Ladle into bowls and top each with 1 tablespoon sour cream and parsley.

SERVES 8: 1¾ CUPS EACH

Calories 338, **Fat** 20g (sat 5g), **Cholesterol** 39mg, **Carbs** 26g, **Total sugars** 5g (added 0g), **Protein** 13g, **Fiber** 4g, **Sodium** 709mg, **Potassium** 974mg.
Nutrition bonus: Vitamin A (132% daily value), Vitamin C (126% dv), Potassium (28% dv), Vitamin B$_{12}$ (23% dv), Folate (20% dv).

Slow-Cooker Chicken Stock

In a 6-quart slow cooker combine 1 medium carrot, 1 celery stalk, and 1 small onion, all cut into 1-inch pieces. Add 4 pounds skinless chicken leg quarters, 6 sprigs fresh parsley, 2 sprigs fresh thyme, 1 bay leaf, 1 crushed garlic clove, and 20 whole peppercorns. Add 9 cups water. Cook on High for 4 hours. Strain and let cool to room temperature before refrigerating in airtight containers for up to 1 week or freezing up to 3 minutes. Makes about 10 cups.

VEGETARIAN STUFFED CABBAGE

ACTIVE: 1¼ HRS **TOTAL:** 2 HRS
TO MAKE AHEAD: Prepare through Step 10 and refrigerate up to 1 day. Let stand at room temperature about 30 minutes before baking.

Although traditionally this dish is made with meat, here Savoy cabbage leaves are stuffed with a combination of rice, mushrooms, onions, garlic and herbs. The stuffed leaves gently bake in a simple tomato sauce. The recipe can be made ahead of time and baked just before serving.

CABBAGE & FILLING

- 1 cup water
- ½ cup short-grain brown rice
- 1 teaspoon extra-virgin olive oil plus 2 tablespoons, divided
- 1 large Savoy cabbage (2-3 pounds)
- 1 pound baby bella mushrooms, finely chopped
- 1 large onion, finely chopped
- 4 cloves garlic, minced
- ½ teaspoon dried rubbed sage
- ½ teaspoon crumbled dried rosemary
- ½ teaspoon salt, divided
- ¼ teaspoon ground pepper plus ⅛ teaspoon, divided
- ½ cup red wine
- ¼ cup dried currants
- ⅓ cup toasted pine nuts (*see Tip page 92*), chopped

SAUCE

- 2 tablespoons extra-virgin olive oil, divided
- 1 small onion, chopped
- 2 cloves garlic, minced
- ¼ teaspoon salt
- ¼ teaspoon ground pepper
- 1 28-ounce can no-salt-added crushed tomatoes (*see Tip*)
- ½ cup red wine

1. To prepare cabbage & filling: Combine water, rice and 1 teaspoon oil in a medium saucepan; bring to a boil. Reduce heat to maintain the barest simmer, cover and cook until the water is absorbed and the rice is just tender, 40 to 50 minutes. Transfer to a large bowl and set aside.

2. Meanwhile, half-fill a large pot with water and bring to a boil. Line a baking sheet with a clean kitchen towel and place near the stove.

3. Using a small sharp knife, remove the core from the bottom of the cabbage. Add the cabbage to the boiling water and cook for 5 minutes. As the leaves soften, use tongs to gently remove 8 large outer leaves. Transfer the leaves to the baking sheet and pat with more towels to thoroughly dry. Set aside.

(continued on page 132)

Sodium in Canned Tomatoes

Sodium amounts vary widely among brands of canned tomatoes. Although it can be hard to find any labeled "no-salt-added," for the best tomato flavor we use brands that have little or no added sodium. Compare nutrition labels and choose one that has 190 mg sodium or less per ½-cup serving.

(continued from page 131)

4. Drain the remaining cabbage in a colander for a few minutes. Finely chop enough to get about 3 cups. (Save any remaining cabbage for another use.)

5. Heat 1½ tablespoons oil in a large skillet over medium-high heat. Add mushrooms, onion, garlic, sage, rosemary and ¼ teaspoon each salt and pepper; cook, stirring, until the mushrooms have released their juices and the pan is fairly dry, 8 to 10 minutes. Add wine and cook, stirring, until evaporated, about 3 minutes more. Add the mixture to the cooked rice along with currants and pine nuts.

6. Heat the remaining ½ tablespoon oil in the skillet over medium-high. Add the chopped cabbage, the remaining ¼ teaspoon salt and ⅛ teaspoon pepper; cook, stirring, until the cabbage is wilted and just beginning to brown, 3 to 5 minutes. Add to the rice mixture.

7. To prepare sauce: Heat 1 tablespoon oil in a large skillet over medium heat. Add onion, garlic, salt and pepper and cook, stirring, until starting to soften, 2 to 4 minutes. Add tomatoes and wine; bring to a simmer and cook until slightly thickened, about 10 minutes.

8. Preheat oven to 375°F.

9. To stuff cabbage: Place a reserved cabbage leaf on your work surface; cut out the thick stem in the center, keeping the leaf intact. Place about ¾ cup filling in the center. Fold both sides over the filling and roll up. Repeat with the remaining 7 leaves and filling.

10. Spread 1 cup of the tomato sauce in a 9-by-13-inch baking dish. Place the stuffed cabbage rolls, seam-side down, on the sauce. Pour the remaining sauce over the rolls and drizzle with the remaining 1 tablespoon oil.

11. Bake, uncovered, basting twice with the sauce, until hot, about 45 minutes.

SERVES 4: 2 ROLLS EACH

Calories 544, **Fat** 24g (sat 3g), **Cholesterol** 0mg, **Carbs** 61g, **Total sugars** 22g (added 0g), **Protein** 14g, **Fiber** 12g, **Sodium** 499mg, **Potassium** 1,833mg.
Nutrition bonus: Vitamin C (118% daily value), Vitamin A (67% dv), Potassium (52% dv), Folate (45% dv), Iron (36% dv), Magnesium (26% dv).

Carrots

Second only to beets in sugar content, carrots make an appearance in every kind of food, from breakfast muffins to dessert and everything in between.

Carrots are probably enjoyed most often in their purest form than in any other way—scrubbed, peeled and munched on raw. They can be eaten whole, sliced, diced, shredded—or pressed to make a powerfully nutritious juice. And delicately flavored pureed carrot soup is wonderful warm or chilled, topped with yogurt.

Carrots are one of a handful of vegetables whose nutrients are actually more accessible to the body cooked than raw. With the exception of carrot juice, raw carrots are harder for the body to break down than cooked carrots.

Most garden-variety carrots are orange, but there are yellow, purple, white and red varieties as well—and they come in an array of shapes and sizes but they all taste the same. Bunches of "rainbow" carrots can be found at farmers' markets—and increasingly supermarkets.

The sweetness of carrots pairs well with the savory members of their plant family, including dill, parsley, chervil, cilantro, coriander, fennel, anise and cumin. (Look at a green carrot top; its resemblance to those herbs—particularly parsley and cilantro—is quite evident.) The sweetness of carrots can be enhanced with honey and orange or balanced by an acid, such as lemon juice or vinegar.

Carrots are a cool-weather crop with two peak seasons—spring and fall. Spring carrots have a more delicate flavor and are sweeter than fall carrots.

Best in spring and fall

AT THE MARKET

⌇ Choose carrots that are firm, with smooth skin and bright color. If the greens are attached, be sure they look fresh, not dry or wilted. (The greens are edible but bitter. Use in small amounts in salads.) Avoid cracked or soft carrots or those with green skin at the top.

⌇ Small carrots have sweeter flavor than large ones. Ideally, choose carrots that are less than 1 inch in diameter.

⌇ "Baby" carrots, sold peeled and prewashed in plastic bags, are not baby carrots at all but rather pieces of large carrots that have been cut down and shaped. Real baby carrots are simply harvested before they reach mature size. True baby carrots have a "shoulder" at the top and often still have some greens attached as well.

⌇ 'Nantes', a French carrot known for its tender texture and extra-sweet flavor, is a favorite. 'Danvers' makes flavorful juice and stores well. If you like tiny carrots, try 'Thumbelina' and 'Paris Market', small round carrots that are harvested when they are the size of a golf ball.

IN YOUR KITCHEN

⌇ If the carrots have greens attached, remove and store separately or discard. Store carrots, unwashed, in a plastic bag in the refrigerator for 2 to 4 weeks.

⌇ Scrub carrots under cool running water with a vegetable brush. Not all carrots need to be peeled. In fact, many nutrients are in or just below the skin. If the carrots are young and fresh, simply scrub, then trim at each end. If the carrots look unappealing, peel with a vegetable peeler, then trim each end.

COOKING BASICS

BOIL Scrub, trim, peel (if desired) and cut carrots into ¼-inch-thick slices. Cook in a small amount of boiling water, covered, until tender-crisp, 7 to 9 minutes. Drain; toss with butter and finely chopped fresh herbs. Season to taste with salt and pepper.

ROAST Scrub, trim, peel (if desired) and cut 2 pounds carrots on the diagonal into ¼-inch-thick slices. In a large bowl combine 4 teaspoons melted butter, 2 teaspoons canola oil, 1 teaspoon ground cardamom, and ½ teaspoon salt. Add carrots and toss well to coat. Spread in an even layer on a rimmed baking sheet. Roast in a 450°F oven until tender and golden, about 30 minutes, stirring twice. Serves 6.

STEAM Scrub, trim, peel (if desired) and cut carrots into ¼-inch-thick slices. Place in a steamer basket over 1 inch of boiling water. Cover and steam, stirring once, until crisp-tender, 5 to 7 minutes. Toss with butter and finely chopped fresh herbs. Season to taste with salt and freshly ground pepper.

NUTRITION

⌇ **1 cup chopped raw carrot:** **Calories** 52, **Fat** 0g (sat 0g), **Cholesterol** 0mg, **Carbs** 12g, **Total sugars** 6g (added 0g), **Protein** 1g, **Fiber** 4g, **Sodium** 88mg, **Potassium** 410mg.

BONUS These root veggies contain falcarinol and falcarindiol, two compounds that lower blood sugar by pulling glucose from your bloodstream into your cells to use for energy.

Grow Your Own

Sow seeds outdoors, 2 to 4 weeks before the last frost, in a sunny spot with loose, fertile soil in raised rows that are 12 inches apart. Lightly cover seeds with ¼ inch of fine soil. Mist soil lightly with water to avoid washing away the seeds. Keep soil consistently moist until seedlings appear. Thin to 1 inch apart when tops are 2 inches high. Thin again to 3 or 4 inches apart 2 weeks later. Mulch to reduce weeds and maintain moisture. Most varieties are ready for harvest 70 to 80 days after planting.

POMEGRANATE MOLASSES-GLAZED CARROTS WITH PISTACHIOS

ACTIVE: 35 MIN **TOTAL:** 35 MIN
TO MAKE AHEAD: Keep warm in a 225°F oven up to 30 minutes.

Instead of a traditional sugar glaze, we glaze spiced carrots with a combination of sweet-tart pomegranate molasses and honey. A touch of butter and a sprinkling of pistachios finish the dish.

    2 pounds carrots, peeled and diagonally sliced (¼-inch)
    ½ cup water
    2 tablespoons pomegranate molasses (*see Tip*)
    2 tablespoons honey
    2 tablespoons butter
    ½ teaspoon ground cinnamon
    ½ teaspoon salt
    ⅓ cup chopped salted pistachios
    2 tablespoons snipped fresh chives

Combine carrots, water, pomegranate molasses, honey, butter, cinnamon and salt in a large skillet. Bring to a boil over medium-high heat. Cover and cook until the carrots are just tender, 6 to 8 minutes. Uncover and cook, stirring frequently, until the liquid is a syrupy glaze, 6 to 8 minutes more. Remove from heat and stir in pistachios and chives. Serve warm.

SERVES 8: ½ CUP EACH

Calories 119, **Fat** 5g (sat 2g), **Cholesterol** 8mg, **Carbs** 17g, **Total sugars** 11g (added 5g), **Protein** 2g, **Fiber** 3g, **Sodium** 241mg, **Potassium** 381mg.
Nutrition bonus: Vitamin A (340% daily value).

Pomegranate Molasses

Pomegranate molasses has a bright, tangy flavor. Find it in Middle Eastern markets and some large supermarkets. To make your own: Simmer 4 cups pomegranate juice, uncovered, in a medium nonreactive saucepan over medium heat until thick enough to coat the back of a spoon, 45 to 50 minutes. (Do not let the syrup reduce too much or it will darken and become too sticky.) Makes about ½ cup. Refrigerate in an airtight container up to 3 months.

DIY Juicing

No juicer? No problem.
Try this DIY version of
blended and strained juice
instead: Coarsely chop all
ingredients. First, place the
soft and/or liquid ingredients
in the blender and process
until liquefied. Then add the
remaining ingredients; blend
until liquefied. Cut two
24-inch lengths of
cheesecloth. Completely
unfold each piece, then stack
the pieces. Fold the double
stack in half for a 4-layer
stack of cloth. Line a large
bowl with the cheesecloth
and pour the contents of
the blender into the center.
Gather the edges of the
cloth together in one hand
and use the other hand to
twist and squeeze the bundle
to extract all the juice from
the pulp.

CARROT-ORANGE JUICE

ACTIVE: 15 MIN **TOTAL:** 15 MIN

In this vibrant, healthful juice, we power-up plain orange juice by adding a yellow tomato, apple and carrots to pack in immune-boosting vitamins A and C.

1 medium yellow tomato, cut into wedges
1 medium orange, peeled and quartered
1 medium apple, cut into eighths
4 large carrots, peeled
  Ice cubes (optional)

1. Working in this order, process tomato, orange, apple and carrots through a juicer according to the manufacturer's directions. *(No juicer? See Tip.)*

2. Fill 2 glasses with ice, if desired, and pour the juice into the glasses. Serve immediately.

SERVES 2: ABOUT 8 OUNCES EACH

Calories 153, **Fat** 1g (sat 0g), **Cholesterol** 0mg, **Carbs** 37g, **Total sugars** 22g (added 0g), **Protein** 3g, **Fiber** 9g, **Sodium** 125mg, **Potassium** 950mg.
Nutrition bonus: Vitamin A (485% daily value), Vitamin C (95% dv), Potassium (27% dv), Folate (20%).

MEXICAN PICKLED CARROTS

ACTIVE: 1¼ HRS **TOTAL:** 1 HR 40 MIN
TO MAKE AHEAD: Store at room temperature up to 1 year if processed in a water bath. **EQUIPMENT:** 4 1-pint (2-cup) canning jars, canning equipment

Use these pickled carrots to top tacos or tostadas or as a side to any south-of-the-border entrée. They are also delicious added to a bowl of soup or tossed with spring greens, feta cheese and just a drizzle of olive oil.

- 3 cups white vinegar
- 1 cup water
- ¾ cup sugar
- 2 tablespoons pickling salt *or* fine sea salt (not iodized)
- 3 pounds small carrots, sliced on the diagonal ⅛ inch thick
- 1 medium red onion, sliced ⅛ inch thick
- 2 fresh jalapeños, sliced into rings ⅛ inch thick
- 2 teaspoons dried oregano, preferably Mexican, divided
- 2 teaspoons cumin seeds, divided
- 2 large cloves garlic, halved

1. Before starting the recipe, gather the needed equipment (*see Tip*).

2. Prepare four 1-pint (2-cup) canning jars and lids: Wash in hot soapy water and rinse well. Place the rack in the pot and place the jars, right-side up, on the rack. Add enough water to fill and cover the jars by at least 1 inch. Cover the pot and bring to a boil; boil, covered, for 10 minutes, then turn off the heat. Keep the jars in the hot water (with the pot covered) while you prepare the recipe.

3. Meanwhile, place the new lids in a small saucepan, cover with water and bring to a gentle simmer. Very gently simmer for 10 minutes (taking care not to boil). Turn off the heat and keep the lids in the water until ready to use.

4. Combine vinegar, water, sugar and salt in a 6- to 8-quart nonreactive pot (stainless-steel) and bring to a boil. Stir until the sugar is dissolved. Add the carrots, onion and jalapeños; return to a boil. Remove from heat and let stand 10 minutes.

5. Meanwhile, remove sterilized jars from the water and place on a clean towel (if they're placed on a cold surface, the jars could crack). Place ½ teaspoon each oregano and cumin seeds in each jar, along with half a garlic clove.

Canning 101

For this recipe, you will need four 1-pint (2-cup) canning jars with rings and new lids, a canning pot with a rack, jar lifter, lid wand or tongs and a clean cloth. Canning equipment is available in hardware stores, online and in most supermarkets, especially during growing season. For more canning tips and information, visit Ball's website, freshpreserving.com.

6. Fill the jars with the vegetables and pickling liquid to within ½ inch of the rim. Wipe the rims with a clean cloth. Use a lid wand (or tongs) to remove the lids from the hot water. Place lids and dry rings on the jars. Tighten until just finger-tight (won't move with gentle pressure), but don't overtighten.

7. To process the filled jars: Using a jar lifter, return jars to the pot with the warm water, placing them on the rack without touching one another or the sides of the pot. If the water does not cover the jars by 1 to 2 inches, add boiling water as needed. Cover the pot and bring to a boil; boil 10 minutes, then turn off the heat, uncover the pot and leave the jars in the water for 5 minutes. Use the jar lifter to transfer the jars to a towel, with some space between each jar. Let stand, without moving, for 24 hours. (If you do not want to process the jars in a boiling-water bath, you can refrigerate the pickles up to 2 months.)

8. After 24 hours, unscrew the rings and test the seals by pressing lightly on the center of each lid. They should have a slight concave indentation and neither yield to your pressure nor pop back. If a seal is not complete, you can process again in boiling water or store any unsealed jars in the refrigerator.

MAKES: ABOUT 8 CUPS (¼-CUP SERVING)

Calories 20, **Fat** 0g (sat 0g), **Cholesterol** 0mg, **Carbs** 5g, **Total sugars** 3g (added 1g), **Protein** 0g, **Fiber** 1g, **Sodium** 81mg, **Potassium** 132mg.
Nutrition bonus: Vitamin A (127% daily value).

Carrots, one of the sweetest of all the root vegetables, are one of the few true vegetables that can be found in every course, from appetizers to dessert.

**Roasted Rainbow Carrots
with Sage Brown Butter**
(see recipe, page 144)

ROASTED RAINBOW CARROTS WITH SAGE BROWN BUTTER

ACTIVE: 15 MIN **TOTAL:** 30 MIN

Cooking butter until it bubbles and starts to turn brown brings out a nutty flavor. That's the 2-minute "secret sauce," along with sage, that makes these carrots special. (Photo: page 143).

  2 pounds small carrots, preferably multicolored
  2 teaspoons extra-virgin olive oil
  ¾ teaspoon salt
  3 tablespoons butter
  2 tablespoons chopped fresh sage *or* 2 teaspoons dried,
      plus more for garnish

1. Position racks in upper and lower thirds of oven; preheat to 450°F.

2. Trim carrots and cut in half lengthwise. Toss with oil and salt in a large bowl. Divide between 2 large rimmed baking sheets and spread in an even layer.

3. Roast the carrots, stirring once and rotating sheets top to bottom and front to back halfway through, until tender, about 15 minutes.

4. Meanwhile, melt butter in a small skillet over medium-high heat. Cook until just starting to brown, 2 to 3 minutes. Remove from heat. When the butter stops bubbling, stir in sage. Transfer the carrots to a serving dish and drizzle the sage brown butter over them. Garnish with fresh sage, if desired.

SERVES 6: 1 CUP EACH

Calories 121, **Fat** 8g (sat 4g), **Cholesterol** 15mg, **Carbs** 13g, **Total sugars** 6g (added 0g), **Protein** 1g, **Fiber** 4g, **Sodium** 384mg, **Potassium** 435mg.
Nutrition bonus: Vitamin A (453% daily value).

HARISSA-RUBBED STEAK & CARROT SALAD

ACTIVE: 35 MIN **TOTAL:** 35 MIN

Harissa is a Tunisian chile paste that adds fiery flavor to grilled steak. Different brands vary in heat, so taste it and use accordingly. Look for it in well-stocked supermarkets or, if you can't find it, rub steak with this mixture to approximate the flavor: 1 minced garlic clove, 1½ teaspoons each ground cumin and paprika, ½ teaspoon olive oil, ¼ teaspoon ground cinnamon and a big pinch of crushed red pepper.

2 tablespoons lemon juice	3 cups thinly sliced carrots (about 1 pound)
1 tablespoon extra-virgin olive oil	
2 cloves garlic, minced	1-1¼ pounds skirt steak (*see Tip*), trimmed and cut into 4 portions
1½ teaspoons ground cumin	
½ teaspoon ground cinnamon	
½ teaspoon paprika	4 teaspoons harissa
¾ teaspoon kosher salt, divided	1 tablespoon chopped fresh parsley *or* cilantro for garnish

1. Preheat grill to medium-high.

2. Whisk lemon juice, oil, garlic, cumin, cinnamon, paprika and ½ teaspoon salt in a microwave-safe medium bowl. Add carrots; stir to coat. Cover and microwave on High until the carrots are tender-crisp, about 2 minutes. Uncover. (*Alternatively, steam carrots over 1 inch of boiling water in a large saucepan fitted with a steamer basket until tender-crisp, 2 to 3 minutes. Toss the carrots with the spice mixture.*)

3. Rub both sides of steak with harissa and sprinkle with the remaining ¼ teaspoon salt. Grill the steak 1½ to 3 minutes per side for medium. Transfer to a clean cutting board and let rest for 5 minutes, then thinly slice across the grain. Serve with spiced carrots, garnished with parsley (or cilantro).

SERVES 4

Calories 270, **Fat** 13g (sat 4g), **Cholesterol** 74mg, **Carbs** 12g, **Total sugars** 5g (added 0g), **Protein** 25g, **Fiber** 4g, **Sodium** 569mg, **Potassium** 763mg.
Nutrition bonus: Vitamin A (343% daily value), Vitamin B$_{12}$ (71% dv), Zinc (39% dv), Potassium (22% dv).

Skirt Steak

Depending on your region, skirt steak may not be something your supermarket regularly carries—call ahead to make sure it's available or ask your butcher to order it. It's usually sold in about 1-pound cuts up to 18 inches long and 5 inches wide but just ¼ inch thick. Before cooking, cut the steak with the grain into several portions to make the long piece more manageable on the grill or in a skillet. Once cooked, be sure to slice it across the grain for maximum tenderness. Hanger steak, flat-iron and flank steak can all be used as substitutes for skirt steak in most recipes.

COCONUT-CARROT MORNING GLORY MUFFINS

ACTIVE: 20 MIN **TOTAL:** 1 HR
TO MAKE AHEAD: Individually wrap in plastic and store at room temperature up to 3 days or freeze up to 3 months. To reheat, remove plastic, wrap in a paper towel and microwave on High 30 to 60 seconds. **EQUIPMENT:** Muffin tin with 12 (½-cup) cups

Make these carrot-flecked, whole-grain muffins ahead so you can hit the ground running on busy mornings.

1 cup whole-wheat *or* white whole-wheat flour
½ cup old-fashioned rolled oats, plus 2 tablespoons for garnish
2 teaspoons baking powder
2 teaspoons ground cinnamon
½ teaspoon salt
¼ teaspoon ground allspice
2 large eggs
1 cup unsweetened applesauce
⅓ cup honey
2 teaspoons vanilla extract
¼ cup coconut oil, melted if necessary *(see Tip)*
2 cups shredded carrots
½ cup unsweetened shredded coconut, plus 2 tablespoons for garnish
½ cup raisins

1. Preheat oven to 350°F. Coat a 12-cup muffin tin with cooking spray.

2. Whisk flour, ½ cup oats, baking powder, cinnamon, salt and allspice in a medium bowl.

3. Whisk eggs, applesauce, honey and vanilla in a large bowl. Whisk in coconut oil. Gently stir in the flour mixture just until moistened. Fold in carrots, ½ cup coconut and raisins.

4. Divide the batter among the muffin cups. Sprinkle with the remaining 2 tablespoons each oats and coconut.

5. Bake the muffins until they spring back when lightly touched and a toothpick inserted in the center comes out with only moist crumbs attached, 30 to 35 minutes. Let stand in the pan for 10 minutes before turning out onto a wire rack. Serve warm or at room temperature.

MAKES: 1 DOZEN MUFFINS

Calories 186, **Fat** 8g (sat 6g), **Cholesterol** 31mg, **Carbs** 28g, **Total sugars** 15g (added 8g), **Protein** 4g, **Fiber** 3g, **Sodium** 206mg, **Potassium** 193mg.
Nutrition bonus: Vitamin A (62% daily value).

Baking with Coconut Oil

Coconut oil is solid at temperatures below 76°F. To melt solidified coconut oil, remove the lid and place the container in a bowl of very hot water; stir frequently until melted. Or just melt the amount you need in the microwave or on the stovetop.

Cauliflower

Cauliflower is a brassica, a close cousin to broccoli and a descendant of a wild cabbage. What sets cauliflower apart from broccoli is how it's grown. Both broccoli and cauliflower have large leaves that surround a head formed by tight flower buds. In cauliflower, this is called the curd. While it's growing, the leaves of white cauliflower are wrapped and tied around the head to create shade to keep it from producing chlorophyll. This process, called blanching, keeps the color of the cauliflower an appealing creamy white.

Although white cauliflower is the most common, there are varieties with vivid colors—including orange, purple and lime green (also called broccoflower, a cross between broccoli and cauliflower). The colored varieties do not require blanching, but they all have the same sweet and nutty flavor and crisp texture. Despite its name, broccoli Romanesco is a type of green cauliflower. Originally cultivated along the Mediterranean coast between Rome and Naples, it looks like a chartreuse sea creature, with swirling clusters of pointed peaks.

Cauliflower is satisfyingly crunchy raw, and it takes to all kinds of cooking methods and flavors. Steamed and buttered with a sprinkle of parsley; pureed in a soup; mashed with herbs and cheese; or roasted until browned and crisp, it is irresistible.

Roast it Italian-style with garlic, crushed red pepper, capers and a squeeze of lemon; or Indian-style, with ginger, cumin, coriander, turmeric, mustard seeds, chile, sugar and a squeeze of lime.

Cauliflower is a cool-weather crop that is harvested in both spring and fall—although it is at peak season from late summer through late fall.

Best in late summer to late fall

AT THE MARKET

🦐 Look for a clean, compact head with tightly closed bud clusters. Avoid heads with loose or crumbly florets, brown spots or dull color. The leaves should look fresh and green.

IN YOUR KITCHEN

🦐 Cauliflower keeps up to 5 days in a plastic bag in the refrigerator. Keep it stem-end up to prevent condensation from forming on the curd, which can cause discoloration and decay.

🦐 Remove the leaves and slice off the thick stem. Remove core *(see Step 2, right)*. Cut head into large florets, then cut or break those into desired size pieces. Rinse in a colander under cool running water; drain.

COOKING BASICS

BAKE Combine 10 cups of water, 2 sliced lemons and 2 tablespoons salt in a large pot. Bring to a boil. Lower a large head of trimmed cauliflower (leave core intact) into pot. Simmer, turning once, until tender, 5 to 7 minutes. Transfer to a colander to drain. Place stem-side down in a baking dish lined with parchment paper. Drizzle with 1 tablespoon olive oil and roast in a 475°F oven until browned all over, 30 to 35 minutes. Serves 4.

BRAISE Heat 1 tablespoon olive oil in a large saucepan over medium-high heat. Add 3 cloves minced garlic, 1 teaspoon dried thyme and ¼ teaspoon crushed red pepper. Cook, stirring, for 1 minute. Add 4 cups cauliflower florets. Cook, stirring, for 2 minutes. Add ½ cup reduced-sodium chicken broth. Reduce heat to medium. Cover and cook, stirring occasionally, until cauliflower is almost tender, 8 to 10 minutes. Uncover and turn heat to medium-high. Cook, shaking the pan occasionally, until the liquid has evaporated and the cauliflower begins to brown, 2 to 4 minutes. Season to taste with salt and pepper. Serves 4.

ROAST Combine 1 tablespoon peanut oil, 1 teaspoon mustard seeds, 1 teaspoon sugar, 1 teaspoon grated fresh ginger, ½ teaspoon ground turmeric, ½ teaspoon ground cumin, ¼² teaspoon salt, and ⅛ teaspoon crushed red pepper in a large bowl. Add 4 cups cauliflower florets. Toss to coat. Roast on a rimmed baking sheet in a 425°F oven until tender and browned, stirring twice, about 30 minutes. Serves 4.

STEAM Bring 1 inch of water to a boil in a large saucepan fitted with a steamer basket. Add 4 cups cauliflower florets, cover and steam until tender-crisp, about 4 minutes. Drizzle with olive oil. Season with salt and pepper. Serve with lemon wedges. Serves 4.

NUTRITION

🦐 **1 cup cauliflower florets: Calories** 28, **Fat** 0g (sat 0g), **Cholesterol** 0mg, **Carbs** 6g, **Total sugars** 2g (added 0g), **Protein** 2g, **Fiber** 2g, **Sodium** 18mg, **Potassium** 176mg.

BONUS Cauliflower is loaded with cancer-thwarting compounds. Orange varieties provide beta-carotene for a stronger immune system and purple types dish up anthocyanins, substances that can help keep your brain sharp.

How to prep

1. Cut off the stem.

2. Turn head upside down and, holding the knife at a 45° angle, slice around the stem to remove the "plug" from center of head *(right)*.

3. Cut the head into large florets, then cut or slice to desired sizes.

CAULIFLOWER STEAKS WITH CHIMICHURRI

ACTIVE: 30 MIN **TOTAL:** 1 HR

Thick slabs of roasted cauliflower are a fine accompaniment to meat. Better still, serve them on their own as a vegetarian alternative. The sides tend to crumble, so for a truly show-stopping presentation, use the center portion of 2 heads and save the rest for another meal.

- 2 tablespoons extra-virgin olive oil
- 2 cloves garlic, minced
- 1 tablespoon minced jalapeño pepper
- ¾ teaspoon salt, divided
- 2 tablespoons finely chopped fresh oregano
- 2 tablespoons finely chopped fresh thyme
- 2 tablespoons water
- 2 teaspoons sherry vinegar
- ½ teaspoon paprika
  Olive *or* canola oil cooking spray
- 1 large head cauliflower (about 3 pounds)
  Ground pepper to taste
- 3 tablespoons finely chopped flat-leaf parsley

1. Combine oil, garlic, jalapeño and ¼ teaspoon salt in a small pan. Cook over medium heat just until the garlic starts to sizzle, 2 to 4 minutes, but don't let it brown. Stir in oregano, thyme, water, vinegar and paprika. Cover and set aside.

2. Preheat oven to 450°F. Line a baking sheet with parchment paper and coat with cooking spray.

3. Remove any outer leaves from the cauliflower, but leave the stem intact. Using a large chef's knife, cut into ½- to ¾-inch-thick slices. The center few slices should remain more or less intact, but the outer slices will crumble into smaller pieces. Place the large and medium pieces on the baking sheet with the cut surfaces touching the pan; sprinkle small pieces in any empty spots. Coat with cooking spray and season with the remaining ½ teaspoon salt and pepper.

4. Roast the cauliflower, gently turning once halfway through, until browned and the stems feel tender when pierced with a knife, 25 to 35 minutes.

5. Just before serving, stir parsley into the reserved herb sauce and season with pepper. Serve the cauliflower steaks with the sauce.

SERVES 4: 1 STEAK (OR ¾ CUP FLORETS) & 2 TBSP. SAUCE EACH

Calories 110, **Fat** 8g (sat 1g), **Cholesterol** 0mg, **Carbs** 8g, **Total sugars** 3g (added 0g), **Protein** 3g, **Fiber** 3g, **Sodium** 479mg, **Potassium** 452mg.
Nutrition bonus: Vitamin C (126% daily value), Folate (20% dv).

DILL-HAVARTI MASHED CAULIFLOWER

ACTIVE: 20 MIN **TOTAL:** 30 MIN

This dish created instant cauliflower converts in our Test Kitchen. The cauliflower is a low-calorie foil for the rich creaminess of Havarti cheese.

  8 cups cauliflower florets (about 1 large head)
  4 cloves garlic, peeled
  1 cup grated dill Havarti *or* Cheddar cheese
¼ cup low-fat milk
  1 tablespoon butter, cubed
  1 teaspoon dried dill
¼ teaspoon salt
¼ teaspoon ground pepper
  2 tablespoons sliced chives *or* scallion greens

1. Bring 1 inch of water to a boil in a large pot fitted with a steamer basket. Add cauliflower and garlic, cover and steam until very tender, 10 to 14 minutes.

2. Transfer the cauliflower and garlic to a food processor. Add cheese, milk, butter, dill, salt and pepper; puree until smooth. Stir in chives (or scallion greens).

SERVES 6: ABOUT ¾ CUP EACH

Calories 137, **Fat** 9g (sat 5g), **Cholesterol** 25mg, **Carbs** 9g, **Total sugars** 3g (added 0g), **Protein** 8g, **Fiber** 3g, **Sodium** 262mg, **Potassium** 479mg.
Nutrition bonus: Vitamin C (117% daily value), Folate (22% dv).

Meyer Lemons

Meyer lemons are a cross between a lemon and an orange. The result is a slightly sweeter, less acidic, almost floral flavor. Look for Meyer lemons from late fall to early spring in well-stocked supermarkets and specialty grocers.

MEDITERRANEAN CAULIFLOWER PIZZA

ACTIVE: 40 MIN **TOTAL:** 1 HR 10 MIN
EQUIPMENT: Parchment paper

Enjoy gluten-free pizza night with this cauliflower-crust pie. The Meyer lemon, olive and sun-dried tomato topping adds a sophisticated twist. Feel free to go with something more traditional, such as marinara sauce and mushrooms.

1 medium head cauliflower (about 2 pounds), trimmed and broken into small florets

1 tablespoon extra-virgin olive oil plus 1 teaspoon, divided

¼ teaspoon salt

2 Meyer lemons *or* 1 regular lemon

6 oil-packed sun-dried tomatoes, drained and coarsely chopped

⅓ cup green *or* black olives, pitted and sliced

1 large egg, lightly beaten

1 cup shredded part-skim mozzarella cheese

½ teaspoon dried oregano

Ground pepper to taste

¼ cup slivered fresh basil

1. Preheat oven to 450°F. Line a rimless baking sheet with parchment paper.

2. Pulse cauliflower in a food processor until reduced to rice-size crumbles. Transfer to a large nonstick skillet. Add 1 tablespoon oil and salt; heat over medium-high, stirring frequently, until the cauliflower begins to soften slightly, 8 to 10 minutes; don't let it brown. Transfer to a large bowl to cool.

3. Meanwhile, with a sharp knife, remove the skin and white pith from the lemon(s). Working over a small bowl, cut the segments from the membranes, letting them drop into the bowl. Drain the juice from the segments (save for another use). Add tomatoes and olives to the segments; toss to combine.

4. Add egg, cheese and oregano to the cooled cauliflower; stir to combine. Spread the mixture onto the prepared baking sheet, shaping into an even 10-inch round. Drizzle the remaining 1 teaspoon oil over the top.

5. Bake the pizza until the top begins to brown, 10 to 14 minutes. Scatter the lemon-olive mixture over the top, season with pepper and continue to bake until nicely browned all over, 8 to 14 minutes more. Scatter basil over the top.

SERVES 4

Calories 200, **Fat** 14g (sat 4g), **Cholesterol** 62mg, **Carbs** 9g, **Total sugars** 2g (added 0g), **Protein** 11g, **Fiber** 3g, **Sodium** 475mg, **Potassium** 451mg.
Nutrition bonus: Vitamin C (94% daily value), Calcium (26% dv).

Tahini

Tahini is a thick paste of ground sesame seeds. Look for it in large supermarkets in the Middle Eastern section or near other nut butters. Sadaf is one of our favorite brands—it's nutty, creamy and never bitter.

ROASTED CAULIFLOWER SALAD WITH WALNUTS

ACTIVE: 35 MIN **TOTAL:** 1 HR
TO MAKE AHEAD: Refrigerate up to 1 day; serve at room temperature.

For this Middle Eastern side dish, walnuts pureed with tahini and lemon make an irresistibly earthy sauce that's tossed with roasted cauliflower, shallot and fresh dill. (Photo: page 8.)

  1 **cup walnuts, divided**
10 **cups cauliflower florets (1- to 2-inch florets, from 1-2 heads)**
1½ **tablespoons extra-virgin olive oil**
  ¾ **teaspoon kosher salt, divided**
  ¼ **cup tahini** *(see Tip)***, at room temperature**
  ¼ **cup lemon juice, plus more to taste**
  2 **tablespoons water, at room temperature, plus more as needed**
  ¼ **cup chopped fresh dill**
  1 **tablespoon minced shallot**

1. Preheat oven to 450°F.

2. Place ½ cup walnuts in a small saucepan and add water to cover by 1 inch. Bring to a simmer. Reduce heat and simmer until slightly softened, about 20 minutes. Drain and let cool to room temperature.

3. Meanwhile, toss cauliflower in a bowl with oil and ¼ teaspoon salt. Spread in a single layer on a baking sheet. Roast until browned on the bottom, about 20 minutes. Transfer to a large bowl and let cool to room temperature.

4. Blend the cooled walnuts, tahini, ¼ cup lemon juice and water in a food processor until very smooth, scraping down the sides a few times. If it's too thick to blend, add additional room-temperature water by the tablespoon until you get a thick sauce.

5. Toast the remaining ½ cup walnuts in a small dry skillet over medium heat for about 5 minutes. Chop and add to the cauliflower along with dill, shallot and the remaining ½ teaspoon salt. Add the dressing; gently toss to coat. Season to taste with more lemon juice, if desired. Serve at room temperature.

SERVES 8: 1 CUP EACH

Calories 200, **Fat** 17g (sat 2g), **Cholesterol** 0mg, **Carbs** 11g, **Total sugars** 3g (added 0g), **Protein** 6g, **Fiber** 4g, **Sodium** 149mg, **Potassium** 513mg.
Nutrition bonus: Vitamin C (114% daily value), Folate (25% dv).

BROCCOLI, CAULIFLOWER & ROMANESCO GRATIN

ACTIVE: 35 MIN **TOTAL:** 1 HR
TO MAKE AHEAD: Prepare through Step 1 and refrigerate florets up to 1 day.
Proceed with Steps 2-5 about 1 hour before serving.

The crumbled cheese crackers on this gratin evoke a classic Thanksgiving casserole. But it gets a modern light spin with a sauce made with low-fat milk and just enough full-flavor cheese to keep it rich without lots of calories.

14 cups bite-size florets from
   2-3 heads broccoli, cauliflower
   and/or romanesco
2 cups low-fat milk
1½ teaspoons Dijon mustard
½ teaspoon garlic powder
½ teaspoon salt
2 tablespoons cornstarch

2 tablespoons water
¾ cup shredded extra-sharp white
   Cheddar cheese
¾ cup shredded Gruyère cheese
¼ cup snipped fresh chives
¾ cup crushed cheese-flavored
   crackers
2 teaspoons extra-virgin olive oil

Go Crackers

When purchasing crackers for casserole toppings—or just for snacking—opt for ones that contain no partially hydrogenated oils.

1. Bring a large pot of water to a boil. Add florets and cook, stirring frequently, for 1 minute. Drain in a colander and immediately rinse with cold water until cool. Drain well. Spread on a baking sheet or kitchen towel and pat with a clean towel to soak up any excess water.

2. Preheat oven to 375°F. Coat a 9-by-13-inch (or similar-size shallow ovenproof dish) with cooking spray.

3. Combine milk, mustard, garlic powder and salt in the large pot; bring to a simmer over medium-high heat. Combine cornstarch and water in a small bowl; whisk into the simmering milk. Bring the mixture to a boil over high heat, whisking. Reduce heat to maintain a simmer and cook, whisking, for 2 minutes. Add Cheddar, Gruyère and chives; whisk until smooth. Remove from heat.

4. Add the florets to the pot and gently stir to coat with the cheese sauce. Transfer to the prepared baking dish. Combine crackers and oil in a small bowl and sprinkle over the vegetables.

5. Bake until the cheese sauce is bubbling and the florets are starting to brown on top, 25 to 30 minutes. Serve warm.

SERVES 12: ⅔ CUP EACH

Calories 218, **Fat** 11g (sat 4g), **Cholesterol** 18mg, **Carbs** 21g, **Total sugars** 5g (added 0g), **Protein** 10g, **Fiber** 3g, **Sodium** 422mg, **Potassium** 313mg.
Nutrition bonus: Vitamin C (88% daily value), Folate (27% dv), Calcium (23% dv).

Celery

Unassuming celery has a lot more going for it than its most familiar uses might suggest. Dismissed as a dieter's staple or swizzle stick for a Bloody Mary, relegated to the crudité tray or narrowly defined as an aromatic that serves only as a flavor base for an array of dishes—its true potential often goes unrecognized.

But celery has more than enough good qualities to be the star of the show. A simple salad of thinly sliced celery dressed with olive oil, vinegar, salt, pepper is crunchy and wonderful with roast chicken or grilled fish. Braised in broth and white wine or cooked in a creamy gratin, celery is surprising and delightful.

There are two types of celery—the pale green 'Pascal' head or bunch celery that is most familiar and the slender and stronger-flavored Chinese celery. Both the stalks and the aromatic, flavorful leaves of regular celery are edible. The celery heart refers to the inner ribs of the bunch. The heart is more tender than the outer stalks, with fewer tough strings.

Celery is part of the same botanical family as carrots, fennel, anise, caraway, chervil, cilantro, dill and parsley—all of which are good flavor companions. It also pairs well with the sweetness of apples and pears, assertive cheeses—especially blue cheese and Parmesan—toasted nuts, olives, cured meats like soppressata and prosciutto, béchamel sauce and lemon.

Celery is a notoriously temperamental crop. It requires fertile soil, cool temperatures and constant moisture. It does not tolerate heat or transplanting very well. It is available year-round but is best in fall to early winter.

Best in fall to early winter

AT THE MARKET

❧ Choose tight, firm bunches with fresh, healthy-looking leaves. The stalks should be straight and rigid and should snap when bent. Avoid stalks that splay out or that have cuts or bruises.

❧ Celery hearts—the tender inner ribs of a bunch of stalks—are often available in packages.

IN YOUR KITCHEN

❧ Store, unwashed, in a plastic bag in the refrigerator up to a week.

❧ Remove stalks from the head as needed. Rinse stalks under cool running water, paying special attention to the base, which—being closest to the soil when growing—is where dirt collects. Cut a thin slice off each end of the stalk.

❧ Because celery is 95 percent water, it can rapidly dehydrate, which leads to limp, rubbery stalks. If this happens, bring it back to its firm state by trimming both ends of each stalk and soaking the stalks in ice-cold water in the refrigerator for 30 minutes to allow the celery to crisp up.

COOKING BASICS

BRAISE Cut a thin slice from the base of each of 2 celery hearts, leaving stalks attached. Trim the tops so the hearts measure 7 to 8 inches long. Slice each heart in half lengthwise. Heat 2 tablespoons extra-virgin olive oil in a large deep skillet over medium heat. Add celery hearts, cut-side down. Cover and cook, turning once, until lightly browned and tender, 8 to 10 minutes. Increase heat to medium-high and add ¼ cup each reduced-sodium chicken broth and dry white wine. Bring to a boil; cook, turning the celery to coat, until the liquid is reduced by half, about 4 minutes. Drizzle with the liquid. Season with ¼ teaspoon salt and pepper to taste. Sprinkle with Parmesan cheese, a squeeze of lemon or chopped fresh herbs, such as dill or parsley. Serves 4.

SAUTÉ Trim and cut 1 bunch celery into ½-inch-thick slices (about 4 cups). Heat 1 tablespoon extra-virgin olive oil in a large skillet over medium heat. Add 2 thinly sliced garlic cloves and cook, stirring, until lightly browned, about 2 minutes. Add the celery and cook, stirring occasionally, until crisp-tender, about 6 minutes. Season with salt to taste and ¼ teaspoon crushed red pepper, if desired. Serves 4.

NUTRITION

❧ **1 cup of chopped raw celery: Calories** 16, **Fat** 0g (sat 0g), **Cholesterol** 0mg, **Carbs** 3g, **Total sugars** 1g (added 0g), **Protein** 1g, **Fiber** 2g, **Sodium** 81mg, **Potassium** 263mg.

BONUS For better blood pressure, munch on some celery. These long and leafy stalks supply a blockbuster cocktail of antioxidants shown to relax blood vessels, decreasing the pressure that can lead to hypertension.

SLIVERED CELERY SALAD WITH BLUE CHEESE DRESSING

ACTIVE: 20 MIN **TOTAL:** 20 MIN

Blue cheese, celery and a dash of hot sauce—it's a tried-and-true combo as an adornment for Buffalo wings. So it's no surprise that the combo in salad form is ideal to serve with turkey burgers and roast chicken.

½ cup buttermilk

½ cup low-fat plain Greek yogurt

½ teaspoon hot sauce, or to taste

¼ teaspoon salt

3 cups diagonally sliced celery (¼ inch)

¼ cup chopped tender celery leaves

½ cup diagonally sliced scallions plus 2 tablespoons, divided

½ cup crumbled blue cheese, divided

1. Whisk buttermilk, yogurt, hot sauce and salt in a medium bowl.

2. Add celery, celery leaves, ½ cup scallions and ¼ cup cheese; fold until blended. Serve sprinkled with the remaining scallions and cheese.

SERVES 6: ABOUT ⅔ CUP EACH

Calories 72, **Fat** 4g (sat 2g), **Cholesterol** 11mg, **Carbs** 4g, **Total sugars** 3g (added 0g), **Protein** 5g, **Fiber** 1g, **Sodium** 334mg, **Potassium** 224mg.

Cut the Strings

The strings along the back of each celery stalk can be fairly tough—especially on large stalks— and can be unpleasant when the celery is eaten raw. If you like, remove them by simply running a vegetable peeler along each stalk, from top to bottom.

CRUNCHY CONFETTI TUNA SALAD

ACTIVE: 25 MIN **TOTAL:** 25 MIN

The herb-infused dressing for this tuna salad calls for equal parts Greek yogurt and low-fat mayo. Lots of fresh veggies, including bell pepper, carrot, radishes and celery, give boosts of flavor, color and nutrition.

DRESSING

- ¼ cup nonfat plain Greek yogurt
- ¼ cup low-fat mayonnaise
- 1 tablespoon whole-grain mustard
- 1 teaspoon lemon juice
- 1 teaspoon chopped fresh dill *or* ¼ teaspoon dried
- ¼ teaspoon kosher salt
  Ground pepper to taste

SALAD

- 2 5-ounce cans chunk light tuna packed in olive oil, drained *(see Tip)*
- 1 small carrot, diced small
- 2 stalks celery, diced small
- ¼ cup coarsely chopped celery leaves *or* parsley
- ¼ cup shredded radishes
- ¼ cup diced yellow bell pepper
- 2 tablespoons minced red onion
- 1 scallion, thinly sliced
- 8 large Bibb lettuce leaves

1. To prepare dressing: Whisk yogurt, mayonnaise, mustard, lemon juice, dill, salt and pepper in a medium bowl.

2. To prepare salad: Place tuna in the bowl and break up with a fork into bite-size chunks. Add carrot, celery, celery leaves (or parsley), radishes, bell pepper, onion and scallion. Stir gently to combine.

3. To serve, stack 2 lettuce leaves on top of one another. Divide the salad among the lettuce leaves.

SERVES 4: ⅔ CUP EACH

Calories 155, **Fat** 7g (sat 1g), **Cholesterol** 12mg, **Carbs** 8g, **Total sugars** 3g (added 1g), **Protein** 15g, **Fiber** 1g, **Sodium** 473mg, **Potassium** 336mg.
Nutrition bonus: Vitamin A (68% daily value), Vitamin C (38% dv).

Better Canned Tuna

For sustainable chunk light tuna, look for the blue Certified Sustainable Seafood label from the Marine Stewardship Council. The certification means the tuna was troll- or pole-and-line caught, which are sustainable for the fish and the environment. We call for chunk light tuna because it's significantly lower in mercury than albacore ("solid white" tuna)—a better choice for health, especially for pregnant women, nursing mothers and children. According to the FDA and EPA, these at-risk groups should limit their consumption of lower-mercury tuna to 12 ounces a week.

CELERY & PARMESAN MINESTRONE

ACTIVE: 35 MIN **TOTAL:** 45 MIN
TO MAKE AHEAD: Refrigerate up to 1 day.

This simple soup cooks quickly with celery stalks, leaves and dried celery seeds to flavor the delicious Parmesan-laced tomato broth.

     2 tablespoons extra-virgin olive oil
     2 cups diced celery
    ½ cup diced carrot
    ½ cup diced onion
     1 clove garlic, chopped
     1 teaspoon celery seeds
    ½ teaspoon ground pepper
     4 cups reduced-sodium chicken broth *or* vegetable broth
    ⅓ cup whole-wheat orzo *or* other small pasta
     1 15-ounce can diced tomatoes
    1¾ cups cooked chickpeas *or* cannellini beans *or* one 15-ounce can, rinsed
        (see *Tip, page 183*)
    ½ cup chopped celery leaves, divided
    ¼ cup packed grated Parmigiano-Reggiano cheese, plus more for serving

1. Heat oil in a large saucepan or soup pot over medium heat. Add celery, carrot, onion, garlic, celery seeds and pepper. Cook, stirring occasionally, until the vegetables are tender, about 10 minutes.

2. Add broth and bring to a boil. Add pasta and cook, uncovered, until the pasta is tender, 8 to 10 minutes. Add tomatoes, chickpeas (or beans), half the celery leaves and ¼ cup cheese. Cook over medium heat until steaming hot, 3 to 5 minutes. Ladle into bowls and garnish with the remaining celery leaves and a light dusting of cheese, if desired.

SERVES 6: ABOUT 1¼ CUPS EACH

Calories 167, **Fat** 7g (sat 1g), **Cholesterol** 3mg, **Carbs** 20g, **Total sugars** 4g (added 0g), **Protein** 8g, **Fiber** 4g, **Sodium** 630mg, **Potassium** 477mg.
Nutrition bonus: Vitamin A (43% daily value).

Celery Root

There is both beauty and beast in this homely root. Its outward appearance is admittedly a little scary—gnarled and knobby and covered in hairy tendrils that are often still matted with soil. Inside, it is creamy white, with a crisp texture and the flavors of celery and parsley and just a touch of the earthy essence of soil.

Celery root (also called celeriac, with the emphasis on the second syllable) is the root of a type of celery that is grown for what develops under the ground rather than for what emerges from it. Celery root grows wild and is cultivated in both the Mediterranean and northern Europe and was once a fairly common vegetable on American tables—most often boiled and topped with cream sauce. Cookbooks throughout the 19th century mentioned it, but it then fell out of favor. Thankfully, it is back.

A classic French preparation is celery root rémoulade—julienned or grated celery root dressed in a Dijon-mayonnaise dressing flavored with tarragon and served as an hors d'oeuvre. Celery root can be grated into a slaw, used in a salad, cooked with other winter vegetables in a hearty stew or cooked and pureed into a creamy, satisfying soup.

It is mild, so companion flavors should not be overpowering if you want to enjoy its clean, fresh taste. It goes well with potatoes, carrots, apples, leeks, mild cheeses, walnuts and hazelnuts.

Celery root is slow-growing. It takes 120 days—all summer and into the fall—to mature. Seeds are started indoors in late winter, and seedlings are transplanted outdoors in late spring. Celery root is in season starting in fall and through late spring.

Best in fall to early spring

AT THE MARKET

❧ Look for firm roots that are heavy for their size and with no soft spots. Choose the roundest roots you can find—the less gnarled, the less waste when trimming. Avoid roots that have a spongy stem end.

IN YOUR KITCHEN

❧ Trim the stalk, if any, and wrap the root in plastic wrap. Store in the refrigerator up to 10 days.

❧ Scrub root with a coarse vegetable brush under cool running water until there is no soil left clinging to the root and water runs clear in the sink. Trim and prepare as shown in the photos, *right*.

COOKING BASICS

PUREE Bring 4 cups low-fat milk, 3 cups water and 2 medium peeled celery roots cut into 1 inch chunks to a boil in a large saucepan over medium heat. Reduce heat and simmer until very tender, about 30 minutes. Reserve 1 cup of the cooking liquid, then drain. Puree celery root, 2 tablespoons butter, ½ teaspoon sea salt and pepper to taste in a food processor until the consistency of thinned mashed potatoes. Add some of the reserved cooking liquid, if necessary, for the right consistency. Serves 4.

BRAISE Heat 1 tablespoon each olive oil and butter in a medium skillet over medium-high heat. Add 1 small minced onion and 1 bay leaf. Cook until onion is tender, 5 minutes. Add 1 medium celery root cut into ½-inch chunks and cook, stirring, until browned, 4 to 5 minutes. Reduce heat to medium and add ¼ cup reduced-sodium chicken broth. Cover and cook, shaking pan occasionally, until celery root is barely tender, 15 to 20 minutes. Season to taste with salt and pepper. Serves 2.

SAUTÉ Heat 1 tablespoon olive oil in a large nonstick skillet over medium heat. Add 1 cup matchstick-cut carrots, 1 cup matchstick-cut leeks (white and light green parts) and 2 cups matchstick-cut celery root. Cook, stirring occasionally, until softened, 3 to 5 minutes. Add ½ cup reduced-sodium chicken broth and 1½ teaspoons chopped fresh thyme. Bring to a simmer. Reduce heat to low. Cover and cook, stirring occasionally, until the vegetables are tender and the broth has evaporated, 10 to 12 minutes. Season with ¼ teaspoon salt and ⅛ teaspoon pepper. Serves 4.

NUTRITION

❧ **1 cup cooked cubed celery root:** Calories 42, **Fat** 0g (sat 0g), **Cholesterol** 0mg, **Carbs** 9g, **Total sugars** 0g (added 0g), **Protein** 2g, **Fiber** 2g, **Sodium** 95mg, **Potassium** 268mg.

BONUS Celery root may guard against breast cancer thanks to apigenin. Apigenin is a phytoestrogen, a kind of plant chemical that suppresses estrogen's ability to encourage breast cancer growth.

How to prep

1. Cut off the stem, leaves and just the top of the root. Cut off a slice from the bottom of the root so it lies flat on the cutting surface.

2. Cut thin slices down the side of the root to remove the knobby peel.

3. Slice or chop as desired. To prevent browning, place pieces in cool water with lemon slices until ready to use *(right)*.

PEAR & CELERY ROOT SLAW

ACTIVE: 30 MIN **TOTAL:** 30 MIN

Use underripe pears to keep the texture crisp in this autumnal slaw. Cutting the pears and celery root by hand into little matchsticks makes a prettier salad, but shred them with a box grater if you're in a hurry (see Tip, page 479).

¼ cup low-fat mayonnaise
2 tablespoons cider vinegar
1 teaspoon sugar
½ teaspoon caraway seeds
¼ teaspoon salt
¼ teaspoon ground pepper
2 slightly underripe pears, julienned (about 4 cups)
1 small celery root, peeled and julienned (about 1 cup)
2 medium carrots, julienned
¼ cup very thinly sliced red onion

Whisk mayonnaise, vinegar, sugar, caraway seeds, salt and pepper in a large bowl. Add pears, celery root, carrots and onion and toss to coat. Serve at room temperature or chilled.

SERVES 6: GENEROUS ¾ CUP EACH

Calories 85, **Fat** 2g (sat 0g), **Cholesterol** 3mg, **Carbs** 17g, **Total sugars** 9g (added 1g), **Protein** 1g, **Fiber** 3g, **Sodium** 219mg, **Potassium** 229mg.
Nutrition bonus: Vitamin A (69% daily value).

MAPLE-BACON ROASTED APPLES & CELERIAC

ACTIVE: 40 MIN **TOTAL:** 40 MIN

Roasted apples and celery root with a maple-bacon glaze is a perfect fall side dish. If you can't find pure maple syrup, use an equal amount of brown sugar plus 1 tablespoon of water in Step 3.

 1 large celery root (celeriac), about 1½ pounds, peeled and cut into
    1-inch pieces
 2 teaspoons extra-virgin olive oil
 ½ teaspoon ground pepper
 ¼ teaspoon salt
 2 apples, cut into 1-inch pieces *(see Tip)*
 2 slices bacon, chopped
 ¼ cup pure maple syrup *(see Tip, page 445)*
 1 teaspoon chopped fresh thyme *or* rosemary *or* ¼ teaspoon dried

1. Preheat oven to 450°F.

2. Toss celery root with oil, pepper and salt and spread on a rimmed baking sheet. Roast until starting to brown, 10 to 12 minutes. Add apples, toss gently and continue roasting until the apples and celery root are tender, 6 to 10 minutes more.

3. Meanwhile, cook bacon in a medium skillet over medium heat, stirring occasionally, until just crispy. Remove to a paper towel-lined plate with a slotted spoon; discard all but 2 teaspoons of the bacon fat. Add maple syrup to the fat in the pan and bring to a boil, scraping up the browned bits. Add the cooked bacon and thyme (or rosemary). When the celery root and apples are tender, gently toss them with the maple-bacon glaze and roast for 5 minutes more.

SERVES 4: ABOUT 1 CUP EACH

Calories 240, **Fat** 8g (sat 2g), **Cholesterol** 9mg, **Carbs** 40g, **Total sugars** 25g (added 13g), **Protein** 4g, **Fiber** 5g, **Sodium** 388mg, **Potassium** 611mg.
Nutrition bonus: Vitamin C (27% daily value).

Apple Picking

All apples are not created equal—at least when it comes to cooking vs. eating them fresh. When cooking with apples—unless you're making applesauce—choose a variety that holds its shape well when exposed to heat (not McIntosh). Good choices for cooking include Granny Smith, Braeburn, Winesap, Jonathan, Jonagold, Golden Delicious and Cortland.

DOUBLE CELERY SOUP

ACTIVE: 15 MIN **TOTAL:** 40 MIN
TO MAKE AHEAD: Refrigerate up to 3 days.

This elegant and delicately flavored soup has an amazingly creamy texture without a drop of dairy. It makes a wonderful, warming first course for an autumnal dinner.

2	cups sliced celery (1-inch pieces)
2	cups diced celery root *or* yellow potatoes (½-inch pieces)
2	shallots, quartered
2	tablespoons extra-virgin olive oil, plus more for serving
¼	teaspoon salt
¼	teaspoon ground pepper
2½	cups low-sodium chicken broth *or* vegetable broth, heated
4	teaspoons celery leaves *or* parsley

1. Preheat oven to 450°F.

2. Toss celery, celery root (or potato), shallots, oil, salt and pepper in a large bowl. Spread evenly on a large rimmed baking sheet. Roast, stirring once, until very tender, about 25 minutes.

3. Puree the vegetables and hot broth in a blender until smooth. (Use caution when blending hot liquids.) Drizzle each portion with oil, if desired, and top with celery leaves (or parsley).

SERVES 4: SCANT 1 CUP EACH

Calories 127, **Fat** 8g (sat 1g), **Cholesterol** 0mg, **Carbs** 10g, **Total sugars** 2g (added 0g), **Protein** 5g, **Fiber** 2g, **Sodium** 289mg, **Potassium** 473mg.

Chard

Once always referred to as "Swiss" chard, that designation is now often dropped from the name for this dark, leafy green. Although it's possible that a 19th-century Swiss botanist named it, we'll go with the more modern "chard." In all likelihood, it was the Sicilians who started cooking with it—and much earlier than the 19th century.

Chard has an earthy flavor similar to beets (which is not surprising since chard is part of the beet family), with a hint of bitterness. Beet greens look very similar to chard and, in fact, are a good substitute in most recipes. Collard greens or spinach leaves (not baby) can also stand in for chard.

Different varieties have white, red, yellow, deep pink or orange stalks. Both the leaves and ribs can be eaten, but in most cases should be cooked separately, as the ribs need more time in the pan.

Like many hearty greens, chard pairs well with legumes—black-eyed peas, lentils, chickpeas and white beans of all kinds—as well as tomatoes and pungent, crumbly cheeses such as feta and aged goat cheese. Chard is lovely tucked into an omelet, stirred into soup or combined with pasta, potatoes or polenta.

Sauté chard in olive oil with a little garlic, crushed red pepper, salt and lemon. Or sauté and stir in toasted pine nuts and raisins. Braise both the stems and leaves in the drippings from bacon or pancetta with a little bit of water or broth. Or cook with onion or other aromatics and chicken broth and puree into a bright, beautiful, very healthful soup.

Chard is available all year long and is at peak from early summer to fall.

Best in early summer to fall

AT THE MARKET

➤ Choose unblemished leaves with no yellowing that are fresh and crisp, not wilted or limp. Avoid very large leaves and ribs. They are overly mature and can have a tough, chewy texture.

➤ The most common variety of chard has deep green leaves and bright red ribs and veins, although green leaves and white ribs are fairly common as well. 'Bright Lights' is a rainbow chard, with multicolor orange, red, deep pink and yellow stems and ribs.

IN YOUR KITCHEN

➤ Chard has high water content and can be rubbery when dehydrated. It's at its very best when cooked immediately after harvesting or purchasing; however, it can be stored short-term. Store unwashed chard in plastic bags in the refrigerator up to 3 days.

➤ Fill a large bowl with cool water. Wash chard in several changes of water, dunking and swirling leaves until no sand or grit is visible on the leaves or in the bottom of the bowl. Pat dry. Hold the rib of each leaf firmly in one hand while using the other hand to strip the leaf from the rib. To chop, stack leaves and roll up; cut the roll into 1-inch strips. Slice the ribs as needed.

COOKING BASICS

BRAISE Wash 1 pound chard, allowing some water to cling to the leaves. Strip leaves from ribs. Trim ribs and slice into ½-inch pieces; set aside. Cut leaves into 1-inch strips. Cook 1½ ounces diced pancetta in a large pot over medium heat until it begins to brown, 4 to 6 minutes. Transfer to a paper towel-lined plate. Add 2 thinly sliced shallots, chard stems and 1 teaspoon chopped fresh thyme to the pan and cook, stirring, until the shallots begin to brown, 4 to 5 minutes. Add chard leaves, ¼ cup water and 1 tablespoon lemon juice and cook, stirring, until wilted, about 2 minutes. Cover and cook until tender, 2 to 4 minutes more. Remove from heat. Stir in pancetta, pepper to taste and 2 tablespoons chopped toasted walnuts. Serves 6.

SAUTÉ Remove ribs from 2 bunches of washed and dried chard. Cut ribs into ½-inch pieces and leaves into 1-inch strips. Heat 1 tablespoon olive oil in a large skillet over medium-high heat. Add ribs and cook, stirring, until just starting to get tender, about 2 minutes. Add 2 cloves minced garlic and cook, stirring constantly, until fragrant, about 1 minute. Add chard leaves and cook, tossing frequently, until they wilt, about 4 minutes. Season with salt and crushed red pepper to taste, if desired. Serve with lemon wedges. Serves 4.

NUTRITION

➤ **1 cup cooked chard: Calories** 35, **Fat** 0g (sat 0g), **Cholesterol** 0mg, **Carbs** 7g, **Total sugars** 2g (added 0g), **Protein** 3g, **Fiber** 4g, **Sodium** 313mg, **Potassium** 961mg.

BONUS These greens are overflowing with vitamin K, a nutrient often lacking in people with arthritis. Just 1 cup of cooked chard delivers more than seven times the daily value for this joint-friendly nutrient. You need a little fat along with vitamin K to absorb it, so use a little oil or butter when you prepare it.

Grow Your Own

Chard thrives in either cool or warm temperatures as long as the soil is well-drained, light and rich in organic matter. Plant seeds outdoors in a sunny spot 2 to 3 weeks before the last spring frost date. Plant seeds at 10-day intervals for 4 weeks for a continuous harvest. (For a fall harvest, plant 40 days before the first fall frost date.) When seedlings are 3 inches tall, thin them to 4 to 6 inches apart. Water consistently. Plants are ready for harvest when 6 to 8 inches tall. Cut off outer leaves 1½ inches above the ground with a sharp knife; new leaves will grow in their place.

Removing the ribs

Hold the rib firmly in one hand while using the other hand to strip off the leaves.

CHARD WITH GREEN OLIVES, CURRANTS & GOAT CHEESE

ACTIVE: 20 MIN **TOTAL:** 20 MIN

Tangy green olives, sweet currants and creamy goat cheese turn chard into a sophisticated treat, just right paired with lamb chops.

  1 tablespoon extra-virgin olive oil
  1 pound chard, stems and leaves separated, chopped
  ¼ teaspoon salt
  ¼ teaspoon ground pepper
  ¼ cup chopped pitted green olives
  ¼ cup currants
  ½ cup crumbled goat cheese (2 ounces)

Heat oil in a large pot over medium heat. Add chard stems, salt and pepper and cook, stirring often, until softened, 3 to 5 minutes. Stir in chard leaves and cook, stirring constantly, until wilted, about 2 minutes. Stir in olives and currants. Dot goat cheese over the top, cover and cook until the chard is tender and the cheese is melted, about 2 minutes more.

SERVES 6: ABOUT ⅔ CUP EACH.

Calories 93, **Fat** 6g (sat 2g), **Cholesterol** 4mg, **Carbs** 7g, **Total sugars** 5g (added 0g), **Protein** 3g, **Fiber** 2g, **Sodium** 346mg, **Potassium** 344mg.
Nutrition bonus: Vitamin A (95% daily value), Vitamin C (38% dv).

BACON CHARD QUESADILLAS

ACTIVE: 35 MIN **TOTAL:** 35 MIN

Smoky bacon, earthy chard and zesty pepper Jack cheese fill these quesadillas. It's a less common filling, but totally delicious. It goes to show you can put just about anything in a quesadilla.

 4 slices center-cut bacon, chopped
 1 small red onion, halved and thinly sliced (about ¾ cup)
 4 cups chopped chard leaves (from 1 bunch)
 ½ teaspoon ground pepper
 1 15-ounce can black beans, rinsed *(see Tip)*
 8 6-inch whole-wheat tortillas
 1 cup shredded pepper Jack cheese

1. Cook bacon in a large nonstick skillet over medium-high heat, stirring often, until crisp, 2 to 3 minutes. Reduce heat to medium, add onion and cook, stirring, until softened, about 2 minutes. Add chard and pepper; cook, stirring, until wilted, 1 to 2 minutes. Add beans and coarsely mash; stir to combine. Remove from heat.

2. Place tortillas on a clean work surface. Spread a generous ¼ cup filling and 2 tablespoons cheese on half of each tortilla. Fold tortillas in half, pressing gently to flatten.

3. Wipe out the pan and return to medium heat. Add 4 quesadillas and cook, turning once, until golden on both sides, 2 to 4 minutes total. Transfer to a platter and tent with foil to keep warm. Reduce heat to medium-low and cook the remaining quesadillas.

SERVES 4: 2 QUESADILLAS EACH

Calories 376, **Fat** 12g (sat 7g), **Cholesterol** 32mg, **Carbs** 58g, **Total sugars** 4g (added 0g), **Protein** 21g, **Fiber** 9g, **Sodium** 748mg, **Potassium** 619mg.
Nutrition bonus: Vitamin A (48% daily value), Calcium (29% dv), Vitamin C (24% dv), Magnesium (23% dv), Iron (22% dv).

Rinse to Reduce Sodium

Canned beans are convenient but tend to be high in sodium. Give them a good rinse before adding to a recipe to reduce some of the sodium (up to 35 percent) or opt for low-sodium or no-salt-added varieties. Or, if you have the time, cook your own beans from scratch *(see Tip page 52)*.

CHARD & CHORIZO FRITTATA

ACTIVE: 40 MIN **TOTAL:** 40 MIN

Frittatas are the ultimate no-fuss dinner, and that's why we love them for busy weeknights. In this one, we sauté earthy chard, chorizo and hash browns in the pan before adding the eggs. The broiler finishes cooking the eggs and turns the top of the frittata a lovely golden brown.

  7 **large eggs**
  3 **scallions, sliced**
 ½ **cup shredded Parmesan cheese**
 ¼ **teaspoon ground pepper**
 ⅛ **teaspoon salt**
  2 **tablespoons extra-virgin olive oil**
  4 **cups chopped chard leaves (from 1 bunch)**
 ½ **cup finely diced Spanish chorizo** *(see Tip)* **or pepperoni (about 2 ounces)**
  3 **cups frozen shredded hash browns**

1. Position rack in upper third of oven; preheat broiler.

2. Whisk eggs, scallions, cheese, pepper and salt in a large bowl.

3. Heat oil in a large cast-iron skillet (or broiler-safe nonstick skillet) over medium-high heat. Add chard and chorizo (or pepperoni) and cook, stirring frequently, until the chard is wilted, 2 to 3 minutes. Stir in hash browns. Pat the mixture into an even layer in the pan.

4. Pour the egg mixture into the pan and evenly spread to the edges. Cook over medium-high heat, lifting around the edges with a heatproof spatula to allow uncooked egg to flow under, until set around the edges, 3 to 4 minutes. Place the pan under the broiler until the top is cooked and the eggs are lightly browned, 3 to 4 minutes. Let stand 5 minutes.

5. To release the frittata from the pan, run the spatula around the edges, then underneath, until you can slide or lift it out onto a cutting board or serving plate. Cut into wedges and serve.

SERVES 4

Calories 434, **Fat** 25g (sat 8g), **Cholesterol** 345mg, **Carbs** 31g, **Total sugars** 1g (added 0g), **Protein** 22g, **Fiber** 3g, **Sodium** 655mg, **Potassium** 805mg.
Nutrition bonus: Vitamin A (57% daily value), Vitamin C (43% dv), Iron & Potassium (23% dv), Calcium (22% dv), Vitamin B₁₂ (20% dv).

Spanish Chorizo

Spanish-style chorizo is a dried, seasoned, fully cooked and smoked pork sausage—different than Mexican-style chorizo, which needs to be cooked. Find it near other cured sausages in well-stocked supermarkets or online at *tienda.com*.

BASIC GREEN SOUP

ACTIVE: 50 MIN **TOTAL:** 1 HR

TO MAKE AHEAD: Prepare through Step 4 (omitting the lemon) and refrigerate up to 3 days. Season with lemon just before serving.

This chard and spinach soup gets complex flavor from slowly cooked onions and lemon juice; a sprinkle of rice gives it body and velvety texture. Serve with a swirl of extra-virgin olive oil for richness.

- 2 tablespoons extra-virgin olive oil, plus more for garnish
- 2 large yellow onions, chopped
- 1 teaspoon salt, divided
- 2 tablespoons water plus 3 cups, divided
- ¼ cup arborio rice
- 1 bunch green chard (about 1 pound)
- 14 cups gently packed spinach (about 12 ounces), trimmed
- 4 cups vegetable broth
  Big pinch of cayenne pepper
- 1 tablespoon lemon juice, or more to taste

1. Heat 2 tablespoons oil in a large skillet over high heat. Add onions and ¼ teaspoon salt; cook, stirring frequently, until the onions begin to brown, about 5 minutes. Reduce the heat to low, add 2 tablespoons water and cover. Cook, stirring frequently until the pan cools down, then occasionally, always covering the pan again, until the onions are greatly reduced and have a deep caramel color, 25 to 30 minutes.

2. Meanwhile, combine the remaining 3 cups water and ¾ teaspoon salt in a large pot; add rice. Bring to a boil. Reduce heat to maintain a simmer, cover and cook for 15 minutes. Strip ribs from chard (save for another use, if desired) and coarsely chop leaves. Coarsely chop spinach.

3. When the rice has cooked for 15 minutes, stir in the chard. Return to a simmer; cover and cook for 10 minutes. When the onions are caramelized, stir a little of the simmering liquid into them; add them to the rice along with the spinach, broth and cayenne. Return to a simmer, cover and cook, stirring once, until the spinach is tender but still bright green, about 5 minutes more.

4. Puree the soup with an immersion blender or in a regular blender, in batches, until smooth. Stir in lemon juice. Garnish each serving with a drizzle of olive oil.

SERVES 8: ABOUT 1¼ CUPS EACH

Calories 100, **Fat** 4g (sat 1g), **Cholesterol** 0mg, **Carbs** 14g, **Total sugars** 4g (added 0g), **Protein** 3g, **Fiber** 3g, **Sodium** 669mg, **Potassium** 425mg.
Nutrition bonus: Vitamin A (148% daily value), Vitamin C (40% dv), Magnesium (20% dv).

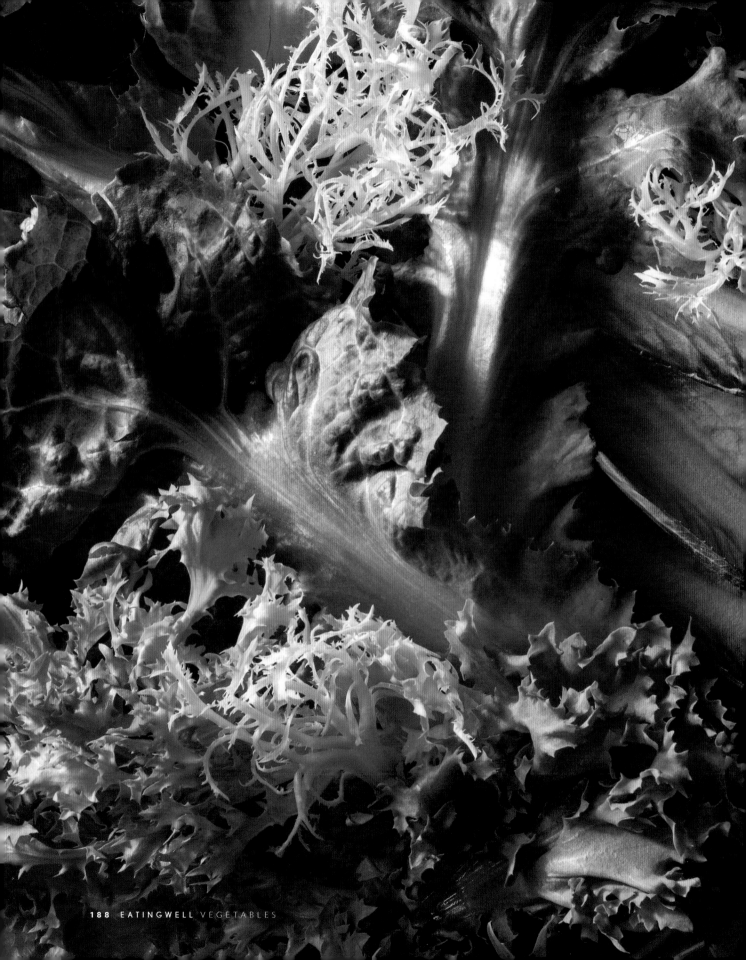

chicories

Plants in the chicory family can be loose-leafed or in tight heads, tapered or round, smooth or frilly. Colors range from white to pale yellow to all shades of green to wine red. Their common characteristics are a structural sturdiness and a distinct bitterness that balances the sweeter, more delicate lettuces with which they are often combined. While they usually find their way into the salad bowl, chicories can be cooked as well.

Common types include curly endive, frisée, escarole, Belgian endive and radicchio. Treviso is a type of radicchio that grows in elongated, rather than round, heads. Puntarelle, an Italian chicory, is more rare but the crucial ingredient in a Roman salad featuring an anchovy-garlic vinaigrette. Curly endive and frisée are quite similar in flavor. Both are most often used raw in cold salads but can be braised or tossed with a hot dressing to wilt and mellow them slightly. *Frisée aux lardons,* a traditional French salad, features frisée tossed with a warm vinaigrette flavored with bacon, Dijon mustard, olive oil and lemon juice. The salad is topped with a poached egg and served with shaved Gruyère and toasted croutons.

Escarole can be used as a salad green, sautéed or lightly braised in garlic and olive oil, or stirred into soup. Although Belgian endive can be sliced and used in salad, braised, sautéed or baked in a gratin, its scoop-shape leaves make it ideal for holding savory fillings on a crudité platter. Crisp, fiercely bitter radicchio is most often a salad ingredient but mellows considerably when roasted, grilled or sautéed in olive oil and tossed with pasta.

All chicories like cool weather and are best during fall through winter.

Best in fall to winter

AT THE MARKET

⚜ All chicories brown slightly where they were cut away from the roots, but there should be no browning anywhere else. Leaves should look crisp and fresh, with no blemishes or bruising. Avoid heads or stems that are very large; they can be tough and very bitter.

IN YOUR KITCHEN

⚜ Store radicchio in a perforated plastic bag in the refrigerator up to 1 week. Store Belgian endive wrapped in a kitchen towel in the refrigerator up to 5 days. Store curly endive, escarole, frisée or puntarelle in a perforated plastic bag in the refrigerator up to 4 days. (Perforated bags allow ethylene to escape, which helps keep produce fresher longer.)

⚜ When using radicchio whole or in wedges, trim base but do not remove core. For slicing, remove core and break off leaves as needed. Wash in cool water and pat dry. When using Belgian endive whole or halved, trim a thin slice off cut end and rinse under cool running water; pat dry. For puntarelle, remove outer leaves (save for a sauté or add to soup). Cut stalks into ¼-inch-thick strips. Soak for 45 minutes in a bowl of ice water. Drain and pat dry. Wash and spin curly endive, escarole and frisée in a salad spinner.

COOKING BASICS

GRILL (RADICCHIO) Trim and quarter 2 heads of radicchio, leaving the cores intact. Brush cut sides generously with 2 tablespoons extra-virgin olive oil. Season to taste with salt and ground pepper. Grill over medium heat, turning frequently, until lightly charred and tender when pierced with a fork, 8 to 12 minutes. Drizzle each piece with ½ teaspoon each extra-virgin olive oil and balsamic vinegar. Adjust seasoning, if desired. Serves 4.

ROAST (RADICCHIO) Trim and quarter 2 heads of radicchio, leaving the cores intact. Arrange the radicchio on a large rimmed baking sheet. Drizzle with 2 tablespoons olive oil, tossing gently to coat. Place each piece cut-side down on the pan. Season to taste with salt and pepper. Roast in a 400°F oven, turning once, until the leaves are wilted and lightly charred, 12 to 15 minutes. Sprinkle with ¼ cup crumbled goat cheese and 1 tablespoon minced fresh chives. Serves 4.

SALAD Combine 8 anchovy fillets, patted dry and minced; 1 tablespoon minced garlic; and ⅓ cup extra-virgin olive oil in a small saucepan. Warm over medium-low heat until fragrant, 2 to 4 minutes. Remove from heat and whisk in an additional ⅓ cup extra-virgin olive oil and ⅓ cup red wine vinegar. Season to taste with ground pepper. For salad, combine 6 cups torn frisée, curly endive or puntarelle leaves or sliced stalks (or a blend) in a large bowl. Toss with ⅓ cup of the dressing. (Refrigerate leftover dressing up to 3 days.) Serves 4.

SAUTÉ (ESCAROLE) Stack washed and dried leaves from 1 head esacarole (about 1 pound) and cut into 1½-inch-wide strips. Heat ¼ cup olive oil in a large deep skillet over medium heat. Add 3 thinly sliced garlic cloves and cook, stirring, until fragrant and golden, about 2 to 3 minutes. Add escarole. Season to taste with salt. Cook, stirring frequently, until escarole is tender, about 10 minutes. Serve with lemon wedges. Serves 4.

NUTRITION

⚜ **1 cup chopped cooked escarole:** **Calories** 28, **Fat** 0g (sat 0g), **Cholesterol** 0mg, **Carbs** 5g, **Total sugars** 0g (added 0g), **Protein** 2g, **Fiber** 4g, **Sodium** 28mg, **Potassium** 368mg.

BONUS Chicories are rich in cichoric acid, a compound that helps your cells soak up glucose from your bloodstream. When your body uses glucose more efficiently, you're less likely to develop insulin resistance, which, if left unchecked, can lead to diabetes.

▲ **Belgian Endive**
The broad, scoop-shape leaves grow in tightly closed tapered heads. There are both white/pale green and white/red varieties.

▲ **Puntarelle (Leaves)**
This Italian chicory has crisp stalks and tender, dandelion-like leaves. Traditionally, the hollow stalks are sliced and eaten as a salad. The leaves can be sautéed in garlic or added to soup.

▲ **Radicchio**
'Chioggia', the most common variety of this intensely flavored chicory, grows in heads of wine-red leaves with bright white veins.

▲ **Frisée**
Very similar in flavor to broader-leaved curly endive, the fine, frizzy leaves of this chicory add interesting texture to salads.

◄ **Escarole**
The large outer leaves of these leafy, lettuce-like heads have a hearty flavor and subtle bitterness, while the pale yellow heart is tender, juicy, and faintly bittersweet.

▲ **Curly Endive**
Sometimes simply called "chicory," this jagged-leafed green is most often used in salads.

SIMPLE GREEN SALAD WITH CITRONETTE

ACTIVE: 15 MIN **TOTAL:** 15 MIN
TO MAKE AHEAD: Refrigerate the dressing (Step 1) up to 3 days. Bring to room temperature and shake before using.

The assertive, slightly bitter tastes of frisée and radicchio match well with mellow-flavor greens, such as red leaf lettuce, baby spinach or even Boston lettuce. Citronette is a light salad dressing made with citrus juice and olive oil—usually lemon juice, but here a mix of lemon and orange.

¼ cup fresh orange juice
¼ cup lemon juice
¼ cup extra-virgin olive oil
1 small shallot, finely chopped
2 teaspoons Dijon mustard
½ teaspoon salt
¼ teaspoon ground pepper
4 cups torn peppery *and/or* bitter greens, such as frisée, radicchio, arugula *or* watercress
8 cups mild greens, such as Boston lettuce, mesclun, baby spinach *or* baby romaine
⅓ cup thinly sliced red onion

1. Combine orange juice, lemon juice, oil, shallot, mustard, salt and pepper in a jar with a tight-fitting lid. Shake until well combined.

2. Place greens and onion in a large salad bowl; toss with ⅓ cup of the dressing.

SERVES 6: ABOUT 1½ CUPS EACH (PLUS ⅔ CUP EXTRA DRESSING)

Calories 43, **Fat** 3g (sat 0g), **Cholesterol** 0mg, **Carbs** 3g, **Total sugars** 1g (added 0g), **Protein** 2g, **Fiber** 1g, **Sodium** 81mg, **Potassium** 270mg.
Nutrition bonus: Vitamin A (63% daily value), Vitamin C (26% dv).

BRAISED ENDIVE

ACTIVE: 15 MIN **TOTAL:** 45 MIN

Slow braising in an aromatic broth tames Belgian endive's sharp flavor and makes it meltingly tender. Serve with roast chicken and acorn squash.

   1 tablespoon extra-virgin olive oil
   ½ cup fresh coarse whole-wheat breadcrumbs *(see Tip, page 18)*
   1 tablespoon chopped fresh parsley
   4 teaspoons butter, divided
   6 medium heads Belgian endive, halved
   1 cup reduced-sodium chicken broth
   1 clove garlic, crushed
   1 sprig fresh thyme
   ½ teaspoon sugar
   ¼ teaspoon salt

1. Heat oil in a large skillet over medium heat. Add breadcrumbs and parsley and cook, stirring, until the breadcrumbs are brown and crispy, 2 to 4 minutes. Transfer to a plate; wipe out the pan.

2. Return the pan to medium heat and melt 2 teaspoons butter. Add 6 endive halves, cut-side down, and cook until beginning to brown, 2 to 3 minutes. Transfer to a cutting board. Repeat with the remaining 2 teaspoons butter and endive.

3. Add the first batch of endive back to the pan. Add broth, garlic, thyme, sugar and salt. Cook, turning the endive every 10 minutes or so, until the liquid has evaporated completely and the endive is glazed, about 30 minutes total. Transfer the endive to a platter. (Discard garlic and thyme.) Serve sprinkled with the reserved breadcrumbs.

SERVES 6: 2 HALVES EACH

Calories 86, **Fat** 5g (sat 2g), **Cholesterol** 7mg, **Carbs** 8g, **Total sugars** 1g (added 1g), **Protein** 3g, **Fiber** 4g, **Sodium** 226mg, **Potassium** 279mg.

CITRUS SALAD WITH OLIVES & RADICCHIO

ACTIVE: 40 MIN **TOTAL:** 40 MIN
TO MAKE AHEAD: Refrigerate onions (Step 1) and dressing (Step 3) in separate containers up to 1 day.

By November the freshest fragrant oranges and grapefruit begin rolling out of groves and into markets. Take advantage of the season by making this gorgeous salad.

- 1 medium red onion, thinly sliced
- 1 cup white-wine vinegar
- 2 tablespoons sugar
- 2 oranges
- 2 pink *or* red grapefruit
- 1 clove garlic, minced
- ¼ teaspoon salt
- ¼ cup extra-virgin olive oil
- 4 cups packed torn escarole leaves
- 4 cups torn radicchio
- 1 cup fresh parsley leaves
- 1 cup shredded Manchego *or* crumbled feta cheese
- 1 cup pitted green olives, quartered

1. Combine onion, vinegar and sugar in a small saucepan. Bring to a boil; cook, stirring occasionally, for 2 minutes. Strain through a fine-mesh sieve, reserving 6 tablespoons of the cooking liquid in a large bowl. (Discard the rest.) Separately set the onion and liquid aside to cool.

2. Meanwhile, peel oranges and grapefruit with a sharp knife, removing all peel and white pith. Slice the fruit into ¼-inch-thick rounds. Remove any seeds.

3. To make the dressing, add garlic and salt to the reserved onion-cooking liquid. Whisk in oil until well combined. Reserve 2 tablespoons of the dressing in a small bowl.

4. Add escarole, radicchio and parsley to the dressing in the large bowl; toss well to coat. Arrange the greens on a large serving platter. Top with the citrus rounds, the reserved onion, cheese and olives. Drizzle the reserved dressing over the top.

SERVES 10: ABOUT 1¼ CUPS EACH

Calories 161, **Fat** 11g (sat 3g), **Cholesterol** 13mg, **Carbs** 13g, **Total sugars** 8g (added 1g), **Protein** 4g, **Fiber** 3g, **Sodium** 458mg, **Potassium** 291mg.
Nutrition bonus: Vitamin C (68% daily value), Vitamin A (34% dv).

PASTA WITH BRAISED RADICCHIO

ACTIVE: 35 MIN **TOTAL:** 35 MIN

Radicchio's main flavor characteristic is bitterness. Here, braised in a garlicky, prosciutto-enriched broth, the powerful bite of this ruby-color green melts to a mellow meatiness.

- 1 tablespoon extra-virgin olive oil
- 3 cloves garlic, slivered
- ¼ teaspoon crushed red pepper
- 2 ounces thinly sliced prosciutto, cut into 2½-inch-long matchsticks
- 2 large heads radicchio, cored and sliced
- Ground pepper to taste
- 1 14-ounce can reduced-sodium chicken broth
- 1 pound whole-wheat linguine *or* spaghetti
- ½ cup freshly grated Parmesan cheese, divided

1. Put a large pot of water on to boil.

2. Heat oil in a large nonstick skillet over medium-low heat. Add garlic and crushed red pepper. Cook, stirring, until tender and fragrant but not brown, 30 to 60 seconds. Add prosciutto and cook, stirring, until lightly browned, 2 to 3 minutes. Add radicchio, increase heat to medium and cook, turning with tongs, until wilted, 4 to 5 minutes. Season with pepper.

3. Pour in broth and bring to a simmer. Reduce heat to low and simmer, stirring occasionally, until the radicchio is tender, about 10 minutes.

4. Meanwhile, cook pasta until just tender, 8 to 10 minutes or according to package directions. Drain and transfer to a serving bowl. Add the sauce and ¼ cup cheese; toss to coat. Serve immediately, passing the remaining ¼ cup cheese separately.

SERVES 6

Calories 356, **Fat** 7g (sat 2g), **Cholesterol** 13mg, **Carbs** 61g, **Total sugars** 3g (added 0g), **Protein** 18g, **Fiber** 10g, **Sodium** 578mg, **Potassium** 443mg.
Nutrition bonus: Magnesium (30% daily value), Folate (22% dv).

WINTER SALAD WITH ROASTED SQUASH & POMEGRANATE VINAIGRETTE

ACTIVE: 45 MIN **TOTAL:** 1 HR
TO MAKE AHEAD: Refrigerate the vinaigrette (Step 2) up to 1 day.

This array of gorgeous colors, textures and tastes is an elegant addition to holiday menus. Sprinkle with Gorgonzola or another creamy blue cheese for an added burst of flavor and richness.

Seeding Pomegranate

To seed a pomegranate, fill a large bowl with water. Lightly score the fruit into quarters from crown to stem end, cutting through the skin but not into the interior of the fruit. Hold the fruit underwater, break it apart and use your hands to gently separate the plump seeds (arils) from the outer skin and white pith. The seeds will drop to the bottom of the bowl and the pith will float to the surface. Discard the pith. Pour the seeds into a colander. Pat dry. Seeds can be frozen up to 3 months.

POMEGRANATE VINAIGRETTE

- 1 tablespoon minced shallot
- 1 tablespoon pomegranate molasses (*see Tip, page 137*)
- 1 tablespoon balsamic vinegar
- 2 teaspoons lemon juice
- 2 teaspoons chopped fresh thyme
- ¼ teaspoon kosher salt
- ¼ cup extra-virgin olive oil
- 2 teaspoons water

SQUASH & SALAD

- 1½-2 pounds winter squash, such as butternut *or* buttercup, peeled, cut into ½-inch pieces
- 2 teaspoons extra-virgin olive oil
- 2 teaspoons fresh thyme leaves
- ½ teaspoon kosher salt
  Ground pepper to taste
- 6 cups torn frisée *or* curly endive
- 6 cups torn radicchio
- ½ cup pomegranate seeds (*see Tip*)
- ⅓ cup pistachios *or* walnuts, toasted (*see Tip, page 92*) and coarsely chopped

1. Preheat oven to 375°F.

2. To prepare vinaigrette: Mix shallot, pomegranate molasses, vinegar, lemon juice, thyme and salt in a small bowl. Whisk in ¼ cup oil, then water.

3. To prepare squash: Place squash on a baking sheet, drizzle with oil and toss to coat. Spread in a single layer and sprinkle with thyme, salt and pepper. Roast, stirring once or twice, until fork-tender, 15 to 25 minutes. Let cool.

4. To prepare salad: Place frisée (or endive), radicchio and the squash in a large bowl. Add the vinaigrette and gently toss to coat. Divide the salad among 6 plates and sprinkle with pomegranate seeds and nuts.

SERVES 6: ABOUT 1¾ CUPS EACH

Calories 214, **Fat** 14g (sat 2g), **Cholesterol** 0mg, **Carbs** 20g, **Total sugars** 6g (added 0g), **Protein** 4g, **Fiber** 6g, **Sodium** 167mg, **Potassium** 669mg.
Nutrition bonus: Vitamin A (238% daily value), Vitamin C (60% dv), Folate (31% dv).

FAVA BEAN PUREE WITH CHICORY

ACTIVE: 20 MIN **TOTAL:** 1 HR 25 MIN

This dish exemplifies the simplicity of the cuisine of Italy's Puglia region. Wild or cultivated chicory is often served raw or cooked, as it is here, with a simple puree of fava beans seasoned solely with olive oil and salt. If you have a special olive oil in your pantry, this is the time to pull it out.

- 8 ounces skinless dried fava beans (about 1½ cups, *see Tip*)
- 1 small red potato, peeled and sliced
- 1 tablespoon extra-virgin olive oil, plus more for serving
- ½ teaspoon salt plus 2 teaspoons, divided
- 2 pounds chicory *or* curly endive (from 2 bunches), trimmed and well washed

1. Place beans and potato in a medium saucepan; add water to cover by ½ inch. Bring to a boil over high heat, skimming off any foam that rises to the surface. Reduce heat to maintain a gentle simmer, cover and cook, stirring occasionally, until the mixture is a thick, soupy consistency, about 1 hour.

2. Transfer the bean mixture to a blender. Add 1 tablespoon oil and ½ teaspoon salt; puree until smooth. Transfer to a platter (or bowl).

3. Put a large pot of water on to boil.

4. Stir the remaining 2 teaspoons salt into the boiling water, then add chicory (or endive) and cook, stirring occasionally, until tender, 6 to 8 minutes. Drain in a colander, pressing to remove excess water.

5. Serve the greens with the fava bean puree, drizzled with a little olive oil, if desired.

SERVES 6: ABOUT ⅔ CUP GREENS & ½ CUP PUREE EACH

Calories 196, **Fat** 3g (sat 1g), **Cholesterol** 0mg, **Carbs** 32g, **Total sugars** 3g (added 0g), **Protein** 12g, **Fiber** 15g, **Sodium** 395mg, **Potassium** 990mg.
Nutrition bonus: Vitamin A (142% daily value), Folate (75% dv), Vitamin C (53% dv), Potassium & Magnesium (28% dv), Iron (21% dv).

Dried Fava Beans

Look for peeled or skinless dried fava beans near other dried beans in the international aisle at well-stocked supermarkets, in natural-foods stores or online from *bobsredmill.com*. The tough outer skins of dried fava beans don't taste particularly good and require soaking and peeling before they're cooked—a very tedious job. Buying them already peeled is a real timesaver.

Collard Greens

When Southerners talk about cooking up a "mess o' greens," it is likely to be a big pot of collards—simmered with ham hocks, bacon or smoked turkey wings and served with peppery hot vinegar.

Collards, a loose-leafed, headless member of the cabbage family with thick, dark green, paddle-shape leaves, have a toothsome texture and mild flavor that is a bit like a cross between cabbage and kale—both close relatives.

Although their affiliation with Southern cooking is strong, it is not unique. Collards are cooked in the Mediterranean, Africa, Asia and in Latin America. *Gomen wat* is an Ethiopian dish of braised collards and onions spiked with ginger, garlic and spices such as turmeric, paprika and allspice. The national dish of Brazil—*feijoada*—is a pork and black bean stew served with rice and garlicky sautéed collard greens. Collards are often the main ingredient in the Portuguese soup *caldo verde* ("green broth").

In addition to an affinity with smoky, salty meats, collards take well to curry, coconut milk, mustard, ginger, vinegar and Asian flavors such as sesame, soy sauce and chili-bean paste or hoisin.

The cut, cooking method and cooking time all have great bearing on the resulting taste and texture of the greens. One traditional Southern method calls for long, slow cooking—sometimes all night—to a soft, silky mass. Thinly sliced and quickly sautéed, they are chewy and fresh-tasting. Simmered or braised in chicken broth for 15 to 30 minutes, they are somewhere in between.

Collards grow well in cool weather. Although they are available all year, they are best in the late fall and winter months.

Best in fall to winter

AT THE MARKET

❧ Look for crisp, dark green leaves with no yellowing or wilting. Choose bunches with deep-color leaves that feel moist but not wet.

IN YOUR KITCHEN

❧ Wrap unwashed leaves in a moist paper towel. Place in a plastic bag and store in the refrigerator up to 5 days.

❧ Wash collard greens in cool water. If sautéing, pat dry. (If braising or boiling, there is no need to do this.) Trim and prepare as shown in photos, *right.*

COOKING BASICS

BRAISE Cut 4 strips of center-cut bacon into ½-inch pieces. Cook in a large skillet over medium-high heat until browned, 3 to 4 minutes. Add 1 sliced medium sweet onion and cook until softened, about 4 minutes. Add 1½ pounds washed, trimmed and chopped collard greens and 1 cup reduced-sodium chicken broth. Reduce heat to low. Cover and cook, stirring occasionally, until the greens are very tender, 20 to 25 minutes. Uncover. If any liquid remains in the pan, continue cooking for another minute or two, until it is nearly evaporated. Season to taste with salt and black pepper.

Sprinkle with hot pepper vinegar to taste, if desired. Serves 4.

SAUTÉ Cut 1½ pounds of washed and trimmed collard greens into ¼- to ½-inch-wide ribbons. Heat 1 tablespoon extra-virgin olive oil in a large skillet over medium-high heat. Add 2 cloves minced garlic and cook, stirring, until fragrant, 1 minute. Add the greens to the pan. Season with ¼ teaspoon salt. Cook, stirring occasionally, until the greens are wilted and tender, 5 to 6 minutes. Season with crushed red pepper to taste, if desired. Serves 4.

NUTRITION

❧ **1 cup of chopped cooked collards:** **Calories** 63, **Fat** 1g (sat 0g), **Cholesterol** 0mg, **Carbs** 11g, **Total sugars** 1g (added 0g), **Protein** 5g, **Fiber** 8g, **Sodium** 28mg, **Potassium** 222mg.

BONUS Collards are loaded with vitamin A, critical for keeping the linings of your lungs, sinuses and gut healthy. One cup of cooked collards delivers three times your daily value of this immune-enhancing nutrient.

How to prep

1. Wash collard greens in cool water; pat dry.

2. Place each leaf on a cutting board and slice along either side of the rib to remove it; discard rib.

3. Roughly chop collard halves or stack and cut crosswise into thick ribbons *(opposite).*

CRUSHED RED POTATOES WITH WINTER GREENS

ACTIVE: 30 MIN **TOTAL:** 30 MIN
TO MAKE AHEAD: Prepare up to 1 hour ahead and keep warm over a larger pan of barely simmering water.

The flavor and texture of this dish change slightly depending on which greens are used. Collards give it a mild cabbage taste; the mustard greens provide a bit of peppery heat. Both broccoli rabe and escarole give it a touch of bitterness—escarole less so than broccoli rabe.

1 pound greens, such as collards, mustard greens, broccoli rabe and/or escarole *(see Tip)*

2 pounds small red potatoes, scrubbed

1 tablespoon extra-virgin olive oil

2 cloves garlic, minced

½ cup nonfat buttermilk

½ teaspoon salt

Ground pepper to taste

1. Remove tough fibrous stems and any wilted or yellow leaves from greens. Wash leaves well and cut into 1-inch pieces.

2. Cook potatoes in a large saucepan of boiling water until tender, about 15 minutes. Remove with a slotted spoon and transfer to a medium bowl. Crush with a potato masher or the back of a large spoon. Add the greens to the boiling water and cook until tender, 2 to 3 minutes. Drain.

3. Heat oil in a large skillet over medium heat. Add garlic and cook, stirring, until fragrant, about 1 minute. Add the cooked greens and toss with the garlic. Stir in the crushed potatoes and buttermilk. Season with salt and pepper.

SERVES 8: ABOUT ¾ CUP EACH

Calories 113, **Fat** 2g (sat 0g), **Cholesterol** 0mg, **Carbs** 21g, **Total sugars** 2g (added 0g), **Protein** 4g, **Fiber** 3g, **Sodium** 186mg, **Potassium** 600mg.
Nutrition bonus: Vitamin C (38% daily value), Vitamin A (36% dv).

Greens Swap

Although other leafy greens, such as mustard greens, kale, chard and escarole, can be substituted for collards in many recipes, watch them carefully during cooking. In general, collard greens can withstand longer cooking times than the other varieties.

BRAISED GREENS & CANNELLINI BEAN PANINI

ACTIVE: 1 HR **TOTAL:** 1 HR
TO MAKE AHEAD: Refrigerate braised greens and bean spread separately up to 3 days.

A creamy spread of cannellini beans cooked with onion, garlic and white wine is the perfect match for tender braised greens. Press the two between pieces of crusty whole-wheat bread and you have an outstanding vegan panini.

BRAISED GREENS

1½ pounds collards *or* kale (about 2 bunches)
  3 tablespoons extra-virgin olive oil
  2 large leeks, sliced ¼ inch thick (*see page 336*), white and light green parts only
  ¼ teaspoon salt
  ¼ teaspoon ground pepper
  ¼ teaspoon crushed red pepper
  1 cup vegetable broth

WHITE BEAN SPREAD & SANDWICH

  2 tablespoons extra-virgin olive oil
  3 shallots, thinly sliced
  2 cloves garlic, thinly sliced
  ½ cup dry white wine
1½ cups cooked cannellini beans *or* one 15-ounce can, rinsed
  ⅛ teaspoon salt
  ⅛ teaspoon ground pepper
  12 slices crusty whole-wheat bread
     Olive oil cooking spray

1. To prepare greens: Strip leaves from stalks. Stack and slice the leaves into 1-inch strips. Thinly slice the stems into ¼-inch pieces. Keep leaves and stems separate. Heat 3 tablespoons oil in a large pot over medium heat. Add leeks and the chopped stems and cook, stirring, until softened, 4 to 5 minutes. Stir in ¼ teaspoon each salt, pepper and crushed red pepper. Add the sliced greens and broth. Reduce heat to low, cover and cook, stirring occasionally, until the greens are very tender and the liquid is nearly evaporated, 20 to 25 minutes.

2. To prepare bean spread: Meanwhile, heat oil in a medium saucepan over medium heat. Add shallots and garlic and cook, stirring occasionally, until tender, 2 to 3 minutes. Add wine and cook until most of it is evaporated, 3 to 6 minutes. Stir in beans, salt and pepper; cook until heated through, 1 to 2 minutes. Puree the bean mixture in a food processor until almost smooth.

3. To prepare panini: Coat one side of the bread with cooking spray. Divide the bean puree among 6 slices (sprayed-side down). Top with the greens and the remaining bread (sprayed-side up). Press in a panini maker until hot and crispy.

SERVES 6: 1 SANDWICH EACH

Calories 392, **Fat** 13g (sat 2g), **Cholesterol** 0mg, **Carbs** 54g, **Total sugars** 2g (added 1g), **Protein** 12g, **Fiber** 7g, **Sodium** 713mg, **Potassium** 448mg.
Nutrition bonus: Vitamin A (154% daily value), Vitamin C (146% dv).

Stovetop Panini

Place four 15-ounce cans and a medium skillet (not nonstick) by the stove. For each batch, heat 1 teaspoon canola oil in a large nonstick skillet over medium heat. Place 2 sandwiches in the pan. Place the medium skillet on top, then weight it down with the cans. Cook the sandwiches until golden on one side, about 2 minutes. Reduce the heat to medium-low, flip the sandwiches, replace the top skillet and cans, and cook until the second side is golden, 1 to 3 minutes more.

Corn

Sweet corn is perhaps the most iconic of American vegetables. More than simply something good to eat, it has become the symbol of summer and all that season brings. Picture the perfect backyard barbecue, and other than the meaty main event—ribs, burgers or brats—in the center of things is always a mountain of sweet corn on a platter.

Corn is actually a cereal grass—one that can grow up to 12 feet tall—that usually produces one or two ears of corn per stalk. Sweet corn is not a high-yield crop proportional to the amount of ground it takes to grow, but the prospect of a just-picked, perfectly cooked and buttered ear spurs gardeners to plant it anyway. Its sweet taste and tender crunch are irresistible—and it's best cooked as soon as possible after picking. An old adage advises to start the water boiling, then head out to the garden to pick the corn. In fact, sweet corn begins to convert its sugars to starch the second it's picked. Heirloom varieties are especially vulnerable to this loss—they can lose 50 percent of their sugars within 12 hours if not refrigerated.

Sweet corn can be boiled, steamed, microwaved, grilled, roasted and sautéed. It can be served creamed, cooked into a chowder and stirred into crispy corn fritters, but it is most often enjoyed straight from the cob. *Elotes*—a much-loved Mexican street food—consists of grilled sweet corn brushed with mayonnaise, rolled in Cotija cheese, sprinkled with chile powder and chopped cilantro, then finished with a squeeze of fresh lime.

Early-, mid- and late-season varieties of sweet corn extend the growing and harvesting season from mid- to late summer.

Best in mid- to late summer

AT THE MARKET

◦ There are hundreds of varieties of sweet corn, both heirloom and modern hybrids. Most are a combination of white, yellow and cream kernels. Choose firm ears with no missing kernels and moist green husks. The silks should look fresh and should be brown at the very top—an indicator that the corn was picked at the right time.

◦ While most feed corn contains genetically modified organisms, very little sweet corn does. For a list of verified non-GMO sweet corn, visit *nongmoproject.org*. You can also buy certified organic to be sure.

◦ While older varieties of sweet corn are grown for local markets and are cooked shortly after harvest, many modern hybrids are shipped long distances. These modern varieties have been bred to have higher sugar content than the older varieties and to retain their sweetness much longer after the corn has been picked.

IN YOUR KITCHEN

◦ Store unhusked ears in a plastic bag in the refrigerator up to 3 days.

◦ Starting at the top of the cob, pull off all the husks and strip off all the silks. Cut off the stem end.

◦ To remove the kernels from an ear of corn, stand the ear on its stem end and slice the kernels off with a sharp knife. You'll get about 1 cup fresh kernels from one large ear of corn. To extract the corn "milk" and get more flavor for sauces, soups or puddings, add another step to the process: After cutting the kernels off, press the dull side of the knife down the length of the ear to push out the rest of the corn and its milk.

COOKING BASICS

BOIL Bring a large tea kettle of water to a boil. Place husked ears of corn in a large skillet. When water comes to a boil, pour it over the corn. Cook over high heat just until water returns to a boil. Immediately drain and serve.

GRILL Preheat grill to medium-high. Brush husked corn lightly with olive oil. Grill the corn, turning occasionally, until some kernels char a little and others are light brown, 6 to 10 minutes.

ROAST Toss 3 cups corn kernels *(see Tip, page 216)* with 2 tablespoons olive oil. Spread on a rimmed baking sheet. Roast in a 450°F oven, stirring once, until some kernels begin to brown, about 20 minutes. Season with salt and pepper. Stir in ½ teaspoon chili powder and 1 tablespoon lime juice or ½ teaspoon smoked paprika and 1 tablespoon sherry vinegar. Serves 4.

NUTRITION

◦ **1 medium ear of sweet corn: Calories** 99, **Fat** 2g (sat 0g), **Cholesterol** 0mg, **Carbs** 22g, **Total sugars** 5g (added 0g), **Protein** 4g, **Fiber** 3g, **Sodium** 1mg, **Potassium** 225mg.

BONUS Corn boasts a low glycemic index, meaning its carbs are slowly released into your bloodstream so they're unlikely to spike blood sugar levels.

How to microwave

1. Cook untrimmed and unhusked corn in microwave on High for 5 minutes. Using a towel to hold the cob, cut off the stem end.

2. Holding the cob at the top end with a towel, shake the ear. The cooked corn will slip right out of the husk, completely free of silks.

Grilled Corn
(see Cooking Basics, opposite)

SWEET CORN SALAD

ACTIVE: 50 MIN **TOTAL:** 2 HRS
TO MAKE AHEAD: Hold at room temperature up to 2 hours.

Freshly harvested corn, charred green chiles and roasted tomatoes make for a salad that tastes like the essence of summer.

- 3 medium green chiles, such as New Mexico (Anaheims) *or* poblanos
- 4 medium plum tomatoes, halved
- 2 tablespoons extra-virgin olive oil, divided
- 1 teaspoon kosher salt, divided
- 8 large ears corn, husked

- 1 tablespoon butter
- 2 tablespoons low-fat mayonnaise
- 2 tablespoons lime juice
- 1 tablespoon chile powder, preferably New Mexico chile
- 1 clove garlic, minced
- ¼ cup chopped fresh cilantro

1. Position rack in upper third of oven; preheat broiler.

2. Place chiles on a rimmed baking sheet. Broil, turning every few minutes, until blackened on all sides, 6 to 10 minutes. Transfer to a medium bowl, cover with plastic wrap and set aside for about 20 minutes to loosen the skins.

3. Reduce oven temperature to 375°F. Toss tomatoes and 1 tablespoon oil in a medium bowl. Arrange on the baking sheet, cut-side up, and sprinkle with ¼ teaspoon salt. Roast in the oven until browned, 1 to 1½ hours.

4. Meanwhile, cut kernels off the cobs *(see page 212)*. Heat butter and the remaining 1 tablespoon oil in a large skillet over medium heat. Add the corn and cook, stirring often, until tender-crisp, 3 to 5 minutes. Transfer to a large bowl.

5. Peel the chiles with your fingers. (It's OK if a little skin is left behind.) Cut them open lengthwise, remove the seeds, stem and white membrane, then chop. Transfer to the bowl with the corn.

6. Whisk mayonnaise, lime juice, chile powder, garlic and the remaining ¾ teaspoon salt in a small bowl.

7. When the tomatoes are done, let cool for 10 minutes, then coarsely chop. Add the tomatoes, the dressing and cilantro to the corn; stir until well combined.

SERVES 8: ABOUT ⅔ CUP EACH

Calories 194, **Fat** 8g (sat 2g), **Cholesterol** 5mg, **Carbs** 31g, **Total sugars** 11g (added 0g), **Protein** 6g, **Fiber** 4g, **Sodium** 212mg, **Potassium** 546mg.
Nutrition bonus: Vitamin C (94% daily value), Vitamin A (22% dv).

Interesting Epazote

Use the Mexican herb epazote in place of the cilantro if you'd like. Its distinctive licorice-like flavor adds another dimension to the dish.

CORN

ROASTED CORN CHEESE DIP

ACTIVE: 15 MIN **TOTAL:** 35 MIN

Inspired by queso fundido—melted Mexican cheese dip—this corn and warm Cheddar cheese dip partners perfectly with toasted baguette or pita chips.

  3 cups corn kernels *(see page 212)*
  8 ounces shredded sharp Cheddar cheese (2 cups)
  8 ounces reduced-fat cream cheese (Neufchâtel), cut into small pieces
  ⅛ teaspoon cayenne *or* chili powder

1. Preheat oven to 375°F.

2. Coat a medium cast-iron skillet with cooking spray; heat over medium-high heat. Add corn; cook, stirring occasionally, until mostly golden brown, 5 to 7 minutes. (Corn kernels may "pop" as they brown.) Remove from heat; stir in Cheddar and cream cheese. Transfer to the oven.

3. Bake until golden and bubbling, 18 to 20 minutes. Sprinkle the cheese dip with cayenne (or chili powder) and serve.

MAKES: 3 CUPS (¼-CUP SERVING)

Calories 155, **Fat** 11g (sat 7g), **Cholesterol** 34mg, **Carbs** 8g, **Total sugars** 3g (added 0g), **Protein** 8g, **Fiber** 1g, **Sodium** 186mg, **Potassium** 146mg.

SUMMER CORN & SCALLOP PASTA

ACTIVE: 45 MINUTES **TOTAL:** 45 MINUTES

Mild, sweet scallops partner beautifully with corn in this light yet creamy pasta.

Buying Sea Scallops

Be sure to buy "dry" sea scallops. "Wet" scallops, which have been treated with sodium tripolyphosphate (STP), are not only mushy and less flavorful but will not brown properly. Some scallops have a small white muscle on the side; remove it before cooking.

8 ounces whole-wheat linguine *or* fettuccine
4 medium ears corn, husked
2 strips bacon, chopped
1 pound dry sea scallops *(see Tip)*, patted dry
½ teaspoon salt, divided
½ teaspoon freshly ground pepper, divided
1 cup chopped red bell pepper
5 cloves garlic, minced
½ cup dry white wine
½ cup reduced-fat sour cream
1 tablespoon all-purpose flour
½ cup chopped fresh basil, plus more for garnish
4 lemon wedges

1. Cook pasta in a large pot of boiling water until just tender, 8 to 10 minutes or according to package directions. Reserve ½ cup cooking liquid; drain pasta.

2. Meanwhile, stand an ear of corn on its stem end in a shallow bowl and slice the kernels off with a sharp, thin-bladed knife. Then press the dull side of the knife down the length of the ear to extract any remaining kernels and corn "milk" into the bowl. Repeat with the remaining 3 ears of corn, catching the kernels and "milk" in the bowl.

3. Cook bacon in a large skillet over medium heat until crispy, 3 to 4 minutes. Remove to a small bowl with a slotted spoon; leave bacon fat in pan.

4. Sprinkle scallops with ¼ teaspoon each salt and pepper. Add the scallops to the pan and cook over medium heat until golden brown, about 2 minutes per side. Transfer to a plate; tent with foil to keep warm.

5. Add corn kernels and "milk," bell pepper and garlic and cook until garlic is fragrant, about 2 minutes. Add reserved cooking liquid and wine and cook, stirring occasionally, until corn is tender, about 3 minutes more. Stir in sour cream and remaining ¼ teaspoon each salt and pepper. Sprinkle flour over mixture. Cook, stirring, until sauce is bubbling and thickened, about 1 minute.

6. Reduce heat to low and return the pasta, bacon and any scallop liquid accumulated on the plate to the pan; toss to coat with the sauce. Stir in basil. Divide the pasta among 4 bowls and top with the scallops. Garnish with more basil, if desired. Serve with lemon wedges.

SERVES 4: ABOUT 1½ CUPS EACH

Calories 473, **Fat** 8g (sat 3g), **Cholesterol** 42mg, **Carbs** 73g, **Total sugars** 11g (added 0g), **Protein** 28g, **Fiber** 10g, **Sodium** 840mg, **Potassium** 832mg.

SWEET CORN ICE CREAM

ACTIVE: 30 MIN **TOTAL:** 4 HRS
TO MAKE AHEAD: Prepare through Step 3 and refrigerate up to 1 day. After freezing, store airtight up to 1 week.

Sweet corn and ice cream are quintessential summer foods. Here's a recipe that combines the two! It may sound strange, but it's an amazing match with fresh blueberries or warm blueberry pie.

1½ teaspoons unflavored gelatin
1 tablespoon water
2 cups corn kernels *(see page 212)*
2 cups low-fat milk
1 14-ounce can nonfat sweetened condensed milk
3 large egg yolks
1 cup buttermilk

1. Sprinkle gelatin over water in a small bowl; let stand, stirring once or twice, while you make the base for the ice cream.

2. Combine corn and milk in a large saucepan. Heat over medium heat until steaming. Whisk condensed milk and egg yolks in a large bowl until combined. Gradually pour the hot milk and corn into the egg yolk mixture, whisking until blended. Return the mixture to the pan and cook over medium heat, stirring with a wooden spoon, until the back of the spoon is lightly coated, 3 to 5 minutes. Do not boil.

3. Remove from heat and puree the custard with an immersion blender or in a regular blender until smooth. (Use caution when pureeing hot liquids.) Strain the custard through a fine-mesh sieve into a clean large bowl; press on the solids to extract the liquid. (Discard solids.) Whisk the gelatin into the custard until melted. Whisk in buttermilk. Transfer to the refrigerator until chilled, at least 2½ hours and up to 1 day.

4. Whisk the ice cream mixture and pour into the canister of an ice cream maker. Freeze according to manufacturer's directions. If necessary, place the ice cream in the freezer to firm up before serving.

SERVES 10: ABOUT ½ CUP EACH

Calories 185, **Fat** 2g (sat 1g), **Cholesterol** 64mg, **Carbs** 34g, **Total sugars** 30g (added 22g), **Protein** 8g, **Fiber** 1g, **Sodium** 95mg, **Potassium** 570mg.
Nutrition bonus: Calcium (20% daily value).

Cucumbers

The saying that someone is "cool as a cucumber" likely has to do with the fact that this fleshy fruit—a type of gourd that is prepared and eaten as a vegetable—is more than 90 percent water. Even at room temperature, all of that moisture makes the interior feel cool and refreshing.

Cucumbers are categorized for slicing or pickling. Within those categories there are four types that are most widely available.

Common slicing cucumbers are the familiar cucumbers found in abundance at supermarkets, usually waxed. Other slicing cucumbers include English cucumbers and Persian cucumbers. English cucumbers are long and slender— they can grow up to 2 feet long—and are usually found in the supermarket wrapped in plastic. Persian cucumbers look similar to English cucumbers but are much shorter—usually just 6 inches in length. Both varieties have no (or very few) developed seeds. Of the pickling cucumbers, the most common variety is Kirby, a short, fat fruit with bumpy, light green skin.

Although sliced Persian cucumbers are sometimes tossed into a stir-fry, cucumbers are usually eaten raw. They're sliced for salads or sandwiches or pureed into a cold soup made creamy with yogurt and flavored with herbs such as dill, tarragon, chives, and mint. Cucumber has an affinity with tangy dairy products such as yogurt, sour cream or buttermilk. Indian raita and Greek tzatziki are both yogurt-based condiments featuring shredded or diced cucumber. At the heart of kappamaki, the simplest of sushi rolls, is a crisp bite of cucumber.

Cucumbers are fast-growing. Most varieties produce fruit 50 to 70 days after they are planted in spring, providing a crisp supply all summer.

▼ *English Cucumbers*

▲ Persian Cucumbers

▲ Pickling Cucumbers, 'Kirby'

AT THE MARKET

⤜ Choose firm cucumbers that feel heavy for their size, with no blemishes, marks, soft spots or too much yellowing on the skin—a sign that they are overmature. (A little bit of yellowing on slicing cucumbers, which they develop from lying on the ground, is fine.) Generally, small cucumbers have crisper flesh and fewer, smaller seeds than large ones.

⤜ Store waxed slicing cucumbers in a plastic bag in the refrigerator up to 1 week. Store unwaxed cucumbers in a plastic bag in the refrigerator up to 5 days.

IN YOUR KITCHEN

⤜ If the skin of the cucumber is thin and/or unwaxed, simply rinse under cool running water. Or, if desired, peel with a vegetable peeler. To remove seeds, cut the cucumber in half lengthwise. Use the tip of a spoon to scrape out the seeds and pulpy center.

COOKING BASICS

SALAD Thinly slice 1 medium cucumber. Toss cucumber slices with 1 tablespoon olive oil, 1 teaspoon fresh lemon juice, 1 teaspoon chopped fresh tarragon, ¼ teaspoon salt and ⅛ teaspoon pepper. Serves 2.

SANDWICH Spread 2 thin slices of soft whole-grain or dark rye bread with 2 teaspoons softened butter. Top one piece of bread with two layers of very thinly sliced cucumber (peel if waxed). Season lightly with salt and pepper. Top with other slice of buttered bread. Cut crusts off bread and discard. Cut sandwich into four triangles. Serves 2.

NUTRITION

⤜ **1 cup sliced cucumber (with peel):** **Calories** 16, **Fat** 0g (sat 0g), **Cholesterol** 0mg, **Carbs** 4g, **Total sugars** 2g (added 0g), **Protein** 1g, **Fiber** 0g, **Sodium** 1mg, **Potassium** 152mg.

BONUS These gourds are the perfect postworkout snack. One cuke boasts more than a cup of water, plus as much fluid-balancing potassium as a banana for optimal rehydration. Each cucumber also packs 11 grams of carbohydrate to help refuel spent muscles.

Grow Your Own

Cucumbers are prolific and easy to grow. A single plant will provide armloads of refreshing cukes all summer. Plant seeds outdoors in a sunny spot in spring after the soil has warmed, no earlier than 2 weeks before the last frost date. Plant in loamy, well-drained soil and give them some space—each plant needs about 6 feet to grow properly. Cucumbers are climbers, so try growing them along trellises or fences. If space is limited, look for a compact bush variety, which has shorter vines. Plant seeds 1 inch deep and water well. When seedlings are 4 inches tall, thin them to 1½ feet apart. To safeguard against pests—particularly cucumber beetles—protect plants with a row cover. As plants grow and fruit sets, water consistently. Lack of water can lead to bitter fruit. Harvest regular slicing cucumbers when they are 6 to 8 inches long. Pickling cucumbers can be harvested when very small—just 2 inches—or up to 6 inches long. Harvest every few days to keep the plants producing.

ROSEMARY-INFUSED CUCUMBER LEMONADE

ACTIVE: 15 MIN **TOTAL:** 15 MIN

Turn fresh rosemary, cucumbers and lemons into grown-up lemonade that will keep you cool on a hot day. Try it with a splash of gin—it's delicious.

  3 large cucumbers
  1 tablespoon chopped fresh rosemary, plus 4 sprigs for garnish
  1 cup water
  ½ cup lemon juice
  3 tablespoons agave syrup *(see Tip)*
     Ice

1. Cut 12 thin slices of cucumber for garnish.

2. Peel and chop the rest of the cucumber; transfer to a food processor, add rosemary and puree. Pour the puree through a fine-mesh strainer set over a medium bowl or large measuring cup. Press on the solids to extract all the juice; discard solids. Add water, lemon juice and agave syrup to the cucumber juice; stir until the agave is dissolved. Divide among 4 ice-filled glasses. Garnish with cucumber slices and rosemary sprigs.

SERVES 4: ABOUT ¾ CUP EACH

Calories 70, **Fat** 0g (sat 0g), **Cholesterol** 0mg, **Carbs** 17g, **Total sugars** 3g (added 0g), **Protein** 1g, **Fiber** 1g, **Sodium** 5mg, **Potassium** 234mg.
Nutrition bonus: Vitamin C (28% daily value).

Agave Syrup

Agave syrup or nectar is made from the naturally sweet juice extracted from the agave plant. It has a lower glycemic index than table sugar, but is even sweeter. Use it in moderation when substituting for table sugar. Look for it near other sweeteners in supermarkets and natural-foods stores.

CUCUMBER & RADISH TZATZIKI

ACTIVE: 25 MIN **TOTAL:** 40 MIN

Thinly sliced radishes lend a peppery bite and pretty pink hue to this traditional Greek cucumber dip. Serve as an appetizer, with pita bread, lavash-style flatbread or vegetable crudités, or as a refreshing sauce with grilled fish.

     1 small cucumber, peeled and seeded (6-7 ounces)
    10 radishes, trimmed
    1½ cups nonfat plain Greek yogurt
     ¼ cup sliced scallions
     2 cloves garlic, minced
     1 teaspoon finely grated lemon zest
     1 tablespoon lemon juice
     2 tablespoons chopped fresh mint
     2 tablespoons chopped fresh dill
     ¼ teaspoon ground coriander
     ½ teaspoon salt
     ¼ teaspoon ground pepper

1. Grate cucumber on the coarse side of a box grater. Transfer to a square of cheesecloth or a clean kitchen towel. Roll up, then twist gently to extract as much liquid as possible. Transfer to a medium bowl.

2. Grate radishes and add to the bowl. Add yogurt, scallions, garlic, lemon zest, lemon juice, mint, dill, coriander, salt and pepper. Stir gently to combine. Cover and refrigerate for 15 minutes to allow flavors to blend.

MAKES: ABOUT 2½ CUPS (¼-CUP SERVING)

Calories 26, **Fat** 0g (sat 0g), **Cholesterol** 2mg, **Carbs** 2g, **Total sugars** 2g (added 0g), **Protein** 4g, **Fiber** 0g, **Sodium** 131mg, **Potassium** 98mg.

WHITE GAZPACHO

ACTIVE: 20 MINUTES **TOTAL:** 2 HOURS 20 MINUTES (INCLUDING 2 HOURS CHILLING TIME)

TO MAKE AHEAD: Prepare through Step 2. Refrigerate up to 1 day. Finish with Step 3 just before serving.

White gazpacho is made with bread, almonds, grapes and garlic and is one of the traditional Spanish gazpacho variations. In this soup, we add cucumbers and honeydew, whir it in a blender and it becomes silky, a little toasty (from the almonds) and refreshing.

2 English cucumbers, divided

2 cups green grapes, divided

2 slices country white bread, crusts removed if desired, torn into pieces

2 cups "no-chicken" broth *(see Tip)* or reduced-sodium chicken broth

1 cup chopped honeydew melon

½ cup sliced blanched almonds, lightly toasted (*see Tip page 92*), divided

1 small clove garlic, halved

2 tablespoons extra-virgin olive oil

2 tablespoons white-wine vinegar

¾ teaspoon salt

1. Dice enough unpeeled cucumber to equal ½ cup and slice enough grapes to equal ½ cup; cover and refrigerate.

2. Peel the remaining cucumbers; cut into chunks. Working in two batches, puree the peeled cucumber, the remaining grapes, bread, broth, melon, 6 tablespoons almonds, garlic, oil, vinegar and salt in a blender until smooth. Transfer to a large bowl, cover and refrigerate until chilled, at least 2 hours and up to 1 day.

3. Serve garnished with the remaining 2 tablespoons almonds and the reserved cucumber and grapes.

SERVES 6: ABOUT 1 CUP EACH

Calories 210, **Fat** 12g (sat 1g), **Cholesterol** 0mg, **Carbs** 23g, **Total sugars** 13g (added 1g), **Protein** 5g, **Fiber** 3g, **Sodium** 541mg, **Potassium** 345mg.

"No-Chicken" Broth

Chicken-flavored broth, a vegetarian broth despite its name, is preferable to vegetable broth in some recipes for its hearty, rich flavor. Sometimes called "no-chicken" broth, it can be found with the soups in the natural-foods section of most supermarkets.

DILL PICKLES

ACTIVE: 25 MIN **TOTAL:** 25 MIN (PLUS 1 DAY MARINATING TIME)
TO MAKE AHEAD: Refrigerate up to 1 month.
EQUIPMENT: 6 pint-size (2-cup) canning jars or similar-size tempered-glass or heatproof-plastic containers with lids

Supermarket dill pickles can't beat the fresh flavor and snap of these homemade refrigerator pickles.

> 3½ pounds pickling cucumbers *or* other small cucumbers, cut into quarters *or* eighths (about 12 cups)
> 1 tablespoon pickling spice *(see Tip)*
> 12-24 sprigs fresh dill
> 3-6 whole large cloves garlic, sliced
> 3 cups distilled white vinegar *or* cider vinegar
> 3 cups water
> 2 tablespoons plus 2 teaspoons sea salt
> 2 tablespoons sugar

1. Divide cucumber spears among 6 pint-size (2-cup) canning jars or similar-size tempered-glass or heatproof-plastic containers with lids. Add ½ teaspoon pickling spice to each jar. Add dill sprigs and garlic slices to taste.

2. Combine vinegar, water, salt and sugar in a large saucepan. Bring to a boil and stir until the salt and sugar dissolve. Let boil for 2 minutes. Remove from heat.

3. Carefully fill jars (or containers) with brine to within ½ inch of the rim, covering the cucumbers completely. (Discard any leftover brine.)

4. Place the lids on the jars (or containers). Refrigerate at least 24 hours before serving. Store in the refrigerator up to 1 month.

MAKES: 6 PINT JARS (¼-CUP SERVING)

Calories 4, **Fat** 0g (sat 0g), **Cholesterol** 0mg, **Carbs** 1g, **Total sugars** 1g (added 0g), **Protein** 0g, **Fiber** 0g, **Sodium** 24mg, **Potassium** 38mg.

Pickling Spice

Pickling spice blends vary depending on the brand, but they are generally some combination of whole or coarse-ground allspice, bay leaves, cardamom, cinnamon, cloves, coriander, dried ginger, mustard seeds and black peppercorns.

PERSIAN CUCUMBER SALAD WITH LENTILS & SPROUTS

ACTIVE: 40 MIN **TOTAL:** 40 MIN

Quick-pickling the cucumbers adds bright flavor to this salad, perfect for a simple lunch or as part of a larger meal.

French Lentils

French green lentils are smaller and rounder than brown lentils and have a distinctive peppery flavor. (*Lentilles du Puy* are the caviar of French lentils.) They also cook more quickly and keep their shape better when cooked, which is ideal in salads. Cook according to package directions—or if you're in a hurry, they are available precooked in packages in the produce sections of some supermarkets.

½ cup champagne vinegar *or* rice vinegar
¼ cup water
1 dried hot chile, such as red Thai *or* chile de arbol, torn
1 teaspoon sugar
¾ teaspoon kosher salt, divided
½ teaspoon dill seeds
2 cups halved and sliced unpeeled small cucumbers, preferably Persian *or* "mini"
2 tablespoons golden raisins
A few sprigs fresh dill

¼ cup nonfat plain Greek yogurt
1½ tablespoons extra-virgin olive oil
Ground pepper to taste
1 cup cooked French green lentils
⅓ cup crumbled feta cheese
4 radishes, halved and thinly sliced
2 scallions, thinly sliced
3 tablespoons coarsely chopped fresh herbs, such as parsley, dill and cilantro
½ cup microgreens *or* mixed sprouts

1. Combine vinegar, water, chile, sugar, ½ teaspoon salt and dill seeds in a small saucepan. Bring to a boil, then simmer for 2 minutes. Let cool slightly.

2. Place cucumbers and raisins in a shallow bowl or glass dish along with dill sprigs. Carefully pour on the hot liquid. Refrigerate, stirring once or twice, for 20 minutes. Strain (reserving the pickling liquid); discard the chile and dill sprigs. Transfer 2 tablespoons of the liquid to a large bowl. (Reserve the remaining pickling liquid to pickle more vegetables or to use in a salad dressing, if desired.)

3. Whisk the 2 tablespoons pickling liquid with yogurt, oil, pepper and the remaining ¼ teaspoon salt. Add the cucumber mixture, lentils, feta, radishes, scallions and herbs; gently toss to combine. Garnish with microgreens (or sprouts).

SERVES 4: ABOUT 1 CUP EACH

Calories 179, **Fat** 9g (sat 3g), **Cholesterol** 12mg, **Carbs** 19g, **Total sugars** 6g (added 0g), **Protein** 8g, **Fiber** 4g, **Sodium** 213mg, **Potassium** 348mg.

Korean Chile Powder

Korean chile powder (gochugaru, gochugalu or Korean "crushed red pepper") is made from thin red peppers that are sun-dried on woven mats or strung together and hung from the eaves of thatch-roofed houses throughout the countryside. Find it in Korean or Asian markets or online from *koamart.com*. Store, airtight, in the refrigerator or freezer indefinitely.

QUICK CUCUMBER KIMCHI

ACTIVE: 30 MIN **TOTAL:** 40 MIN (PLUS 12-24 HRS MARINATING TIME)
TO MAKE AHEAD: Refrigerate for up to 1 week.

While slowly fermented cabbage and pungent garlic are the ingredients most people associate with kimchi, there are dozens of other versions of Korea's national dish, featuring all manner of vegetables, such as these quickly pickled cucumbers with just a trace of garlic.

2 pickling cucumbers *or* other small cucumbers (about 8 ounces)
1 teaspoon kosher salt
2 cloves garlic, finely chopped
2 scallions, white and light green parts only, finely chopped
1 ¼-inch piece fresh ginger, peeled and finely chopped
2 tablespoons rice vinegar
1 tablespoon Korean chile powder *(see Tip)*
2 teaspoons sugar
½ teaspoon fish sauce *(see Tip, page 105)*

1. Cut cucumbers in half lengthwise and then crosswise into ⅛-inch-thick half moons. Place in a medium bowl and mix thoroughly with salt. Let stand at room temperature about 30 minutes.

2. Meanwhile, combine garlic, scallions, ginger, vinegar, chile powder, sugar and fish sauce in a medium nonreactive bowl (stainless steel, enamel-coated or glass).

3. Drain the cucumbers (discard the liquid). Stir the cucumbers into the vinegar mixture. Cover and refrigerate for 12 to 24 hours before serving.

MAKES: 1½ CUPS (¼-CUP SERVING)

Calories 8, **Fat** 0g (sat 0g), **Cholesterol** 0mg, **Carbs** 2g, **Total sugars** 1g (added 0g), **Protein** 0g, **Fiber** 0g, **Sodium** 62mg, **Potassium** 61mg.

GRILLED CHICKEN THIGHS WITH CUCUMBER-MINT SALAD

ACTIVE: 35 MIN **TOTAL:** 35 MIN

The cumin-and-coriander rub on this chicken pairs deliciously with a minty cucumber salad. Chicken thighs vary widely in size. Ask your butcher to hand-select 4 large thighs for this recipe. If you can only find small thighs, cook 2 per person and reduce the grill time slightly.

⁓
Broiler Variation

Coat a broiler pan with cooking spray and place the seasoned chicken thighs on it. Broil 3 to 4 inches from the heat source until no longer pink in the middle, 5 to 6 minutes per side.
⁓

- 2 cups diced, seeded English cucumber (about 1 large)
- 6 tablespoons chopped fresh mint
- 3 tablespoons finely chopped red onion
- 3 tablespoons extra-virgin olive oil, divided
- 2 tablespoons white-wine vinegar
- ¾ teaspoon salt, divided
- 3 cloves garlic, minced
- 1 teaspoon ground coriander
- 1 teaspoon ground cumin
- 4 large boneless, skinless chicken thighs (about 1¼ pounds), trimmed

1. Preheat grill to medium-high. *(No grill? See Tip.)*

2. Combine cucumber, mint, onion, 2 tablespoons oil, vinegar and ¼ teaspoon salt in a medium bowl. Set aside.

3. Mash garlic and the remaining ½ teaspoon salt in a small bowl until it becomes a paste. Stir in the remaining 1 tablespoon oil, coriander and cumin. Rub the mixture on both sides of each chicken thigh.

4. Grill the chicken thighs until an instant-read thermometer inserted into the thickest part registers 165°F, 3 to 5 minutes per side. Serve the chicken with the cucumber salad.

SERVES 4: 1 CHICKEN THIGH & ½ CUP SALAD EACH

Calories 323, **Fat** 21g (sat 4g), **Cholesterol** 94mg, **Carbs** 5g, **Total sugars** 2g (added 0g), **Protein** 27g, **Fiber** 1g, **Sodium** 520mg, **Potassium** 358mg. **Nutrition bonus:** Zinc (20% daily value).

▶ Italian, 'Angela'

▲ Asian, 'Orient Express'

▼ Italian, 'Nadia'

▲ Italian, 'Barbarella'

▼ Asian, 'Orient Charm'

Eggplant

Glossy, eye-catching eggplant takes on a wonderful variety of textures depending on how it's cooked. Sliced and grilled, broiled or pan-fried, it has the toothsome quality of a steak or pork chop. Grilled whole and pureed with garlic, lemon juice and tahini, it becomes *baba ghanoush*, the lusciously creamy, spreadable Middle Eastern dip.

Eggplant is commonly used in Mediterranean, Middle Eastern, Indian, African, Southeast Asian and French cooking. It is a close relative of the tomato—a fellow member of the nightshade family with whom it makes a fine companion—and has a similar growing habit, with heavy fruit dangling from vines in the heat of summer.

While the most familiar eggplant is the glossy, deep purple, shiny globe variety (the most common of which is 'Black Beauty'), eggplants come in an array of shapes, sizes and colors. They can be white, light purple or lavender, striated, orange or green. The flesh is either white and creamy or pale green. They range from golf-ball-size rounds to pear-shape specimens measuring 8 inches long and 4 inches in diameter to long, thin violet-hued Asian varieties.

Some of the most well-known dishes made with eggplant are Eggplant Parmesan, ratatouille, moussaka and the Chinese dish of eggplant with garlic sauce. While it may be most familiar in the company of tomatoes, olive oil, onion and garlic, eggplant is equally at home with Asian flavors such as curry, peanut sauce, chiles, lime, miso, ginger, mint, cilantro, Thai basil and soy sauce.

Eggplant is a tropical and subtropical plant that thrives in warm or hot weather and sandy soil, so of course it's best from midsummer to early fall.

▼ *Italian, 'Nadia'*

▲ *Asian, 'Orient Express'*

▼ *'Fairy Tale'*

Best in midsummer to early fall

AT THE MARKET

ᗡ► Choose eggplants that are firm and feel heavy for their size, with glossy, taut skin. The flesh should give slightly, then bounce back, when pressed. Avoid eggplant with soft spots, cracks or signs of shriveling. Smaller eggplants with fewer seeds are often sweeter and more tender than larger ones.

IN YOUR KITCHEN

ᗡ► Eggplant is best prepared when at its plumpest, right after it's purchased or harvested; it starts to dehydrate as it sits. Store in a plastic bag in a cool place for up to 2 days. It can also be stored in a perforated plastic bag in the warmest part of the refrigerator up to 2 days.

ᗡ► Small, tender-skinned eggplants need only to be rinsed under cool running water and have the cap trimmed. Larger eggplants may need to be peeled if the skin is thick and tough.

COOKING BASICS

GRILL Cut 1 medium eggplant into ½-inch rounds. Brush both sides of each slice with 1 tablespoon olive oil. Season with ¼ teaspoon salt and pepper to taste. Grill over medium-high heat until tender and marked, 3 to 5 minutes per side. Serves 4.

ROAST Cut 2 medium eggplants into 1-inch cubes. Toss with 2 tablespoons olive oil, ¼ teaspoon salt and pepper to taste on a large rimmed baking sheet. Roast in a 475°F oven until lightly browned and tender, about 25 minutes. Toss with 1 tablespoon red-wine vinegar and 2 tablespoons finely chopped fresh parsley or basil. Serves 6.

SAUTÉ Cut 1 medium eggplant into ½-inch dice. Heat 2 tablespoons olive oil in a large skillet over medium-high heat. Add eggplant and cook, stirring occasionally, until just tender, about 8 minutes. Add 1 minced garlic clove and 1 tablespoon chopped fresh oregano and cook, stirring occasionally, until the garlic is fragrant and the eggplant is golden and tender. Transfer to a serving bowl. Season with ¼ teaspoon salt, pepper to taste and 1 tablespoon finely grated Parmesan cheese, if desired. Serves 4.

NUTRITION

ᗡ► **1 cup of cooked cubed eggplant:** Calories 35, **Fat** 0g (sat 0g), **Cholesterol** 0mg, **Carbs** 9g, **Total sugars** 3g (added 0g), **Protein** 1g, **Fiber** 3g, **Sodium** 1mg, **Potassium** 122mg.

BONUS Eggplant skin is a prime source of nasunin, an antioxidant believed to scavenge your brain for harmful free radicals that can attack and damage the outer membranes of brain cells, impairing their ability to function at their peak.

———— ≈ ————

Grow Your Own

Eggplant is not difficult to grow, but it is highly sensitive to temperature, so planting at the right time is crucial. Eggplant seeds germinate best when air temperatures are above 75°F.

If your summer is long, nearly any variety will work. If your summers are short, choose early-maturing varieties. Start seeds indoors 6 weeks before your last spring frost—or buy seedlings from a nursery right before planting. Plant 3- to 4-inch seedlings 24 to 30 inches apart in loose, well-drained soil (mix in a little sand if necessary) in full sun. Water well and stake any plants more than 24 inches tall. Harvest 16 to 24 weeks after sowing the seed, when the skin is shiny and taut.

———— ≈ ————

Pork & Shrimp Stuffed Eggplant
(see recipe, page 242)

SICILIAN EGGPLANT CAPONATA

ACTIVE: 1½ HRS **TOTAL:** 1½ HRS
TO MAKE AHEAD: Refrigerate up to 1 week. Serve at room temperature.

If you use dark purple eggplant and don't mind a little skin, peel in alternating thin strips for a striped effect.

2 pounds eggplant, peeled and cut into ½-inch cubes
1 tablespoon sea salt
½ cup extra-virgin olive oil, divided
3 bay leaves
1 pound onions, chopped
1 pound celery, sliced ½ inch thick
1 pound cherry tomatoes, halved
¼ cup capers, preferably salt-packed, well rinsed (*see Tip*)

20 large green olives, pitted and very coarsely chopped
2 fresh hot red chile peppers, halved, seeded and thinly sliced
½ cup red-wine vinegar
1 tablespoon honey
2 tablespoons chopped flat-leaf parsley
2 tablespoons chopped fresh basil

1. Combine eggplant and salt in a large bowl. Transfer to a colander and cover with a plate weighted down with cans. Set in the sink to drain for 1 hour.

2. Meanwhile, heat ¼ cup oil in a large skillet over medium heat. Add bay leaves and let sizzle for about 1 minute. Stir in onions and celery. Reduce heat to medium-low and cook, stirring occasionally, until the vegetables are soft, about 30 minutes; do not let them brown. Add tomatoes and capers, increase heat to medium and cook, stirring occasionally, just until the tomatoes start to break down, about 5 minutes. Stir in olives; transfer everything to a large bowl.

3. Rinse the eggplant to get rid of as much salt as possible; dry thoroughly. Heat the remaining ¼ cup oil in the skillet over medium heat until very hot. Add the eggplant and cook, tossing and stirring, until browned on all sides, 10 to 15 minutes. Add chiles and cook, stirring, until softened, 5 to 10 minutes. Transfer to the bowl with the tomato mixture and gently stir to combine.

4. Whisk vinegar and honey in a small saucepan; bring to a boil over medium heat. Simmer until thickened and reduced to about ¼ cup, about 5 minutes. Stir into the vegetables along with parsley and basil. Serve at room temperature.

SERVES 10: SCANT 1 CUP EACH

Calories 181, **Fat** 13g (sat 2g), **Cholesterol** 0mg, **Carbs** 16g, **Total sugars** 9g (added 2g), **Protein** 2g, **Fiber** 5g, **Sodium** 365mg, **Potassium** 544mg.
Nutrition bonus: Vitamin C (45% daily value).

Salt-Packed Capers

Capers are the unopened buds of *Capparis spinosa*, a plant native to the Mediterranean. Most capers are sold packed in a vinegar brine, but they are sold dry-cured in salt as well. Salt-packed capers have a less acidic, fresher flavor and firmer texture than softer brined capers. Rinse before using: Swish in tepid water to remove salt. Let stand for 1 minute, then scoop them out with a small sieve. Rinse under cool running water. If they are still too salty, repeat the process.

GRILLED EGGPLANT & BABA GHANOUSH

ACTIVE: 45 MIN **TOTAL:** 55 MIN
TO MAKE AHEAD: Hold at room temperature for up to 2 hours.

This eggplant appetizer pairs grilled eggplant slices with smoky eggplant dip. Serve with garlic-rubbed grilled bread.

    3 small eggplants (about 8 ounces each)
 1½ teaspoons kosher salt, divided
    3 cloves garlic, divided
    4 tablespoons extra-virgin olive oil, divided
    1 tablespoon butter, melted
    1 large eggplant (about 1½ pounds)
  ½ cup tahini
  ¼ cup lemon juice
  ½ teaspoon ground pepper
  ⅓ cup crumbled goat cheese
    1 tablespoon coarsely chopped parsley

1. Preheat grill to medium.

2. Cut small eggplants into ½-inch-thick rounds. Sprinkle on both sides with ½ teaspoon of the salt and let stand for 10 minutes. Mince 1 garlic clove and combine with 2 tablespoons oil and butter in a small bowl. Brush on both sides of the eggplant slices.

3. Pierce large eggplant in several places with a fork. Grill, turning frequently, until starting to char on all sides, 15 to 20 minutes total. Move to a cooler spot and continue to cook, turning once, until very tender, 8 to 10 minutes more.

4. Meanwhile, grill the eggplant slices, turning once or twice, until tender and well-marked, 6 to 10 minutes total.

5. Cut the large eggplant in half. Scoop the flesh into a food processor. Add the remaining 1 teaspoon salt, 2 cloves garlic and 2 tablespoons oil, tahini, lemon juice and pepper. Process until almost smooth.

6. To serve, place the dip and eggplant slices on a platter. Sprinkle with goat cheese and parsley.

SERVES 10: ¼ CUP DIP & 2 SLICES EGGPLANT EACH

Calories 180, **Fat** 14g (sat 3g), **Cholesterol** 5mg, **Carbs** 11g, **Total sugars** 5g (added 0g), **Protein** 4g, **Fiber** 4g, **Sodium** 372mg, **Potassium** 382mg.

MARINATED EGGPLANT WITH GREEN CHERMOULA

ACTIVE: 1 HR **TOTAL:** 2 HRS
TO MAKE AHEAD: Let stand at room temperature up to 2 hours or refrigerate up to 1 day (bring to room temperature before serving).

A chermoula is a North African marinade that usually includes lemon, garlic, cumin and salt. Here it gets a hit of color and herbal freshness from cilantro and parsley.

8 cups cold water
⅓ cup kosher salt
4 Asian eggplants
   (about 2 pounds)
¼ cup chopped fresh cilantro
¼ cup chopped flat-leaf parsley

12 tablespoons extra-virgin olive
   oil, divided
   Zest and juice of 1 lemon
1 clove garlic, finely grated *or*
   minced
1 tablespoon ground coriander
1 tablespoon ground cumin

1. Combine water and salt in a large container, whisking to dissolve the salt. Cut eggplants in half lengthwise, then slice into ½-inch-thick half-moons. Add to the water. Fit a plate on top of the eggplant and place something heavy on it, such as a can, to keep the eggplant submerged. Soak for at least 1 hour and up to 2 hours.

2. Meanwhile, combine cilantro, parsley, 3 tablespoons oil, lemon zest and juice, garlic, coriander and cumin in a large bowl; set aside.

3. Drain the eggplant; thoroughly pat dry. Line a baking sheet with paper towels. Heat 3 tablespoons oil in a large cast-iron skillet over medium heat. Add a third of the eggplant; cook, turning once, until dark golden brown and almost charred, 3 to 5 minutes per side. (If you think it's done, give it another minute or two so it's really creamy inside and crisp outside.) Transfer to the prepared baking sheet to drain. Repeat with the remaining oil and eggplant in two more batches.

4. Gently stir the eggplant into the herb sauce. Let marinate at room temperature for at least 15 minutes and up to 2 hours before serving.

SERVES 8: ½ CUP EACH

Calories 226, **Fat** 21g (sat 3g), **Cholesterol** 0mg, **Carbs** 8g, **Total sugars** 4g (added 0g), **Protein** 1g, **Fiber** 4g, **Sodium** 286mg, **Potassium** 284mg.

Soaking Eggplant

Before cooking a soak in saltwater, as is done in this recipe, firms up the eggplant so it can stand up to stir-frying by collapsing air pockets in its spongy flesh. Not only does the saltwater soak allow the eggplant to get creamy on the inside and crisp on the outside, it results in using less cooking oil because it is less absorbent.

EGGPLANT PARMESAN

ACTIVE: 45 MIN **TOTAL:** 2½ HRS
TO MAKE AHEAD: Prepare through Step 6 and freeze (unbaked) up to 3 months. Thaw in the refrigerator 2 days. Bake, uncovered, at 400°F for 40 to 45 minutes.

Eggplant Parmesan doesn't have to include layers of deep-fried eggplant and mountains of cheese. This version has just enough melty mozzarella between layers of breaded baked eggplant. Don't skip the step of salting the eggplant, especially if you want to freeze one of the casseroles. (This recipe is designed to make two 8x8 casseroles, one to eat tonight and one for later.) Salting helps draw out extra moisture so the eggplant holds up better in the freezer.

- 2 eggplants (about 1 pound each), cut into 12 slices each
- 1½ teaspoons kosher salt, divided
- ¾ cup whole-wheat flour
- ¾ cup liquid egg whites *or* 6 large egg whites
- 2½ cups fine dry breadcrumbs (*see Tip*), preferably whole-wheat
- 3 tablespoons Italian seasoning, divided
- 4 tablespoons extra-virgin olive oil, divided
  Olive oil cooking spray
- 2 28-ounce cans crushed tomatoes
- 1½ cups shredded part-skim mozzarella cheese, divided
- 4 tablespoons finely shredded Parmigiano-Reggiano cheese, divided
  Fresh basil for garnish

1. Place 2 layers of paper towels on a baking sheet or cutting board. Place half the eggplant slices on the paper towels. Sprinkle with ¾ teaspoon salt. Cover with another double layer of paper towels. Top with the remaining eggplant slices and sprinkle with the remaining ¾ teaspoon salt. Cover with another double layer of paper towels. Let stand at room temperature for 1 hour.

2. Position oven racks in upper and lower positions and place a large baking sheet on each rack to heat; preheat to 425°F.

3. Blot the eggplant slices with more paper towels. Put flour in one shallow dish, egg whites in another. Combine breadcrumbs and 2 tablespoons Italian seasoning in a third dish. Dip each slice of eggplant in the flour, shaking off excess. Dip in the egg, letting the excess drip off, then press into the breadcrumbs.

Fine Dry Breadcrumbs

Fine dry breadcrumbs are available at the supermarket, but you can easily make your own. Trim crusts from firm sandwich bread. Tear the bread into pieces and process in a food processor until very fine crumbs form. Spread on a baking sheet and bake at 250°F until dry, about 10 to 15 minutes. One slice of bread makes about ⅓ cup dry breadcrumbs.

4. Remove the heated baking sheets from the oven and add 2 tablespoons oil to each, tilting to coat. Place half the eggplant on each baking sheet, not letting the slices touch. Generously coat the tops with cooking spray. Bake for 15 minutes. Flip the slices over and continue baking until golden brown, about 15 minutes more.

5. Combine crushed tomatoes and the remaining 1 tablespoon Italian seasoning in a medium bowl.

6. To assemble: Coat two 8-inch-square baking dishes with cooking spray. Spread ½ cup of the tomatoes in each prepared baking dish. Make a layer of 6 eggplant slices over the sauce. Spread with 1 cup of tomatoes and sprinkle with ¼ cup mozzarella. Top with the remaining 6 slices of eggplant, a generous 1 cup tomatoes, ½ cup mozzarella and 2 tablespoons Parmesan.

7. To serve: Bake until the sauce is bubbling and the cheese is melted, about 15 minutes. Serve garnished with basil, if desired. To freeze: Let unbaked casserole(s) cool to room temperature. Tightly wrap with heavy-duty foil (or freezer paper) and freeze. (To prevent foil from sticking to the cheese, coat with cooking spray first.)

MAKES: 2 CASSEROLES, 4 SERVINGS EACH (ABOUT ¾ CUP)

Calories 295, **Fat** 13g (sat 4g), **Cholesterol** 13mg, **Carbs** 33g, **Total sugars** 9g (added 0g), **Protein** 14g, **Fiber** 8g, **Sodium** 459mg, **Potassium** 715mg.
Nutrition bonus: Vitamin C (35% daily value), Calcium (28% dv), Iron & Potassium (20% dv).

PORK & SHRIMP STUFFED EGGPLANT

ACTIVE: 1½ HRS | **TOTAL:** 1½ HRS

Plump eggplants are perfect for stuffing. This Thai-inspired filling is generously seasoned with lemongrass and green curry. (Photo: page 235.)

Lemongrass

Look for lemongrass—a woody, scallion-shape herb with aromatic lemon flavor—in the produce department of well-stocked supermarkets or Asian food shops. To use, trim off the root end and grassy top. Peel off the woody outer leaves. Thinly slice the softer inner stalk, then finely chop.

EGGPLANT & STUFFING

- 3 eggplants (1-1¼ pounds each)
- 2 tablespoons plus 1 teaspoon peanut *or* canola oil, divided
- 1 tablespoon minced fresh ginger
- 1 tablespoon minced garlic
- 1 tablespoon finely chopped jalapeño pepper
- 2 teaspoons finely chopped lemongrass *(see Tip)*
- ½ cup chopped scallions
- ¼ cup finely chopped cilantro stems (save leaves for sauce & garnish)
- 1 pound lean ground pork *(see Tip, page 458)*
- 6 ounces peeled raw shrimp, coarsely chopped
- 1 cup cooked brown jasmine rice
- 2 tablespoons Thai green curry paste
- 1 tablespoon fish sauce *(see Tip, page 105)*
- 1 teaspoon dark brown sugar
- 1 teaspoon freshly grated lime zest
- 1 large egg, lightly beaten

SAUCE

- 2 teaspoons peanut oil *or* canola oil
- ¼ cup finely chopped shallots
- ¼ cup finely chopped scallion, white part only
- 2 teaspoons minced garlic
- 1 teaspoon minced fresh ginger
- 1 tablespoon Thai green curry paste
- 1 13-ounce can "lite" coconut milk
- 3 tablespoons lime juice
- 1 tablespoon fish sauce
- 2 teaspoons dark brown sugar
- ¼ cup whole cilantro leaves

1. Preheat oven to 400°F.

2. To prepare eggplant: Halve eggplants lengthwise, keeping stems intact. Using a paring knife, score the cut sides in a crisscross pattern, taking care not to cut into the skin. Brush the cut sides with 1½ tablespoons oil. Place the eggplants cut-side down in a large roasting pan. Brush the skins with ½ tablespoon oil.

3. Bake for 15 minutes. Turn eggplants over and bake until the flesh is quite tender, 15 to 20 minutes more; remove from the oven. Reduce temperature to 350°F.

4. To prepare stuffing & stuff eggplant: Meanwhile, heat the remaining 1 teaspoon oil in a small skillet over medium heat. Add ginger, garlic, jalapeño and lemongrass; cook, stirring, for 2 minutes. Add scallions and cilantro stems; cook, stirring, 1 minute more. Transfer to a medium bowl.

5. When the eggplants are cool enough to handle, scoop out the pulp, leaving about ¼ inch of pulp in the skin. Chop the eggplant pulp; add to the bowl. Stir in pork, shrimp, rice, 2 tablespoons curry paste, fish sauce, brown sugar, lime zest and egg. Return eggplants to the roasting pan. Mound about 1 cup stuffing into each.

6. Bake the eggplants until the stuffing is firm and registers 165°F on an instant-read thermometer, about 30 minutes.

7. To prepare sauce: Meanwhile, heat 2 teaspoons oil in a small saucepan over medium heat; stir in shallots, scallion whites, garlic and ginger; cook, stirring, until soft, about 3 minutes. Add 1 tablespoon curry paste and cook, stirring, for 1 minute. Pour in coconut milk, 3 tablespoons lime juice, fish sauce and 2 teaspoons brown sugar. Bring to a simmer.

8. When the eggplants are done, pour the sauce over them and bake 5 minutes more. Serve garnished with cilantro leaves.

MAKES: 6 SERVINGS, ½ EGGPLANT & ABOUT ⅓ CUP SAUCE EACH

Calories 379, **Fat** 17g (sat 6g), **Cholesterol** 115mg, **Carbs** 36g, **Total sugars** 12g (added 2g), **Protein** 25g, **Fiber** 6g, **Sodium** 735mg, **Potassium** 616mg.

Fennel

Fans of economy, meet fennel: All parts—the bulb, stem and feathery fronds—can be consumed. Fans of accuracy, take note: Some food markets incorrectly label fennel bulbs "anise." Although both have a faintly sweet licorice-like flavor—and both are members of the carrot family—they are two different plants. The plant with feathery fronds is fennel. Anise is an aromatic flowering herb whose seeds are used for flavoring cookies, cakes and liqueurs.

To further clarify, it is helpful to know that there are two kinds of fennel. Herb fennel is cultivated for its fern-like leaves as well as the seeds used to flavor Italian sausage, pork roast, cookies and breads. Florence fennel—also called bulb fennel or *finocchio* in Italian—develops a crisp, licorice-flavored bulb that is eaten as a vegetable. While it has the same type of feathery foliage as herb fennel, it does not have the same type of seeds.

Fennel is native to the Mediterranean. Although it has been incorporated into most of the cuisines of that region, the Italians seem to have taken a particular liking to it. It is integral to many cooked dishes and enjoyed raw as well as a palate cleanser and digestive aid after a hearty meal—or with soft goat cheese and ripe figs as dessert.

Fennel is lovely in the tomatoey, saffron-infused broth of *cioppino*—the seafood stew created by Italian-American fishermen in San Francisco. Thin slices of crunchy raw fennel combined with peak-season citrus, drizzled with good olive oil and seasoned with a little sea salt and freshly ground black pepper makes a refreshing winter salad.

Garnish soup with the fronds, add to salads or chop and sprinkle over a seared or grilled fish fillet.

It takes three months for fennel to go from seed to harvestable bulb. Planted in spring, it comes into season in late summer or early fall and stays in season through winter.

Best in fall to early spring

AT THE MARKET

❧ Choose smooth bulbs with no cuts, cracks or blemishes. Sniff the bulb; it should have a fresh anise scent. The fronds (if attached) should be bright green in color and look fresh, not wilted or slimy.

IN YOUR KITCHEN

❧ Store fennel bulbs with fresh-looking fronds attached for up to 5 days in a plastic bag in the refrigerator. If the fronds look less than perfectly fresh, remove them before storing.

❧ Cut off the stalk and feathery fronds, reserving the fronds, if desired. Cut off the root end of the bulb. If the outer layer of the bulb is tough, peel the surface of it with a vegetable peeler. If it is very tough, remove the whole layer. If using sliced or chopped, cut the bulb in quarters and remove the core from each quarter.

COOKING BASICS

GRILL Trim the stalks and fronds from 1 fennel bulb. Cut a thin slice off the root end, leaving core intact. Cut bulb in half vertically from top to bottom. Cut each half vertically into four thin slices. Brush slices on both sides with 1 tablespoon olive oil. Season with ¼ teaspoon salt and pepper to taste. Grill over medium-high heat until lightly charred and tender, 2 to

3 minutes per side. Transfer to a serving platter. Squeeze half of a lemon over the fennel. Top with a few shavings of Parmesan cheese. Serves 2.

SAUTÉ Slice 2 heads fennel. Heat 2 tablespoons olive oil in a large skillet over medium-high heat. Add fennel and 1 clove sliced garlic. Cook, stirring occasionally, until fennel is tender and golden brown, 8 to 10 minutes. Season with salt and pepper to taste. Serve with lemon wedges, if desired. Serves 4.

NUTRITION

❧ **1 cup of sliced raw fennel: Calories** 27, **Fat** 0g (sat 0g), **Cholesterol** 0mg, **Carbs** 6g, **Total sugars** 3g (added 0g), **Protein** 1g, **Fiber** 3g, **Sodium** 45mg, **Potassium** 360mg.

BONUS This bulb could help skin look younger. Fennel contains anethole, a compound that prevents the breakdown of collagen, a protein that keeps skin firm and supple. It's also high in vitamin C, another collagen booster.

How to prep

1. Cut off the stalk and leaves on top of the bulb, retaining fronds for garnish if desired. Cut ½-inch off the root end on the bottom of the bulb.

2. Cut bulb in quarters.

3. Cut out the core from each of the quarters. Slice or chop as desired.

GRAPE & FENNEL SALAD

ACTIVE: 30 MIN **TOTAL:** 30 MIN

This bright flavored, crunchy salad studded with toasted almonds has a double dose of fennel—thin slices of the bulb in the salad itself and lightly crushed fennel seeds in the champagne vinaigrette.

  2 tablespoons extra-virgin olive oil
  2 tablespoons champagne vinegar *or* white-wine vinegar
  ½ teaspoon fennel seeds, lightly crushed
  ¼ teaspoon salt
  ¼ teaspoon ground pepper
  5 cups red and green seedless grapes (about 1¾ pounds), halved
  1 large fennel bulb, halved, cored and thinly sliced
  3 stalks celery, thinly sliced on the diagonal
  4 scallions, thinly sliced on the diagonal
  3 tablespoons slivered almonds, toasted *(see Tip page 92)*

Whisk oil, vinegar, fennel seeds, salt and pepper in a large bowl. Add grapes, fennel, celery and scallions; toss to coat. Serve topped with almonds.

SERVES 8: ABOUT 1 CUP EACH

Calories 127, **Fat** 5g (sat 1g), **Cholesterol** 0mg, **Carbs** 21g, **Total sugars** 15g (added 0g), **Protein** 2g, **Fiber** 3g, **Sodium** 103mg, **Potassium** 384mg.

≈

Anise Liqueur

Nearly all of the countries that rim the Mediterranean make some sort of anise liqueur. The aromatic flowering herb grows all over the region, and its seeds are used to flavor all kinds of foods, sweets and liqueurs. France has Pernod, pastis and absinthe. Italy has sambuca, Greece has ouzo, Spain has chinchon, and Turkey, raki. The liqueurs vary in their degree of sweetness and are consequently not interchangeable in savory recipes. Sambuca is much sweeter than either Pernod or ouzo and should be reserved as an after-dinner drink, not used as an ingredient in a main course.

≈

FENNEL GRATIN

ACTIVE: 30 MIN **TOTAL:** 1½ HRS

Topped with Parmesan and breadcrumbs, this simple gratin is a tasty accompaniment to most any roast meat or simply prepared fish.

- 5 medium fennel bulbs (about 1¼ pounds each)
- 2 teaspoons extra-virgin olive oil
- 2 cloves garlic, very finely chopped
- 1 cup reduced-sodium chicken broth *or* vegetable broth
- 1 tablespoon lemon juice
- 1 tablespoon anise-flavored liqueur, such as Pernod *or* ouzo (optional)
- ¼ teaspoon salt
- ¼ teaspoon ground pepper
- ½ cup freshly grated Parmesan cheese
- 1 cup fresh breadcrumbs *(see Tip, page 18)*
  Chopped fennel fronds *or* parsley for garnish

1. Preheat oven to 400°F. Coat a 1½-quart gratin dish or other shallow baking dish with cooking spray.

2. Trim off stalks and tough outer layers from fennel. Cut the bulbs in half lengthwise. Then cut each half into 4 wedges. Heat oil in a large nonstick skillet over medium-high heat. Add the fennel and cook, stirring occasionally, until it begins to brown, 3 to 4 minutes. Add garlic and cook, stirring, about 1 minute more. Pour in broth, lemon juice and anise liqueur (if using); cook, stirring occasionally, until the liquid is reduced by half, 4 to 5 minutes. Season with salt and pepper and transfer to the prepared dish.

3. Bake until the fennel is very tender, about 45 minutes. Combine Parmesan and breadcrumbs; sprinkle over the fennel. Continue baking until the top is golden, about 10 minutes more. Sprinkle with chopped fennel fronds (or parsley), if desired.

SERVES 6

Calories 153, **Fat** 4g (sat 1g), **Cholesterol** 6mg, **Carbs** 24g, **Total sugars** 1g (added 1g), **Protein** 7g, **Fiber** 7g, **Sodium** 476mg, **Potassium** 877mg.
Nutrition bonus: Vitamin C (41% daily value), Potassium (25% dv), Calcium (22% dv).

ROASTED FENNEL WITH OLIVE TAPENADE, FETA & MINT

ACTIVE: 25 MIN **TOTAL:** 1½ HRS
TO MAKE AHEAD: Refrigerate the roasted fennel (Steps 2-3) and tapenade (Step 4) in separate containers up to 1 day. Bring to room temperature before serving.

Slow-roasting fennel caramelizes its natural sugars and softens what in a raw state is a very crisp texture to that of a rich roasted onion. Topped with olive tapenade, feta and mint, it makes a unique side dish. Recipe adapted from Tyler Florence Family Meal *by Tyler Florence (Rodale, 2010).*

6 large bulbs fennel, with tops
5 tablespoons extra-virgin olive oil, divided
¼ teaspoon kosher salt
¼ teaspoon ground pepper
2 cups pitted green olives
¼ cup chopped flat-leaf parsley
¼ cup chopped fresh tarragon

3 small cloves garlic, peeled
2 tablespoons chopped rinsed capers
1 tablespoon red-wine vinegar
1 teaspoon crushed red pepper
¾ cup crumbled feta cheese
1 cup torn fresh mint leaves

1. Preheat oven to 375°F.

2. Cut off and discard fennel stalks; coarsely chop the fronds and reserve for garnish. Halve each fennel bulb lengthwise, trim the base and remove the tough outer layer. Rub the bulb halves with 2 tablespoons oil, salt and pepper. Place cut-side down in a roasting pan.

3. Roast the fennel until soft and caramelized, 1 to 1¼ hours.

4. Meanwhile, to make the olive tapenade, combine the remaining 3 tablespoons oil, olives, parsley, tarragon, garlic, capers, vinegar and crushed red pepper in a food processor and pulse until chunky.

5. To serve, arrange the roasted fennel on a serving platter and top with the tapenade, then sprinkle with feta, mint and the reserved fennel fronds.

SERVES 12: ½ FENNEL BULB & 2½ TBSP. TAPENADE EACH

Calories 151, **Fat** 11g (sat 3g), **Cholesterol** 8mg, **Carbs** 11g, **Total sugars** 1g (added 0g), Protein 3g, **Fiber** 5g, **Sodium** 538mg, **Potassium** 557mg.
Nutrition bonus: Vitamin C (29% daily value).

MEDITERRANEAN SAUTÉED SHRIMP & FENNEL

ACTIVE: 25 MIN **TOTAL:** 25 MIN

This sautéed fennel and shrimp with a tomato-caper sauce is very versatile. Serve in whatever way suits your fancy—with pasta, whole grains, such as bulgur or brown rice, or even mashed potatoes.

    1 tablespoon extra-virgin olive oil
    1 large fennel bulb, cored and cut into 2-inch-long strips (about 4 cups)
    1 15-ounce can diced tomatoes, preferably fire-roasted
    1 tablespoon chopped fresh oregano *or* 1 teaspoon dried
    1 pound peeled and deveined raw shrimp (21-25 per pound) (*see Tip*)
    2 tablespoons capers, rinsed
    ¼ teaspoon ground pepper
    ¼ cup crumbled feta cheese

Heat oil in a large skillet over medium heat. Add fennel and cook, stirring occasionally, until starting to brown, 6 to 8 minutes. Add tomatoes and oregano and cook, stirring and scraping up any browned bits, about 30 seconds. Add shrimp and cook, stirring occasionally, until pink and just cooked through, about 4 minutes. Stir in capers and pepper. Serve sprinkled with feta.

SERVES 4

Calories 179, **Fat** 6g (sat 2g), **Cholesterol** 167mg, **Carbs** 9g, **Total sugars** 3g (added 0g), **Protein** 23g, **Fiber** 3g, **Sodium** 449mg, **Potassium** 717mg.
Nutrition bonus: Vitamin C (42% daily value), Vitamin B$_{12}$ (27% dv).

Shrimp Sizes

Shrimp is usually sold by the number needed to equal one pound. For example, "21-25 count" means there will be 21 to 25 shrimp in a pound. Size names, such as "large" or "extra-large," are not standardized, so to get the size you want, order by the count per pound.
Both wild-caught and farm-raised shrimp can damage the surrounding ecosystems when not managed properly. Fortunately, it is possible to buy shrimp that have been raised or caught with sound environmental practices. Look for fresh or frozen shrimp certified by an independent agency, such as the Marine Stewardship Council. If you can't find certified shrimp, choose wild-caught shrimp from North America— it's more likely to be sustainably caught.

Garlic

Most people are not fence-sitters on the topic of garlic. Generally, if you love garlic, you really love it. With rare exception, most of the world's cuisines have made it a central ingredient. What would Caesar salad be without garlic? Or hummus? Or intensely flavored Chinese XO Sauce? Or Cuban mojo? Or really half of the Italian dishes you can think of?

When used raw, garlic is pungent and spicy. Cooked, it mellows to varying degrees, depending on the method. Although garlic is used mostly as a flavoring, it could be argued that when roasted until creamy and sweet and spread on bread, meat or vegetables, the latter serves simply as a vehicle for the former.

There are about 600 varieties of this member of the lily family that range in color from white to purple, and they all fall into one of three categories.

Softneck varieties grow layers of cloves around a stem. They have necks that stay soft after harvest (this is the type that is braided). It has the strongest flavor of the three types and stores the longest. It is best adapted to where winters are mild.

Hardneck varieties grow one ring of cloves around a stem and often have milder flavor than softnecks. They do well in cold climates and in late spring and early summer produce curly green garlic scapes on top that can be used in cooking.

Elephant garlic is very large and has only about 4 cloves to a bulb. It is more closely related to the leek than to other varieties of garlic and has a milder flavor than regular garlic.

Most garlic requires 40 days below 40°F for a clove to turn into a bulb. The biggest, most flavorful bulbs are planted in the fall for harvest in summer.

Best in summer

AT THE MARKET

≫ Choose garlic heads that are firm with no soft or mushy cloves. Avoid cloves with scars, nicks or blemishes or dark, powdery patches under the skin.

IN YOUR KITCHEN

≫ Store garlic in a cool, dry, dark spot with good air circulation. Garlic can be stored in a mesh bag hanging from a pantry or (dry) basement ceiling. In proper conditions, garlic can be stored up to 3 months.

≫ Remove garlic clove from head. Place clove on a work surface. Place the broad side of a chef's knife on top of it and gently press down. The papery skin will crack and can easily be removed.

COOKING BASICS

BRAISE Separate a garlic head into cloves. Bring 1 cup water to a boil in a small saucepan. Drop cloves in water and simmer for 1 minute; drain and peel. Heat 1 tablespoon olive oil in pan over low heat. Sauté the cloves until tender, about 10 minutes. Add ½ cup reduced-sodium chicken broth to pan. Season with a pinch of salt and pepper. Simmer over low until meltingly tender, 5 minutes. Use in mashed potatoes or toss with cooked pasta or vegetables.

GARLIC BREAD Combine 2 tablespoons butter and ½ cup olive oil in a small saucepan over medium heat. Add 2 cloves minced garlic and 2 tablespoons finely chopped parsley. Heat until butter melts. Cut a whole-grain baguette in half horizontally. Brush cut sides with olive oil mixture. Season with salt and sprinkle with 2 tablespoons grated Parmesan cheese. Bake in a 450°F oven until golden, about 10 to 15 minutes. Serves 10 to 12.

ROASTING For roasting method, see page 258.

NUTRITION

≫ **3 raw garlic cloves: Calories** 13, **Fat** 0g (sat 0g), **Cholesterol** 0mg, **Carbs** 3g, **Total sugars** 0g (added 0g), **Protein** 1g, **Fiber** 0g, **Sodium** 2mg, **Potassium** 36mg.

BONUS Garlic is packed with allicin, a natural blood thinner that promotes heart health by preventing blood clots from forming. To get an even bigger bump from your cloves, chop them about 10 minutes before cooking to release enzymes that activate allicin.

Grow Your Own

In the north, plant in the fall, three weeks before the first frost; mulch well. Elsewhere, plant in early spring as soon as the soil can be worked. Plant cloves 3 inches apart and 2 inches deep in full sun in loose, well-drained soil. Water every 3 to 5 days the first 3 weeks. After that, water when dry. When the tops turn brown, stop watering. When the tops die down, dig up gently with a pitchfork—but only during a dry spell. Allow heads to dry on the ground for 1 week. Clip roots to ½ inch long. Wait 1 more week before clipping the stems off hardneck varieties.

How to make garlic paste

1. Use the broad side of a chef's knife to crush the clove. Remove papery skin, then trim root end.

2. Coarsely chop the garlic and sprinkle with a dash of salt.

3. Use the broad side of a chef's knife, pressing and smearing, to make paste.

◄ **Common Garlic (Purple)**
Milder, sweeter and less sulfurous than common white garlic, these purple and white bulbs are considered the best type for roasting.

▲ **Garlic Scapes**
These are the green spiral-shape sprouts that appear on top of garlic plants in the spring. Regular garlic cloves can be used as a substitute for garlic scapes.

▲ **Common Garlic (white)**
The most familiar type of garlic has heads comprised of large juicy cloves that have the distinctive fiery bite beloved by fans of "the stinking rose."

GARLIC SCAPE PESTO

ACTIVE: 10 MIN **TOTAL:** 10 MIN
TO MAKE AHEAD: Refrigerate in an airtight container up to 2 weeks or freeze up to 6 months.

During the spring when garlic scapes are plentiful at farmers' markets and farm stands, this is one way to savor scapes and their gorgeous garlicky flavor for weeks. Try the pesto with pasta, stir-fries, grilled fish, poultry and steak. If you don't have garlic scapes, make this pesto with regular garlic cloves.

  ½ cup chopped garlic scapes *or* garlic cloves
  ½ cup extra-virgin olive oil

Pulse garlic scapes (or garlic) in a food processor until well chopped. Add oil and process until somewhat smooth.

MAKES: ABOUT ⅔ CUP (1-TBSP. SERVING)

Calories 103, **Fat** 10g (sat 1g), **Cholesterol** 0mg, **Carbs** 2g, **Total sugars** 0g (added 0g), **Protein** 0g, **Fiber** 0g, **Sodium** 1mg, **Potassium** 25mg.

Scape Season

Most garlic growers and gardeners clip the scapes off to direct more of the plant's energy into growing a large bulb rather than the flower heads that will appear if left on the plant. Garlic scapes are not waste. When harvested at a young and tender stage, they are delicious, with a mild garlicky flavor and crisp, asparagus-like texture.

ROASTED GARLIC & ASPARAGUS SALAD

ACTIVE: 40 MIN **TOTAL:** 1 HR
TO MAKE AHEAD: Refrigerate roasted garlic cloves in oil (Steps 1-3) up to 3 days; bring to room temperature before finishing Step 3.

The dressing for this salad uses two kinds of garlic—mellow, sweet roasted garlic cloves and mild-tasting fresh garlic scapes. Use chopped fresh garlic in the dressing if you can't find garlic scapes.

2 heads garlic

3 tablespoons extra-virgin olive oil, divided

½ teaspoon salt, divided

½ teaspoon ground pepper, divided

¼ cup minced fresh chives

2 tablespoons finely chopped fresh garlic scapes *or* 2 teaspoons finely chopped garlic cloves

¼ cup lemon juice

2 bunches asparagus, trimmed

2 teaspoons freshly grated lemon zest

½ cup walnut halves, toasted and chopped *(see Tip, page 92)*

1. Preheat oven to 400°F.

2. Slice the tips off the garlic heads, exposing the cloves. Place the heads on a square of aluminum foil. Pour 2 tablespoons oil over them and sprinkle with ¼ teaspoon each salt and pepper. Roast until the garlic feels soft when you squeeze the bulb, 40 to 50 minutes, depending on size.

3. When cool enough to handle, gently squeeze cloves from the skins into a small bowl (discard skins). Add chives and garlic scapes. Swirl in lemon juice.

4. Peel the tough outer layer off the bottom half of asparagus stalks, if desired. Place the asparagus on a rimmed baking sheet; drizzle with the remaining 1 tablespoon oil and sprinkle with lemon zest and ¼ teaspoon each salt and pepper. Roast, shaking the pan halfway through, until the asparagus is just tender, 10 to 20 minutes. Let stand for 5 minutes.

5. Divide the warm asparagus among 6 plates. Top each portion with about 2 tablespoons roasted garlic vinaigrette and 1 generous tablespoon walnuts.

SERVES 6

Calories 133, **Fat** 10g (sat 1g), **Cholesterol** 0mg, **Carbs** 9g, **Total sugars** 2g (added 0g), **Protein** 4g, **Fiber** 2g, **Sodium** 206mg, **Potassium** 268mg.
Nutrition bonus: Folate (31% daily value), Vitamin C (25% dv).

SOLE WITH GARLIC-ALMOND-CAPER SAUCE

ACTIVE: 35 MIN **TOTAL:** 35 MIN

Here, seasoned fillets of sole (or flounder) are sautéed in a hot skillet, then topped with a simple sauce of sautéed garlic, slivered almonds, capers and lemon juice—a riff on sole meunière. This is a very simple dish, but all the ingredients need to be ready by the stove because it cooks very quickly once you turn on the heat.

Sustainable Sole

For sustainably fished sole or flounder, look for wild-caught fish from the U.S. Pacific. For more information on choosing the best fish and shellfish options for both your health and the health of the ocean, visit *seafoodwatch.org.*

¾ cup all-purpose flour

½ cup sliced almonds, divided

¾ teaspoon ground pepper, divided

½ teaspoon salt

2 large egg whites

2 tablespoons water

8 small fillets of sole *or* flounder (1-1¼ pounds total; *see Tip*)

2 tablespoons canola oil, divided

1 tablespoon extra-virgin olive oil

¼ cup thinly sliced garlic

2 tablespoons capers, rinsed

3 tablespoons lemon juice

4 lemon wedges for serving

1. Preheat oven to 250°F.

2. Pulse flour, ¼ cup almonds, ½ teaspoon pepper and salt in a food processor until the almonds are finely chopped. Transfer to a large plate. Whisk egg whites and water in a shallow dish. Dip fish fillets in the egg mixture, then into the flour mixture, coating well on both sides. Shake off any excess.

3. Heat 1 tablespoon canola oil in a large nonstick or cast-iron skillet over medium heat. The oil should be quite hot: When you drop a bit of the seasoned flour into it, it should sizzle up immediately.

4. Add half the fish to the pan and cook until golden brown, 2 to 4 minutes per side. Transfer the fish to a large baking sheet and keep warm in the oven. Repeat with remaining canola oil and fish. Remove the pan from the heat. Transfer the fish to the baking sheet.

5. Add olive oil to the pan and return to low heat. Add garlic and the remaining ¼ cup almonds; cook, stirring, for 15 seconds. Remove from the heat; stir in capers, lemon juice and the remaining ¼ teaspoon pepper. Divide the fish among 4 plates and top with the sauce. Serve with lemon wedges, if desired.

SERVES 4: 2 FISH FILLETS & ABOUT 2 TBSP. SAUCE EACH

Calories 297, **Fat** 17g (sat 2g), **Cholesterol** 44mg, **Carbs** 18g, **Total sugars** 1g (added 0g), **Protein** 18g, **Fiber** 2g, **Sodium** 550mg, **Potassium** 317mg.

GARLIC CHICKEN

ACTIVE: 40 MIN **TOTAL:** 40 MIN

Whole garlic cloves are mild when simmered with chicken in a simple white wine-mustard sauce. Serve with smashed potatoes with buttermilk and sautéed green beans.

  2 heads garlic, cloves separated
  8 chicken drumsticks (about 2½ pounds), skin removed, trimmed
      (see Tip)
  ½ teaspoon salt, divided
  ¼ teaspoon ground pepper
  3 tablespoons extra-virgin olive oil
  ⅓ cup white wine
  1 cup reduced-sodium chicken broth
  2 teaspoons Dijon mustard
  2 teaspoons all-purpose flour
  ⅓ cup chopped scallion greens *or* fresh chives

1. Lightly smash garlic cloves with the side of a large knife to loosen the skins. Peel; cut larger ones in half. Sprinkle chicken with ¼ teaspoon salt and pepper.

2. Heat oil in a large skillet over medium heat. Add the garlic and cook, stirring, until beginning to brown, about 2 minutes. Remove to a plate with a slotted spoon.

3. Add chicken to the pan and cook until browned on one side, about 4 minutes. Turn it over and return the garlic to the pan. Add wine and cook for 1 minute.

4. Whisk broth, mustard, flour and the remaining ¼ teaspoon salt in a small bowl. Add the mixture to the pan; bring to a boil, then reduce the heat to maintain a lively simmer. Cover and cook until the chicken is cooked through, 8 to 10 minutes. Serve sprinkled with scallion greens or chives.

SERVES 4: 2 DRUMSTICKS & ABOUT ⅓ CUP SAUCE EACH

Calories 336, **Fat** 18g (sat 3g), **Cholesterol** 168mg, **Carbs** 7g, **Total sugars** 1g (added 0g), **Protein** 32g, **Fiber** 0g, **Sodium** 618mg, **Potassium** 483mg.
Nutrition bonus: Zinc (23% daily value).

Skinning Chicken Legs

To remove the skin from raw chicken drumsticks, grip the skin from the meaty end of the drumstick with a paper towel and pull down toward the exposed bone until it comes off completely.

Jerusalem Artichokes

The Jerusalem artichoke is neither an artichoke nor does it have anything specifically to do with Jerusalem. Like many common botanical labels, its name is likely the result of inaccurate translations, misnomers and mispronunciations through centuries and across continents.

Sunchoke—its alternate name—more accurately reflects its true nature. The knobby tuber of a perennial sunflower that grows between 6 and 10 feet tall and produces beautiful yellow blooms, the vegetable looks a bit like gingerroot. It has a crisp, ivory-colored interior that has a clean, nutty, slightly sweet flavor.

Jerusalem artichokes are an indigenous North American crop introduced by Native Americans to early settlers, who introduced them to Europe.

Very thin raw slices are lovely as a crudité with dips or sauces. They can be lightly steamed or briefly boiled and tossed with a little butter and salt or with a vinaigrette. Or they can be cooked until very soft and pureed into a creamy, delicate soup. They take beautifully to roasting—turning crisp and browned on the outside and tender on the inside.

A caveat: Jerusalem artichokes can have a breezy effect on the digestive system. They contain a carbohydrate called inulin, which humans do not have the enzymes to digest. The task falls to "friendly" intestinal bacteria, which do a fine job— but they create carbon dioxide in the process. Start with a small portion and see how it goes.

Most varieties require between 120 and 150 days from planting to harvest. Planted in the spring, Jerusalem artichokes come into season in the fall—and are best left in the ground until needed, stretching the season through the winter.

Best in fall through winter

AT THE MARKET

➣ Choose Jerusalem artichokes that are firm, with no soft or spongy spots and no shriveling.

IN YOUR KITCHEN

➣ Store Jerusalem artichokes wrapped in paper towels (to absorb excess moisture and cushion them because they bruise easily). Place in a plastic bag and store in the refrigerator for up to 1 week.

➣ Cut off any dark or spongy spots. Peeling is optional—it depends on the thickness of the skin. Thin-skinned tubers need only a good scrubbing with a vegetable brush under cool running water. If the skins are thick and need peeling, use a paring knife to remove the skin and work around the knobbiness. Slice, chop or dice as desired. Place cut Jerusalem artichokes in water with lemon slices as you work to prevent browning.

COOKING BASICS

BRAISE Cut 1 pound Jerusalem artichokes into 1-inch chunks. Melt 1 tablespoon each butter and olive oil in a medium skillet over medium heat. Add the Jerusalem artichokes and toss gently to coat. Season with ¼ teaspoon salt and pepper to taste. Cook and stir for 1 to 2 minutes. Add ½ cup reduced-sodium chicken broth and ¼ cup white wine. Increase heat to medium-high and cook until the liquid bubbles at the edges. Reduce heat to medium-low. Cover and cook until crisp-tender, about 10 minutes. Uncover, increase heat to medium and cook until the liquid is reduced to a glaze, about 1 minute. Toss with 1½ teaspoons minced fresh parsley and ½ teaspoon finely grated lemon zest. Serves 4.

ROAST Peel 1½ pounds Jerusalem artichokes; cut in half if large. Toss with 2 tablespoons olive oil, 1 tablespoon minced fresh rosemary, ½ teaspoon pepper and ¼ teaspoon salt on a large rimmed baking sheet. Spread into a single layer and roast in a 425°F oven, stirring once, until just tender when pierced with a knife, 18 to 20 minutes. Stir in 2 ounces coarsely chopped prosciutto and ½ cup coarsely chopped walnuts. Roast until the prosciutto is crisp and the Jerusalem artichokes are very tender, 10 to 15 minutes more. Sprinkle with additional fresh rosemary, if desired. Serves 4.

SAUTÉ Thinly slice 1 pound Jerusalem artichokes. Heat 1 tablespoon butter and 2 tablespoons olive oil in a medium pan over medium-high heat. Add the Jerusalem artichokes and cook, stirring frequently, until browned and crisp on all sides, about 5 minutes. Season with ¼ teaspoon salt and pepper to taste. Sprinkle with finely chopped parsley, if desired. Serves 4.

NUTRITION

➣ **1 cup sliced raw Jerusalem artichokes: Calories** 110, **Fat** 0g (sat 0g), **Cholesterol** 0mg, **Carbs** 26g, **Total sugars** 14g (added 0g), **Protein** 3g, **Fiber** 2g, **Sodium** 6mg, **Potassium** 644mg.

BONUS Sunchokes are full of energy-boosting iron, a nutrient many women and children don't consume enough of. One cup supplies 28 percent of the daily recommendation for this mineral. To soak up even more of these tubers' iron, pair them with vitamin C-heavy vegetables, such as potatoes and tomatoes.

Roasted Jerusalem Artichokes with Crispy Prosciutto & Walnuts
(see Cooking Basics, opposite)

JERUSALEM ARTICHOKE-POTATO SOUP WITH CRISPY CROUTONS

ACTIVE: 35 MIN **TOTAL:** 1 HR

With just the tiniest touch of half-and-half, this soup is incredibly creamy and rich-tasting—in large part due to the combination of the Jerusalem artichokes with Yukon Gold potatoes. Serve as a starter before a fall or winter dinner.

- 3 tablespoons extra-virgin olive oil, divided
- 1 large leek *or* 2 small leeks, cleaned and thinly sliced *(see page 336)*
- 3 cloves garlic, minced
- 5 cups reduced-sodium chicken *or* vegetable broth
- 1 pound Jerusalem artichokes, peeled and chopped
- 8 ounces Yukon Gold potatoes, peeled and diced
- ¾ teaspoon salt
- ½ cup half-and-half
- 2 teaspoons fresh thyme leaves, plus more for garnish
- 3 cups cubed whole-wheat bread
- ½ teaspoon garlic powder
- ½ teaspoon ground pepper

1. Heat 1 tablespoon oil in a large saucepan or pot over medium heat. Add leek and cook, stirring, until softened, about 5 minutes. Stir in garlic. Cook 1 minute more. Add broth, Jerusalem artichokes, potatoes and salt; bring to a boil. Reduce heat and simmer, covered, until the vegetables are very tender, 20 to 25 minutes.

2. Puree soup with an immersion blender or in a regular blender. (Use caution when pureeing hot liquids.) Stir in half-and-half and thyme.

3. Meanwhile, preheat oven to 425°F. Place bread cubes on a baking sheet. Drizzle with the remaining 2 tablespoons oil, then sprinkle with garlic powder and pepper; toss to coat. Bake, stirring once halfway through, until browned and crisp, 15 to 20 minutes.

4. Serve the soup topped with the croutons and thyme leaves, if desired.

SERVES 8: ABOUT 1 CUP EACH

Calories 185, **Fat** 8g (sat 2g), **Cholesterol** 6mg, **Carbs** 24g, **Total sugars** 6g (added 0g), **Protein** 6g, **Fiber** 3g, **Sodium** 663mg, **Potassium** 481mg.

Jicama

The appeal of humble jicama lies in its refreshing crunch and surprising versatility. Jicama [HEE-kah-mah]—also called Mexican turnip or Mexican yam bean—is the root of a legume native to Central America. The vines that grow above the ground of this member of the morning glory family (sweet potato is a cousin) can reach up to 20 feet in length. The root has a juicy, crisp, slightly sweet flesh covered by a rough brown peel.

It is most commonly consumed raw—crunchy jicama sticks with a squeeze of fresh lime juice and a dusting of hot red chile powder are a popular Mexican street snack. But it can be cooked as well. The best methods are roasting, grilling and sautéing. Because it has a texture similar to water chestnuts, it easily fits into stir fries and stays pleasantly crisp.

Top half slices or thin wedges of jicama with white bean dip, hummus, guacamole, or whipped herbed goat cheese and serve as a cocktail snack. Julienne or chop and toss into a salad, shred and add to slaw or dice and toss into fresh salsa. Combine cubed jicama with fruits—mangoes, watermelon, cantaloupe and oranges—with a drizzle of olive oil, salt and a little black pepper or chile powder.

Jicama grows in frost-free regions. Although some gardeners in the very southernmost part of the United States grow them, most jicama in American markets are imported from Mexico and South America. They are available year-round but are best in fall through spring.

Best in fall through spring

AT THE MARKET

➤ Choose small to medium jicama that feel heavy for their size. The skin should be as smooth and thin as possible, with a slight sheen. Avoid roots with bruises, nicks or soft spots.

IN YOUR KITCHEN

➤ Store uncut jicama in the refrigerator up to 2 weeks. Once cut, store in a tightly sealed plastic bag in the refrigerator up to 1 week.

➤ Jicama always needs to be peeled. Scrub the jicama with a stiff vegetable brush under cool running water. Use a vegetable peeler or sharp paring knife to remove the skin and the fibrous first layer under it. Cube, chop, dice, slice or shred according to how you will use it.

COOKING BASICS

GRILL Quarter a medium peeled jicama and slice each quarter into ¼-inch-thick slices. Brush both sides of slices with olive oil. Season with ¼ teaspoon salt and chile powder to taste, if desired. Grill over medium-high heat until golden brown, turning once, about 1 minute per side. Serve with fresh lime wedges. Serves 2.

ROAST Toss 2 cups of peeled cubed jicama (1 inch) with 1 tablespoon olive oil, ¼ teaspoon salt and pepper to taste. Spread in a single layer on a large rimmed baking sheet. Roast in a 400°F oven, stirring every 15 minutes, until golden brown and tender, about 45 minutes to 1 hour. The last 10 minutes of roasting time, toss with 2 cloves minced garlic. When jicama is done, toss with 2 teaspoons finely chopped fresh parsley, if desired. Serves 2.

SAUTÉ Cut a 1-pound peeled jicama into thin matchsticks. Heat 1 tablespoon olive oil in a medium skillet over medium-high heat. Add the jicama to the pan and cook, stirring frequently, about 3 minutes. Add 1 clove minced garlic and cook, stirring frequently, until the jicama is translucent, about 2 minutes more. Remove from heat. Season with ¼ teaspoon salt and pepper to taste. Stir in ½ teaspoon finely grated lemon zest and 1 teaspoon fresh lemon juice. Serves 2.

NUTRITION

➤ **1 cup sliced raw jicama: Calories** 46, **Fat** 0g (sat 0g), **Cholesterol** 0mg, **Carbs** 11g, **Total sugars** 2g (added 0g), **Protein** 1g, **Fiber** 6g, **Sodium** 5mg, **Potassium** 180mg.

BONUS Munching on jicama can fill you up for very few calories and improve your digestive health too. One cup of raw jicama provides 6 grams of fiber. That's three times the amount you'd get from a slice of whole-wheat bread for about half the calories.

JICAMA-APPLE SLAW

ACTIVE: 35 MIN **TOTAL:** 35 MIN

Some stores carry jicama that has already been peeled; by all means use it if you can find it. For best flavor and appearance, serve the slaw soon after it's made.

⅓ cup packed chopped fresh cilantro, plus leaves for garnish

2 tablespoons chopped fresh mint, plus leaves for garnish

1-2 tablespoons minced jalapeño pepper

1 teaspoon sugar

¾ teaspoon salt

½ teaspoon ground cumin

¼ cup lime juice

⅓ cup extra-virgin olive oil

1 1-pound jícama

1 tart green apple

2 navel oranges

2 avocados, diced

1. Place ⅓ cup cilantro, 2 tablespoons mint, jalapeño to taste, sugar, salt, cumin and lime juice in a food processor. Process until finely chopped, about 30 seconds, stopping once to scrape down the sides. With the motor running, slowly add oil through the feed tube until the dressing is well combined. Transfer the dressing to a large bowl. Change to the shredding disk.

2. Using a small sharp knife, carefully peel jicama, making sure to remove both the papery brown skin and the layer of fibrous flesh just underneath. Cut the jicama and apple into pieces (remove core) that will fit comfortably through the processor feed tube. Shred the jicama and apple in the processor. Add to the bowl with the dressing.

3. Using a sharp knife, remove the peel and pith from the oranges. Working over the bowl (to catch any juice), cut the orange segments from the surrounding membranes, letting them drop into the bowl. Squeeze any remaining juice into the slaw. (Discard membranes and peel.) Add avocados; gently toss to combine. Serve immediately, garnished with cilantro and mint leaves.

SERVES 6: GENEROUS 1 CUP EACH

Calories 287, **Fat** 22g (sat 3g), **Cholesterol** 0mg, **Carbs** 23g, **Total sugars** 9g (added 1g), **Protein** 3g, **Fiber** 10g, **Sodium** 300mg, **Potassium** 563mg.
Nutrition bonus: Vitamin C (90% daily value), Folate (21% dv).

Spiralize This

Yes, spiralizers can make faux noodles from zucchini and parsnip. But they also provide a way to quickly and uniformly process vegetables for pretty presentation. Similar to using a pencil sharpener, with just a few turns of a crank the vegetable advances in the feed tube and comes out as beautifully curled vegetable ribbons—ready for salads, stir-fries or shoestring fries.

SPICY JICAMA & RED ONION SHOESTRINGS WITH HERBED CHIPOTLE AIOLI

ACTIVE: 35 MIN **TOTAL:** 1 HR
EQUIPMENT: Vegetable spiralizer

Guests will gobble up these tender-crisp shoestrings embellished with Parmesan and breadcrumbs and served with spicy mayo. Serve on small plates with appetizer forks for easy eating and a pretty presentation.

- 1 large jicama (about 2 pounds), peeled
- 1 small red onion, trimmed and peeled
- 2 tablespoons extra-virgin olive oil
- 3 slices whole-grain bread, lightly toasted
- ¼ cup grated Parmesan cheese
- ½ teaspoon ground pepper
- ¼ teaspoon cayenne pepper
- ½ cup low-fat mayonnaise
- 1 tablespoon minced fresh herbs, such as parsley, cilantro *and/or* chives
- 1 clove garlic, minced
- ¼-½ teaspoon ground chipotle pepper

1. Position racks in upper and lower thirds of oven; preheat to 425°F.

2. Using a vegetable spiralizer, spiralize jicama and onion *(see Tip)*. Place in a large bowl and toss with oil to coat.

3. Pulse bread in a food processor into crumbs. Add to the bowl along with Parmesan, pepper and cayenne; toss to coat. Divide the mixture between 2 large rimmed baking sheets.

4. Bake on the upper and lower racks, stirring and rotating the pans top to bottom halfway through, until browning in spots, about 30 minutes.

5. Meanwhile, combine mayonnaise, herbs, garlic and chipotle pepper to taste in a small bowl. Serve the shoestrings with the aioli.

SERVES 8: ½ CUP SHOESTRINGS & 1 TBSP. AIOLI EACH

Calories 151, **Fat** 8g (sat 1g), **Cholesterol** 6mg, **Carbs** 18g, **Total sugars** 4g (added 0g), **Protein** 3g, **Fiber** 6g, **Sodium** 209mg, **Potassium** 208mg.
Nutrition bonus: Vitamin C (35% daily value).

Kale

No vegetable has been more venerated in recent years than kale. Its seemingly magical powers have been touted in every form of media—and on T-shirts that proclaim "Kale, Yeah!" and "Eat More Kale"—and perhaps the most unfettered expression of fandom, simply "KALE." And it is not just for smoothie-sipping yogis. A chicken sausage and Tuscan kale sandwich was on the menu at the 2014 Super Bowl. Captain Kale is a Halloween costume.

There is truth behind the hoopla. Kale is supernutritious and versatile. It can be sautéed, braised, steamed, boiled, blitzed raw in a smoothie—or baked into crispy chips.

The four most common types of this nonheading member of the cabbage family are curly kale, Tuscan kale (also called dinosaur kale or lacinato kale), Russian Red—a variety with flat frilly-edged leaves—and flowering kale. Flowering kale grows in gorgeous rosettes of green, white, purple and pink leaves. It is primarily used as a visual element in ornamental gardens but is edible as well. 'Salad Savoy' is the market name for this type of kale.

Season kale with garlic, smoked paprika, smoked salt, vinegar, lemon or chile. Sauté in toasted sesame oil and season with a little sea salt and toasted sesame seeds. The strong cabbagey flavor pairs well with potatoes, white beans, olives, rich cheeses, ham, bacon and chorizo. Stir it into bean soup, sauté and tuck it into an omelet with goat cheese or feta or toss with pasta. Use it as a stand-in for spinach in spanakopita, the flaky Greek phyllo pie.

Kale is available all year but is most tender and flavorful during the cold months, and actually tastes even better after a frost.

Best in late fall through winter

AT THE MARKET

ᕧ Choose kale with small or medium-size leaves—they are the most tender and have the best flavor—and with dark green leaves that are relatively soft, with crisp edges. Avoid leaves that are wilted, yellowing or slimy.

IN YOUR KITCHEN

ᕧ Store kale, unwashed, in a plastic bag in the coldest part of the refrigerator up to 2 days.

ᕧ Wash and prepare kale as shown in the photos, *below.*

COOKING BASICS

CREAMED Heat 2 tablespoons olive oil in a large pot over medium heat. Add 1 cup sliced leek (white and light green parts only) and cook, stirring frequently, until starting to soften, 1 to 2 minutes. Add 12 cups chopped kale, 2 cloves minced garlic, ¾ teaspoon salt and ½ teaspoon pepper. Cook, stirring often, until very soft, 10 to 20 minutes, adding water ¼ cup at a time if the greens start to stick. Sprinkle with 2 tablespoons all-purpose flour and cook, stirring, for 30 seconds. Stir in 1½ cups reduced-fat milk and a pinch of nutmeg. Cook, stirring, until just starting to boil and thicken, 1 to 2 minutes. Serves 4.

SAUTÉ Heat 1 tablespoon extra-virgin olive oil in a large pot over medium heat. Add 1 large bunch coarsely chopped kale (about 16 cups) and cook, tossing, until bright green, about 1 minute. Add ½ cup water, reduce heat to medium-low, cover and cook, stirring occasionally, until the kale is tender, 12 to 15 minutes. Push the kale to one side; add 1 teaspoon olive oil to the empty side and cook 2 cloves minced garlic and ¼ teaspoon crushed red pepper until fragrant, 30 seconds to 1 minute. Remove from heat. Stir in 1 to 2 teaspoons sherry vinegar or red-wine vinegar and ¼ teaspoon salt. Serves 4.

NUTRITION

ᕧ **1 cup chopped cooked kale:** Calories 36, **Fat** 1g (sat 0g), **Cholesterol** 0mg, **Carbs** 7g, **Total sugars** 2g (added 0g), **Protein** 2g, **Fiber** 3g, **Sodium** 30mg, **Potassium** 296mg.

BONUS Detoxify with kale in your salad or smoothie. These power greens supply indole-3 carbinol, a compound found in certain cruciferous vegetables that helps cleanse and rid your body of carcinogens, drugs and toxins.

How to prep

1. Wash kale in cool water to remove sand and grit.

2. Slice along each side of the stem or hold onto it and pull off the leaves.

3. Chop or tear leaves to desired size.

▼ *Tuscan Kale (aka Dinosaur, Lacinato)*
The bubbly surface on these dark green, glossy leaves mostly disappears when cooked. It has a milder flavor than curly kale.

▲ *Curly Kale*
This variety, with frilly-edged, dusky green leaves is the most common kale at the supermarket.

◄ *Curly Red Kale*
There are two common kale varieties that have a splash of red in their veins—curly red (shown above) and Russian Red, whose leaves are shaped like large oak leaves.

───── ≈ ─────

Flax Power

Flaxseed delivers more heart-healthy alpha-linolenic acid (ALA) than any other plant source—but the seeds have to be ground in order for the body to reap the benefits. Look for ground flaxseeds (or flaxmeal) in the natural-foods section of supermarkets or in natural-foods stores. Store in the refrigerator or freezer. Or grind fresh from whole seeds in a clean coffee grinder or food processor. Blend into a smoothie or sprinkle over yogurt, cereal and salad.

───── ≈ ─────

GREEN SMOOTHIE

ACTIVE: 10 MIN **TOTAL:** 10 MIN

Get your daily dose of dark leafy greens any time of day with this delicious green smoothie. Ground flaxseed adds omega-3s. Pour any extra into a freezer-pop mold and have it later as a frozen green smoothie pop.

 2 ripe medium bananas
 1 ripe pear *or* apple, peeled if desired, chopped
 2 cups chopped kale leaves, tough stems removed
 ½ cup cold orange juice
 ½ cup cold water
 12 ice cubes
 1 tablespoon ground flaxseed *(see Tip)*

Place bananas, pear (or apple), kale, orange juice, water, ice cubes and flaxseed in a blender. Pulse a few times, then puree until smooth, scraping down the sides as necessary.

SERVES 2: ABOUT 1¾ CUPS EACH

Calories 238, **Fat** 3g (sat 0g), **Cholesterol** 0mg, **Carbs** 54g, **Total sugars** 28g (added 0g), **Protein** 6g, **Fiber** 8g, **Sodium** 35mg, **Potassium** 1,014mg.
Nutrition bonus: Vitamin C (209% daily value), Vitamin A (138% dv), Potassium (29% dv), Magnesium (24% dv).

KALE CHIPS

ACTIVE: 25 MIN **TOTAL:** 25 MIN
TO MAKE AHEAD: Store in an airtight container at room temperature up to 2 days.

Not a fan of kale? These crispy baked kale chips will convert you! For the best result, allow the greens plenty of space in the pans.

> 1 large bunch kale, tough stems removed, leaves torn into pieces (about 16 cups)
> 1 tablespoon extra-virgin olive oil
> ¼ teaspoon salt

1. Position racks in upper third and center of oven; preheat to 400°F.

2. If kale is wet, very thoroughly pat dry with a clean kitchen towel; transfer to a large bowl. Drizzle the kale with oil and sprinkle with salt. Using your hands, massage the oil and salt onto the kale leaves to evenly coat. Fill 2 large rimmed baking sheets with a layer of kale, making sure the leaves don't overlap. (If all the kale won't fit, make the chips in batches.)

3. Bake until most leaves are crisp, rotating the pans back to front and top to bottom halfway through, 8 to 12 minutes total. (If baking a batch on just one sheet, start checking after 8 minutes to prevent burning.)

SERVES 4: ABOUT 2 CUPS EACH

Calories 110, **Fat** 5g (sat 1g), **Cholesterol** 0mg, **Carbs** 16g, **Total sugars** 4g (added 0g), **Protein** 5g, **Fiber** 6g, **Sodium** 210mg, **Potassium** 642mg.
Nutrition bonus: Vitamin A (767% daily value), Vitamin C (192% dv), Calcium (20% dv).

Flavored Chips

Add flavor to kale chips by tossing with a hit of cayenne pepper, black pepper, smoked paprika or onion, garlic or chili powder. Or substitute toasted sesame oil for the olive oil.

MASSAGED KALE SALAD WITH ROASTED GARLIC DRESSING

ACTIVE: 20 MIN **TOTAL:** 1 HR

Using a whole head of sweet roasted garlic creates an irresistible dressing that gets "massaged" into raw leaves of kale. Roasting the garlic ahead of time cuts preparation time in half. This salad is a good match for pizza.

  1 head garlic
2½ tablespoons extra-virgin olive oil, divided
  1 large red onion, thinly sliced
     Pinch of salt
  1 tablespoon reduced-sodium soy sauce
  2 tablespoons lemon juice
  8 kale leaves, chopped (about 1 small bunch)

1. Position a rack in the upper third of oven; preheat to 400°F.

2. Rub off excess papery skin from garlic head without separating the cloves. Slice the tip off the head, exposing the cloves. Place the head on a piece of foil, drizzle with ½ tablespoon oil and wrap into a package. Place the package on the upper rack and roast until the garlic is very soft, 40 to 50 minutes. (It's OK if the garlic starts roasting as the oven preheats.)

3. Meanwhile, toss onion in a bowl with 1 tablespoon oil and salt. Spread on a large baking sheet. Place on the upper rack alongside garlic and roast, stirring once halfway through, until golden brown, about 15 minutes. Let the garlic and onion cool for 5 minutes.

4. Gently squeeze cloves from garlic head into a large bowl (discard skins). Whisk in soy sauce, lemon juice and the remaining 1 tablespoon oil until combined. Add kale and, with clean hands, firmly squeeze the ingredients together until the leaves break down and the volume has been reduced by about half. Add onion and toss to coat.

SERVES 4: 1 CUP EACH

Calories 142, **Fat** 9g (sat 1g), **Cholesterol** 0mg, **Carbs** 13g, **Total sugars** 2g (added 0g), **Protein** 4g, **Fiber** 2g, **Sodium** 198mg, **Potassium** 429mg.
Nutrition bonus: Vitamin C (147% daily value), Vitamin A (134% dv).

Massaging Kale

Mellow sturdy greens, such as kale, with the power of massage. A few minutes of judicious massaging not only tenderizes them but also softens the bitter edge. The process breaks down cell walls, releasing enzymes that split apart bitter-tasting compounds.

KALE SALAD WITH BACON-BLUE CHEESE VINAIGRETTE

ACTIVE: 30 MIN **TOTAL:** 30 MIN

Hot roasted potatoes wilt the kale in this salad just enough to tenderize the kale, then bacon and blue cheese layer on smoke and salt to stand up to the flavor. Go for a big-flavored blue here—we enjoy the tanginess of Maytag. Serve with steak or chicken.

- 1 pound Yukon Gold potatoes, scrubbed, cut into 1-inch chunks
- 3 tablespoons extra-virgin olive oil, divided
- ½ teaspoon dried thyme
- ½ teaspoon salt, divided
- ½ teaspoon ground pepper, divided
- 6 cups kale, stems removed, torn into bite-size pieces
- 3 tablespoons cider vinegar
- 3 tablespoons crumbled blue cheese
- 2 tablespoons minced shallot
- 1 tablespoon honey mustard
- 1 tablespoon minced fresh parsley
- 3 pieces center-cut bacon, cooked and crumbled
- 2 Belgian endives, cored and sliced
- ¼ cup currants *or* sweetened dried cranberries

1. Preheat oven to 400°F.

2. Toss potatoes, 1 tablespoon oil, thyme and ¼ teaspoon each salt and pepper in a large bowl. Spread on a large baking sheet. Roast the potatoes, stirring once or twice, until tender and browned, 15 to 20 minutes.

3. Place kale in the large bowl, add the hot potatoes and let stand for several minutes, tossing occasionally, until the potatoes are warm but not hot.

4. Meanwhile, whisk the remaining 2 tablespoons oil, vinegar, blue cheese, shallot, mustard, parsley and the remaining ¼ teaspoon salt and pepper in a small bowl. Drizzle the dressing over the warm salad. Add bacon, endive and currants (or cranberries); toss to combine. Serve immediately.

SERVES 6: ABOUT 1⅓ CUPS EACH

Calories 214, **Fat** 11g (sat 2g), **Cholesterol** 7mg, **Carbs** 26g, **Total sugars** 6g (added 1g), **Protein** 7g, **Fiber** 4g, **Sodium** 376mg, **Potassium** 881mg.
Nutrition bonus: Vitamin C (151% daily value), Vitamin A (150% dv), Potassium (25% dv), Folate (21% dv).

Mashing Beans

When mashing beans—as is done to thicken this soup— you can add a bit of broth to make the mashing easier.

RIBOLLITA SOUP

ACTIVE: 1 HR **TOTAL:** 1¼ HRS

Ribollita, a hearty Tuscan soup, uses day-old bread to add body. This version uses a bean mash, which keeps the soup gluten-free and adds fiber.

1 14-ounce can whole peeled plum tomatoes

2 15-ounce cans cannellini beans, rinsed, divided *(see Tip, page 183)*

3 tablespoons extra-virgin olive oil, divided

1 medium leek, halved lengthwise and sliced *(see page 336)*, white and light green parts only

¼ cup thinly sliced garlic

½ teaspoon ground pepper, divided

1 cup diced carrots

1 cup diced celery

1 cup diced zucchini

¼ teaspoon salt, divided

1 bunch kale *or* chard, tough stems removed and cut into 2-inch-wide slices

¼ head Savoy *or* green cabbage, cut into 1-inch cubes

2 cups diced russet potatoes

3 cups vegetable broth

2 cups water

½ teaspoon dried thyme

1 bay leaf

⅛ teaspoon celery seeds

Crushed red pepper to taste

1. Drain the tomatoes, reserving the liquid. Dice the tomatoes. Using a potato masher, mash half the beans into a paste. Set the tomatoes and beans aside.

2. Heat 2 tablespoons oil in a large pot over medium heat. Add leek and garlic; cook, stirring, until tender, 2 to 3 minutes. Do not brown. Season with ⅛ teaspoon pepper. Stir in carrots, celery, zucchini and the remaining 1 tablespoon oil; cook, stirring, until the vegetables are nearly tender, 3 to 5 minutes. Season with ⅛ teaspoon each salt and pepper.

3. Stir in kale and cabbage. Cover and cook, stirring occasionally, until wilted, 4 to 6 minutes. Add potatoes, broth, water, tomatoes and juice, the bean puree and whole beans, thyme and bay leaf. Bring to a simmer over medium heat. Season with celery seeds, crushed red pepper and the remaining ¼ teaspoon pepper and ⅛ teaspoon salt. Cover and cook, stirring occasionally and reducing the heat to maintain a gentle simmer, until all the vegetables are tender, 15 to 20 minutes.

SERVES 8: ABOUT 1¾ CUPS EACH

Calories 198, **Fat** 6g (sat 1g), **Cholesterol** 0mg, **Carbs** 33g, **Total sugars** 5g (added 0g), **Protein** 8g, **Fiber** 9g, **Sodium** 551mg, **Potassium** 574mg.
Nutrition bonus: Vitamin A (112% daily value), Vitamin C (84% dv).

Kohlrabi

This tentacled orb can confound even the most experimental cook. With its Sputnik-like appearance and exotic name, surely no vegetable prompts the question, "What the heck do I do with it?" more often than kohlrabi. The answer to that question, fortunately, is all kinds of delicious things.

Kohlrabi looks a bit like a turnip growing above ground, with leaf-topped stalks protruding from the bulb (often cut off by the time they reach the market), which is actually a swollen stem. The skin can be either white, pale green or purple—but the crisp flesh inside is always creamy white.

Skin color has no bearing on the flavor, which is similar to that of a broccoli stem—yet delicately peppery and a little sweet. Kohlrabi can be eaten raw or cooked. Kohlrabi is popular in Eastern Europe and Germany, where it is often prepared steamed and topped with a nutmeg-spiced white sauce. Although its name is derived from the German names for cabbage *kohl* and turnip *rübe*, it is not a cross between the two—though it is a member of the brassica family. It is also popular in China and India, where it is cooked in curries or pickled with salt, turmeric, dry mustard, vinegar and oil.

Use a mandoline to cut paper-thin slices and dress with good olive oil, a squeeze of lemon and a sprinkle of sea salt. Or top raw slices with a sharp cheese, such as blue cheese or goat cheese, and serve as an appetizer. Shred and sauté in butter with curry powder, boil and top with sour cream and fresh dill or mash like potatoes.

Kohlrabi planted in early spring takes 45 to 60 days to mature to perfect eating size and is most abundant through the summer into early fall.

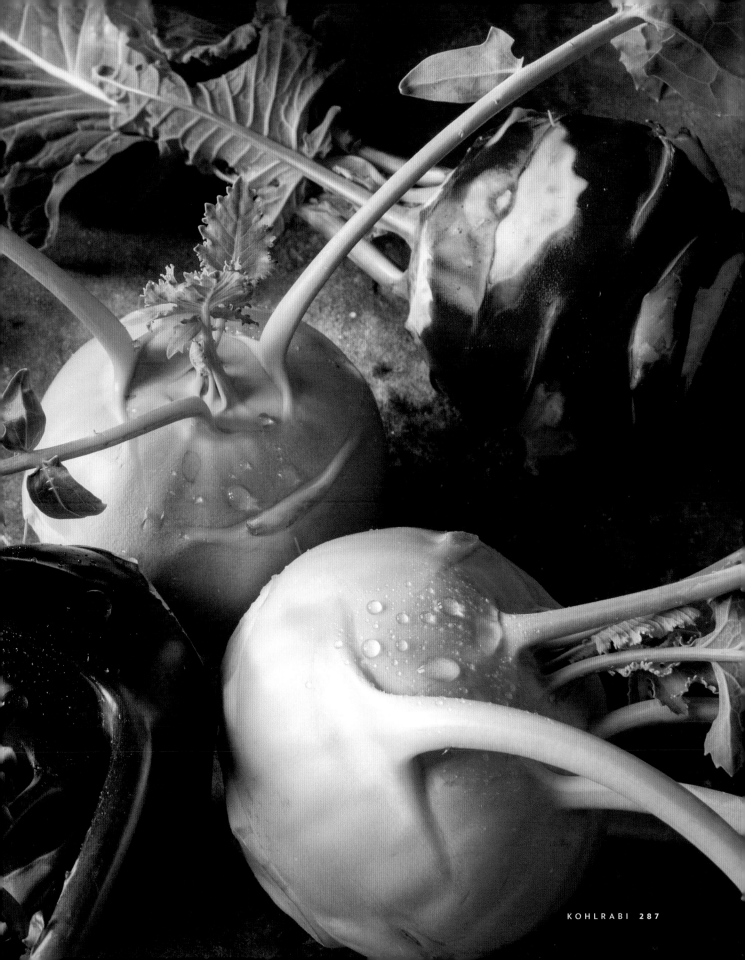

Best in summer and early fall

AT THE MARKET

❧ Choose kohlrabi that are 2 to 3 inches in diameter for the most tender texture—and make sure they are round, not elongated. (As the stems stretch as they grow, they tend to get woody.) Choose kohlrabi that feel heavy for their size. If the leaves are still attached, they should look fresh, not wilted. Avoid kohlrabi with cracks, cuts or shriveling.

IN YOUR KITCHEN

❧ Store kohlrabi in a plastic bag in the refrigerator up to 1 week.

❧ Cut off the stalks, if present, and peel the fibrous skin with a vegetable peeler or paring knife. Rinse in cool water.

❧ The smaller, newer leaves of kohlrabi are edible. Trim the ends and rinse in cool water. Pat or spin dry. (Cook as you would spinach or beet greens.)

COOKING BASICS

GRILL Cut 3 medium peeled kohlrabi into ½-inch slices. Bring 1 inch of water to a boil in a large saucepan fitted with a steamer basket. Add kohlrabi. Cover and steam until tender-crisp, 5 to 6 minutes. Stir together 2 tablespoons each olive oil, minced garlic and balsamic vinegar. Dip each slice of kohlrabi in the mixture, turning to coat. Season lightly with salt and pepper to taste. Grill over medium heat until tender and lightly charred, about 2 minutes per side. If desired, sprinkle with finely grated Parmesan cheese. Serves 2.

ROAST Cut 3 medium peeled kohlrabi into ½-inch cubes. Toss with 1 tablespoon olive oil, ¼ teaspoon salt and pepper to taste. Roast at 450°F in a single layer on a rimmed baking sheet until golden brown and tender when pierced with a fork, about 30 minutes, stirring every 10 minutes. Serves 2.

SAUTÉ Cut 3 medium peeled kohlrabi into ¼-inch cubes. Heat 1 tablespoon olive oil in a medium nonstick skillet over medium heat. Add kohlrabi and cook, stirring frequently, until light golden, about 5 minutes. Add 1 minced shallot and cook until the kohlrabi is tender, about 5 minutes more. Season with ¼ teaspoon salt and pepper to taste. Stir in 2 tablespoons minced fresh herbs, such as parsley and/or chives. Serves 2.

NUTRITION

❧ **1 cup of diced raw kohlrabi: Calories** 36, **Fat** 0g (sat 0g), **Cholesterol** 0mg, **Carbs** 8g, **Total sugars** 4g (added 0g), **Protein** 2g, **Fiber** 5g, **Sodium** 27mg, **Potassium** 472mg.

BONUS Kohlrabi is smart food for your smile. One cup of raw kohlrabi serves up nearly one and a half times the daily value for vitamin C, a nutrient that keeps gums healthy. It's also plentiful in fiber, which works like nature's toothbrush to scrub teeth and reduce the risk of gum disease.

CIDER & HONEY KOHLRABI SLAW WITH RADICCHIO

ACTIVE: 15 MIN **TOTAL:** 15 MIN
TO MAKE AHEAD: Refrigerate up to 2 hours; top with sunflower seeds just before serving.

This crunchy confetti-color slaw is an exceptionally good accompaniment to grilled chicken and pork chops.

¼ cup cider vinegar

3 tablespoons honey

1 teaspoon Dijon mustard

½ teaspoon celery seeds

½ teaspoon salt

½ teaspoon ground pepper

3 tablespoons extra-virgin olive oil

2 medium kohlrabi (about 1¼ pounds), peeled

2 medium carrots

1 small head radicchio

¼ cup roasted unsalted sunflower seeds

1. Whisk vinegar, honey, mustard, celery seeds, salt and pepper in a large bowl. Slowly whisk in oil until combined.

2. Use a box grater or a food processor fitted with a shredding disk to coarsely shred kohlrabi and carrots. Cut radicchio in half lengthwise, core and thinly slice. Add the vegetables to the bowl and toss well to combine.

3. Sprinkle with sunflower seeds.

SERVES 8: ¾ CUP EACH

Calories 118, **Fat** 7g (sat 1g), **Cholesterol** 0mg, **Carbs** 12g, **Total sugars** 8g (added 6g), **Protein** 2g, **Fiber** 2g, **Sodium** 181mg, **Potassium** 278mg.
Nutrition bonus: Vitamin C (104% daily value), Vitamin A (103% dv).

Keep It Crunchy

Add toasted nuts or seeds to salads right before serving so they stay delightfully crunchy.

KOHLRABI-CORN FRITTERS WITH HERBED YOGURT SAUCE

ACTIVE: 40 MIN **TOTAL:** 40 MIN

We call for Madras curry powder in these crisp fritters because it's moderately spicy. If you'd like more heat, look for hot Madras curry.

1 large kohlrabi (about 1 pound), peeled

2 eggs, lightly beaten

½ cup corn kernels, fresh *or* frozen (thawed)

1 scallion, finely chopped

3 tablespoons all-purpose flour

3 tablespoons chopped fresh basil, divided

1 teaspoon Madras curry powder

½ teaspoon baking powder

½ teaspoon salt plus a pinch, divided

Pinch of cayenne pepper (optional)

3 tablespoons extra-virgin olive oil, divided

¾ cup nonfat Greek yogurt

1 tablespoon chopped fresh cilantro

1. Preheat oven to 300°F.

2. Coarsely shred kohlrabi in a food processor fitted with a shredding disk or through the large holes of a box grater. (You should have about 3 cups shredded.) Place on a clean kitchen towel, gather up the edges and squeeze out as much liquid as possible. Combine eggs, corn, scallion, flour, 2 tablespoons basil, curry powder, baking powder, ½ teaspoon salt and cayenne (if using) in a large bowl; add the kohlrabi and stir just until combined.

3. Heat 1 tablespoon oil in a large nonstick skillet over medium-high heat. Using a scant ¼ cup batter for each fritter, drop 4 fritters into the pan and flatten with a spatula into 2½-inch patties. Cook until golden brown, 2 to 3 minutes per side. Transfer to a baking sheet to keep warm in the oven. Reduce heat to medium and cook the remaining batter in 2 batches, using 1 tablespoon oil per batch.

4. Meanwhile, combine yogurt, cilantro, the remaining 1 tablespoon basil and the remaining pinch of salt in a small bowl. Serve the fritters with the herbed yogurt.

SERVES 6: 2 FRITTERS & 1 TBSP. SAUCE EACH

Calories 140, **Fat** 9g (sat 2g), **Cholesterol** 63mg, **Carbs** 9g, **Total sugars** 3g (added 0g), **Protein** 7g, **Fiber** 2g, **Sodium** 302mg, **Potassium** 237mg.
Nutrition bonus: Vitamin C (39% daily value).

Lettuces & Salad Greens

A big green salad is the little black dress of the culinary world. It suits nearly any occasion, can be simple or sophisticated, dressed up or down. The foundation of most salads is a broad spectrum of lettuces and salad greens—and there is a distinction between the two. Lettuces are a subset of salad greens.

Lettuces are categorized by growing form—in heads of varying shapes and sizes. The three main types are crisphead, butterhead, and loose-leaf. Crisphead lettuces, iceberg the most familiar, grow in very tightly clasped round heads. Romaine lettuce grows in elongated heads. Each leaf has a substantial rib running along the center. Loose round rosettes of tender butterhead leaves take well to light dressings, such as a simple shallot-mustard vinaigrette. Mildly flavored loose-leaf lettuces grow in open layers in very loosely formed heads and often have ruffly leaves. Common loose-leaf lettuces are red and green oakleaf.

Salad greens comprise a larger group of leafy vegetables—some of which are covered in this book in chapters of their own, such as arugula, watercress and the chicories. (Here we touch on a few salad greens not addressed elsewhere.)

Salads can be made all or primarily from one type of lettuce—the crunchy romaine in a Caesar salad, for instance—or from a colorful mélange of lettuces and salad greens, each of which contributes texture and flavor for a perfectly balanced salad.

Lettuces and salad greens thrive in cool weather and are at their best in spring and fall.

Best in spring and fall

AT THE MARKET

❧ Choose dense, heavy head lettuces with bright color and no browning on the outer leaves. Choose loose-leaf lettuces that have crisp leaves with no signs of wilting. Salad greens should have good color with no yellowing, wilting or brown spots.

IN YOUR KITCHEN

❧ Store lettuces in a plastic bag in the crisper in the refrigerator. Crisphead and romaine lettuces can be stored up to 1 week. More delicate butterhead and loose-leaf lettuces can be stored up to 5 days. Store loose salad greens in a plastic bag wrapped in a paper towel in the crisper in the refrigerator up to 3 days.

❧ Separate the leaves of head lettuces and loose-leaf lettuces. Rinse leaves in cool water and spin dry in a salad spinner or dry on paper towels.

COOKING BASICS

BUTTERMILK RANCH DRESSING Whisk ½ cup buttermilk, ¼ cup reduced-fat mayonnaise, 2 tablespoons champagne or white-wine vinegar, ½ teaspoon granulated garlic and ½ teaspoon each salt and pepper in a small bowl until smooth. Stir in ⅓ cup chopped fresh herbs, such as chives, tarragon, basil or dill. Makes 1 cup. Use 1 tablespoon dressing for every 1 cup of salad.

GARLIC-DIJON VINAIGRETTE Combine ½ cup olive oil, ½ cup lemon juice, ½ cup red-wine vinegar, ¼ cup Dijon mustard and 4 cloves of peeled and minced garlic in a blender, a jar with a tight-fitting lid or a medium bowl. Blend, shake, or whisk until smooth. Season with ½ teaspoon salt and pepper to taste. Makes 1¾ cups.

HOISIN-SESAME DRESSING Place ⅓ cup canola oil, 3 tablespoons rice vinegar, 2 tablespoons hoisin sauce, 1 tablespoon toasted sesame oil, 1 tablespoon toasted sesame seeds and 1 minced scallion in a bowl or jar with a tight-fitting lid; whisk or shake until well combined. Makes ¾ cup.

NUTRITION

❧ **2 cups of shredded romaine lettuce:** Calories 16, **Fat** 0g (sat 0g), **Cholesterol** 0mg, **Carbs** 3g, **Total sugars** 1g (added 0g), **Protein** 1g, **Fiber** 2g, **Sodium** 8mg, **Potassium** 232mg.

BONUS Lettuce is an outstanding source of vitamin K, a nutrient that may help keep bones strong. Just 1 cup of iceberg or romaine gives you 22 to 60 percent, respectively, of your day's worth of K.

Grow Your Own

Lettuces and salad greens are perhaps the easiest of all vegetables to grow. Picking a beautiful salad from your backyard minutes before a meal is deeply satisfying. Start head lettuces indoors 6 weeks before the last frost date and transplant outdoors 3 weeks before the last frost date. Sow other types of lettuces and salad greens directly in the soil in early spring or fall. Choose a site with loose, well-drained soil, enriched with compost, in sun to part shade. Keep the soil moist, cool and free of weeds. As seedlings grow, thin to 4 to 6 inches apart (eat the young plants as you thin them). Harvest lettuces and salad greens when they reach the desired size. Cut head lettuces about 1 inch above the lowest leaves. As soon as loose-leaf and romaine lettuces are big enough to spare a few leaves, snap off individual leaves from the outer edges of the head. Baby lettuce blends or mesclun can be cut with scissors about 1 inch above the lowest leaves.

▼ Red-Leaf Lettuce
The red-tipped leaves of this loose-leaf lettuce are a variant of green-leaf lettuce. They add a spark of color to salads.

◀ Romaine Lettuce
The crisp, elongated leaves of this lettuce are the main ingredient in classic Caesar salad.

▼ Iceberg Lettuce
Created in the 1940s for its ability to travel long distances, this crunchy lettuce is the base for two salads—the chopped salad and the wedge salad—that are now considered cornerstones of American comfort food.

◀ Butterhead Lettuce
These beautiful rosette-like heads have soft, buttery-textured leaves. Common varieties include Boston, Bibb, and Buttercrunch.

▲ Green-Leaf Lettuce
The ruffly, mild-flavor leaves of this loose-leaf lettuce are good for both salads and layering on sandwiches.

▼ Dandelion Greens
The leaves of this common "weed" contribute pleasant bitterness to salads. Some varieties have leaves with smooth edges—others are jagged. Puntarelle, a type of chicory (see page 191), has a similar taste and appearance.

▲ Mesclun
This mix of tender young greens can include leafy lettuces, arugula, frisée, spinach, chard, dandelion, mustard, radicchio and mâche, and soft-stemmed herbs such as parsley, dill and chervil.

▶ Mâche
These tiny leaves—also called lamb's lettuce or corn salad—have a nutty flavor and delicate texture.

GREEN SALAD WITH PEACHES, FETA & MINT VINAIGRETTE

ACTIVE: 30 MIN **TOTAL:** 30 MIN

This recipe follows an essential formula for superb salads: Toss greens with fruit, nuts and cheese. Later in the summer, melons are a good alternative to the stone fruit.

MINT VINAIGRETTE

- ¼ cup chopped fresh mint
- 3 tablespoons lemon juice
- ⅓ cup extra-virgin olive oil
- 2 tablespoons red-wine vinegar
- 1 teaspoon honey
- ½ teaspoon kosher salt

SALAD

- 12 cups bitter greens, such as arugula, mizuna *and/or* watercress, tough ends trimmed
- ½ cup packed slivered fresh mint
- ¼ teaspoon kosher salt
- 6 ripe peaches *or* nectarines, sliced
- ⅓ cup sliced *or* slivered almonds, toasted
- ¾ cup crumbled feta *or* goat cheese (about 3 ounces)

1. To prepare vinaigrette: Combine chopped mint and lemon juice in a small saucepan. Bring to a boil and remove from heat. Let steep about 10 minutes. Strain into a large bowl, pressing on the leaves to extract all the liquid. (You should have about 3 tablespoons liquid after straining.) Add oil, vinegar, honey and ½ teaspoon salt; whisk until well combined.

2. To prepare salad: Add greens and slivered mint to the bowl with the vinaigrette and sprinkle with salt. Add peaches (or nectarines) and almonds; gently toss to combine. Serve the salad topped with feta (or goat cheese).

SERVES 6: ABOUT 1½ CUPS EACH

Calories 270, **Fat** 19g (sat 4g), **Cholesterol** 13mg, **Carbs** 22g, **Total sugars** 15g (added 1g), **Protein** 7g, **Fiber** 6g, **Sodium** 329mg, **Potassium** 730mg.
Nutrition bonus: Vitamin A (77% daily value), Vitamin C (53% dv), Folate (38% dv), Potassium (21% dv).

A Balanced Salad

Bitter greens such as those called for in this salad—arugula, mizuna and watercress—are a foil to the sweetness of the fruit and the salty tang of the feta cheese.

ROMAINE WEDGES WITH SARDINES & CARAMELIZED ONIONS

ACTIVE: 30 MIN **TOTAL:** 30 MIN
TO MAKE AHEAD: Refrigerate the dressing (Step 2) up to 2 days.

This crunchy knife-and-fork salad features romaine-lettuce boats filled with savory sardines, sweet caramelized onions and juicy cherry tomatoes all drizzled with a creamy dressing.

Good-for-You Sardines

Wild-caught sardines from the Pacific are one of the most healthful foods we can consume, from both a nutritional and environmental standpoint. A 2-ounce serving provides 22 percent of the daily value for calcium and 157mg omega-3s—more per serving than tuna, salmon or just about any other food—plus they're packed with vitamin D. And it just so happens that their rich meaty flavor is the perfect foil to crisp and crunchy greens.

1 tablespoon canola oil
1 large sweet onion, sliced
⅛ teaspoon salt plus ½ teaspoon, divided
2 tablespoons balsamic vinegar
½ cup reduced-fat plain Greek yogurt
2 tablespoons low-fat mayonnaise
2 tablespoons white-wine vinegar
4 teaspoons minced shallot
¼ teaspoon ground pepper
2 hearts of romaine, halved lengthwise and cored
2 4-ounce cans sardines with bones, packed in olive oil, drained
1 cup halved grape *or* cherry tomatoes

1. Place oil, onion and ⅛ teaspoon salt in a small saucepan over medium heat. Cover and cook, stirring occasionally, until the onion is very soft and starting to brown, 12 to 15 minutes. Reduce heat to medium-low if they brown too quickly. Stir in balsamic vinegar and simmer, uncovered, until it is reduced to a glaze, 1 to 3 minutes.

2. Whisk yogurt, mayonnaise, white-wine vinegar, shallot, pepper and the remaining ½ teaspoon salt in a small bowl.

3. Divide romaine halves among 4 dinner plates or place on a large platter. Spoon the dressing over the salads. Break sardines into two or three pieces each and divide among the romaine halves. Top with the caramelized onions and tomatoes.

SERVES 4: 1 WEDGE EACH

Calories 202, **Fat** 10g (sat 2g), **Cholesterol** 60mg, **Carbs** 13g, **Total sugars** 7g (added 0g), **Protein** 14g, **Fiber** 3g, **Sodium** 648mg, **Potassium** 598mg.
Nutrition bonus: Vitamin A (201% daily value), Vitamin B$_{12}$ (59% dv), Folate (42% dv), Calcium (22% dv), Vitamin C (21% dv).

CHIMICHURRI GRILLED STEAK SALAD

ACTIVE: 1 HR **TOTAL:** 1 HR (PLUS MARINATING TIME)
TO MAKE AHEAD: Prepare through Step 1 up to 1 day ahead.

Chimichurri is a zingy Argentinean sauce made with garlic, parsley, vinegar and oil. Here it doubles as marinade for flank steak and as salad dressing.

1 cup packed flat-leaf parsley leaves	1 pound flank steak, trimmed
5 tablespoons extra-virgin olive oil, divided	2 hearts of romaine *or* 2 small heads
¼ cup white vinegar	1 large bell pepper, quartered
1 small clove garlic, chopped	1 small red onion, sliced ½ inch thick
¾ teaspoon salt, divided	

1. Puree parsley, 1 tablespoon oil, vinegar, garlic and ¼ teaspoon salt in a blender. Pat 1 tablespoon of the mixture on each side of steak. Put the steak on a plate, cover and refrigerate at least 1 hour and up to 24 hours. Add 3 tablespoons oil to the herb mixture remaining in the blender; pulse to blend. Transfer to a bowl, cover and refrigerate if not using right away.

2. Twenty minutes before you are ready to grill, preheat grill to medium-high.

3. Cut each heart (or head) of romaine in half lengthwise, leaving the root end intact. Brush lettuce, bell pepper and onion with the remaining 1 tablespoon oil. Sprinkle with ¼ teaspoon salt. Sprinkle the steak with remaining ¼ teaspoon salt. Let the dressing come to room temperature if necessary while you grill.

4. Oil the grill rack *(see Tip)*. Put steak, lettuce, bell pepper and onion on the grill, placing the steak on the hottest part. Grill the steak, turning once, until desired doneness, 6 to 8 minutes per side for medium. Grill the pepper and onion, turning occasionally, until charred and tender, about 10 minutes total. Grill the lettuce, turning once, until lightly charred, about 2 minutes per side.

5. Let the steak rest on a clean cutting board for 5 minutes, then thinly slice against the grain. Chop the bell pepper and onion. Divide the lettuce, steak, pepper and onion among 4 plates. Drizzle with the reserved dressing.

SERVES 4

Calories 363, **Fat** 24g (sat 5g), **Cholesterol** 70mg, **Carbs** 9g, **Total sugars** 4g (added 0g), **Protein** 27g, **Fiber** 4g, **Sodium** 518mg, **Potassium** 864mg.
Nutrition bonus: Vitamin A (249% daily value), Vitamin C (131% dv), Folate (54% dv), Zinc (34% dv), Potassium (25% dv), Iron (22% dv), Vitamin B$_{12}$ (20% dv).

Oiling the Grill

Oiling a grill rack before you grill foods helps ensure that the food won't stick. Oil a folded paper towel, hold it with tongs and rub it over the rack. (Do not use cooking spray on a hot grill.) When grilling delicate foods such as tofu and fish, it is helpful to coat the food with cooking spray.

DANDELION SALAD WITH GOAT CHEESE & TOMATO DRESSING

ACTIVE: 35 MIN **TOTAL:** 1 HR 10 MIN
TO MAKE AHEAD: Refrigerate the dressing (Step 1) up to 3 days.

Cultivated dandelion greens are a bit milder than their wild cousins, but they still have some bite. Their peppery nature blends beautifully with sweet baby spinach and the salty-savory flavors of bacon and cheese in this salad.

Foraging for Dandelion Greens

Although it might be tempting to pick the dandelion greens that proliferate in abundance in parks and by roads, train tracks or telephone poles, they may not be fit for consumption. If you can't gather enough greens from your own (pesticide-free) yard, buy bunches of dandelion greens at the market.

DRESSING

- ¼ cup crumbled goat cheese
- 2 tablespoons white-wine vinegar
- 2 teaspoons maple syrup
- ¼ cup extra-virgin olive oil
- 2 plum tomatoes, seeded and chopped
- ½ teaspoon salt
  Ground pepper to taste
- 1 tablespoon chopped fresh tarragon

SALAD

- 8 ounces orecchiette *or* small pasta shells, preferably whole-wheat
- 2 slices bacon
- 1 tablespoon extra-virgin olive oil
- 1 medium red onion, thinly sliced
- 2 cups dandelion greens *or* arugula, any tough stems removed
- 2 cups baby spinach
- ¼ cup grated Parmesan cheese

1. To prepare dressing: Combine goat cheese, vinegar and maple syrup in a blender or food processor and blend until combined. Add ¼ cup oil and tomatoes and blend until smooth. Season with salt and pepper. Stir in tarragon.

2. To prepare salad: Bring a large saucepan of water to a boil. Add pasta and cook according to package directions. Drain, rinse with cold water and set aside.

3. Cook bacon in a large skillet over medium heat until crisp, about 4 minutes. Drain on a paper towel. Crumble when cool. Wipe out the pan. Add 1 tablespoon oil and onion and cook, stirring, over medium heat until soft, about 5 minutes. Let cool.

4. Toss bacon and onion in a large bowl with dandelion greens, spinach, Parmesan and ½ cup dressing. Drizzle more dressing over each serving, if desired. (Cover and refrigerate the remaining ½ cup dressing up to 3 days.)

SERVES 4: ABOUT 2 CUPS EACH

Calories 377, **Fat** 16g (sat 4g), **Cholesterol** 11mg, **Carbs** 49g, **Total sugars** 4g (added 1g), **Protein** 14g, **Fiber** 6g, **Sodium** 340mg, **Potassium** 374mg.
Nutrition bonus: Vitamin A (89% daily value), Vitamin C (30% dv).

▼ *White Button*

▲ *Portobello*

▲ *Oyster*

◄ *Shiitake*

► *Dried Morels*

Mushrooms

Meaty mushrooms are an anomaly. Unlike all other foods eaten as vegetables, they are not plants. Because they lack the chlorophyll necessary to create their own food, the sun doesn't do them much good. Mushrooms—members of the Kingdom of Fungi—flourish in cool, dim, damp places.

Although delicious sautéed in olive oil and garlic or sprinkled on top of a pizza, their primary purpose in the wild is to break down and recycle plant material. Mushrooms are the fruit—the reproductive organs—of a fungus, an organism that grows mostly underground. As an apple carries seeds, each mushroom carries millions of spores.

While the most common cultivated mushroom is the white button, the array of mushrooms that grow in the wild is vast and impossible to quantify.

Mushrooms are both regional and seasonal. Foraging is a favorite activity in spring and fall—when most seasonally specific types of mushrooms spring up in the woods, usually at the base of trees or on decomposing wood. (Never eat a mushroom that has not been identified by an expert.)

The spring arrival of distinctively scrolled morels —with their nutty flavor and chewy texture—to the woods of the Midwest and East creates excitement among those in the know. If you accompany a forager, you will be sworn to secrecy as to the location of the patch.

Porcini ("the piglets" in Italian) rule the fall. This mushroom, in its most common market form, is dried, which intensifies its extraordinarily rich flavor and aroma. Revel in it in risotto, stews, and braises.

Cultivated mushrooms such as white button, cremini, large and meaty portobello and fragrant and flavorful shiitake are available all year. Specific varieties of wild mushrooms are available during spring, summer and fall.

◄ *Cremini*

▲ *Trumpet Royale*

◄ *Hen of the Woods*

◄ *Chanterelle*

Best in spring and fall

AT THE MARKET

❧ Choose mushrooms that have firm, fresh-looking flesh. They should be moist but not slimy—and not dry. Avoid mushrooms with blemishes, spots or splits. They should smell earthy and have tight gills.

IN YOUR KITCHEN

❧ Store fresh mushrooms in a paper bag or loosely covered container in the refrigerator and use within 1 or 2 days. Remove the plastic wrap from packaged button mushrooms and wrap the container with clean paper towels; store in the refrigerator for 1 to 2 days.

❧ Store dried mushrooms in a cool, dark place up to 1 year.

❧ Clean mushrooms right before you use them. Wipe with a damp paper towel—or use a mushroom brush—to remove any loose dirt. You can also rinse them briefly under cool running water. (This must be done to morels.) Pat dry with paper towels and use immediately.

❧ Trim and discard the ends of soft stems—then slice or chop the mushroom. Shiitakes have inedible woody stems. Cut or snip the stems where they meet the mushroom cap and discard the stems.

❧ Removing the gills is optional. Because the dark gills on portobellos can turn foods with which they are combined black, you may opt to scrape them out with a spoon.

❧ Soak dried mushrooms in hot water to cover for 20 to 30 minutes until softened. Remove mushrooms from water with your fingers or a spoon and rinse in a strainer under cool running water to wash away any remaining sand and grit. Strain liquid through a paper towel, coffee filter or cheesecloth to remove grit. Use the liquid to add flavor to soups, sauces and braising liquids.

COOKING BASICS

GRILL (PORTOBELLOS) Mash 1 garlic clove with ¼ teaspoon salt until it is a smooth paste *(see page 254)*. Mix the paste with 1 tablespoon olive oil. Brush the flavored oil over both sides of 4 portobello mushroom caps. Season with pepper. Grill over medium-high until tender, 4 minutes per side. Drizzle with balsamic vinegar and sprinkle with chopped fresh parsley, basil or dill. Serves 4.

ROAST Combine 2 tablespoons each sesame oil and reduced-sodium soy sauce, 1 tablespoon each grated fresh ginger and minced garlic, 4 teaspoons rice vinegar and pepper to taste in a large bowl. Add 1½ pounds thickly sliced mixed mushrooms (such as shiitake, oyster and white) and 2 bunches scallions cut into 2-inch pieces. Transfer to a roasting pan. Roast in a 450°F oven until browned and cooked through, stirring once or twice, about 25 minutes. Sprinkle with 1 tablespoon toasted sesame seeds. Serves 6.

SAUTÉ Cook 2 slices chopped bacon in a large skillet over medium heat until beginning to brown, about 4 minutes. Add 1½ pounds thinly sliced mixed mushrooms (such as cremini, shiitake and portobello), 2 cloves minced garlic, 1½ teaspoons chopped fresh rosemary, ¼ teaspoon salt and pepper to taste. Cook, stirring occasionally, until almost dry, 8 to 10 minutes. Add ¼ cup dry white wine and cook until most of the liquid has evaporated, 30 seconds to 1 minute. Serves 6.

NUTRITION

❧ **1 cup of sliced raw white mushrooms:** Calories 15, **Fat** 0g (sat 0g), **Cholesterol** 0mg, **Carbs** 2g, **Total sugars** 1g (added 0g), **Protein** 2g, **Fiber** 1g, **Sodium** 4mg, **Potassium** 223mg.

BONUS Fungi are filled with cancer-fighting proteins called lectins. There are as many as 105 lectins believed to wage war on cancer by reducing inflammation, bolstering immunity and reducing its ability to metastasize.

MUSHROOM PÂTÉ

ACTIVE: 25 MIN **TOTAL:** 25 MIN
TO MAKE AHEAD: Refrigerate up to 3 days. Serve at room temperature.

Brown-skinned cremini mushrooms are immature portobellos. They have only a slightly stronger flavor than white button mushrooms. Serve this vegetarian pâté recipe as an appetizer with crackers and pickled onions or try it as a sandwich spread.

　1　teaspoon extra-virgin olive oil plus 2 tablespoons, divided
　¼　cup minced shallots
　1　pound cremini mushrooms (baby bella), coarsely chopped
　2　tablespoons chopped fresh sage, plus more for garnish
　¼　teaspoon salt
　¼　teaspoon ground pepper
　3　tablespoons dry sherry
　½　cup walnuts, toasted *(see Tip, page 92)*
　2　tablespoons nutritional yeast *(see Tip) or* Parmesan cheese

1. Heat 1 teaspoon oil in a large skillet over medium-high heat. Add shallots and cook, stirring, until starting to lightly brown, about 30 seconds. Add mushrooms and cook, stirring frequently, until their liquid is almost evaporated, 4 to 5 minutes. Add sage, salt and pepper and cook, stirring, for 2 minutes more. Add sherry, scraping up any browned bits, and cook until the liquid evaporates, 2 to 3 minutes.

2. Transfer the mixture to a food processor. Add the remaining 2 tablespoons oil, walnuts and nutritional yeast (or Parmesan) and pulse until very finely chopped, about 30 seconds. Serve garnished with sage, if desired.

MAKES: 2 CUPS (2-TBSP. SERVING)

Calories 56, **Fat** 5g (sat 1g), **Cholesterol** 0mg, **Carbs** 3g, **Total sugars** 1g (added 0g), **Protein** 2g, **Fiber** 1g, **Sodium** 39mg, **Potassium** 175mg.

Nutritional Yeast

Nutritional yeast has long been used by vegans as a naturally dairy-free cheese stand-in because of its nutty, earthy, umami qualities. But it now attracts even more fans because of its stellar nutrition profile. Nutritional yeast is not the same as yeast used to make bread—it's heated and dried so it doesn't rise. Two tablespoons of the flakes provides about 3 grams of protein and 2 grams of fiber. Plus, it's a good source of minerals and B vitamins. Look for the golden flakes and powder—they can be used interchangeably—at natural-food stores, in bulk bins or online.

The unique sculptural form and flavor of each type of mushroom imbues them with a bit of mystery. Although there are about 10 million species identified worldwide, biologists agree that there are thousands more yet to be discovered.

Sautéed Mushrooms with Caramelized Shallots
(see recipe, page 310)

Grapeseed Oil

Grapeseed oil contains compounds that preliminary research suggests may have anti-cancer properties. Grapeseed oil also has a high smoke point and, with its mild flavor, is an all-purpose cooking oil. In addition to using it for cooking, try it in a simple raspberry vinaigrette tossed with fresh greens or drizzled over melon wedges.

SAUTÉED MUSHROOMS WITH CARAMELIZED SHALLOTS

ACTIVE: 30 MIN **TOTAL:** 30 MIN
TO MAKE AHEAD: Clean, trim and halve the mushrooms and refrigerate up to 1 day.

You might want to add a splash of excellent vinegar or some freshly grated lemon zest to these mushrooms, but neither is necessary.

  1 tablespoon grapeseed oil *(see Tip)* or canola oil
  1 cup cubed (¼-inch) thick-cut bacon
  1 cup thinly sliced shallots
  8 cups trimmed and halved mixed mushrooms, such as chanterelle, shiitake, oyster, black trumpet *and/or* cremini (1¼-1½ pounds)
  2 tablespoons water
  2 tablespoons thinly sliced fresh sage
  1 tablespoon unsalted butter, at room temperature
  ¼ teaspoon sea salt
  ¼ teaspoon ground pepper

1. Heat oil in a large heavy skillet over medium heat. Add bacon. Cook, stirring occasionally, until beginning to brown, 3 to 5 minutes. Add shallots and cook, stirring occasionally, until softened and browned, 3 to 4 minutes.

2. With a slotted spoon, transfer the bacon and shallots to a plate lined with a paper towel to drain.

3. Remove about half the fat from the pan. Return the pan to medium heat, add mushrooms, cover and cook, stirring once, until the mushrooms release their liquid, 3 to 4 minutes. Uncover and cook until the liquid evaporates, about 1 minute. Add water and scrape up any browned bits.

4. Return the bacon and shallots to the pan and cook about 1 minute. Stir in sage, butter, salt and pepper. Serve warm.

SERVES 8: ABOUT ½ CUP EACH

Calories 86, **Fat** 5g (sat 2g), **Cholesterol** 9mg, **Carbs** 7g, **Total sugars** 2g (added 0g), **Protein** 4g, **Fiber** 1g, **Sodium** 121mg, **Potassium** 474mg.

ARTICHOKE & PARMESAN STUFFED MUSHROOMS

ACTIVE: 25 MIN **TOTAL:** 45 MIN
TO MAKE AHEAD: Prepare through Step 3 up to 2 hours ahead.

For this recipe, marinated artichokes and Parmesan cheese are mixed with thyme and panko for a delicious filling. If serving at a party, consider doubling the recipe. These babies will be devoured quickly!

24 medium cremini (baby bella) *or* white mushrooms
 4 teaspoons extra-virgin olive oil, divided
 2 tablespoons minced shallot
 2 cloves garlic, minced
½ cup drained marinated artichoke hearts, chopped
 3 tablespoons panko breadcrumbs, divided *(see Tip)*
 2 tablespoons grated Parmesan cheese
 2 tablespoons low-fat mayonnaise
⅛ teaspoon dried thyme
¼ teaspoon salt
¼ teaspoon ground pepper

1. Position rack in upper third of oven; preheat broiler to low. Coat a 9-by-13-inch metal baking pan with cooking spray.

2. Remove and finely chop mushroom stems. Heat 1 teaspoon oil in a medium skillet over medium heat. Add the stems, shallot and garlic and cook, stirring, until the liquid is evaporated, about 5 minutes. Transfer to a bowl and stir in artichoke hearts, 2 tablespoons breadcrumbs, Parmesan, mayonnaise and thyme.

3. Toss the mushroom caps in another bowl with 2 teaspoons oil, salt and pepper. Stuff each with filling and place in the prepared pan. Combine the remaining 1 tablespoon breadcrumbs and 1 teaspoon oil and sprinkle on the mushrooms.

4. Broil on the upper rack until the mushrooms are soft and the breadcrumbs are golden, 15 to 20 minutes.

SERVES 8: 3 MUSHROOMS EACH

Calories 64, **Fat** 3g (sat 1g), **Cholesterol** 2mg, **Carbs** 7g, **Total sugars** 1g (added 0g), **Protein** 3g, **Fiber** 1g, **Sodium** 170mg, **Potassium** 284mg.

Panko Breadcrumbs

Panko breadcrumbs, also known as Japanese breadcrumbs or bread flakes, are coarser in texture than other dried breadcrumbs. They produce a crispy crust and are less likely to become soggy than finely ground breadcrumbs. Look for panko in the Asian section or natural-foods section of large supermarkets and in Asian markets.

WILD MUSHROOM & POLENTA CASSEROLE

ACTIVE: 50 MIN **TOTAL:** 1¾ HRS
TO MAKE AHEAD: Prepare through Step 4 and refrigerate up to 1 day. Let stand, uncovered, at room temperature 1 hour before finishing with Step 5.

Choose morels or maitake mushrooms for a more "meaty" experience, chanterelles for a more buttery texture.

2¾ cups water
1¼ cups medium- to coarse-ground yellow cornmeal *(see Tip)*
½ teaspoon kosher salt
2 tablespoons extra-virgin olive oil
1½ pounds mushrooms, preferably wild, trimmed and thickly sliced
1 small red onion, finely chopped
⅔ cup dry white wine *or* low-sodium vegetable broth

1½ tablespoons chopped fresh rosemary
1½ tablespoons chopped fresh sage
¼ teaspoon ground pepper
6 ounces Taleggio *or* fontina cheese, finely diced
½ cup freshly grated Parmigiano-Reggiano cheese

1. Bring water to a boil in a large saucepan. Gradually whisk in cornmeal and salt. Reduce heat to low and cook, stirring constantly, until the polenta is very thick, 4 to 5 minutes. Scrape onto a clean cutting board and spread into an 8-inch-wide slab.

2. Preheat oven to 350°F. Coat an 8-inch baking dish with cooking spray.

3. Heat oil in a large skillet over medium heat. Add mushrooms and cook, stirring occasionally, until they start to brown, 12 to 15 minutes. Add onion and cook, stirring, until softened, 3 to 5 minutes. Stir in wine (or broth), rosemary, sage and pepper and cook for 1 minute. Remove from heat.

4. Cut the cooled polenta into 12 pieces about ½ inch wide. Arrange half the strips in the prepared dish. Top with half the mushroom mixture, half the Taleggio (or fontina) and half the Parmigiano. Top with the remaining polenta, mushroom mixture and cheeses.

5. Bake until brown and bubbling, 40 to 45 minutes. Let cool for 10 minutes. Cut into 6 pieces to serve.

SERVES 6: ABOUT 1 CUP EACH

Calories 336, **Fat** 17g (sat 7g), **Cholesterol** 39mg, **Carbs** 28g, **Total sugars** 2g (added 0g), **Protein** 16g, **Fiber** 5g, **Sodium** 460mg, **Potassium** 609mg.
Nutrition bonus: Iron (83% daily value), Calcium (29% dv), Zinc (27% dv).

Polenta

Any type of cornmeal can be used for polenta, but we like medium- or coarse-ground cornmeal for its texture. Usually labeled "cornmeal," some brands are labeled "polenta." Look for it near whole-grain flours. Store it in an airtight container in the freezer if you don't plan to use it quickly.

QUINOA MUSHROOM SOUP

ACTIVE: 40 MIN **TOTAL:** 1 HR

Reminiscent of old-fashioned mushroom-barley, this soup gets a modern update with nutrient-packed quinoa.

½ ounce dried porcini mushrooms

1 cup boiling water

1 tablespoon extra-virgin olive oil plus 2 teaspoons, divided

12 ounces mixed mushrooms, thinly sliced

¼ teaspoon ground pepper

¼ cup dry sherry *or* dry vermouth

1 large onion, finely chopped

2 stalks celery, chopped

1 large carrot, halved lengthwise and thinly sliced

½ small red bell pepper, chopped

4 cups mushroom broth *or* low-sodium chicken broth

¾ cup canned no-salt-added crushed tomatoes *or* tomato puree

½ cup quinoa

1 tablespoon dried marjoram *or* oregano

1 bay leaf

2 teaspoons reduced-sodium soy sauce

1. Combine porcini and boiling water in a small bowl; cover and set aside.

2. Meanwhile, heat 1 tablespoon oil in a large pot over medium-high heat. Add fresh mushrooms, sprinkle with pepper and cook without stirring for 2 minutes. Stir and continue to cook, stirring once or twice, until the mushrooms have given off their liquid and are well browned, about 4 minutes more. Add sherry (or vermouth) and cook, stirring, for 1 minute.

3. Add the remaining 2 teaspoons oil to the pot along with onion, celery, carrot and bell pepper and cook, stirring frequently, until the onion is tender and translucent, about 4 minutes.

4. When mushrooms have soaked for 20 minutes, line a sieve with a paper towel, place over a bowl and strain the porcini; reserve the liquid. Chop the porcini and add to the pot along with the strained liquid. Add broth, tomatoes, quinoa, marjoram and bay leaf; bring to a boil. Reduce heat to a simmer, cover and cook for 20 minutes. Remove from heat and stir in soy sauce.

SERVES 4: 2 CUPS EACH

Calories 229, **Fat** 8g (sat 1g), **Cholesterol** 0mg, **Carbs** 31g, **Total sugars** 8g (added 0g), **Protein** 8g, **Fiber** 6g, **Sodium** 661mg, **Potassium** 778mg.
Nutrition bonus: Vitamin A (76% daily value), Vitamin C (32% dv), Potassium (22% dv), Folate & Iron (20% dv).

ASPARAGUS & MUSHROOM RISOTTO

ACTIVE: 1 HR **TOTAL:** 1 HR

We think this deep rich red-wine risotto is best made with mushroom broth (find it in well-stocked supermarkets), but any vegetarian broth works well.

The Parmigiano-Reggiano Difference

Parmigiano-Reggiano is a specific type of Parmesan that's full of flavor. Many of our recipes that call for Parmesan specify Parmigiano-Reggiano so that you can use just a little bit and get a lot of flavor. If you can't find it, your best bet is to buy any hard grating cheese imported from Italy and grate it fresh just before using.

4 cups mushroom *or* vegetable broth

1 cup water

1 bunch asparagus (about 1 pound), trimmed, cut into 1-inch pieces

1 tablespoon extra-virgin olive oil

⅓ cup chopped shallots

3 cloves garlic, minced

1 tablespoon chopped fresh thyme *or* 1 teaspoon dried

8 ounces shiitake mushrooms, stemmed, caps sliced

1 cup arborio rice

1 cup Cabernet Sauvignon *or* other full-bodied dry red wine

½ cup finely shredded Parmigiano-Reggiano cheese, plus more for garnish *(see Tip)*

¼ cup chopped fresh parsley, plus more for garnish

¼ teaspoon ground pepper

1. Bring broth and water to a boil in a medium saucepan. Add asparagus and cook until tender-crisp, about 4 minutes. Remove to a bowl with a slotted spoon and set aside. Reduce the heat to maintain a gentle simmer.

2. Heat oil in a large pot over medium-low heat. Add shallots, garlic and thyme; cook, stirring often, until starting to soften, 2 minutes. Add mushrooms and cook, stirring frequently, until softened, 3 to 4 minutes. Add rice; cook, stirring, for 1 minute. Add wine and cook, stirring often, until the wine is absorbed, 2 to 3 minutes.

3. Add 1½ cups of the simmering broth and cook, stirring, until it is absorbed. Continue to cook on medium-low, adding broth in ½-cup increments and stirring frequently after each addition, until most of the liquid is absorbed. The risotto is done when all the broth is used and the rice is creamy and just tender, 24 to 28 minutes total.

4. Stir in the reserved asparagus and cook for 1 minute. Remove from the heat and stir in cheese, parsley and pepper. Serve immediately, sprinkled with more cheese and parsley, if desired.

SERVES 4: 1½ CUPS EACH

Calories 335, **Fat** 7g (sat 2g), **Cholesterol** 7mg, **Carbs** 48g, **Total sugars** 3g (added 0g), **Protein** 10g, **Fiber** 4g, **Sodium** 721mg, **Potassium** 462mg.
Nutrition bonus: Folate (26% daily value), Vitamin A (23% dv), Vitamin C (20% dv).

KOREAN STEAK & MUSHROOM TACOS WITH KIMCHI

ACTIVE: 45 MIN **TOTAL:** 45 MIN

These tacos were inspired by Kogi—the L.A. food trucks that spawned the Korean barbecue-meets-Mexican craze. The spicy, pickled flavor and crunchy texture of kimchi, the Korean cousin to sauerkraut, is just right on a taco. Look for jars of kimchi near refrigerated Asian ingredients or near sauerkraut or refrigerated pickles in well-stocked supermarkets or natural-foods stores. Serve with steamed brown rice and sautéed bok choy with chile-garlic sauce.

- 2 tablespoons reduced-sodium soy sauce
- 1 tablespoon toasted sesame oil
- 1 tablespoon packed light brown sugar
- 1 tablespoon mirin *(see Tip, page 84)*
- 1 tablespoon gochujang *(see Tip)*
- 2 cloves garlic, minced

- 12 ounces skirt steak *(see Tip, page 145)*, trimmed and cut into 3 pieces
- 8 ounces shiitake mushrooms, stemmed
- 8 corn tortillas, warmed
- 1 cup prepared kimchi, drained and chopped
- 1 cup shredded carrot
- 2 scallions, cut into thirds and thinly sliced lengthwise

1. Preheat grill to medium-high.

2. Combine soy sauce, sesame oil, brown sugar, mirin, gochujang and garlic in a small saucepan. Bring to a simmer over medium heat and cook, stirring, until slightly thickened, about 3 minutes. Remove from heat and cover to keep warm.

3. Grill steak 1½ to 3 minutes per side for medium. Transfer to a clean cutting board and let rest for 5 minutes. Grill mushroom caps until soft and charred around the edges, 1 to 2 minutes per side. Thinly slice the steak across the grain. Slice the mushrooms. Add the steak and mushrooms to the sauce and stir to combine.

4. To assemble tacos, divide the steak and mushrooms among tortillas. Top with kimchi, carrot and scallions.

SERVES 4

Calories 354, **Fat** 12g (sat 3g), **Cholesterol** 55mg, **Carbs** 37g, **Total sugars** 8g (added 3g), **Protein** 24g, **Fiber** 6g, **Sodium** 649mg, **Potassium** 709mg.
Nutrition bonus: Vitamin A (93% daily value), Vitamin B$_{12}$ (53% dv), Zinc (37% dv), Potassium (20% dv).

Gochujang

Also called hot pepper paste, gochujang or kochujang, Korean chile paste is a fermented spicy condiment made from red chiles, soybeans and salt. Find it in Korean or Asian markets or online from *koamart.com*. It keeps indefinitely in the refrigerator. To make a substitute, combine 2 tablespoons each white miso and Asian-style chile sauce, such as sriracha, and 2 teaspoons molasses.

Mustard Greens

Metaphorically speaking, mustard greens are the members of your social circle that can have a dauntingly strong personality—but that you're glad to have in your corner.

The most assertively flavored of the leafy brassicas (which include kale and collards), this peppery, spicy green can be eaten raw in salads when young (such as the baby greens shown here) and cooked when more mature—usually steamed, sautéed or boiled. A quick turn in the sauté pan best retains its nutrients—which are many. More mature mustard greens can be eaten raw in a salad if massaged first *(see Tip, page 282)*.

While the frilly-leaved Southern or American variety is the type found in most supermarkets, mustard greens do not have a single shape, size or flavor. Leaves range from glowing chartreuse to deep purple, crinkly to silky smooth, mildly mustardy to spicy hot and chewy to delicately tender. Chinese mustard greens—also called *gai choy*—look similar to bok choy. Some varieties of mustard are grown for their leaves; others for the seeds that are ground and turned into the bright yellow condiment; or used whole in pickling spice—or on their own.

Mustard greens are delicious with garlic, onions, bacon, vinegar and brown sugar, and golden raisins. Try them Indian-style, sautéed in ghee with minced chile, garlic and garam masala—or Asian-style, cooked in sesame oil with garlic and ginger, a splash of reduced-sodium soy sauce and mirin, and a sprinkle of toasted sesame seeds. Lightly braise and combine with beans, potatoes or grains.

Mustard greens, available throughout the year, are best from midwinter to spring. Greens grown in the heat of summer are hotter in flavor than spring or fall greens.

Best in midwinter to spring

AT THE MARKET

❧ Choose mustard greens with crisp, rich green leaves. Avoid greens with any yellowing or wilting.

❧ Mustard greens have an array of leaf types. 'Southern Giant Curled' is a traditional type, with very frilly bright green leaves. 'Giant Red' has deep red-purple leaves with green undersides. 'Green Wave' has heavily curled leaves and a particularly mustardy-hot flavor that mellows when cooked.

IN YOUR KITCHEN

❧ Wrap, unwashed, in moist paper towels and place in a plastic bag in the refrigerator. Store up to 3 days in the refrigerator.

❧ Rinse leaves in cool water, swirling through the water to remove soil and grit. Gently shake off excess water. Place each leaf on a cutting board and slice along either side of the center stem to remove it; discard stem. Chop or tear leaves as desired.

COOKING BASICS

BRAISE Cook 3 slices diced bacon in a large skillet over medium heat until it begins to brown. Add 1 diced onion, 1 clove minced garlic and ½ teaspoon crushed red pepper and cook until the onion is soft, about 6 minutes. Add ¼ cup reduced-sodium chicken broth, 2 tablespoons cider vinegar and 1 tablespoon brown sugar. Bring to a boil. Add 1½ pounds washed and dried, roughly chopped mustard greens, stirring to coat. Reduce heat to medium-low and cook, stirring often, until the greens are tender and most of the liquid has evaporated, 10 to 12 minutes. Season with ½ teaspoon salt and pepper to taste. Serves 4.

SALAD Tear the leaves from 2 washed and dried bunches of mustard greens into small pieces and place in a large bowl. Add ½ cup freshly grated Parmesan cheese, ⅓ cup olive oil, ¼ cup fresh lemon juice, 3 cloves minced garlic, 1 tablespoon reduced-sodium sauce, 1 minced anchovy fillet or ½ teaspoon anchovy paste (optional), ½ teaspoon pepper and ¼ teaspoon salt. With clean hands, firmly massage and crush the greens to work in the flavoring until volume of greens is reduced by about half. Taste and adjust seasonings if desired. Serves 6.

NUTRITION

❧ **1 cup of chopped cooked mustard greens: Calories** 36, **Fat** 1g (sat 0g), **Cholesterol** 0mg, **Carbs** 6g, **Total sugars** 2g (added 0g), **Protein** 4g, **Fiber** 3g, **Sodium** 13mg, **Potassium** 227mg.

BONUS Mustard greens are full of nutrients that protect your eyes. One cooked cup contains 60 percent of your day's worth of vitamin C to shield against macular degeneration. They're also high in lutein and zeaxanthin, antioxidants that help prevent cataracts.

STIR-FRIED MUSTARD GREENS WITH EGGS & GARLIC

ACTIVE: 15 MIN **TOTAL:** 15 MIN

This Southeast Asian dish originated in China and is essentially a garlicky stir-fry of any kind of leafy green. Asian cooks customize it with ingredients such as sambal olek chile, eggs, meat, mushrooms, tofu, crispy baby anchovies or shrimp. It is usually served as part of a Sunday family meal with other dishes, such as clear soup, grilled fish, stewed pork, and steamed jasmine rice.

3	tablespoons canola *or* peanut oil
4	cloves garlic, thinly sliced
1	teaspoon shredded fresh ginger
1	fresh red chile pepper, sliced
2	large eggs
10-12	ounces mustard greens, chopped (about 1 bunch)
1	tablespoon fish sauce *or* oyster sauce, plus more to taste
1	pinch white pepper powder
	Crispy fried baby anchovies *or* bonito flakes for garnish (optional) *(see Tip)*

1. Heat a 14-inch flat-bottom carbon-steel wok or large cast-iron skillet over high heat until it just starts to smoke. Add oil, followed by garlic, ginger and chile. Cook, stirring, until the garlic starts looking golden brown on the edges, about 1 minute.

2. Crack eggs into the pan and scramble for a few seconds. Add mustard greens and stir to combine with the egg mixture. Season with fish (or oyster) sauce and pepper and cook just to wilt the greens, 1 to 3 minutes. Serve topped with crispy fried baby anchovies (or bonito flakes), if desired.

SERVES 4: ½ CUP EACH

Calories 162, **Fat** 13g (sat 2g), **Cholesterol** 93mg, **Carbs** 6g, **Total sugars** 2g (added 0g), **Protein** 6g, **Fiber** 3g, **Sodium** 349mg, **Potassium** 357mg.
Nutrition bonus: Vitamin C (111% daily value), Vitamin A (48% dv).

Crispy Fish

Both crispy fried baby anchovies and bonito flakes—made from dried smoked bonito tuna—are used in many Japanese, Chinese and Southeast Asian dishes to add flavor and texture. Bonito flakes are an integral ingredient in *dashi*—Japanese broth—for miso soup. Look for crispy fried baby anchovies and bonito flakes at Asian markets.

≈
Hot Chiles, Cool Effect

Hot chile peppers—such as the serranos in this dish—might awaken your taste buds and make you sweat, but they add more than just heat to your meal. Hot chiles (and zesty spices like cayenne and crushed red pepper) have health benefits, too, as they help trigger the body's natural cooling system and rev up metabolism.
≈

INDIAN-STYLE MUSTARD GREENS & KALE WITH TOASTED NAAN

ACTIVE: 40 MIN **TOTAL:** 40 MIN

To serve this appetizer flatbread-style, brush whole naan lightly with olive oil and toast on a grill pan until lightly charred on both sides. Top with the greens.

- 6 8-inch whole-grain naan flatbreads
- 4 tablespoons extra-virgin olive oil, divided
- 1-1¼ pounds mustard greens, stemmed and coarsely chopped
- 8 ounces kale, stemmed and coarsely chopped
- 2 tablespoons cornmeal
- 1 medium sweet onion, finely chopped
- 4 small cloves garlic, minced
- 1-2 serrano chile peppers, seeded and finely chopped
- 1 tablespoon minced fresh ginger
- ½ teaspoon ground turmeric
- 2 tablespoons lemon juice
- ¾ teaspoon salt
- 4 ounces paneer cheese, torn, *or* crumbled feta cheese (about 1 cup)

1. Position racks in upper and lower thirds of oven; preheat to 425°F.

2. Lightly brush naan on both sides with 2 tablespoons oil. Cut each into 6 wedges and arrange on 2 large baking sheets. Bake, turning once and rotating top to bottom, until lightly browned, 8 to 10 minutes. Remove from oven. Turn broiler to high.

3. Meanwhile, bring a large pot of water to a boil. Add mustard greens and kale. Cook for 2 minutes. Transfer to a colander and drain well, pressing with a spoon to remove excess water. Place the greens in a food processor and process until very finely chopped. Add cornmeal and pulse to combine.

4. Heat the remaining 2 tablespoons oil in a large broiler-safe skillet over medium-high heat. Reduce heat to medium; add onion, garlic, chile pepper to taste and ginger. Cook, stirring frequently, until soft and golden, 6 to 8 minutes. Add turmeric; cook, stirring, for 1 minute. Add the greens and cook, stirring, until the moisture evaporates, 1 to 2 minutes more. Stir in lemon juice and salt. Sprinkle with cheese. Broil until the cheese melts, 1 to 2 minutes. Serve the greens with the toasted naan wedges for scooping.

SERVES 12: 3 NAAN WEDGES & ¼ CUP GREENS EACH

Calories 251, **Fat** 11g (sat 4g), **Cholesterol** 9mg, **Carbs** 31g, **Total sugars** 4g (added 0g), **Protein** 9g, **Fiber** 5g, **Sodium** 495mg, **Potassium** 354mg.
Nutrition bonus: Vitamin C (73% daily value), Vitamin A (49% dv).

Okra

The slippery quality of okra that makes some steer clear of this crunchy pod is actually one of its most useful attributes. It comes from mucilage, a natural thickener made up of sugar residues and proteins that gives body to all kinds of soups and stews, including that most iconic of New Orleans dishes, gumbo. (In fact, okra is known as "gombo" in much of West Africa—a pretty strong clue as to how the dish got its name.)

Although okra is synonymous with the American South, this seedpod of a tropical plant related to both hibiscus and cotton is prevalent in the cuisines of Africa, India, Southeast Asia, the Middle East, the Caribbean and South America as well.

There are many varieties of okra, from those with short, squat pods to slender fruit measuring more than a foot long. Most varieties have pods that range in color from light to dark green, though there are some that produce red or crimson-streaked pods.

Okra is most commonly stewed—or battered and deep-fried. Because the viscosity of mucilage increases with exposure to heat, quick-cooking methods, such as sautéing, grilling and roasting, help retain the fresh, crisp texture of the raw pod as well as the pleasant "pop" of the seeds inside.

The flavor of okra (which hints of artichoke and asparagus) and its glutinous quality are balanced by acids, such as tomato, lemon and vinegar, as well as heat from both fresh and dried chiles. It is also enhanced by garlic, onion, ginger and aromatic seeds such as cumin, coriander, anise and fennel.

Okra thrives in hot, steamy weather and is at peak season from mid- to late summer in most parts of the country. Prior to producing the succulent green pods, the plants are awash in blooms that—not surprisingly—look like hibiscus flowers.

Best in late summer

AT THE MARKET

➣ Choose okra pods that are firm and dry. Avoid those that are mushy, slimy or have blemishes. The skin coating should have a peach-fuzz appearance.

IN YOUR KITCHEN

➣ Store okra in a paper bag in the warmest part of the refrigerator up to 3 days.

➣ Trim the stem ends, being careful not to expose the seeds (unless pods will be sliced) and rinse well under cool running water. For roasting, grilling or sautéing, be sure okra is very dry to ensure the best texture. Pat dry with paper towels. Leave whole, slice or cut in half horizontally, as desired.

COOKING BASICS

ROAST Toss 1 pound trimmed okra with 2 tablespoons olive oil, ½ teaspoon salt, ¼ teaspoon ground cayenne pepper and pepper to taste. Spread in a single layer on a large rimmed baking sheet. Roast in a 450°F oven until lightly browned and tender, shaking the pan every 5 minutes, for about 15 minutes. Serves 4.

SAUTÉ Slice 1 pound trimmed okra into ½-inch-thick pieces. Cook 2 slices bacon in a large skillet over low heat until crisp. Drain on a paper towel-lined plate. Increase heat to medium-high. Add 1 thinly sliced small sweet onion to the pan and cook, stirring occasionally, until slightly softened, about 2 minutes. Add the okra and cook, stirring frequently, until tender-crisp and with bright color, 5 to 6 minutes. Season with ¼ teaspoon salt and pepper to taste. Crumble the bacon over the okra; serve immediately. Serves 4.

STEW Combine 1 pound trimmed okra and 2 chopped medium tomatoes in a large heavy skillet. Pierce 1 habanero chile (or 2 jalapeños) with a fork and add to the pan. Bring to a boil. Cover and cook over medium heat until the okra is tender, 8 to 13 minutes. Season with ¼ teaspoon salt and pepper to taste. Serves 4.

NUTRITION

➣ **1 cup sliced cooked okra: Calories** 36, **Fat** 0g (sat 0g), **Cholesterol** 0mg, **Carbs** 7g, **Total sugars** 4g (added 0g), **Protein** 3g, **Fiber** 4g, **Sodium** 10mg, **Potassium** 216mg.

BONUS This vegetable has a long folk history of helping to manage blood sugar in people with diabetes. One reason could be its antioxidants, quercetin and isoquercetin, shown to block enzymes that break down sugars, hindering their ability to enter the bloodstream.

Stewed Okra
(see Cooking Basics, opposite)

GRILLED OKRA & HOT PEPPERS

ACTIVE: 20 MIN **TOTAL:** 20 MIN
EQUIPMENT: Grill basket

The fire of the grill gives okra a tender texture and subtle smokiness. Adjust the level of spiciness in this side dish by choosing chiles that are tame, incendiary or anywhere in between.

1 pound okra, stem ends trimmed
2 fresh chile peppers, sliced ¼ inch thick
1 tablespoon extra-virgin olive oil
½ teaspoon salt
¼ teaspoon ground pepper

1. Place a grill basket on the grill and preheat on high for 10 minutes. (Or position oven rack 5 inches from heat source; preheat broiler to high.)

2. Combine okra, peppers, oil, salt and pepper in a large bowl. Transfer to the grill basket (or to a rimmed baking sheet).

3. Grill (or broil) until the okra is bright green and just tender, stirring occasionally, 8 to 10 minutes.

SERVES 4: ABOUT 1 CUP EACH

Calories 71, **Fat** 4g (sat 1g), **Cholesterol** 0mg, **Carbs** 9g, **Total sugars** 2g (added 0g), **Protein** 2g, **Fiber** 4g, **Sodium** 299mg, **Potassium** 358mg.
Nutrition bonus: Vitamin C (57% daily value).

INDIAN-STYLE SAUTÉED OKRA

ACTIVE: 25 MIN **TOTAL:** 25 MIN

Sautéing the spices in a little bit of additional ghee toasts them and heightens their flavor.

2	tablespoons ghee *(see Tip)* or extra-virgin olive oil, divided
1	pound fresh okra, trimmed
½	teaspoon salt
1	small red onion, chopped
1-2	fresh Thai chiles, seeded and minced
2	cloves garlic, minced
1	tablespoon minced fresh ginger
1	teaspoon cumin seeds
½	teaspoon ground turmeric
½	teaspoon ground coriander
2	tablespoons chopped fresh cilantro
1	teaspoon freshly grated lemon zest
1	tablespoon lemon juice

1. Heat 1 tablespoon ghee (or oil) in a large skillet over medium heat. Add okra and sprinkle with salt. Cover and cook, stirring occasionally, until the okra is beginning to soften, 3 to 4 minutes. Add the remaining 1 tablespoon ghee (or oil), onion, chile to taste, garlic, ginger, cumin, turmeric and coriander. Cover and cook, stirring occasionally, until softened, about 5 minutes more.

2. Remove from heat. Add cilantro, lemon zest and lemon juice and stir until the okra is coated.

SERVES 4: 1 CUP EACH

Calories 117, **Fat** 7g (sat 1g), **Cholesterol** 0mg, **Carbs** 12g, **Total sugars** 3g (added 0g), **Protein** 3g, **Fiber** 4g, **Sodium** 301mg, **Potassium** 408mg.
Nutrition bonus: Vitamin C (57% daily value).

Ghee

Ghee is a type of clarified butter that originated in India. Butter is slowly melted so milk solids sink to the bottom of the pan while the golden liquid rises to the surface. The liquid is simmered until most of the moisture evaporates and the solids begin to caramelize, giving ghee a nutty flavor and aroma. The solids are then extracted. Removing the lactose and casein (a milk protein) makes ghee better tolerated by those who have dairy sensitivities. A little goes a long way to add flavor to foods.

Buying Crab

Pasteurized crab is available in a range of grades. Splurge on large, more expensive grades like colossal lump, jumbo lump and backfin for recipes in which crab is the focus. Use small, less expensive grades, such as special, claw meat or claw fingers, for other recipes. Look for crab in a supermarket seafood department or canned-fish section packaged in large cans, plastic tubs or sealed foil pouches. Before using, be sure to pick out any stray shells or cartilage. To make sure you're getting sustainably caught crab, avoid anything from Russia. For the most up-to-date information check seafoodwatch.org.

SEAFOOD GUMBO

ACTIVE: 1 HR 20 MIN **TOTAL:** 2¼ HRS

This crab and shrimp gumbo comes from Eula Mae Doré, who was the cook at the Commissary on Avery Island, home to the Tabasco company. Just as most cooks of her generation, she learned Cajun cooking by watching, rather than from cookbooks. Serve with brown rice. (Recipe adapted from Eula Mae's Cajun Kitchen *by Eula Mae Doré and Marcelle R. Bienvenu; Harvard Common Press, 2007.)*

5 tablespoons canola oil, divided
1 pound okra, fresh *or* frozen (thawed), trimmed and cut into ¼-inch-thick rounds
4 teaspoons distilled white vinegar
⅓ cup all-purpose flour
2 cups chopped green bell peppers
1¼ cups chopped yellow onions
1¼ cups chopped scallions, divided
1 cup chopped celery
1 clove garlic, minced
1 28-ounce can diced tomatoes with their juice
2 cups seafood stock *or* water
½ cup cubed boiled deli ham
2 bay leaves
2 sprigs fresh thyme *or* ½ teaspoon dried
1 tablespoon Worcestershire sauce
1 teaspoon hot sauce
⅛ teaspoon salt
1 pound peeled and deveined raw shrimp (26-30 count) *(see Tip, page 249)*
½ pound lump crabmeat, any shells *or* cartilage removed *(see Tip)*
2 tablespoons chopped parsley

1. Heat 1 tablespoon oil in a large nonstick skillet over medium heat. Add okra and cook, stirring often, until it starts to turn dark brown, 18 to 22 minutes. Add vinegar and cook, stirring frequently, until the okra is browned and no longer has "sticky strings" attached, 2 to 3 minutes more. Set aside.

2. Heat the remaining 4 tablespoons oil in a large heavy pot over medium heat for 2 minutes. Add flour and cook, stirring slowly and constantly, until the mixture smells very toasty and is the color of peanut butter, 5 to 10 minutes.

3. Add bell peppers, onions, 1 cup scallions, celery and garlic and cook, stirring often, until the vegetables are tender and lightly golden, 10 to 12 minutes. Stir in the okra, tomatoes, stock (or water), ham, bay leaves,

thyme, Worcestershire, hot sauce and salt. Reduce the heat to medium-low, cover and simmer, adjusting the heat as necessary to maintain a slow, steady simmer, for 45 minutes.

4. Add shrimp and crabmeat to the pot and simmer, uncovered, until the shrimp are cooked through, about 8 minutes. Discard the bay leaves and thyme. Garnish with parsley and the remaining scallions.

SERVES 8: ABOUT 1½ CUPS EACH

Calories 244, **Fat** 10g (sat 1g), **Cholesterol** 104mg, **Carbs** 18g, **Total sugars** 6g (added 0g), **Protein** 22g, **Fiber** 5g, **Sodium** 620mg, **Potassium** 734mg.
Nutrition bonus: Vitamin C (98% daily value), Potassium (21% dv).

Onions

A world without onions would be dull indeed. Countless dishes start with some type of onion sautéing in a pan. Onions and their cousins—shallots, leeks, scallions and the wild springtime leeks called ramps—are all alliums, an offshoot of the lily family.

The most common are globe-shape, or storage, onions that are white, yellow or red. The name is apt. Storage onions are harvested, then kept under cool, dry, dark conditions that maintain freshness for months. Although storage onions are considered to be at peak season in fall, they are harvested year-round. Spring/summer onions are available March through August and have a milder, sweeter flavor than those harvested in fall and winter.

Members of the onion family that are used fresh (not stored long-term) include leeks, scallions, spring onions, and ramps (wild leeks).

All types of onions grow best in soil that is rich in sulfur. Peeling the skin or chopping the flesh releases an enzyme that binds with the sulfur. It's that chemical reaction that makes you sniffle and weep—and that also imbues the onion with its pungency and flavor. Although raw onions add an enticing bite on a bowl of chili or a burger, their best qualities come out when they are cooked. As the water content in the onion evaporates during cooking, its natural sugars are intensified and the flavor becomes much sweeter. This is especially true when the onion is caramelized—cooked low and slow until it becomes beautifully golden.

Best in fall: onions & shallots. Best in spring: leeks, scallions, ramps.

ONIONS

AT THE MARKET

🖙 Choose onions and shallots that are firm with bright-color outer skin that is dry and papery. Avoid onions and shallots that have bruises or those that have begun to sprout.

🖙 Choose leeks, ramps and scallions with roots intact, firm whites with no cracks or bruises and fresh green leaves that are not withered.

IN YOUR KITCHEN

🖙 Store onions and shallots in a cool, dark, well-ventilated place up to a month. Do not store in plastic bags or refrigerate. To prepare an onion or shallot, keep the root end intact and cut off the top, then remove the dry, papery layers. Remove and discard the outer layer of skin.

🖙 Store leeks and scallions in a slightly open plastic bag in the refrigerator up to 1 week. To prepare leeks, cut off the root and dark green tops. Cut stem in half lengthwise. Swish in cool water to release any sand or soil. Drain and repeat until no grit remains. For scallions, cut off the root end and rinse.

🖙 Store uncleaned ramps at room temperature with bulbs submerged in water up to 3 days. Cleaned ramps will last up to 5 days in the refrigerator, loosely wrapped in moist paper towels in a sealable bag. To prepare ramps, trim root ends and remove any loose or wilted layers around the white and pink

stems. Rinse ramps under cool running water to remove dirt and grit; pat dry.

COOKING BASICS

BRAISE (LEEKS) Trim and clean 4 large leeks. Place leek halves in a large skillet with ½ cup vegetable broth (or reduced-sodium chicken broth) and 1 sprig fresh rosemary. Bring to a simmer over high heat. Cover, reduce heat and cook until tender, about 12 minutes. Serves 4.

CARAMELIZE Add 1 tablespoon olive oil or butter per onion to a skillet. Heat over medium-high heat. Cook sliced onions, stirring frequently, until tender and starting to brown, 5 to 7 minutes. Cover and continue to cook over medium-low heat, stirring occasionally, until golden brown, 13 to 15 minutes. Uncover and cook over medium-high until golden, 3 to 5 minutes.

GRILL Cut trimmed and peeled onions into ½- to 1-inch-thick slices. Run a

metal skewer though each slice to keep them intact. Brush with olive oil and season with salt and pepper. Grill over medium heat until tender, turning once or twice, 15 to 20 minutes.

ROAST Trim and peel onions, leaving just enough root to keep the onions intact. Cut into wedges. Toss with olive oil, salt and pepper. Spread on a rimmed baking sheet. Roast in a 400°F oven until the onions are tender and browned, 30 to 45 minutes.

NUTRITION

🖙 **½ cup chopped cooked onion:** **Calories** 41, **Fat** 0g (sat 0g), **Cholesterol** 0mg, **Carbs** 11g, **Total sugars** 5g (added 0g), **Protein** 1g, **Fiber** 2g, **Sodium** 3mg, **Potassium** 175mg.

BONUS Onions are rich in organosulfides, compounds that help prevent cancers of the mouth, esophagus, stomach and colon.

How to dice an onion

1. Cut off stem end, leaving root end intact, then cut onion in half through the root end. Peel the onion.

2. Place flat end of one onion half on the cutting board. Make one or two cuts lengthwise from stem toward root end.

3. Make a series of lengthwise cuts through onion half, from top to bottom. Cut crosswise into dice.

▲ **Spring Onions**
These immature globe onions are left in the ground longer than scallions, hence the larger bulbs. They are milder than mature storage onions but stronger than scallions.

◀ **Leeks**
Related to both garlic and bulbing onions, these fragrant stalks taste a bit like a blend of the two. Often only the white and light green parts are used. However, the dark green is also edible.

▲ **Ramps**
These fragrant and pungent wild leeks have a brief season in spring—usually just a few weeks. One aspect of their specialness is scarcity. The wild plants can take up to four years to flower and reproduce.

◀ **Scallions**
Also called green onions (although there are purple varieties too), these mild onions can be either immature bulbing onions or a type of onion that never forms bulbs.

▲ **White Onion**
The sharpest and most pungent of the storage onions, these tend to have the firmest texture and thinnest skin. Although they can be cooked just like yellow onions, they are the best choice for using raw in salsa.

▼ **Red Onion**
These jewel-tone onions have a strong flavor but are sweeter than yellow or white onions; a popular choice for using raw in salads and dips and on burgers and sandwiches.

▼ Cipolline

These small saucer-shape Italian onions—usually just 1 to 3 inches in diameter—have firm texture and pungent, semisweet flavor. They soften considerably when cooked. They are also popular for pickling.

◄ Yellow Onion

This is the all-purpose storage onion for cooking or using raw. Milder than white onions, they have a good balance between astringency and sweetness.

▼ Shallot

Milder and sweeter than onions, these small teardrop-shape bulbs with delicate papery skin have a hint of garlic.

▼ Pearl Onion

Small in size partially because they are densely planted and picked at a stunted size, pearl onions have crisp, juicy flesh and a mild onion flavor. They are commonly used in stews and braises or are pickled. There are both yellow and white varieties (*see lower left*).

◄ Sweet Onion

The most common varieties are Vidalia, Walla Walla and Maui. They lack the astringency of regular storage onions and—as the name suggests—are sweeter as well.

CURRIED ONION DIP

ACTIVE: 25 MIN **TOTAL:** 35 MIN
TO MAKE AHEAD: Refrigerate up to 2 days.

*Skip the standard onion soup-mix dip and serve up this healthy homemade
version with your favorite chips or crudités.*

  1 tablespoon extra-virgin olive oil
  1 large onion, diced
  2 tablespoons water
  ¾ teaspoon curry powder
  ½ teaspoon garlic powder
  ½ teaspoon salt, divided
  ¾ cup reduced-fat sour cream
  3 ounces reduced-fat cream cheese, at room temperature

1. Heat oil in a large skillet over medium-high heat. Add onion and cook,
stirring occasionally, until starting to color, 5 to 7 minutes. Reduce heat to
medium and continue cooking, stirring occasionally, until golden brown, 8 to
10 minutes more. Add water, curry powder, garlic powder and ¼ teaspoon salt
and cook, stirring constantly, until the spices are very fragrant, 30 seconds to
1 minute.

2. Transfer the onions to a large bowl and let cool for 10 minutes. Whisk in
sour cream, cream cheese and the remaining ¼ teaspoon salt.

MAKES: ABOUT 1¾ CUPS (2-TBSP. SERVING)

Calories 47, **Fat** 4g (sat 2g), **Cholesterol** 10mg, **Carbs** 2g, **Total sugars** 1g (added 0g),
Protein 1g, **Fiber** 0g, **Sodium** 115mg, **Potassium** 44mg.

BEER-BATTERED ONION RINGS WITH ROASTED PEPPER AIOLI

ACTIVE: 30 MIN **TOTAL:** 45 MIN

Cornmeal adds crispness to these onions rings and a touch of brown ale in the batter adds subtle malt flavor. While the rings bake, zest up plain mayo into a dipping sauce with roasted red peppers and a clove of garlic.

2 tablespoons canola oil
¼ cup all-purpose flour
1 tablespoon cornstarch
½ teaspoon garlic powder
¼ teaspoon cayenne pepper
¼ teaspoon salt
½ cup brown ale
1 cup fine yellow cornmeal

1 large sweet onion, sliced into ½-inch-thick rings
Canola *or* olive oil cooking spray

ROASTED RED PEPPER AIOLI
1 clove garlic, minced
⅛ teaspoon salt
⅓ cup low-fat mayonnaise
¼ cup sliced jarred roasted red peppers

1. Preheat oven to 450°F. Brush a large rimmed baking sheet with oil.

2. Whisk flour, cornstarch, garlic powder, cayenne and ¼ teaspoon salt in a medium bowl. Whisk in ale until combined. Place cornmeal in a shallow bowl. Separate onion slices into rings and dip in the batter, letting excess drip off, then dredge in cornmeal. Place on the prepared baking sheet. Coat the onion rings with cooking spray.

3. Bake until browned on the bottom, about 12 minutes. Turn, coat the other side with cooking spray and bake until browned and crispy, 10 to 12 minutes more.

4. To prepare aioli: Mash garlic and ⅛ teaspoon salt into a paste on a cutting board. Transfer the paste to a bowl and stir in mayonnaise and red peppers. Serve with the onion rings.

SERVES 4: 6-7 ONION RINGS & 1½ TBSP. AIOLI EACH

Calories 223, **Fat** 9g (sat 1g), **Cholesterol** 5mg, **Carbs** 32g, **Total sugars** 3g (added 1g), **Protein** 3g, **Fiber** 2g, **Sodium** 417mg, **Potassium** 135mg.

Sweet Onion Season

Certain onion varieties lack the astringency of common yellow or white onion, so have a sweeter flavor. Referred to as "sweet onions," they are the best choice for onion rings. The most common varieties of sweet onion are Vidalia (in season April through June), Walla Walla (in season June through August) and Maui (in season May through December).

MINI ONION GRATINS

ACTIVE: 15 MIN **TOTAL:** 45 MIN

Turn a couple of big onions into an easy and cool-looking vegetable side dish with crunchy gratin-like topping. The nutty taste of fontina cheese is a good match for the onions, but you can use any melty cheese you have on hand.

- 2 large white onions, cut into 4 thick rounds each
- 2 tablespoons extra-virgin olive oil plus 2 teaspoons, divided
- ½ teaspoon ground pepper, divided
- ¼ teaspoon salt
- ¾ cup fine fresh breadcrumbs, preferably whole-wheat (see Tip, page 18)
- ½ cup shredded fontina cheese
- 1 teaspoon crumbled dried rosemary *or* 1 tablespoon chopped fresh

1. Preheat oven to 450°F.

2. Keeping onion rounds intact, place on a rimmed baking sheet. Combine 2 tablespoons oil, ¼ teaspoon pepper and salt in a small bowl. Brush both sides of the onions with the oil mixture. Bake, turning once, for 15 minutes.

3. Meanwhile, combine breadcrumbs, cheese, rosemary, the remaining 2 teaspoons oil and ¼ teaspoon pepper in a small bowl.

4. Turn the onions over again and top each with some of the breadcrumb mixture. Reduce oven temperature to 400°F and continue baking until lightly browned, 12 to 15 minutes more.

SERVES 4: 2 ROUNDS EACH

Calories 216, **Fat** 14g (sat 4g), **Cholesterol** 16mg, **Carbs** 15g, **Total sugars** 4g (added 1g), **Protein** 7g, **Fiber** 3g, **Sodium** 333mg, **Potassium** 172mg.

≋

Stale Bread

To stale bread naturally, store at room temperature in a paper (not plastic) bag for 2 to 5 days. If you don't want to wait, bake sliced or cubed bread on a large baking sheet at 250°F until crisped and dry, 15 to 20 minutes. One 1-pound loaf (12 to 14 slices) yields 8 to 10 cups of 1-inch cubes.

≋

ROASTED GARLIC & LEEK BREAD CASSEROLE

ACTIVE: 50 MIN **TOTAL:** 1 HR 20 MIN

This stuffing-like casserole is inspired by the vegetable tians of Provence.

1 large head garlic

3 tablespoons extra-virgin olive oil, divided

3 cups water plus 2 tablespoons, divided

8 slices stale bread, crusts removed (*see Tip*)

4 cups halved and thinly sliced leeks (about 2 large leeks), white and light green parts only (*see page 336*)

½ teaspoon kosher *or* sea salt, divided

1 cup shredded raclette *or* Gruyère cheese

1 tablespoon chopped fresh thyme

¼ teaspoon ground pepper

1. Preheat oven to 375°F.

2. Remove excess papery skin from garlic and place the head in a small baking dish. Drizzle with ½ teaspoon oil. Add ¼ inch water to the dish. Roast, uncovered, until tender but still firm, about 30 minutes. Peel the cloves and thinly slice; set aside.

3. Meanwhile, bring 3 cups water to a boil. Place bread in a heatproof dish in a single layer. Pour in water to nearly submerge it. Let stand until it is saturated, 3 to 5 minutes. Transfer to a colander in batches and press out the liquid. The bread should be moist, not dripping. Tear into pieces and place in a large bowl.

4. Heat 1 tablespoon oil in a large skillet over medium heat. Add leeks, 2 tablespoons water and ¼ teaspoon salt; partially cover and cook, stirring occasionally, until the leeks are tender but still bright green, 5 to 7 minutes.

5. Add the leeks to the bowl of bread along with the garlic, 1½ tablespoons oil, cheese, thyme, pepper and the remaining ¼ teaspoon salt; gently combine with your hands or a spoon. Spread the mixture in a 1-inch layer in a shallow baking dish. Drizzle with the remaining 1 teaspoon oil.

6. Bake until crisp and golden in spots, about 30 minutes. Serve warm.

SERVES 6: ABOUT ¾ CUP EACH

Calories 275, **Fat** 14g (sat 5g), **Cholesterol** 20mg, **Carbs** 26g, **Total sugars** 5g (added 2g), **Protein** 12g, **Fiber** 4g, **Sodium** 321mg, **Potassium** 240mg.
Nutrition bonus: Calcium (27% daily value), Vitamin A (24% dv).

SCRAMBLED EGGS WITH RAMPS & BACON

ACTIVE: 15 MIN **TOTAL:** 15 MIN

A small amount of bacon fat is enough to cook the ramps, shallots and eggs while adding enticing smoky flavor. This recipe, quick enough for breakfast, makes a satisfying supper as well.

6-8 ramps *(see page 337)*
  2 slices bacon, chopped
  2 tablespoons minced shallot
  4 large eggs
  ⅛ teaspoon salt
     Ground pepper to taste

1. Rinse ramps well and pat dry. Trim the stem ends and cut the greens from the stems. Thinly slice the stems and the greens; keep separate.

2. Cook bacon in a medium nonstick skillet over medium heat until crisp, 5 to 6 minutes. Transfer to a paper towel-lined plate to drain. Reserve 1 teaspoon of the drippings in the pan, discarding the rest.

3. Add shallot and the ramp stems to the drippings and cook, stirring constantly, until tender, 1 to 2 minutes. Push to one side. Add the ramp greens and cook, stirring, just until slightly wilted. Reserve about 1 tablespoon of the greens for topping.

4. Whisk eggs, salt and pepper in a medium bowl until well blended. Add to the pan along with the bacon and cook over medium heat, gently lifting and folding with a rubber spatula, until very softly set and still slightly wet-looking, about 2 minutes.

5. Divide between 2 plates. Top with the reserved greens. Serve immediately.

SERVES 2: ABOUT ¾ CUP EACH

Calories 199, **Fat** 12g (sat 4g), **Cholesterol** 379mg, **Carbs** 6g, **Total sugars** 2g (added 0g), **Protein** 16g, **Fiber** 1g, **Sodium** 405mg, **Potassium** 333mg.
Nutrition bonus: Vitamin A (22% daily value), Folate (20% dv).

SPRING SALAD WITH PEAS & FRIZZLED SHALLOTS

ACTIVE: 40 MIN **TOTAL:** 40 MIN

This simple spring salad combines red-leaf lettuce and frisée with fresh peas and crispy fried shallots tossed with a light tarragon-infused vinaigrette. The fried shallots give this salad a unique, crunchy flavor. And compared with store-bought fried onions, they have half the calories and a fraction of the saturated fat and sodium.

1½ cups thinly sliced shallots
 6 tablespoons extra-virgin olive oil
 3 tablespoons white-wine vinegar
 1 tablespoon whole-grain mustard
 1 tablespoon chopped fresh tarragon *or* 1 teaspoon dried
 ¼ teaspoon salt
 ¼ teaspoon ground pepper
 6 cups torn red-leaf lettuce
 4 cups torn frisée
 1 cup shelled fresh peas *or* frozen peas (thawed)
 2 large hard-boiled eggs, shredded *or* chopped

1. Separate shallot slices into rings. Heat oil in a small stainless-steel skillet (or small saucepan) over medium-high heat until shimmering. (To test if your oil is hot enough, add a shallot ring; if it starts sizzling on contact, the oil is ready.) Add half the shallots and cook, stirring frequently, until browned, 4 to 8 minutes. With the pan off the heat, use a slotted spoon to transfer the shallots to a plate lined with paper towels. Cook the remaining shallots and transfer to the plate. (The shallots will get crispier as they cool.)

2. Pour the hot oil into a large, heat-resistant bowl; let cool for 10 minutes. Whisk in vinegar, mustard, tarragon, salt and pepper until well combined. Add lettuce, frisée, peas and eggs and toss to combine. Divide among 6 plates or bowls. Top each portion with about 3 tablespoons frizzled shallots.

SERVES 6: ABOUT 1⅓ CUPS SALAD & 3 TBSP. SHALLOTS EACH

Calories 203, **Fat** 16g (sat 3g), **Cholesterol** 62mg, **Carbs** 9g, **Total sugars** 2g (added 0g), **Protein** 5g, **Fiber** 3g, **Sodium** 201mg, **Potassium** 292mg.
Nutrition bonus: Vitamin A (74% daily value), Folate (22% dv).

POTATO-LEEK BISQUE

ACTIVE: 50 MIN **TOTAL:** 50 MIN
TO MAKE AHEAD: Refrigerate the bisque and the crouton topping up to 3 days.

It's hard to believe how rich and creamy this soup is, even though there's not a drop of cream in it. Croutons topped with anchovy, olives and leek are a crunchy, savory foil to the soup. But skip them if you like and incorporate all the cooked leeks into the soup instead.

2 tablespoons extra-virgin olive oil
3 pounds leeks, white and light green parts only, sliced
¾ teaspoon salt, divided
1½ pounds Yukon Gold potatoes, peeled and diced
3 cups nonfat *or* low-fat milk
2 cups reduced-sodium chicken broth
3 tablespoons lemon juice

¼ teaspoon ground white pepper, or to taste
Thinly sliced fresh chives for garnish

CROUTONS

¼ cup minced pitted oil-cured olives
3 anchovies, minced
¼ teaspoon ground pepper
8 slices baguette, preferably whole-wheat, toasted

1. To prepare bisque: Heat oil in a large pot over medium heat. Add leeks and ¼ teaspoon salt. Cook, stirring occasionally, until very tender but not brown, 20 to 30 minutes. Adjust heat as necessary and add a bit of water if needed to prevent sticking. Set aside ⅓ cup of the leeks in a small bowl.

2. Add potatoes, milk and broth to the pot. Bring to a simmer (do not boil) and cook, stirring occasionally, until the potatoes are very tender, 10 to 15 minutes.

3. To prepare croutons: Meanwhile, add olives, anchovies and black pepper to the reserved leeks; mix well. Divide evenly among the toasted baguette slices.

4. When the potatoes are tender, remove from the heat. Puree the soup with an immersion blender or in batches in a standing blender. (Use caution when pureeing hot liquids.) Season with the remaining ½ teaspoon salt, lemon juice and white pepper. Divide among 8 soup bowls and float a crouton on top of each. Garnish with chives, if desired.

SERVES 8: ABOUT 1 CUP EACH

Calories 276, **Fat** 6g (sat 1g), **Cholesterol** 3mg, **Carbs** 48g, **Total sugars** 9g (added 0g), **Protein** 9g, **Fiber** 3g, **Sodium** 740mg, **Potassium** 606mg.
Nutrition bonus: Vitamin C (31% daily value), Vitamin A (29% dv).

SHALLOT, TARRAGON & LEMON VINEGAR

ACTIVE: 40 MIN **TOTAL:** 3-4 WEEKS
TO MAKE AHEAD: Refrigerate the vinegar up to 1 year.
EQUIPMENT: 3 pint-size (2-cup) glass canning jars; cheesecloth

Stir a little of this infused vinegar and some fresh chopped tarragon into reduced-fat cream cheese and try it as a spread for crackers. Top with a piece of smoked salmon for an instant appetizer. Or combine the vinegar with a little olive oil, low-fat mayonnaise and chopped celery and use as a dressing for tuna salad. The recipe makes enough vinegar to have enough extra to decant into a decorative bottle or two to give as a simple homemade gift.

12 sprigs fresh tarragon
6 strips of zest from 2 lemons
   (see Tip)
3 shallots, peeled and quartered

6 cups cider vinegar
   Additional fresh tarragon,
   lemon zest *and/or* shallots for
   decoration (optional)

Peeling Citrus

Use a vegetable peeler to remove strips of the outer skin (zest), leaving the bitter white pith behind.

1. Wash 3 pint-size (2-cup) heatproof glass canning jars (or similar containers) and their lids with hot soapy water. Rinse well with hot water. Fill a large, deep pot (such as a water-bath canner) about half full with water. Place the jars upright into the pot; add enough additional water to cover by 2 inches. Bring the water to a boil; boil jars for 10 minutes. Add the lids to the pot, then remove the pot from the heat. Let the jars and lids stay in the hot water as you prepare the flavoring and vinegar. (Keeping the jars warm minimizes breakage when filling with hot liquid.)

2. Thoroughly rinse tarragon and zest with water and pat dry with a clean towel. Remove the jars from the water bath with a jar lifter or tongs. Divide shallots, zest and tarragon among the jars. Heat vinegar in a large saucepan to a bare simmer (at least 190°F). Carefully divide the vinegar among the prepared jars, leaving at least ¼ inch of space between the top of the jar and the vinegar. Remove lids from the water bath, dry with a clean towel and screw tightly onto the jars.

3. Store the jars in a cool, dark place, undisturbed, for 3 to 4 weeks. Strain vinegar through cheesecloth into another container. Repeat as needed until all the sediment is removed and the vinegar is clear. Discard all solids and pour the strained vinegar back into rinsed jars or divide among sterilized decorative bottles. Decorate with fresh tarragon, strips of zest and/or quartered shallots, if desired.

MAKES: 6 CUPS (1-TBSP. SERVING)

Calories 3, **Fat** 0g (sat 0g), **Cholesterol** 0mg, **Carbs** 0g, **Total sugars** 0g (added 0g), **Protein** 0g, **Fiber** 0g, **Sodium** 1mg, **Potassium** 11mg.

Parsnips

Ivory-hued parsnips look like a white carrot, yet deliver sweeter, more intense flavor than their more commonly used relative. They can be shaved raw onto salads when small and tender and roasted, steamed, sautéed or prepared any way other root vegetables are.

The sweet and pungent qualities of parsnips make them a good match for fragrant spices like curries and chiles but also give them the flavor fortitude to stand up to bold ingredients, such as horseradish and mustards. When used in soups, stews and casseroles they add a sugary richness. Temper intense parsnips by mixing them with mild-mannered roots, such as potatoes and celery root. If you can't get parsnips, consider using celery root or carrots instead.

Unlike carrots, parsnips tend to grow in more irregular shapes and sizes and can be more challenging to prep. The root is often very wide at the base, tapering to a fine point at the tip, plus they have a core that can be tough and fibrous, all of which means doing a little extra knife work to get them into uniform pieces that will cook evenly.

Parsnips need to be planted early in the spring and harvested after a hard frost in the fall, which transforms their starches into sugars. Some aficionados prefer spring-dug parsnips, which have spent the winter under the frosty soil developing even more intense flavors. And because they spend so much time in the ground (taking up valuable garden real estate), parsnips are usually more costly than carrots and, not surprisingly, rarely come with good-looking green tops attached.

Best in fall to spring

AT THE MARKET

➣ Choose parsnips that are firm and have no soft spots or discoloration. Don't expect the greens (if there are any) to look fresh. For ease of prep, look for parsnips that don't have any secondary roots that will be difficult to peel around.

➣ Most markets carry the standard All America variety of parsnips, but look at farmers' markets for heirloom varieties, such as the Harris Model and Hollow Crown, which grow in different sizes and have varying levels of sweetness.

IN YOUR KITCHEN

➣ Refrigerate unwashed parsnips in a sealed bag. They'll keep at least 2 weeks if not longer.

➣ Peel parsnips as you would a carrot using a peeler. Parsnips have a core that can be tough and fibrous, especially when they're large. If necessary, cut the parsnip into quarters and simply slice out the core using a sharp knife. Once peeled and cut, parsnips will start to turn brown rather quickly. If you're not going to use them right away or just want to preserve their pretty ivory color, soak them in water spiked with an acid, such as lemon juice or vinegar.

COOKING BASICS

BRAISE Peel and cut 1½ pounds of parsnips lengthwise in ½-inch sticks. Layer in a 2½-quart covered casserole dish. Brush with 1 tablespoon melted butter and add 1 cup of vegetable or reduced-sodium chicken broth. Bake, covered, at 350°F for 1 hour, stirring once to uncover the submerged parsnips. Remove with a slotted spoon and top with chopped fresh parsley. Serves 4.

PURÉE Simmer evenly sized pieces of peeled and cut parsnip in lightly salted water until tender, about 20 minutes; drain. Puree until smooth.

ROAST Peel and cut 1 pound of parsnips into ½-inch-by-2-inch pieces, toss with 1 tablespoon olive oil and roast at 400°F until tender and golden, 25 to 25 minutes. Serves 3.

SAUTÉ Peel and cut 1½ pounds parsnips in quarters lengthwise. Heat 1 tablespoon olive oil in a large skillet over medium-high heat. Add parsnips, ½ teaspoon salt and pepper to taste and cook, stirring occasionally, until parsnips begin to brown at the edges, about 12 minutes. Add 1 tablespoon butter, 1 tablespoon chopped fresh rosemary and 1 tablespoon honey to pan. Cook, stirring occasionally, over medium heat until the vegetables are coated, about 5 minutes. Serves 4.

NUTRITION

➣ **½ cup cooked sliced parsnips: Calories** 55, **Fat** 0g (sat 0g), **Cholesterol** 0mg, **Carbs** 13g, **Total sugars** 4g (added 0g), **Protein** 1g, **Fiber** 3g, **Sodium** 8mg, **Potassium** 286mg.

BONUS Eat one parsnip and you'll rack up 40 percent more blood-pressure-lowering potassium than you'd get from a banana. You'll also score a third of your day's vitamin C to help blood vessels stay relaxed and pliable.

Grow Your Own

Parsnips are easy to grow, but it's very important that you start with fresh seeds you've just purchased—not from a packet saved from a previous year. Parsnips require a long growing season, so plant in early spring as soon as the soil can be worked. Sow seeds about ½ inch apart and ½ inch deep in soft, loamy soil so the roots grow straight and don't fork. When seedlings emerge—in 2 to 3 weeks— thin to between 3 and 6 inches apart. Water during the heat of summer if you get less than 1 inch of rainfall per week. Harvest in the fall after at least one hard frost.

CREAMY PARSNIPS & PEARS

ACTIVE: 20 MIN **TOTAL:** 50 MIN
TO MAKE AHEAD: Refrigerate up to 2 days or freeze up to 1 month. Reheat in a covered casserole at 350°F for 35 to 45 minutes.

For a delightful change from mashed potatoes, try this velvety puree made with earthy parsnips and sweet autumn pears. This recipe freezes well and can be easily doubled. Thin leftovers with broth and enrich with sour cream for a delicious soup.

2 pounds parsnips, peeled and cut into 2-inch pieces
1 large pear (Bartlett *or* Anjou), peeled, cored and halved
4 cloves garlic, peeled
1 tablespoon butter
2 teaspoons lemon juice
¼ teaspoon salt
Ground pepper to taste

1. Place parsnips, pear and garlic in a large saucepan and cover with lightly salted water. Bring to a boil. Reduce heat to medium-low, cover and simmer until the parsnips are tender and can be easily pierced with a knife, 20 to 25 minutes.

2. Drain and transfer to a food processor. Add butter, lemon juice, salt and pepper. Process until completely smooth. Scrape into a serving bowl and serve hot. (To keep puree hot up to 1 hour, cover with parchment or wax paper and set the bowl in a pan of barely simmering water.)

SERVES 8: ½ CUP EACH

Calories 113, **Fat** 2g (sat 1g), **Cholesterol** 4mg, **Carbs** 24g, **Total sugars** 8g (added 0g), **Protein** 2g, **Fiber** 5g, **Sodium** 85mg, **Potassium** 471mg.

Perfect Pears

Most pears don't significantly change in color when ripe, so go by touch: Ripe pears are soft when gently pressed near the stem. Store ripe pears in the coldest part of the refrigerator to prevent overripening.

PARSNIP-CELERY ROOT PANCAKES WITH PANCETTA

ACTIVE: 45 MIN **TOTAL:** 45 MIN

Serve these crispy sweet-savory pancakes as a side dish to a big roast or pork chops.

2 slices pancetta

3 medium parsnips, peeled and cored if necessary *(see page 352)*

1 small celery root (about 1 pound), peeled and halved

2 large eggs, lightly beaten

⅓ cup nonfat milk

¼ cup white whole-wheat flour *(see Tip)*

2 tablespoons chopped fresh chives, plus more for garnish

1 teaspoon whole-grain mustard

½ teaspoon ground pepper

¼ teaspoon salt

4 tablespoons extra-virgin olive oil, divided

6 tablespoons crème fraîche

1. Preheat oven to 300°F. Cook pancetta in a small skillet over medium heat until crisp, about 5 minutes per side. Let cool on a paper towel-lined plate; crumble.

2. Coarsely shred parsnips and celery root halves in a food processor fitted with the shredding disk. Combine eggs, milk, flour, chives, mustard, pepper and salt in a large bowl. Stir in the shredded vegetables and the pancetta.

3. Wipe out the skillet; add 2 tablespoons oil and heat over medium heat. Cook 4 pancakes per batch, using about ¼ cup of batter for each and flattening with a spatula to make them 3 to 4 inches in diameter. Cook until golden, 2 to 3 minutes per side. Transfer to a baking sheet and keep warm in the oven. Repeat with the remaining batter to make 16 pancakes, using the remaining 2 tablespoons oil for the last 2 batches.

4. To serve, top each pancake with 1 teaspoon crème fraîche and sprinkle with additional chives, if desired.

SERVES 8: 2 PANCAKES & 2 TSP. CRÈME FRAÎCHE EACH

Calories 220, **Fat** 14g (sat 5g), **Cholesterol** 59mg, **Carbs** 18g, **Total sugars** 4g (added 0g), **Protein** 5g, **Fiber** 4g, **Sodium** 411mg, **Potassium** 409mg.
Nutrition bonus: Vitamin C (20% daily value).

The Whole-Wheat Difference

Milled from hard white winter wheat rather than the hard red winter wheat of traditional whole-wheat flours, this white cousin claims the same healthful nutritional profile without the bitter tannins. The benefits of whole-wheat flours are a direct result of milling the nutrient-rich germ and bran of the wheat berry along with the endosperm. In all-purpose flour only the endosperm is used.

Peas

If you're looking for a reason to slow down, buy fresh shelling peas. Popping the plump little orbs out of the pods is a job best done sitting down, on the porch if you have one. A bowl full of just-shelled peas is an anticipation of pure pleasure—if the peas make it into the bowl at all, sweet and crunchy as they are.

The key to preserving the wonderfully sweet flavor and crisp texture of peas is to barely cook them. Briefly boiled or steamed fresh English peas need very little embellishment—just a small bit of butter and a little salt, maybe chopped mint or basil. Sauté snow peas in sesame oil and sprinkle with toasted sesame seeds and salt. Crunch on crisp and juicy sugar snap peas—an edible-pod pea that is a cross between snow peas and English peas—raw with dip or slice into thin ribbons and toss with coarsely shredded radishes and vinaigrette or sauté them in olive oil and toss with a little salt, coarsely ground pepper and chopped toasted cashews.

As soon as peas are picked, their sugars start to convert to starch, so the quicker they make it into the pot or pan (or your mouth), the sweeter they'll be. The short shelf life of English peas in particular means they can be difficult to find fresh. Outside of growing your own, a farmstand or farmers' market is your best bet.

Peas thrive in the cool weather of spring, although snow peas—despite their name—do a little better in warmer weather than English peas or sugar snap peas. Pea season is sweet but fleeting. When temperatures reach above 80°F, it's over.

▼ *English Peas*

▼ *Snow Peas*

Best in spring

AT THE MARKET

For all three varieties, choose pods that are crisp, glossy and bright green, with fresh-looking ends. Avoid pods that are dull, faded, yellowing, blemished, limp or overly mature.

IN YOUR KITCHEN

Store fresh English peas, unshelled, in a perforated plastic bag in the refrigerator up to 2 days. Shell right before cooking. Store snow peas and sugar snap peas in a plastic bag in the refrigerator up to 3 days.

English peas require shelling. *(See photos.)* Although some varieties of sugar snap peas and snow peas are stringless, most need to have the strings removed from both sides of the pod. Using your fingers or a paring knife, snap off the stem end, then pull the string off along the length of both sides of the pod. Rinse snow peas and sugar snap peas in a colander under cool running water.

COOKING BASICS

BOIL Bring 1 cup of water for each cup of shelled English peas or edible-pod peas (snow peas or sugar snap peas) to a boil in a pot; add peas. Cover and cook until tender-crisp, 2 to 4 minutes; drain. Toss with butter, salt and chopped fresh tarragon.

MICROWAVE Place 3 cups shelled English peas in a microwave-safe bowl. Add 2 tablespoons water. Cover and microwave on High for 4 to 5 minutes, stirring once. For snow peas or sugar snap peas, place 2 cups peas in a microwave-safe bowl. Add 2 tablespoons water. Cover and microwave on High for 2 to 4 minutes, until tender-crisp. Drain and season as desired. Serves 6 (English peas) or 2 (snow peas or sugar snap peas).

STEAM Bring 1 inch of water to a boil in a saucepan fitted with a steamer basket. Add shelled English peas. Cover and steam until tender-crisp, about 10 to 12 minutes. For snow peas or sugar snap peas, cover and steam until tender-crisp, about 2 to 4 minutes; drain. Toss with olive oil, salt and freshly grated lemon zest.

NUTRITION

½ cup of cooked English peas: Calories 67, **Fat** 0g (sat 0g), **Cholesterol** 0mg, **Carbs** 12g, **Total sugars** 5g (added 0g), **Protein** 4g, **Fiber** 4g, **Sodium** 3mg, **Potassium** 217mg.

BONUS Technically legumes, peas are a key source of nutrients that support heart health, especially fiber and vegetable protein. Toss one cup into pasta, rice or quinoa and you'll pick up 5 grams.

≈

Grow Your Own

Plant peas in rich, well-drained soil 6 weeks before the last frost, in a spot protected from the midday sun when temperatures are higher than 80°F. Most varieties require support from a stake or trellis. Peas take 50 to 70 days to mature.

≈

How to prep English peas

1. Cut off the stem end of the pea pod; remove strings.

2. Open the pod.

3. Pop the peas out by running your thumb down the length of the pod *(right)*.

PEA, PANCETTA & TARRAGON CROSTINI

ACTIVE: 1 HR **TOTAL:** 1 HR

Pancetta—unsmoked Italian bacon—is a flavorful alternative to cured bacon. It comes in thinly sliced rounds and small chunks that are better for dicing— which is what you want for this recipe.

CROSTINI

- 1 10-ounce baguette, sliced ¼ inch thick (about 45 slices)
- 5 tablespoons extra-virgin olive oil
- ½ teaspoon kosher salt
  Ground pepper to taste

PEAS

- 2 cups shelled English peas, fresh or frozen (thawed)
- 2 ounces diced pancetta
- 1 tablespoon minced shallot
- 2 tablespoons extra-virgin olive oil
- 3 tablespoons chopped fresh tarragon
- 1 tablespoon finely grated lemon zest
- ¼ teaspoon kosher salt
  Ground pepper to taste
- 8 ounces soft goat cheese

1. To prepare crostini: Position racks in upper and lower thirds of oven; preheat to 350°F. Arrange bread on 2 large rimmed baking sheets. Brush both sides of bread with oil; season one side with ½ teaspoon salt and pepper. Bake the crostini, turning them over and rotating the pans top to bottom halfway through, until toasted, 15 to 20 minutes. Cool completely on the pans.

2. To prepare peas: Meanwhile, bring a medium saucepan of water to a boil over high heat. Add peas and cook until tender, about 3 minutes. Drain immediately.

3. Cook pancetta in a large skillet over medium heat, stirring frequently, until crisp, 5 to 6 minutes. Remove with a slotted spoon and drain on a paper towel-lined plate. Reserve 1 teaspoon of the drippings in the pan.

4. Cook shallot in the drippings for 30 seconds. Add the peas and pancetta along with oil, tarragon, lemon zest, salt and pepper. Cook, stirring occasionally, until heated through, 1 to 2 minutes. Remove from heat. Lightly crush the peas with a fork and stir to combine.

5. Spread about 1 teaspoon of goat cheese on each crostini. Top with a generous 1 teaspoon of the pea mixture. Serve immediately.

SERVES 15: 3 CROSTINI EACH

Calories 154, **Fat** 9g (sat 3g), **Cholesterol** 10mg, **Carbs** 12g, **Total sugars** 1g (added 0g), **Protein** 7g, **Fiber** 3g, **Sodium** 285mg, **Potassium** 32mg.

PEAS & LETTUCE

ACTIVE: 20 MIN **TOTAL:** 20 MIN

A take on the French technique of cooking peas with a little lettuce, this light springtime dish goes well with mildly seasoned seafood or chicken. Because it has a sweet, mellow flavor, it would be overwhelmed by intense spicing.

4 teaspoons extra-virgin olive oil
2 cups shelled English peas (3 pounds unshelled)
1 tablespoon finely chopped fresh mint
4 cups thinly sliced Boston lettuce (about 1 small head)
¼ teaspoon salt
Ground pepper to taste

Heat oil in a large nonstick skillet over medium-low heat. Add peas and stir to coat with oil. Cover and cook, stirring once or twice, until beginning to brown, about 4 minutes. Stir in mint and cook for 30 seconds. Add lettuce, cover and cook, stirring once or twice, until wilted, 1 to 2 minutes. Remove from the heat and season with salt and pepper.

SERVES 6: ABOUT ½ CUP EACH

Calories 68, **Fat** 3g (sat 0g), **Cholesterol** 0mg, **Carbs** 7g, **Total sugars** 2g (added 0g), **Protein** 3g, **Fiber** 3g, **Sodium** 131mg, **Potassium** 141mg.
Nutrition bonus: Vitamin A (44% daily value).

GARLIC STIR-FRIED SNOW PEAS & PEA GREENS

ACTIVE: 15 MIN **TOTAL:** 15 MIN

A favorite in stir-fries, snow peas are grown primarily for their crunchy delicate pods—the tiny seeds inside are almost incidental. This fresh stir-fry is fragrant with garlic and ginger. Adding a little puree of garlic scapes at the end gives an added subtle garlicky flavor, but the dish is delicious without it as well.

1	tablespoon canola oil
2	tablespoons chopped garlic
2	tablespoons chopped fresh ginger
2	cups snow peas *or* snap peas, trimmed
2	packed cups pea greens *or* pea sprouts
1-3	teaspoons Garlic Scape Pesto (*page 259*; optional)
1	tablespoon reduced-sodium soy sauce

Heat oil in a large flat-bottomed carbon-steel wok or large heavy skillet over high heat until shimmering. Add garlic and ginger; cook, stirring, until fragrant, 10 to 15 seconds. Add peas; cook, stirring, until bright green and the garlic is light brown, about 1 minute. Stir in pea greens (or sprouts) and Garlic Scape Pesto to taste (if using). Add soy sauce; cook, stirring, until the pea greens are starting to wilt, 30 seconds to 1 minute.

MAKES: 4 SERVINGS, ABOUT ⅔ CUP EACH

Calories 129, **Fat** 4g (sat 0g), **Cholesterol** 0mg, **Carbs** 21g, **Total sugars** 1g (added 0g), **Protein** 7g, **Fiber** 3g, **Sodium** 148mg, **Potassium** 328mg.
Nutrition bonus: Vitamin C (44% daily value), Folate (25% dv).

Pea Shoots

Pea greens, also known as pea shoots, are the leaves, tendrils and flowers of a mature pea plant. They have a mild sweetness akin to snap and snow peas. Look for pea shoots at farmers' markets or Asian markets. Pea sprouts are smaller sprouted pea leaves and are easier to find—many large supermarkets stock them year-round.

SNAP PEA & CHERRY TOMATO STIR-FRY

ACTIVE: 25 MIN **TOTAL:** 25 MIN

Serve this lightly spicy, colorful side with grilled shrimp or salmon. If you like you can use snow peas instead or a mix of the two.

- 2 tablespoons reduced-sodium soy sauce
- 2 tablespoons rice vinegar
- 1 tablespoon toasted sesame seeds
- 2 teaspoons chili-garlic sauce
- 2 tablespoons toasted sesame oil
- 4 cups snap peas (about 12 ounces), trimmed
- 1 pint cherry *or* grape tomatoes
- ¼ teaspoon salt

Whisk soy sauce, vinegar, sesame seeds and chili-garlic sauce in a large bowl; place near the stove. Place a large carbon-steel wok or large skillet over high heat until very hot. Swirl in oil and add snap peas and cherry tomatoes. Sprinkle with salt and stir-fry until the peas are tender-crisp and the tomatoes are softened, 4 to 5 minutes. Transfer to the bowl with the soy sauce mixture; toss to combine.

SERVES 4: 1 CUP EACH

Calories 127, **Fat** 8g (sat 1g), **Cholesterol** 0mg, **Carbs** 11g, **Total sugars** 5g (added 0g), **Protein** 4g, **Fiber** 3g, **Sodium** 420mg, **Potassium** 386mg.
Nutrition bonus: Vitamin C (103% daily value), Vitamin A (31% dv).

PEAS & HAM PASTA SALAD

ACTIVE: 35 MIN **TOTAL:** 35 MIN
TO MAKE AHEAD: Refrigerate salad and dressing separately up to 1 day. Toss with the dressing about 1 hour before serving.

The creamy dill-and-garlic buttermilk dressing made with low-fat mayo makes this picnic-perfect pasta salad lower in fat and calories than the original version of this old-school favorite. For the best flavor, combine the pasta salad with the dressing about 1 hour before serving, then chill.

DRESSING

1 clove garlic, minced
¼ teaspoon salt
½ cup buttermilk
¼ cup low-fat mayonnaise
3 tablespoons chopped fresh dill *or* 1 tablespoon dried
1 tablespoon distilled white vinegar

PASTA SALAD

10 ounces (about 2 cups) whole-wheat elbow noodles
1¾ cups sliced button mushrooms
1¾ cups peas, fresh *or* frozen (thawed)
1 cup diced ham
¼ cup finely chopped sweet onion, such as Vidalia
2 large hard-boiled eggs *(see Tip)*, chopped
½ cup diced Cheddar cheese
Ground pepper to taste

1. To prepare dressing: Mash garlic and salt in a medium bowl with the back of a spoon into a chunky paste. Add buttermilk, mayonnaise, dill and vinegar; whisk until combined.

2. To prepare pasta salad: Cook pasta in a large pot of boiling water according to package directions. Drain, transfer to a large bowl and let cool. Add mushrooms, peas, ham, onion, eggs, cheese, pepper and the dressing; toss to coat.

SERVES 6: ABOUT 1⅓ CUPS EACH

Calories 337, **Fat** 9g (sat 4g), **Cholesterol** 88mg, **Carbs** 46g, **Total sugars** 4g (added 0g), **Protein** 21g, **Fiber** 6g, **Sodium** 636mg, **Potassium** 377mg.
Nutrition bonus: Magnesium (23% daily value), Vitamin A (21% dv).

Hard-Boiled Eggs

To hard-boil eggs, place in a single layer in a saucepan; cover with 1 inch of water. Bring just to a simmer over medium-high heat. Reduce heat to low and cook at the barest simmer for 10 minutes. Remove from heat, immediately pour out hot water and cover the eggs with ice-cold water. Let stand in the water until cool.

SEARED SALMON WITH SUGAR SNAP-FENNEL SLAW

ACTIVE: 35 MIN **TOTAL:** 35 MIN

The light and summery snap-pea-and-fennel slaw is a crisp bed for seared salmon (or any firm fish). The delicate fennel fronds add more mild licorice flavor to the dish.

¼ cup lemon juice
3 tablespoons extra-virgin olive oil, divided
2 tablespoons minced shallot
½ teaspoon light brown sugar
¾ teaspoon salt, divided

½ teaspoon ground pepper, divided
1 large fennel bulb, with fronds
2 cups sugar snap peas, trimmed
1¼ pounds wild Alaskan salmon, skinned *(see Tip)*
2 teaspoons minced fresh chives

1. Combine lemon juice, 2½ tablespoons oil, shallot, brown sugar, ½ teaspoon salt and ¼ teaspoon pepper in a large bowl. Set aside 4 teaspoons of the dressing in a small bowl.

2. Slice top off fennel bulb. Discard or reserve stems for another use. Chop 2 tablespoons of the fronds and add to the large bowl. (Reserve remaining fronds for garnish.) Halve, core and thinly slice the bulb. Thinly slice snap peas into long matchsticks. Toss the fennel and peas with the dressing in the large bowl; let stand while you cook the salmon.

3. Cut salmon into 4 portions and season with the remaining ¼ teaspoon each salt and pepper. Heat the remaining 1½ teaspoons oil in a large nonstick skillet over medium-high heat. Add the salmon and cook for 2 minutes. Gently turn and continue cooking until just opaque in the center, 2 to 4 minutes more.

4. Divide the slaw and salmon among 4 plates. Drizzle each portion with 1 teaspoon of the reserved dressing and top with ½ teaspoon chives and fennel fronds, if desired.

SERVES 4: 4 OZ. SALMON & 1 CUP SLAW EACH

Calories 308, **Fat** 16g (sat 3g), **Cholesterol** 66mg, **Carbs** 10g, **Total sugars** 3g (added 1g), **Protein** 30g, **Fiber** 3g, **Sodium** 539mg, **Potassium** 889mg.
Nutrition bonus: Vitamin B_{12} (100% daily value), Vitamin C (68% dv), Potassium (25% dv), Omega-3s.

Salmon Buying Guide

All wild salmon—and now some farmed—are considered a sustainable choice for the environment. For farmed, ask for fish that's raised in land- or tank-based systems. For more information about choosing sustainable seafood, go to *seafoodwatch.org*.

▲ Serrano

▲ Poblano

▼ Jalapeño

▼ Fresno

▲ Bell Peppers
(Sweet Peppers)

Peppers

◄ *Thai Bird Chile*

The fruits of the Capsicum genus—peppers, in common parlance—are a rainbow of colors and bring bold, highly distinctive flavor to foods.

Peppers are either sweet or hot. The sweet-pepper category is very small, comprised only of bell peppers. Each of the many varieties of hot peppers resides somewhere along a fiery continuum known as the Scoville Scale. The heat comes from a chemical called capsaicin (*cap-SAY-a-sin*). The Scoville Scale measures the hotness of peppers in multiples of 100 Scoville heat units (SHU). It ranges from 0 (bell peppers) to more than 1,000,000 for the Indian chile called Naga Jolokia (also known as the Ghost Pepper, presumably because if you eat one it may cause your soul to take flight). In more moderately hot peppers, the spiciness is a pleasant accent to the flavor of the chile, which can be fruity, grassy, nutty or woodsy, depending on the variety.

While bell peppers can be the featured ingredient—stuffed or sliced for a colorful side-dish sauté of sweet pepper strips—hot peppers play a supporting but very important role, adding their unique brand of fire to soups, stews, salsas, sauces and stir-fries. Hot chiles are integral to the flavors of Latin American, Thai, Korean, Southeast Asian and Indian cooking.

Peppers—which originated in the Amazon basin of South America—thrive in heat and humidity. Although they are available in supermarkets year-round, they peak from midsummer to early fall.

▲ *Cubanelle/Italian*

◄ *Habanero*

◄ *New Mexico*

Best in midsummer to early fall

AT THE MARKET

❧ Choose firm, bright-color peppers with glossy skin. Avoid peppers with nicks, soft spots or blemishes.

IN YOUR KITCHEN

❧ Store peppers in a plastic bag in the refrigerator up to 1 week.

❧ Rinse peppers under cool running water. For bell peppers, cut off all four sides of the pepper. Discard stem and seeds. Slice or chop as desired. *(For hot peppers, see photos, right.)* Take precaution when preparing hot peppers as the volatile oils can be transferred to your skin. Avoid rubbing your eyes and wash your hands well when you're done—or wear plastic or rubber gloves.

COOKING BASICS

FISH SAUCE WITH CHILES Chop ½ cup stemmed Thai bird chiles with a knife or in a food processor. (Wear gloves.) Transfer to a jar with a tight-fitting lid. Add 1 cup fish sauce; cover and shake well. Store in refrigerator. Use in place of soy sauce when you want a punch of salty and spicy.

GRILL Toss quartered bell peppers with olive oil, salt and pepper to taste. Grill skin-side up over medium heat until the peppers begin to soften, 4 to 5 minutes. Turn them and continue to cook until slightly charred, 3 to 4 minutes more. If desired, toss with chopped fresh parsley or basil.

ROAST Place a wire rack on a large baking sheet. Arrange whole peppers on the rack. Roast at 450°F, turning

occasionally with tongs, until blackened in places, 30 to 40 minutes. Transfer to a large bowl and cover with plastic wrap. Let steam for 10 minutes. Uncover and let cool. Remove stems, skins and seeds. Slice or chop.

SAUTÉ Heat 2 tablespoons extra-virgin olive oil in a large skillet over medium heat. Add 6 sliced red, yellow and/or orange bell peppers and cook, stirring occasionally, until softened, 5 to 8 minutes. Stir in 1 teaspoon dried oregano, ¼ teaspoon salt and pepper to taste. Cook, stirring occasionally and adjusting heat if necessary so the peppers don't burn, until tender, 12 to 15 minutes. Serves 6.

NUTRITION

❧ **1 medium red bell pepper: Calories** 37, **Fat** 0g (sat 0g), **Cholesterol** 0mg, **Carbs** 7g, **Total sugars** 5g (added 0g), **Protein** 1g, **Fiber** 3g, **Sodium** 35mg, **Potassium** 251mg.

BONUS Red, green or yellow, peppers are bursting with vitamin C, a nutrient that helps build collagen to keep your skin firm.

Grow Your Own

Plant peppers in a sunny spot where the temperature during the day will be 70°F or higher and no lower than 60°F at night. Start seeds indoors in late winter or buy pepper seedlings. Plant sweet and hot pepper varieties as far apart as possible to avoid cross-pollination. Stake young plants to keep them upright and supported when they start producing fruit.

How to prep hot peppers

1. Cut off the stem end.

2. Cut the pepper in half lengthwise.

3. Use a small sharp knife to remove membrane and seeds, avoiding contact with your hands as much as possible.

Fish Sauce with Chiles
(see Cooking Basics, opposite)

SICILIAN PEPPER SALAD

ACTIVE: 30 MIN **TOTAL:** 30 MIN
TO MAKE AHEAD: Hold temperature up to 2 hours or refrigerate up to 1 day; bring to room temperature before serving.

The defining taste of this pepper salad is the generous addition of vinegar and sugar that give it the pop of sweet and sour that's so common in Sicilian cooking. Sweet currants reflect the Arabic influence in Sicilian cuisine.

- 3 tablespoons extra-virgin olive oil
- 3 medium red bell peppers, sliced ¾ inch thick
- 5 Italian frying peppers, Cubanelles *or* banana peppers, sliced ¾ inch thick
- 4 cloves garlic, very thinly sliced
- 1 tablespoon dry white wine *or* water
- ⅓ cup white-wine vinegar
- 1 tablespoon sugar
- ¾ teaspoon kosher salt
- ½ cup currants
- ⅓ cup pine nuts, toasted
- 2 tablespoons chopped fresh parsley

Heat oil in a large skillet or pot over medium-high heat. Add peppers; cook, stirring often, for 5 minutes. Add garlic and wine (or water); cook, stirring occasionally, until almost tender, 3 to 5 minutes more. Add vinegar, sugar and salt; cook, stirring, for 1 minute. Remove from heat. Gently stir in currants and pine nuts. Sprinkle with parsley just before serving.

SERVES 8: ¾ CUP EACH

Calories 142, **Fat** 9g (sat 1g), **Cholesterol** 0mg, **Carbs** 14g, **Total sugars** 10g (added 2g), **Protein** 2g, **Fiber** 3g, **Sodium** 112mg, **Potassium** 294mg.
Nutrition bonus: Vitamin C (138% daily value), Vitamin A (32% dv)

Cooling the Fire

Capsaicin—the chemical in chiles that makes them hot—is an oil-like substance that does not wash away with water. If you need to cool the inferno in your mouth, a sip of cold milk or beer will do you more good than cold water. Studies have shown that capsaicin stimulates the production of endorphins—which may explain why some hot-pepper fans report feelings of euphoria after eating spicy food.

HOMEMADE HOT SAUCE

ACTIVE: 30 MIN **TOTAL:** 2 HRS (INCLUDING COOLING TIME)
TO MAKE AHEAD: Refrigerate up to 1 month or freeze in an airtight container up to 6 months.

This sauce makes good use of bountiful tomatoes, onions and peppers in your garden or farmers' market. Adjust the heat to your preference: In our tests, two habaneros yield a pleasantly spicy sauce without excessive heat—for spicy-food fans, take it up a notch by adding extra hot peppers.

    2 tablespoons extra-virgin olive oil
    1 cup diced onion
    2 medium chile peppers, such as poblano, New Mexico *or* Anaheim, diced
  2-4 habanero peppers *or* other small hot chile peppers, stemmed, halved and seeded *(see page 372)*
    4 cloves garlic, minced
    1 pound tomatoes, diced (about 3 cups)
    1 cup distilled white vinegar
    2 teaspoons salt
  1-3 teaspoons sugar

1. Heat oil in a large saucepan over medium-high heat. Add onion, chile peppers, habaneros to taste and garlic and cook, stirring, until the onion is soft and beginning to brown, 3 to 4 minutes.

2. Reduce heat to medium. Add tomatoes, vinegar, salt and sugar to taste. Cook, stirring occasionally, until the tomatoes begin to break down, about 5 minutes.

3. Carefully transfer the tomato mixture to a food processor or blender. Puree until smooth. (Use caution when pureeing hot ingredients.) Set a fine-mesh sieve over a medium bowl; pour the pureed mixture through the sieve, pushing on the solids with a wooden spoon to extract all the liquid. (Discard solids.) Let the sauce cool to room temperature, about 1½ hours.

MAKES: ABOUT 2⅔ CUPS (1-TBSP. SERVING)

Calories 12, **Fat** 1g (sat 0g), **Cholesterol** 0mg, **Carbs** 1g, **Total sugars** 1g (added 0g), **Protein** 0g, **Fiber** 0g, **Sodium** 110mg, **Potassium** 37mg.

PAPRIKA & RED PEPPER SOUP WITH PISTACHIOS

ACTIVE: 30 MIN **TOTAL:** 50 MIN
TO MAKE AHEAD: Refrigerate up to 2 days.

Richly satisfying, this luscious soup combines capsaicin from both paprika and its hot-blooded sibling Thai chile. A gift from Spain, Hungary and South America, paprika along with chiles infuse the soup with robust color and gentle heat. For an extra-nutty flavor, puree an additional ¼ cup shelled pistachios with ¼ cup water and serve the soup with a dollop of pistachio puree on top.

2 tablespoons canola oil
1 small onion, diced
2 large red bell peppers, seeded and diced
1-2 fresh green Thai *or* serrano chiles, stemmed and coarsely chopped
2 teaspoons sweet Hungarian paprika
1 teaspoon kosher *or* sea salt
½ teaspoon ground cardamom
½ cup unsalted shelled pistachios
2 cups vegetable broth *or* water
1 cup buttermilk
2 tablespoons whipping cream
¼ cup finely chopped fresh cilantro *or* basil

1. Heat oil in a large saucepan or pot over medium-high heat. Add onion, bell peppers and chiles to taste. Cook, stirring, until the vegetables release some of their juices and the onion is lightly browned around the edges, 3 to 5 minutes. Sprinkle the vegetables with paprika, salt and cardamom and cook, stirring, until the spices are very fragrant, 1 to 2 minutes.

2. Stir in pistachios and broth (or water). Bring to a boil. Reduce the heat to medium-low and simmer, covered, stirring occasionally, until the peppers are fork-tender, 20 to 25 minutes. Remove from the heat; let cool 5 minutes.

3. Transfer the soup to a blender (in batches if necessary) and puree until smooth. (Use caution when pureeing hot liquids.) Return the soup to the pan.

4. Whisk buttermilk and cream in a bowl; stir into the soup. Gently warm over low heat. Serve sprinkled with cilantro (or basil).

SERVES 4: ABOUT 1 CUP EACH

Calories 246, **Fat** 17g (sat 3g), **Cholesterol** 9mg, **Carbs** 18g, **Total sugars** 10g (added 0g), **Protein** 7g, **Fiber** 5g, **Sodium** 574mg, **Potassium** 415mg.
Nutrition bonus: Vitamin C (179% daily value), Vitamin A (77% dv).

SOUTH TEXAS STEAK FAJITAS

ACTIVE: 40 MIN **TOTAL:** 40 MIN (PLUS 8-24 HRS MARINATING TIME)

Bottled Italian salad dressing is a tasty (and convenient) part of the marinade. Pick one with a short ingredient list.

STEAK & MARINADE

- 3 fresh jalapeño peppers, stems and seeds removed
- 1 small onion, quartered
- ¼ cup fresh cilantro
- ¾ cup pale ale *or* lager
- ½ cup Italian salad dressing
- ⅓ cup lime juice
- 1 tablespoon Worcestershire sauce
- 1½ teaspoons garlic powder
- 1 teaspoon salt
- ½ teaspoon ground cumin
- 1 pound skirt steak *(see Tip, page 145)*
- 1 bay leaf

FAJITA VEGETABLES

- 1 tablespoon canola oil
- 3 New Mexican green chiles *or* poblano peppers *(see Tip)*, seeded and cut into ½-inch strips
- 1 medium onion, halved and cut into ½-inch-wide strips
- ⅛ teaspoon salt
- 8 6-inch flour tortillas, heated

1. To marinate steak: Place jalapeños, onion and cilantro in a blender or food processor and blend until finely chopped. Add remaining marinade ingredients (except bay leaf); puree until smooth. Place steak and bay leaf in a gallon-size sealable plastic bag and pour marinade over it. Close and refrigerate, turning occasionally, for 8 hours to 24 hours.

2. To grill steak: Preheat grill to medium-high.

3. Remove the steak from the marinade and place on the grill. (Discard marinade.) Grill 3 to 4 minutes per side for medium. Remove the steak to a clean cutting board and let rest for 5 minutes.

4. To prepare vegetables: Meanwhile, heat oil in a large skillet over high heat until shimmering. Add chiles and onion strips, sprinkle with ⅛ teaspoon salt and cook, stirring, until blackened in spots and just softened, 4 to 6 minutes.

5. Holding a knife at a 45-degree angle to the steak, very thinly slice. Serve the steak and vegetables on a platter with the tortillas so everyone can make fajitas at the table.

SERVES 4: 2 FAJITAS (WITH ½ CUP FILLING) EACH

Calories 453, **Fat** 19g (sat 5g), **Cholesterol** 74mg, **Carbs** 40g, **Total sugars** 7g (added 0g), **Protein** 30g, **Fiber** 3g, **Sodium** 819mg, **Potassium** 711mg.

Pepper Lexicon

New Mexico chiles (aka Anaheim chiles) are 7 to 10 inches long, ripen from green to red and are mildly spicy. Poblano peppers (sometimes called pasilla peppers) are dark green in color, about 6 inches long and can be fiery or relatively mild; there's no way to tell until you taste them. The two can be used interchangeably and are found at most large supermarkets.

CHILES RELLENOS WITH CHICKEN

ACTIVE: 1¾ HRS **TOTAL:** 1¾ HRS
TO MAKE AHEAD: Prepare through Step 4 and refrigerate up to 2 days.

This pan-fried (instead of deep-fried) version of chiles rellenos (stuffed fried peppers) has a chicken and corn filling. Serve with salsa or tomatillo enchilada sauce.

16 medium-to-large poblano peppers *or* large New Mexico green chiles
2 cups shredded cooked chicken
2 cups frozen corn, thawed
2 cups shredded Mexican cheese blend
1 bunch scallions, chopped
½ cup nonfat *or* low-fat plain yogurt
1½ teaspoons salt, divided
⅔ cup all-purpose flour
6 large egg whites
4 tablespoons canola oil, divided

1. Preheat broiler.

2. Place peppers (or chiles) on a large baking sheet. Broil 4 to 6 inches from the heat source, turning once or twice, until the skins blacken and blister, about 10 minutes total. Transfer to a large bowl, cover with a kitchen towel and let stand until cool enough to handle. Remove the blistered skin, leaving stems intact. Make a slit lengthwise in each pepper and remove the seeds. Set aside.

3. Combine chicken, corn, cheese, scallions, yogurt and 1 teaspoon salt in a medium bowl. Fill each roasted pepper with about ¼ cup of the mixture. Fold the pepper over to completely enclose the filling.

4. Combine the remaining ½ teaspoon salt and flour in a shallow dish. Beat egg whites in another shallow dish until frothy. Dip each pepper in the flour mixture to coat on all sides, brush off any excess, then dip into the egg whites.

5. Heat 1 tablespoon oil in a large nonstick skillet over medium heat. Carefully set 4 peppers into the hot oil and cook until the cheese is melted and the peppers are golden brown, 2 to 3 minutes per side. Remove to a platter; tent with foil (or transfer to a 250°F oven) to keep warm. Repeat with the remaining oil and peppers, reducing the heat as necessary to prevent overbrowning. Serve warm.

SERVES 8: 2 RELLENOS EACH

Calories 343, **Fat** 18g (sat 7g), **Cholesterol** 60mg, **Carbs** 24g, **Total sugars** 8g (added 0g), **Protein** 23g, **Fiber** 3g, **Sodium** 671mg, **Potassium** 608mg.
Nutrition bonus: Vitamin C (370% daily value), Vitamin A (31% dv), Calcium (27% dv).

MOROCCAN-STYLE STUFFED PEPPERS

ACTIVE: 30 MIN **TOTAL:** 30 MIN

Aromatic savory-and-sweet stuffed peppers are a satisfying supper, thanks to lean beef, brown rice and bell pepper in each bite. Serve with rainbow chard sautéed with olive oil, garlic and parsley.

- 1 8- to 10-ounce bag microwavable brown rice *or* 1⅔ cups hot cooked brown rice
- 4 medium-to-large bell peppers, tops cut off and seeded
- 1 pound lean (90% *or* leaner) ground beef (*see Tip*)
- 4 cloves garlic, minced
- ½ cup currants
- 2 teaspoons ground cumin
- 1 teaspoon ground cinnamon
- 2½ cups low-sodium vegetable juice, such as V8, divided
- ¼ cup chopped fresh mint, plus more for garnish
- 1 teaspoon freshly grated orange zest
- ¾ teaspoon salt
- ¼ teaspoon ground pepper

1. Heat rice according to package directions. (If using cooked rice, skip to Step 2.)

2. Place peppers upside-down in a round microwave-safe casserole dish just large enough to fit them. Add ½ inch water to the dish and cover with a lid or inverted dinner plate. Microwave on High until the peppers are tender but still hold their shape, 3 to 6 minutes. Drain the water and turn the peppers right-side up.

3. Meanwhile, cook beef and garlic in a large nonstick skillet over medium-high heat, breaking up the beef with a wooden spoon, until no longer pink, 4 to 6 minutes. Stir in currants, cumin and cinnamon; cook for 1 minute. Stir in the rice and cook for 30 seconds more. Remove from the heat and stir in ½ cup vegetable juice, ¼ cup mint, orange zest, salt and pepper.

4. Spoon the beef mixture into the peppers. Pour the remaining 2 cups vegetable juice into the dish and cover. Microwave on High until the juice and filling are hot, 2 to 3 minutes. Serve the peppers with the sauce; garnish with mint, if desired.

SERVES 4

Calories 401, **Fat** 11g (sat 4g), **Cholesterol** 69mg, **Carbs** 48g, **Total sugars** 22g (added 0g), **Protein** 27g, **Fiber** 7g, **Sodium** 591mg, **Potassium** 1,304mg.
Nutrition bonus: Vitamin C (334% daily value), Vitamin A (105% dv), Zinc (42% dv), Potassium (37% dv), Vitamin B$_{12}$ (35% dv), Iron (28% dv), Magnesium (20% dv).

Potatoes

If an award were given out for the most versatile vegetable, the potato would have it locked. This humble tuber—a member of the nightshade family—can be baked, roasted, steamed, hashed, mashed and fried. It's the shapeshifter of the vegetable world.

Although there are no hard-and-fast rules about which type of potato to use in a particular dish, there are some differences in size, shape, texture, and water and starch content among the varieties that point to the right spud for the job.

Waxy potatoes, such as red-skinned potatoes and fingerlings, have moist, dense flesh. They hold their shape better than other varieties when cooked and work well in salads and soups.

Russet potatoes—also called baking potatoes—have drier, starchier flesh. Ideal for baking or mashing, they cook up into a wonderfully fluffy texture. Cut into chunks or wedges, tossed with olive oil, salt and pepper and roasted at high heat, they make perfect home fries—crisp on the outside and ethereally light on the inside.

Both Yukon Gold and white potatoes (also called chef's potatoes) fall somewhere in the middle between waxy potatoes and russets and are considered to be all-purpose potatoes that work well in most recipes.

The diversity of potatoes is vast. There are hundreds of varieties of heirloom and specialty potatoes with blue, red, purple or vibrant yellow flesh. Bite-size petite potatoes (also called pearl potatoes) are a new addition to the panoply.

There are two peak seasons for potatoes. Baby or new potatoes are planted in early spring and are harvested in mid- to late spring, before they reach full maturity. They have especially tender flesh. Late-season potatoes are planted in midsummer and are harvested in the fall and early winter, when they are fully mature.

Best in spring and fall to early winter

AT THE MARKET

❧ Choose potatoes that are firm to the touch, with no soft spots, cuts or green coloration of the skin. Avoid potatoes that have started to sprout.

IN YOUR KITCHEN

❧ Potatoes should never be refrigerated. Store them in a cool, dark place with good air circulation—ideally between 40°F and 50°F—to discourage softening, sprouting and spoiling. If they come in a plastic bag, remove from the bag and store in an open paper bag or cardboard box. Properly stored, potatoes will keep 10 to 12 weeks. Small, thin-skinned potatoes and new potatoes should be used within a few days.

❧ Most potatoes require only a good scrubbing with a stiff brush under cool running water. Depending on how you use the potato—and your own personal preferences—you can peel or not.

❧ If potatoes begin to sprout during storage but are still firm, remove the sprouts and eyes that are beginning to sprout before eating. Potatoes may turn green when exposed to light, which is a sign of increased alkaloid levels. Peel away any green skin or flesh before preparing. It is not only bitter-tasting but can cause digestive problems.

COOKING BASICS

BAKE (RUSSET) Prick potatoes all over with a fork. Place directly on the rack in a 425°F oven. (If you like softer skin, rub the potatoes all over with olive oil and wrap each separately in foil before baking.) Bake until tender, 40 to 60 minutes. Cool about 10 minutes. Roll each potato under a towel to slightly mash the flesh. (If baked in foil, remove it first.)

MICROWAVE (RUSSET) Prick 2 medium potatoes all over with a fork. Microwave on Medium, turning once or twice, until soft, about 20 minutes. Serves 2.

ROAST (RUSSET) Cut 2 pounds russet potatoes into ¾-inch chunks (peel, if desired). Toss on a large rimmed baking pan with 1 tablespoon olive oil, ½ teaspoon salt and pepper to taste. Roast in a 450°F oven, turning occasionally, until golden brown and tender, 30 to 35 minutes. Serves 6.

SMASHED & PAN-FRIED (BABY/NEW) Place 2 pounds baby or new potatoes in a large saucepan. Cover with cold water. Bring to a boil. Reduce heat; cover and cook until tender, about 15 minutes. Preheat oven to 200°F. Drain and arrange potatoes on a large baking sheet. With a potato masher, lightly crush each potato to about a ¾-inch-thickness. Heat ¼ cup olive oil in a large skillet over medium-high heat. Working in batches, fry potatoes in hot oil until golden brown, turning once, about 10 to 12 minutes. Keep cooked potatoes warm in the oven. Season lightly with salt and pepper. Serves 6.

STEAM (BABY/NEW) Bring 1 inch of water to a boil in a large saucepan fitted with a steamer basket. Add 2 pounds new potatoes (quarter or halve large ones). Cover and steam until tender when pierced with a fork, 18 to 20 minutes. (Check water level near end of steaming. Add more boiling water as needed.) Toss with 2 tablespoons butter, ¼ cup finely chopped parsley, ¾ teaspoon salt and pepper.

NUTRITION

❧ **1 medium baked russet potato with skin: Calories** 168, **Fat** 0g (sat 0g), **Cholesterol** 0mg, **Carbs** 37g, **Total sugars** 2g (added 0g), **Protein** 5g, **Fiber** 4g, **Sodium** 24mg, **Potassium** 952mg.

BONUS Potatoes contain resistant starch, a type your body can't digest which keeps you feeling full. Volunteers in a study who downed a resistant-starch supplement with breakfast and lunch ate 10 percent fewer calories over the following 24 hours.

▲ *'Kennebec'*
These thin-skinned white-fleshed potatoes are perfect for frying.

◄ *'Norland'*
This white-fleshed potato was developed for the short growing season in northern climates. It stores well and is good for roasting and boiling.

▲ *'Adirondack Red'*
The moist and dense flesh of this waxy potato is red, unlike other red potatoes, which have white flesh.

▲ *'Green Mountain'*
Similar to a russet, this heirloom variety introduced around 1885 has a floury texture.

◄ *'Adirondack Blue'*
The recently created hybrid has intensely hued flesh due to anthocyanins.

▲ *'Laratte'*
The satiny flesh of these fingerlings is exceptionally creamy when steamed.

◄ *'Keuka Gold'* & *'Yukon Gold'*
The yellow flesh of these potatoes (*left, far left*) is a perfect balance of flouriness and waxiness.

▲ *'Red Clouds'*
The flesh of these red-skinned potatoes is uncommonly dry, making it an ideal boiling potato.

▲ *'Red Golds'*
These waxy potatoes keep their shape when boiled, perfect for salads.

Tahini

Tahini is a thick paste of ground sesame seeds. Look for it in large supermarkets in the Middle Eastern section or near other nut butters.

POTATOES WITH GREEN TAHINI SAUCE

ACTIVE: 35 MIN **TOTAL:** 2¼ HRS (INCLUDING 1½ HOURS COOLING TIME)
TO MAKE AHEAD: Prepare through Step 2; refrigerate potatoes and sauce separately. Finish Step 3 and hold at room temperature up to 2 hours or refrigerate up to 8 hours.

The cilantro- and lemon-laced tahini sauce is a bold partner for potatoes; it would also be good tossed with roasted carrots or broccoli.

3 pounds small new potatoes, scrubbed
2 tablespoons kosher salt plus ½ teaspoon, divided
1 bunch fresh cilantro, coarsely chopped
½ cup tahini *(see Tip)*, at room temperature
¼ cup lemon juice
2 tablespoons water at room temperature, plus more as needed
2 tablespoons chopped fresh parsley
2 teaspoons extra-virgin olive oil

1. Place potatoes in a large pot, add 2 tablespoons salt and cover with cold water by about 2 inches. Bring to a boil. Reduce heat and simmer until tender, about 15 minutes. Let the potatoes cool to room temperature in the water, 1½ to 2 hours. Drain and cut the potatoes in half.

2. Combine cilantro, tahini, lemon juice and water in a food processor (or blender); process until very smooth, adding additional room-temperature water by the tablespoon as needed for a smooth sauce.

3. Toss the potatoes in a large bowl with the tahini sauce, parsley and the remaining ½ teaspoon salt. Drizzle with oil just before serving.

SERVES 8: ABOUT 1 CUP EACH

Calories 239, **Fat** 9g (sat 1g), **Cholesterol** 0mg, **Carbs** 36g, **Total sugars** 2g (added 0g), **Protein** 5g, **Fiber** 4g, **Sodium** 189mg, **Potassium** 612mg.
Nutrition bonus: Vitamin C (28% daily value).

≈

Smoked Paprika

Smoked paprika, made from
smoke-dried red peppers,
adds earthy, smoky flavor
to foods and can be used
in many types of savory
dishes. Look for it at large
supermarkets.

≈

CRISPY POTATOES WITH SPICY TOMATO SAUCE

ACTIVE: 40 MIN **TOTAL:** 40 MIN
TO MAKE AHEAD: Refrigerate the sauce (Step 1) up to 1 week.

This recipe is a tribute to our love of the Spanish tapa Patatas Bravas—crispy bites of potatoes sometimes served with spicy tomato sauce. If you're not in the mood for spicy sauce, just add a tiny pinch of crushed red pepper or omit it altogether. The recipe makes lots of the zesty sauce—which will hold well for a few days. Try it in an omelet or as a sandwich spread.

  1 teaspoon extra-virgin olive oil plus 2 tablespoons, divided
  6 cloves garlic, minced
  1 15-ounce can crushed tomatoes, preferably fire-roasted
  ½ teaspoon smoked paprika *(see Tip)*, optional
  ½ teaspoon crushed red pepper
  ½ teaspoon salt, divided
  1½ pounds new *or* baby potatoes, scrubbed and cut into ¾- to 1-inch cubes
  ¼ teaspoon ground pepper

1. Heat 1 teaspoon oil in a medium saucepan over medium heat. Add garlic and cook, stirring, for 1 minute. Add tomatoes, paprika, crushed red pepper and ¼ teaspoon salt. Adjust heat so the sauce is simmering and cook, stirring occasionally, until thickened to the consistency of ketchup, 16 to 20 minutes.

2. Meanwhile, toss potatoes, pepper and the remaining ¼ teaspoon salt in a medium bowl. Heat the remaining 2 tablespoons oil in a large nonstick skillet over medium-high heat. Reduce heat to medium, add the potatoes and toss to coat. Cook, stirring frequently, until the potatoes are dark golden brown and tender, 15 to 20 minutes. Serve the potatoes with the sauce for dipping.

SERVES 4: ABOUT ¾ CUP POTATOES & 2 TBSP. SAUCE EACH

Calories 212, **Fat** 8g (sat 1g), **Cholesterol** 0mg, **Carbs** 33g, **Total sugars** 4g (added 0g), **Protein** 4g, **Fiber** 4g, **Sodium** 274mg, **Potassium** 873mg.
Nutrition bonus: Vitamin C (30% daily value), Potassium (25% dv).

MAMA'S POTATO SALAD

ACTIVE: 1 HR **TOTAL:** 1¼ HRS
TO MAKE AHEAD: Refrigerate up to 2 days.

This is the classic potato salad that has been served on paper plates nestled in wicker plate holders for many a summer picnic.

- 5 russet potatoes (about 3 pounds)
- 1½ teaspoons salt, divided
- ½ cup white-wine vinegar
- 4 large eggs
- 1¼ cups low-fat mayonnaise
- 4 stalks celery, finely chopped
- 1 Vidalia *or* other sweet onion, finely chopped
- ¼ cup sweet *or* dill pickle relish
- Ground pepper to taste

1. Peel potatoes and cut into ½-inch cubes. Place in a large pot and add water to cover; season with 1 teaspoon salt. Bring to a boil over high heat. Reduce the heat and simmer until very tender, 15 to 20 minutes. Drain well. While still warm, transfer the potatoes to a baking sheet and drizzle with vinegar. Set aside to cool to room temperature.

2. Meanwhile, place eggs in a medium saucepan and add water to cover by 1 inch. Bring to a simmer over medium-high heat. Reduce heat to low and cook at the barest simmer for 10 minutes. Remove from heat, pour out the hot water and cover the eggs with ice-cold water. Let stand until cool enough to handle before peeling.

3. Once the eggs have cooled, remove the shells. Grate the eggs through the large holes on a box grater or finely chop them.

4. Combine mayonnaise, celery, onion, pickle relish, the remaining ½ teaspoon salt and pepper in a large bowl. Add the cooled potatoes and grated eggs; stir to combine. Serve at room temperature or chilled.

SERVES 12: ABOUT ¾ CUP EACH

Calories 197, **Fat** 6g (sat 1g), **Cholesterol** 68mg, **Carbs** 32g, **Total sugars** 5g (added 1g), **Protein** 4g, **Fiber** 2g, **Sodium** 447mg, **Potassium** 448mg.

Perfect Potato Salad

While many potato salad recipes call for waxy potatoes—which have firm texture and hold their shape when cooked—some people prefer to use russets, as in this recipe. The result is that the potatoes break down just slightly for a blend of larger pieces with a little bit of creamy mash.

WARM POTATO SALAD WITH BACON-MUSTARD DRESSING

ACTIVE: 40 MIN **TOTAL:** 40 MIN

This German potato salad gets an update with tart Granny Smith apples, which hold their shape when roasted.

- 2 pounds fingerling potatoes, scrubbed and cut in half lengthwise
- 2 tablespoons extra-virgin olive oil
- 1½ tablespoons chopped fresh rosemary
- ¾ teaspoon salt, divided
- ½ teaspoon ground pepper, divided
- 1 medium onion, cut into ¼-inch-thick slices
- 2 medium Granny Smith apples, peeled and thinly sliced
- 3 slices center-cut bacon *(see Tip)*
- ¼ cup cider vinegar
- 2 tablespoons whole-grain mustard

1. Preheat oven to 450°F. Coat a large roasting pan with cooking spray.

2. Toss potatoes, oil, rosemary, ½ teaspoon salt and ¼ teaspoon pepper in the pan. Arrange cut-side down; roast for 10 minutes. Scatter onion on top (do not stir); cook until the potatoes are golden brown on the bottom, 10 to 15 minutes more. Stir in apples; cook until tender but still holding their shape, about 5 minutes more.

3. Meanwhile, cook bacon in a large skillet over medium heat, turning once, until crisp, about 10 minutes. Drain on a paper towel-lined plate; crumble. Off the heat, whisk vinegar, mustard and the remaining ¼ teaspoon each salt and pepper into the drippings in the pan, scraping up any browned bits.

4. Drizzle the apples and vegetables with the dressing, sprinkle with bacon and stir to coat. Serve hot or at room temperature.

SERVES 10: ABOUT ¾ CUP EACH

Calories 129, **Fat** 4g (sat 1g), **Cholesterol** 2mg, **Carbs** 22g, **Total sugars** 6g (added 0g), **Protein** 2g, **Fiber** 3g, **Sodium** 294mg, **Potassium** 450mg.

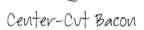

Center-Cut Bacon

Center-cut bacon comes from the center of the pork belly. It has up to one-third less fat than bacon cut from the ends.

GOAT CHEESE MASHED POTATOES

ACTIVE: 30 MIN **TOTAL:** 40 MIN

TO MAKE AHEAD: Prepare the mashed potatoes and keep them warm up to an hour by setting the pan in a larger pan of barely simmering water with a piece of parchment or wax paper on the surface of the potatoes. Or reheat in the microwave.

Goat cheese adds a creamy, slightly tart dimension to mashed potatoes. If you like to keep your potatoes pure white and add an assertive spiciness, use white pepper instead of black.

2½	pounds potatoes, preferably Yukon Gold, peeled and cut into chunks
1	tablespoon salt
3	ounces creamy goat cheese (chèvre), cut into small pieces
½-⅔	cup nonfat milk, heated
⅛	teaspoon salt
	Ground pepper to taste

1. Place potatoes in a large saucepan, cover with cold water and add 1 tablespoon salt. Bring to a boil and cook until the potatoes are tender, about 10 minutes. Drain and return the potatoes to the pan. Shake the pan over low heat to dry the potatoes slightly. Remove the pan from the heat.

2. Mash the potatoes with a potato masher, ricer or food mill. Stir in goat cheese and enough hot milk to make a smooth mixture. Season with the ⅛ teaspoon salt and pepper.

SERVES 6

Calories 197, **Fat** 3g (sat 2g), **Cholesterol** 7mg, **Carbs** 37g, **Total sugars** 3g (added 0g), **Protein** 6g, **Fiber** 3g, **Sodium** 327mg, **Potassium** 619mg.
Nutrition bonus: Vitamin C (22% daily value).

CHEESY POTATO CASSEROLE

ACTIVE: 25 MIN **TOTAL:** 1¾ HRS
TO MAKE AHEAD: Prepare through Step 3; refrigerate up to 1 day. Let casserole stand at room temperature while preheating the oven. Proceed with Step 4.

The original version of this cheesy potato casserole stars canned soup, full-fat sour cream, a stick of butter and a crust of crushed potato chips. We lightened it considerably by using homemade white sauce instead of canned soup and swapping nonfat Greek yogurt for sour cream. Crushed cornflakes replace potato chips. Dig in!

Canola oil cooking spray
2 pounds red potatoes, scrubbed and diced
1 cup low-fat milk
2 tablespoons cornstarch
8 ounces sharp Cheddar cheese, shredded (about 2 cups)
1 cup nonfat Greek yogurt
1 medium onion, chopped
½ teaspoon salt plus a pinch, divided
½ teaspoon ground pepper
2 cups crushed unsweetened cornflakes

1. Preheat oven to 350°F. Coat a 9-by-13-inch (or similar-size) baking dish with cooking spray.

2. Place potatoes in a large pot, add water to cover and bring to a boil. Immediately drain and rinse with cold water; drain well. Return to the pot.

3. Meanwhile, whisk milk and cornstarch in a large saucepan. Bring to a boil over medium-high heat, whisking often, until bubbling and thickened enough to coat the back of a spoon, 2 to 4 minutes. Remove from the heat and stir in Cheddar, yogurt, onion, ½ teaspoon salt and pepper until combined. Pour the sauce over the potatoes and mix well. Spread evenly in the prepared pan.

4. Sprinkle the casserole with cornflakes. Using short bursts, coat the cornflakes with cooking spray; sprinkle with the remaining pinch of salt. Bake until browned and bubbling at the edges, about 1 hour. Let cool for 20 minutes before serving.

SERVES 10: ABOUT ¾ CUP EACH

Calories 233, **Fat** 8g (sat 5g), **Cholesterol** 25mg, **Carbs** 30g, **Total sugars** 5g (added 1g), **Protein** 11g, **Fiber** 2g, **Sodium** 397mg, **Potassium** 510mg.
Nutrition bonus: Iron (24% daily value), Calcium (22% dv).

—≈—

Conscientious Caviar

Caviar labeled "Caspian" or "Beluga" should be avoided; both have been banned from import into the United States due to pollution and overfishing. Sustainable alternatives are available closer to home. Sterling Caviar, from white sturgeon farmed in northern California, is an admirable stand-in for its Russian and Iranian cousins. Along with other American caviars, including paddlefish, salmon and trout, it gets a green light from environmentalists—and a thumbs-up from our kitchen.

—≈—

TWICE-BAKED POTATOES WITH HORSERADISH & CAVIAR

ACTIVE: 15 MIN **TOTAL:** 1½ HRS

Here, twice-baked potatoes put on their fancy pants. If oven space is limited, these can be made in the microwave.

  2 medium russet potatoes, scrubbed
  ½ cup reduced-fat sour cream, divided
  ¼ cup low-fat milk
  2 tablespoons prepared horseradish
  1 tablespoon chopped fresh chives
  1 teaspoon chopped fresh dill, plus sprigs for garnish
  ¼ teaspoon salt
  ¼ teaspoon ground pepper
  2 teaspoons caviar *(see Tip)*

1. Preheat oven to 400°F.

2. Pierce potatoes in several places with a fork. Bake directly on the center rack until tender, 40 to 60 minutes. (Alternatively, microwave on Medium, turning once or twice, until soft, about 20 minutes.)

3. Reduce oven temperature to 375°.

4. When the potatoes are cool enough to handle, cut in half and scoop the flesh into a bowl, leaving a thin layer of flesh next to the skin so potatoes hold their shape when stuffed. Place the skins in a small baking dish. Add ¼ cup sour cream, milk, horseradish, chives, chopped dill, salt and pepper to the potato flesh. Beat with an electric mixer or mash with a potato masher until smooth; divide among the potato skins.

5. Bake the stuffed potatoes until the filling is hot, 15 to 20 minutes. (Or microwave until hot, 2 to 4 minutes.)

6. To serve, top each half with 1 tablespoon of the remaining sour cream, ½ teaspoon caviar and a dill sprig.

SERVES 4: ½ POTATO EACH

Calories 142, **Fat** 4g (sat 2g), **Cholesterol** 28mg, **Carbs** 22g, **Total sugars** 2g (added 0g), **Protein** 4g, **Fiber** 2g, **Sodium** 262mg, **Potassium** 565mg.

Radishes

Crunchy, peppery radishes offer one of the first refreshing bites of spring. Although they are thought of as being round, red and small—as in the Red Globe radishes that are often the sole option in the supermarket—the array of shapes, colors and sizes is dizzying. There are the large round and very assertive 'Black Spanish' radishes and long white, mild 'Icicle' radishes. Pink-and-white French breakfast radishes are petite—about the size of a finger. The Japanese daikon radish—seen most often in the market weighing in at about 1 pound—can reach upwards of 60 pounds. Watermelon radishes—a stunningly beautiful root with pale green skin and striated pink and white flesh—can range from golf ball-size to softball-size.

Radishes are most commonly eaten raw. A classic French hors d'oeuvre features thinly sliced radishes on slices of buttered bread with a sprinkle of sea salt. Paper-thin slices of mixed radishes drizzled with good olive oil, sprinkled with chopped fresh chervil or snipped chives and seasoned with coarse salt makes a clean-tasting and beautiful spring salad. Along with shredded cabbage, radishes add crunch as a garnish for a steaming bowl of posole, the Mexican hominy stew.

These relatives of the turnip can be gently cooked as well. Roasting, braising or sautéing mellows the peppery bite and enhances juiciness. A touch of salt and a sprinkle of fresh herbs, such as chives, parsley, basil or tarragon, heightens the distinctive flavor.

Radishes are a cool-weather crop with two seasons—one in spring and the other in fall.

Best in late spring

AT THE MARKET

➳ Choose radishes with bright color and firm, plump skin that has a sheen to it. Radishes sold in bunches with the tops still attached—as opposed to those that have been trimmed and packaged in plastic bags—will taste much fresher. Greens should not be excessively wilted. Avoid radishes with bruises, nicks or sponginess. Overly mature radishes will have cracks and a woody texture.

IN YOUR KITCHEN

➳ Remove green foliage, if present, because leaving it attached will dehydrate the radishes. The greens are edible. If you plan to use them, store them separately. Trim the tip of the root and the top of each radish.

➳ Rinse radishes under cool running water, rubbing with your fingers. Some large radishes may require scrubbing with a brush. Store, lightly wrapped in damp paper towels, in a tightly sealed plastic bag in the refrigerator up to 5 days. If the skin is thick and tough on large radishes (such as black radishes), they may require peeling right before you use them.

COOKING BASICS

BRAISE Cut two bunches (1 to 1½ pounds total) trimmed radishes in half. (Leave ½ inch of green top, if desired.) Melt 1 tablespoon butter in a large skillet over medium heat. Add radishes. Cook, stirring occasionally, until the radishes begin to soften, 5 to 6 minutes. Add ⅔ cup reduced-sodium chicken broth. Bring to a simmer. Cover and cook until the radishes are tender-crisp, 5 to 6 minutes. Add 1 tablespoon balsamic vinegar and ½ teaspoon salt. Turn heat to high. Uncover and cook, stirring occasionally, until the liquid is reduced to a glaze, 2 to 3 minutes. Season with freshly ground pepper to taste. Stir in 2 tablespoons minced fresh parsley. Serves 4.

SAUTÉ Cut two bunches (1 to 1½ pounds) trimmed radishes in half. (Leave ½ inch of green top if desired.) Melt 1 tablespoon butter in a large skillet over medium-high heat. Add the radishes and cook, shaking the pan occasionally, until just tender and golden brown, 6 to 7 minutes. If desired, stir in 1 tablespoon chopped chives or snipped fresh tarragon. Season with ½ teaspoon salt and freshly ground pepper to taste. Serves 4.

NUTRITION

➳ **½ cup sliced raw red radishes: Calories** 9, **Fat** 0g (sat 0g), **Cholesterol** 0mg, **Carbs** 2g, **Total sugars** 1g (added 0g), **Protein** 0g, **Fiber** 0g, **Sodium** 23mg, **Potassium** 135mg.

BONUS With 95 percent of their weight coming from water, radishes are super-filling, yet they're one of the lowest-calorie foods. With only 1 calorie per large radish, enjoy an entire cupful of slices for 19 calories.

Grow Your Own

Radishes offer nearly immediate gratification. Some varieties are ready to harvest just 3 weeks after planting. Sow seed in early spring, 2 to 4 weeks before the last frost date, in a sunny spot in loose, fertile soil. Dampen soil before planting to prevent seeds from blowing away. Cover with ¼ inch of fine soil. Keep soil moist with a mister to prevent seeds from washing away. Sow seeds every 1 to 2 weeks. 'French Breakfast'—a lightly spicy radish with white-tipped scarlet roots—is a good variety to plant in succession. It fares better than some others when the weather warms in early summer. When seedlings are 2 inches tall, thin to 3 inches apart. Harvest when radishes are large enough to eat.

SPRING RADISH SALAD

ACTIVE: 15 MIN **TOTAL:** 15 MIN

For this utterly simple spring salad look for colorful varieties of radishes such as watermelon, green, French breakfast and Easter egg. (Photo: page 401.)

- 2 bunches mixed spring radishes (about 1 pound), trimmed and thinly sliced
- 1 tablespoon fresh chervil *and/or* snipped chives
- 2 teaspoons extra-virgin olive oil
- ¼ teaspoon coarse salt

Arrange sliced radishes on a platter or individual serving plates. Sprinkle with herbs, drizzle with oil and sprinkle with salt.

SERVES 4: ABOUT ½ CUP EACH

Calories 39, **Fat** 2g (sat 0g), **Cholesterol** 0mg, **Carbs** 4g, **Total sugars** 2g (added 0g), **Protein** 1g, **Fiber** 2g, **Sodium** 114mg, **Potassium** 266mg.
Nutrition bonus: Vitamin C (29% daily value).

Chervil

Chervil (from the Greek for "herb of rejoicing") has a mild flavor between those of parsley and anise. It doesn't dry well, so is best used fresh.

Round and red may be the first descriptors that come to mind when ruminating on radishes—but these crisp and peppery roots come in a gorgeous array of shapes and colors.

Spring Radish Salad
(see recipe, page 399)

RADISH CANAPÉS WITH CREAMY DILL SPREAD

ACTIVE: 20 MIN **TOTAL:** 20 MIN

Every bite of these pretty canapés offers the creaminess of herbed cream cheese and the peppery crunch of radish. Serve them as part of an appetizer buffet at a spring party.

　4　ounces reduced-fat cream cheese *or* creamy goat cheese
　2　tablespoons chopped fresh dill, plus sprigs for garnish
　1　tablespoon capers, rinsed and chopped *(see Tip, page 236)*
　⅛　teaspoon ground pepper, plus more for garnish
　12　slices cocktail-size thin pumpernickel *or* rye bread
6-8　medium radishes, thinly sliced

Mash cream cheese (or goat cheese), chopped dill, capers and ⅛ teaspoon pepper in a small bowl until well combined. Spread about 2 teaspoons of the mixture on each piece of bread. Top each with a few radish slices, a sprig of dill and a generous grinding of pepper.

SERVES 6: 2 CANAPÉS EACH

Calories 84, **Fat** 5g (sat 2g), **Cholesterol** 14mg, **Carbs** 8g, **Total sugars** 1g (added 0g), **Protein** 3g, **Fiber** 1g, **Sodium** 163mg, **Potassium** 71mg.

ROASTED RADISHES & LEEKS WITH THYME

ACTIVE: 20 MIN **TOTAL:** 30 MIN

Radishes become sweet and tender when roasted in a hot oven. If the roasting doesn't mellow the bite of the radish enough for your taste, stir in a sprinkle of sugar or a drizzle of honey along with the butter and thyme.

2 bunches radishes (about 1 to 1½ pounds), trimmed, halved if small, quartered if large
1 tablespoon extra-virgin olive oil
½ teaspoon salt
¼ teaspoon ground pepper
1 large leek, white and light green part only, halved and thinly sliced *(see page 336)*
1 tablespoon butter
1 teaspoon finely chopped fresh thyme *or* ¼ teaspoon dried

1. Preheat oven to 450°F.

2. Combine radishes, oil, salt and pepper in a large roasting pan.

3. Roast for 10 minutes. Stir in leek. Continue roasting until the radishes are lightly browned and tender, 10 to 15 minutes more. Stir in butter and thyme; serve warm.

SERVES 4: ABOUT ⅔ CUP EACH

Calories 89, **Fat** 7g (sat 2g), **Cholesterol** 8mg, **Carbs** 7g, **Total sugars** 3g (added 0g), **Protein** 1g, **Fiber** 2g, **Sodium** 340mg, **Potassium** 308mg.
Nutrition bonus: Vitamin C (33% daily value).

Spinach

Lush, succulent spinach epitomizes the power of green. The first of the leafy vegetables to emerge in the spring—sometimes pushing through late-winter snow—brings bright color to a gray landscape and can survive a frost, even temperatures as low as 15°F. Spinach is also a nutritional powerhouse—rich in iron, folate and vitamin C.

A relative of both beets and chard, spinach is classified into one of three basic types. Flat-leaf spinach has smooth, broad leaves. Savoy spinach, with dark green, curly and deeply crinkled leaves, is more difficult to clean than flat-leaf because sand and grit can get caught in its crevices; the taste and texture of its crisp leaves are worth the effort. Then there is Semi-Savoy spinach—a hybrid variety that has slightly crinkled leaves.

Baby spinach, harvested early in its growth stage, has small leaves and a more tender texture and sweeter taste than mature spinach. Baby spinach is best raw—in salads and on sandwiches. For cooking, mature spinach is best—but when it's fresh and crisp, it's also great eaten raw.

Spinach has a water content of between 80 and 90 percent. When it is cooked—even for the briefest time—it loses considerable volume. Flavor and texture also suffer from overcooking, so in general, the shorter the cook time, the better.

Spinach is classic with eggs—in omelets, frittatas and soufflés. Complementary flavors include garlic, sesame, ginger and chile; lemon, vinegar and Kalamata olives; and bacon and nutmeg.

Spinach thrives in sandy soil in cool weather, with peak seasons in both spring and fall.

Best in spring and fall

AT THE MARKET

❧ Spinach is sold loose, in bunches and in plastic bags or containers. Look for slender stalks and crisp, dark green leaves with no signs of yellowing, wilting or sliminess. Spinach sold in bunches stays fresh longer than spinach sold in plastic bags. Fresh spinach should smell sweet, not sour or musty.

IN YOUR KITCHEN

❧ Store unwashed spinach in a plastic bag in the refrigerator up to 4 days. If desired, add a dry paper towel to the bag to absorb extra moisture and extend the life of the spinach.

❧ Cut any woody stems from mature spinach. (Baby spinach does not require stemming.) Swirl the leaves in a bowl of cool water. Let stand for 3 minutes. The sand and dirt will settle to the bottom. Repeat as needed. On the final rinse, use warm water. The warmth relaxes the crinkles in the leaves and allows any remaining bits of sand to be washed away. Spin dry or pat dry with clean kitchen towels.

COOKING BASICS

SAUTÉ Heat 2 tablespoons olive oil in a large pot over medium heat. Add 4 cloves thinly sliced garlic and cook until beginning to brown, 1 to 2 minutes. Add 20 ounces mature spinach, stemmed and rinsed; toss to coat. Cover and cook until wilted, 3 to 5 minutes. Remove from heat and toss with 1 tablespoon lemon juice and ¼ teaspoon each crushed red pepper and salt. Serves 4.

MICROWAVE Place 1 pound stemmed and rinsed (but not dried) mature spinach in a large microwave-safe dish. Cover and microwave on High until the spinach begins to wilt, about 2 minutes, depending on the strength of your microwave. (Drain in a mesh strainer, pressing with the back of a spoon to extract as much liquid as possible, and return to the bowl.) Toss with 1 tablespoon toasted sesame seeds and 2 teaspoons each toasted sesame oil and reduced-sodium soy sauce. Serves 3.

NUTRITION

❧ **1 cup of cooked spinach: Calories** 41, **Fat** 0g (sat 0g), **Cholesterol** 0mg, **Carbs** 7g, **Total sugars** 1g (added 0g), **Protein** 5g, **Fiber** 4g, **Sodium** 126mg, **Potassium** 839mg.

BONUS If you battle migraine headaches, spinach could help thanks to its ample magnesium, a mineral often in short supply among migraine sufferers. In one study, people who downed a daily 600 mg magnesium supplement (one and a half times the daily value) for three months experienced 41 percent fewer migraines. One cup of cooked spinach provides 39 percent of your day's worth, or 1 57 milligrams.

Grow Your Own

Spinach sprints from the garden soil to the table in just about 40 days, making it satisfying to grow. Semi-savoy spinach is generally the best type for home gardeners, because it is more disease-resistant than other types—and its leaves are easier to clean. Spinach needs 6 weeks of cool weather from seeding to harvest. Sow seeds in loose, well-drained soil in full sun to light shade 4 to 6 weeks before the last frost in the spring and 6 to 8 weeks before the first frost in the fall. Plant every couple of weeks during early spring to prolong the harvest. When seedlings are 2 inches tall, thin to 4 inches apart. Keep soil moist; mulch to retain moisture and prevent weeds. Harvest when leaves are big enough to eat.

How to wash spinach

Rinse stemmed spinach in several changes of cool water, ending with warm water to relax the leaves and release any remaining sand and grit.

~~~~

White Balsamic Vinegar

White balsamic vinegar is an unaged balsamic made from Italian white wine grapes and grape musts (unfermented crushed grapes). Its mild flavor and clear color make it ideal for salad dressings. Look for it at large supermarkets and specialty-food stores.

SPINACH & WARM MUSHROOM SALAD

ACTIVE: 30 MIN **TOTAL:** 30 MIN

Skip baby spinach for this hearty salad—sturdy mature spinach leaves hold up better when tossed with the warm mushroom and bacon vinaigrette.

  8 cups mature spinach, tough stems removed
  2 cups coarsely chopped radicchio
  2 tablespoons extra-virgin olive oil, divided
  2 slices bacon, chopped
  1 large shallot, halved and sliced (½ cup)
  3 cups sliced mixed mushrooms, such as shiitake, oyster *and/or* cremini, or whole enoki
  ¼ teaspoon salt
  ¼ teaspoon ground pepper
  2 tablespoons white balsamic vinegar *(see Tip)*
  ½ teaspoon honey

1. Combine spinach and radicchio in a large bowl.

2. Heat 1 tablespoon oil in a large skillet over medium heat. Add bacon and shallot and cook, stirring, until the bacon is crisp, 4 to 5 minutes. Add mushrooms, salt and pepper and cook, stirring, until the mushrooms are tender, 5 to 7 minutes. Remove from heat and stir in the remaining 1 tablespoon oil, vinegar and honey, scraping up any browned bits. Immediately pour the warm vinaigrette over the spinach mixture and toss to coat.

SERVES 4: ABOUT 2 CUPS EACH

Calories 137, **Fat** 9g (sat 1g), **Cholesterol** 3mg, **Carbs** 11g, **Total sugars** 4g (added 1g), **Protein** 5g, **Fiber** 3g, **Sodium** 260mg, **Potassium** 618mg.
Nutrition bonus: Vitamin A (117% daily value), Folate (35% dv), Vitamin C (33% dv).

GREEN CURRY SOUP

ACTIVE TIME: 1¼ HRS **TOTAL:** 1¼ HRS

This soup is dark green with spinach plus all sorts of other green vegetables.

Green Curry Paste

Look for prepared green curry paste—a fiery mixture of green chiles and Thai seasonings—in the Asian section of large supermarkets. The heat and salt level can vary widely depending on brand. Be sure to taste as you go; if you like your curry very spicy, you can turn up the heat by using a little more fresh serrano chile.

- 2 medium yellow onions
- 2 tablespoons extra-virgin olive oil plus 2 teaspoons, divided
- ½ teaspoon salt, divided
- 2 tablespoons Thai green curry paste *(see Tip)*
- 4-5 cups low-sodium vegetable broth
- 8 cups spinach (about 6 ounces), tough stems trimmed, divided
- 2 cups water
- 2 large cloves garlic, chopped
- 2½ cups oyster *or* shiitake mushrooms (about 4 ounces), cut into ¼-inch strips
- 1½ cups chopped green beans (1-inch)
- 1 cup thinly sliced peeled broccoli stems
- 5 scallions, sliced
- 1 tablespoon minced lemongrass
- 1 cup chopped fresh cilantro
- 1 serrano chile, finely chopped
- 2 tablespoons fresh lemon juice

1. Quarter onions lengthwise, then thinly slice crosswise. Heat 2 tablespoons oil in a large pot over medium-high heat. Add onions and ¼ teaspoon salt; cook, stirring often, until beginning to brown, 6 to 8 minutes. Stir in curry; cook, stirring, for 3 minutes. Stir in 4 cups broth; bring to a simmer.

2. Meanwhile, coarsely chop 4 cups spinach. Puree the remaining 4 cups spinach with water in a blender until it is chopped to confetti.

3. Heat remaining 2 teaspoons oil in a large skillet over medium heat. Add garlic; cook, stirring until fragrant, about 30 seconds. Add mushrooms; cook, stirring, until the liquid evaporates and the mushrooms color, 4 to 6 minutes.

4. Stir the mushrooms and green beans into the pot; simmer for 5 minutes. Stir in broccoli stems, scallions and lemongrass; simmer for 3 minutes more. Stir in chopped and pureed spinach, cilantro and a big pinch of serrano. Return to a simmer, cover and cook 1 minute. Add more broth, if desired. Add lemon juice. Season with more salt, serrano, and/or lemon juice to taste.

SERVES 6: ABOUT 1 ⅔ CUPS EACH

Calories 117, **Fat** 7 g (sat 1g), **Cholesterol** 0mg, **Carbs** 13g, **Total Sugars** 5g (added 0g), **Protein** 3g, **Fiber** 4g, **Sodium** 408mg, **Potassium** 375mg.
Nutrition bonus: Vitamin A (60% daily value), Vitamin C (35% dv), Folate (20% dv).

CREAMED SPINACH CASSEROLE

ACTIVE: 25 MIN **TOTAL:** 1¼ HRS
TO MAKE AHEAD: Prepare Steps 2 & 3; refrigerate up to 1 day. Bring to room temperature before folding in egg whites.

This casserole is the sophisticated cousin of creamed spinach. Serve with roast beef or at the holidays.

- 3 10-ounce packages frozen spinach, thawed
- 1 cup low-fat milk
- ¼ cup all-purpose flour
- ¼ teaspoon salt
- ¼ teaspoon ground white pepper
- ⅛ teaspoon ground nutmeg
- 1 cup extra sharp Cheddar cheese, divided
- 1 cup low-fat cottage cheese
- 3 large egg whites

1. Preheat oven to 350°F. Coat a shallow 2-quart baking dish with cooking spray.

2. Press spinach in a mesh strainer to get out as much moisture as possible. Pulse in a food processor until very finely chopped.

3. Combine milk, flour, salt, pepper and nutmeg in a large saucepan. Cook over medium heat, whisking, until thickened, 2 to 4 minutes. Remove from the heat and stir in ½ cup Cheddar, cottage cheese and the spinach.

4. Beat egg whites in a large bowl with an electric mixer, slowly increasing the speed, until they begin to foam. Continue to beat until the whites hold their shape; do not overbeat. (You'll know they are ready when you lift the beaters out and the peak doesn't flop over.)

5. Gently fold the whites into the spinach mixture with a rubber spatula until uniform. (It's OK if a few white streaks remain.) Transfer to the prepared baking dish.

6. Bake for 35 minutes. Top with the remaining ½ cup Cheddar; continue baking until the cheese is melted, about 10 minutes more. Let stand for 5 minutes.

SERVES 8: ABOUT 1 CUP EACH

Calories 142, **Fat** 6g (sat 3g), **Cholesterol** 17mg, **Carbs** 10g, **Total sugars** 3g (added 0g), **Protein** 14g, **Fiber** 3g, **Sodium** 388mg, **Potassium** 476mg.
Nutrition bonus: Vitamin A (254% daily value), Folate (42% dv), Calcium (30% dv), Magnesium (23% dv).

Summer Squash

It's good that so many things can be done with summer squash—it is the most enthusiastic producer in the garden.

Zucchini, in particular, is prolific. One plant can produce between 6 and 10 pounds of fruit over a season. Gardeners tell stories of furtively leaving bags of zucchini at their neighbors' front doors, in a desperate move to not be overrun by the bounty.

Summer squash are members of the cucurbit family—fruits that have high water content and lots of seeds—that includes cucumbers, gourds, melons, pumpkins and winter squash. Unlike winter squash, summer squash is harvested at an immature stage when the skin and seeds are still edible.

The most common types of summer squash include zucchini, yellow squash and the diminutive pattypan. Chayote [chi-OH-tay], becoming more well known and available, can be prepared the same ways other summer squashes—sautéed, grilled, roasted or stuffed and baked.

Zucchini lends moisture and texture to baked goods when grated and stirred into the batter for quick breads, muffins and cakes. In Italy, *fritelle di fiori di zucca*— batter-fried zucchini blossoms—are a crisp, ethereal delicacy. Only the male blossoms—those with a long, thin stem—are harvested. It is the female flowers—those with a slight swelling at the bottom—that, once pollinated, produce the squash.

Summer squash originated in the tropics and thrives in warm, humid weather. They are best quality in the height of summer.

Best in summer

AT THE MARKET

➤ Choose summer squash that feel heavy for their size and that have glossy, unblemished skin.

➤ Zucchini and yellow squash have the best taste and texture when no bigger than about 6 inches long; pattypan squash should be no bigger than 2 to 3 inches wide. As summer squash get larger, they get pulpy, seedy and bitter.

IN YOUR KITCHEN

➤ Store unwashed summer squash in a plastic bag in the refrigerator up to 5 days.

➤ Rinse summer squash under cool running water, rubbing gently if there is any residual soil. Trim off both ends, then slice, cut or grate as desired.

COOKING BASICS

GRILL Slice 2 trimmed medium summer squash or zucchini (about 1 pound) diagonally into ¼-inch-thick slices. Brush both sides with olive oil. Season lightly with salt and pepper to taste. Grill over medium-high heat until browned and tender, about 2 to 3 minutes per side. Top with basil pesto. Serves 4.

ROAST Slice 4 trimmed medium summer squash or zucchini (about 2 pounds) diagonally into ½-inch-thick slices. Toss with ¼ cup olive oil, 1 teaspoon salt, ¼ teaspoon crushed red pepper and black pepper to taste. Add 1 cup finely grated Parmesan cheese; toss to coat. Set a rack on a large rimmed baking sheet and spray it with cooking spray. Arrange the squash on the rack. Roast in a 425°F oven, rotating the pan halfway through cooking, until tender and lightly caramelized, about 12 minutes. Transfer the squash to a platter or serving plates. Serve with lemon wedges. Serves 8.

SAUTÉ Cut 1 medium zucchini and 1 medium yellow squash (about 1 pound total) in half lengthwise; slice. Heat 1 tablespoon olive oil in a large nonstick skillet over medium heat. Add 1 halved and sliced medium onion and 2 cloves minced garlic. Cook, stirring, until beginning to soften, about 3 minutes. Add the squash, 1 tablespoon chopped fresh oregano, ¼ teaspoon salt and pepper to taste. Reduce heat to low, cover and cook, stirring once, until the vegetables are tender-crisp, 3 to 5 minutes. Stir in 2 medium chopped tomatoes and 1 tablespoon red-wine vinegar. Remove from heat. Stir in ⅓ cup finely grated Parmesan cheese. Serves 4.

NUTRITION

➤ **1 cup of sliced cooked zucchini:** Calories 27, **Fat** 1g (sat 0g), **Cholesterol** 0mg, **Carbs** 5g, **Total sugars** 3g (added 0g), **Protein** 2g, **Fiber** 2g, **Sodium** 5mg, **Potassium** 475mg.

BONUS Feasting on summer squash could spell seasonal allergy relief. It's loaded with vitamin C, a natural antihistamine. Eat just one medium zucchini and you'll net 58 percent of the vitamin C you need in a day.

Grow Your Own

Sow seeds 2 to 3 weeks after the last spring frost date in full sun in loose, fertile, well-drained soil. Plant seeds 2 or 3 feet apart in a traditional garden bed or plant several seeds sown closer together in a slight mound or hill—the soil is warmer when slightly elevated. (Allow 5 or 6 feet between hills.) Keep plants well watered and mulch to retain moisture and keep weeds at bay. Harvest zucchini and yellow squash when about 6 inches long. Harvest pattypan squash when about 2 to 3 inches wide. Cut, do not pull, the fruit from the vines. Check plants daily and harvest frequently for the best fruit and to increase production.

◄ Zucchini
A native of Italy, this squash is most often found in cylindrical form, but there are round, or globe, varieties as well.

◄ Pattypan
The flesh of these scallop-edge, flying saucer-shape squashes tastes very much like zucchini or yellow squash.

▼ Chayote
About the size of a large pear, this gourd-like squash, native to Mexico, has white flesh wrapped around a single large seed.

◄ Yellow Squash (Straightneck)
There are both crookneck and straightneck varieties of this mild-flavor squash.

SHAVED ZUCCHINI-FENNEL SALAD

ACTIVE: 20 MIN **TOTAL:** 20 MIN

Long strips of raw zucchini and shaved fennel absorb the lemony vinaigrette in this refreshing summer salad. Serve right away after tossing with the dressing to keep the zucchini crisp.

1 pound zucchini (2 medium), trimmed
1 large bulb fennel, quartered and cored, fronds reserved
2 tablespoons extra-virgin olive oil
2 tablespoons lemon juice
¾ teaspoon salt
¼ teaspoon ground pepper
¼ cup slivered red onion
6 tablespoons shredded Manchego *or* Asiago cheese

1. Very thinly slice zucchini lengthwise into long strips with a vegetable peeler, mandoline or knife. Place the strips on a double layer of paper towels and let stand while you prepare the rest of the salad.

2. Very thinly slice fennel bulb with a knife or mandoline. Chop enough fronds to equal about ¼ cup. Whisk oil, lemon juice, salt and pepper in a large bowl. Add the zucchini, fennel, fronds and onion; gently stir to coat well. Serve sprinkled with cheese.

SERVES 6: ABOUT 1 CUP EACH

Calories 97, **Fat** 7g (sat 2g), **Cholesterol** 6mg, **Carbs** 6g, **Total sugars** 2g (added 0g), **Protein** 3g, **Fiber** 2g, **Sodium** 384mg, **Potassium** 362mg.
Nutrition bonus: Vitamin C (33% daily value).

STRING BEANS & SUMMER SQUASH

ACTIVE: 25 MIN **TOTAL:** 25 MIN

Cooking beans and summer squash in seasoned broth adds flavor with minimal effort. Try any fresh herb you have on hand and swap out yellow summer squash for zucchini if you prefer.

- 1 tablespoon extra-virgin olive oil
- 1 pound green *and/or* yellow wax beans, trimmed and halved
- 1 large summer squash, halved lengthwise, then cut crosswise into ½-inch slices
- 2 medium cloves garlic, minced
- ¼ teaspoon salt
- ¼ teaspoon ground pepper
- ½ cup reduced-sodium chicken broth *or* vegetable broth
- 1 teaspoon dried marjoram *or* 2 teaspoons fresh chopped

1. Heat oil in a large skillet over medium-high heat. Add beans, squash, garlic, salt and pepper and cook, stirring occasionally, until the vegetables are beginning to brown, about 3 minutes.

2. Add broth, cover and reduce the heat to medium. Cook until the beans are tender-crisp, 4 to 5 minutes. Remove from the heat and stir in marjoram.

SERVES 6: ABOUT ¾ CUP EACH

Calories 59, **Fat** 3g (sat 0g), **Cholesterol** 0mg, **Carbs** 8g, **Total sugars** 2g (added 0g), **Protein** 2g, **Fiber** 3g, **Sodium** 145mg, **Potassium** 273mg.
Nutrition bonus: Vitamin C (28% daily value).

ZUCCHINI BREAD PANCAKES

ACTIVE: 35 MIN **TOTAL:** 35 MIN

Shredded zucchini adds fiber and nutrients to whole-grain pancakes. If you want, top with maple syrup and more pecans.

≈

Homemade Pumpkin Pie Spice

If you don't have pumpkin pie spice, use ½ teaspoon cinnamon, ¼ teaspoon ground ginger and ⅛ teaspoon each ground nutmeg and cloves in this recipe.

≈

- 2 cups shredded zucchini
- 1¼ cups white whole-wheat flour *or* all-purpose flour
- 2 teaspoons baking powder
- 1 teaspoon pumpkin pie spice blend *(see Tip)*
- ¼ teaspoon salt
- 2 large eggs
- 1 cup plus 2 tablespoons low-fat milk
- 2 tablespoons melted butter
- 2 tablespoons light brown sugar
- 1 teaspoon vanilla extract
- ½ cup toasted pecans *(see Tip, page 92)*, chopped

1. Put shredded zucchini in a clean kitchen towel and squeeze to remove as much moisture as possible.

2. Whisk flour, baking powder, pumpkin pie spice and salt in a large bowl. Whisk eggs, milk, butter, brown sugar and vanilla in a medium bowl. Make a well in the center of the dry ingredients, add wet ingredients and whisk until combined. Fold in the zucchini and nuts.

3. Coat a large nonstick skillet (or griddle) with cooking spray; heat over medium heat. Cook pancakes in batches, using a scant ⅓ cup batter for each and spreading to about 4 inches wide. Cook until bubbles dot the surface, 1 to 3 minutes. Flip and brown on the other side, 1 to 2 minutes more. Reduce the heat if the pancakes are browning too quickly. Serve hot.

MAKES: 5 SERVINGS, 2 PANCAKES EACH

Calories 300, **Fat** 15g (sat 5g), **Cholesterol** 89mg, **Carbs** 34g, **Total sugars** 10g (added 5g), **Protein** 10g, **Fiber** 4g, **Sodium** 369mg, **Potassium** 311mg.
Nutrition bonus: Iron (28% daily value), Calcium (21% dv).

SAUSAGE-&-QUINOA-STUFFED ZUCCHINI

ACTIVE: 40 MIN **TOTAL:** 40 MIN

Here's another way to make a dent in that bumper crop of zucchini this summer: Stuff them with turkey-sausage-and-tomato-studded quinoa. Fresh marjoram lends floral notes to the stuffing, but any fresh herb will work.

1 tablespoon extra-virgin olive oil

3 links sweet *or* hot turkey sausage, casings removed

1 small onion, chopped

½ cup quinoa

1 cup water

1 cup quartered grape *or* cherry tomatoes

1 tablespoon chopped fresh marjoram *or* 1 teaspoon dried

4 medium zucchini

¼ teaspoon ground pepper

⅛ teaspoon salt

⅓ cup finely shredded Parmesan cheese

1. Heat oil in a large saucepan over medium-high heat. Add sausage and onion and cook, breaking the sausage into small pieces, until no longer pink, about 5 minutes. Add quinoa and water and bring to a boil. Reduce heat to maintain a simmer, cover and cook, stirring once or twice, until the water is absorbed and the quinoa is tender, 15 to 20 minutes. Remove from heat and stir in tomatoes and marjoram.

2. Meanwhile, cut zucchini in half lengthwise. Cut a thin slice off the bottoms so each half sits flat. Scoop out the pulp, leaving a ¼-inch shell. (Discard the pulp.) Place the zucchini in a microwave-safe dish and sprinkle with pepper and salt. Cover and microwave on High until tender-crisp, 3 to 4 minutes. Uncover.

3. Position rack in upper third of oven; preheat broiler to high.

4. Transfer the zucchini to a broiler-safe pan (or pans). Fill with the quinoa mixture and sprinkle with cheese. Broil on the upper rack until the cheese is melted, about 2 minutes.

SERVES 4: 2 ZUCCHINI HALVES EACH

Calories 293, **Fat** 13g (sat 3g), **Cholesterol** 58mg, **Carbs** 23g, **Total sugars** 7g (added 0g), **Protein** 22g, **Fiber** 4g, **Sodium** 626mg, **Potassium** 911mg.
Nutrition bonus: Vitamin C (68% daily value), Potassium (26% dv), Magnesium & Zinc (25% dv), Folate (24% dv).

Quinoa

This nutty-tasting whole grain is packed with fiber and protein—more protein than any other grain—and with fewer carbohydrates than most grains. In fact, it provides a complete protein—defined as providing all 8 essential amino acids.

FUSILLI WITH YELLOW SQUASH & GRAPE TOMATOES

ACTIVE: 25 MIN **TOTAL:** 25 MIN

Corkscrew-shape pasta tossed with silky sautéed summer squash and ripe red tomatoes is a feast for the eyes as well as the palate.

- 3 tablespoons extra-virgin olive oil
- 1 medium sweet yellow onion, halved and thinly sliced
- 1 pound summer squash (about 1 pound)
- 1 tablespoon chopped fresh thyme
- ½ teaspoon salt plus 1 tablespoon, divided
- ¼ teaspoon ground pepper
- 2 cups grape tomatoes (about 6 ounces), halved lengthwise
- 12 ounces fusilli *or* other corkscrew-shape pasta

1. Put 2 quarts of water on to boil in a large pot.

2. Heat oil in a large skillet over medium-high heat. Add onion and cook, stirring frequently, until lightly browned, 4 to 8 minutes.

3. Meanwhile, if the yellow squash has a crookneck, cut off the neck, halve it lengthwise and cut into ¼-inch slices; quarter the wider part lengthwise and cut into ¼-inch slices. If the squash is shaped like a zucchini, quarter it lengthwise and cut into ¼-inch slices.

4. When onion is lightly browned, add squash, thyme, ½ teaspoon salt and pepper. Cook over medium-high heat, stirring frequently, until squash releases most of its liquid and begins to brown, 7 to 10 minutes. Add tomatoes and cook, stirring occasionally, until they begin to break down, 4 to 6 minutes more.

5. Meanwhile, add the remaining 1 tablespoon salt to the boiling water, stir in pasta and cook according to package instructions until just tender. Drain well and toss with the sauce.

SERVES 6: ABOUT 1⅓ CUPS EACH

Calories 311, **Fat** 9g (sat 1g), **Cholesterol** 0mg, **Carbs** 49g, **Total sugars** 5g (added 0g), **Protein** 10g, **Fiber** 4g, **Sodium** 339mg, **Potassium** 407mg.
Nutrition bonus: Vitamin C (36% daily value), Folate (34% dv).

MEXICAN BISON & SQUASH STEW

ACTIVE: 1 HR **TOTAL:** 3 HRS
TO MAKE AHEAD: Prepare through Step 2; let cool and refrigerate up to 2 days. Skim any fat from the top, reheat and finish with Step 4.

Mexican cooks are adept at turning tough chunks of meat into delicious and tender stews. This stew, which uses tough cuts of bison, such as chuck or brisket, is flavored with chili powder, cumin and tequila. Serve with warm tortillas.

3 tablespoons chili powder, divided
2 teaspoons kosher salt
1 teaspoon ground cumin
2 pounds bison chuck *or* brisket, trimmed and cut into 2-inch pieces
2 tablespoons extra-virgin olive oil, divided
2 cups chopped onion
3 mild green chiles, such as Anaheim *or* poblano, seeded and cut into ½-inch pieces
1 tablespoon chopped garlic
½ cup tequila *or* water

1 15-ounce can white *or* yellow hominy, rinsed *(see Tip)*
2 cups diced tomatoes
1 cup reduced-sodium chicken broth
1 cup orange juice
2 tablespoons lime juice
3 cups diced (1-inch pieces) pattypan, chayote *or* summer squash
Ground pepper to taste

GARNISHES
8 lime wedges
½ cup fresh cilantro leaves
2 cups finely shredded cabbage
1 cup finely chopped red onion

1. Combine 1½ tablespoons chili powder, salt and cumin in a large bowl. Add bison and toss to coat. Heat 1 tablespoon oil in a large pot over medium-high heat. Reduce heat to medium, add half the meat and brown on all sides, 5 to 7 minutes. Transfer to a plate. Add the remaining 1 tablespoon oil and brown the rest of the meat. Transfer to the plate.

2. Add onion to the pot and cook, stirring, until starting to soften, 3 to 5 minutes. Add chiles and garlic; cook, stirring, for 2 to 3 minutes more. Add the remaining 1½ tablespoons chili powder and stir until the vegetables are well coated. Add tequila (or water), scrape up any browned bits and simmer until most of the liquid is evaporated. Stir in hominy, tomatoes, broth, orange juice, lime juice and the reserved bison. Return to a simmer, reduce heat, cover and cook until the bison is easily pierced with a fork, 1½ to 2 hours.

≈
Hominy
≈

Hominy, white or yellow corn treated with lime to remove the tough hull and germ, is toothsome and pleasantly chewy. Canned cooked hominy can be found in the Latin section of large supermarkets—near the beans—or at Latin markets.

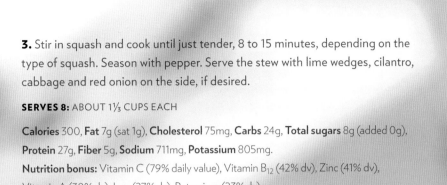

3. Stir in squash and cook until just tender, 8 to 15 minutes, depending on the type of squash. Season with pepper. Serve the stew with lime wedges, cilantro, cabbage and red onion on the side, if desired.

SERVES 8: ABOUT 1⅓ CUPS EACH

Calories 300, **Fat** 7g (sat 1g), **Cholesterol** 75mg, **Carbs** 24g, **Total sugars** 8g (added 0g), **Protein** 27g, **Fiber** 5g, **Sodium** 711mg, **Potassium** 805mg.
Nutrition bonus: Vitamin C (79% daily value), Vitamin B_{12} (42% dv), Zinc (41% dv), Vitamin A (30% dv), Iron (27% dv), Potassium (23% dv).

Winter Squash

On the outside, the array of winter squash is a sculptural mélange of sizes and forms—from elegant cylinders to squatty globes to teardrop shapes. Skins can be smooth or corrugated, in solid shades of green, yellow, orange, and white, or patterns of stripes, spots or mottling. Inside, they are different as well—but not as. All winter squash share the characteristics of having flesh in some hue of yellow, orange or gold, with varying degrees of density and sweetness.

The most common winter squash include acorn, butternut, carnival, delicata, hubbard, kabocha, spaghetti squash and culinary pumpkins.

While some winter squash—such as acorn and delicata—need only to be split, seeded and baked with a little brown sugar and butter, most types (with the exception, perhaps, of spaghetti squash) can be turned into velvety soups, pies and fruit butters. Firm squash, such as butternut, are good for roasting and grilling as well.

The natural sweetness of winter squash is enhanced by sweet spices such as cinnamon, cloves, nutmeg, as well as earthy, toasty spices such as fennel, cumin, coriander, chile and curry powder.

Winter squash and summer squash are all part of the same family, but they are harvested at different stages of maturity. While summer squash are harvested when both skin and seeds are still tender and edible, winter squash is harvested later in the growing season, in the fall, when the sugars in the flesh and a hard outer shell have developed (though the shells of thinner-skinned winter squash are edible as well). In either case, the hard shell lengthens the shelf life of winter squash, making it an ideal storage vegetable for cold winter months.

Best in fall

AT THE MARKET

➤ Choose winter squash that feel heavy for their size, with no soft spots, bruises or nicks.

IN YOUR KITCHEN

➤ Store hard-shelled winter squash—acorn, butternut, hubbard, kabocha, pumpkin and spaghetti squash—in a cool, dry, well-ventilated spot up to 2 months. (All winter squash stores best at temperatures between 50°F and 60°F.) Store delicata in the same conditions up to 2 weeks.

➤ Use a sharp knife to carefully cut the squash in half. Use a spoon to scrape out seeds and pulpy fibers. Trim base and stem ends. The skins vary in toughness. For example, delicata's is always tender. If desired, use a sharp knife or peeler to remove the skin.

COOKING BASICS

BAKE (ACORN) Spray a baking pan with cooking spray. Brush cut sides of a halved seeded acorn squash with olive oil. Season with salt and pepper. Bake, cut-side down, in a 400°F oven until tender, 35 to 45 minutes. If desired, stir together 3 tablespoons warmed pure maple syrup, 1 teaspoon butter and ¼ teaspoon ground cinnamon to drizzle on the squash. Serves 2.

GRILL (DELICATA) Cut 2 halved and seeded delicata squash into 1-inch-thick half-moons. Toss with 1 tablespoon olive oil, ½ teaspoon garam masala, ¼ teaspoon salt and pepper to taste. Grill over medium heat until tender and lightly charred on both sides, about 5 minutes per side. Serves 4.

ROAST Toss 2 to 3 pounds peeled and cubed winter squash (such as butternut, kabocha or hubbard) with 1 tablespoon olive oil, ½ teaspoon salt and pepper to taste. Spread on a large rimmed baking sheet and roast in a 375°F oven until tender and lightly browned, 30 to 45 minutes. In a small skillet cook 2 cloves minced garlic in 2 teaspoons olive oil until fragrant, 30 seconds to 1 minute. Toss the squash with the garlic and 1 tablespoon chopped Italian parsley. Serves 4.

NUTRITION

➤ **1 cup cooked cubed butternut squash: Calories** 82, **Fat** 0g (sat 0g), **Cholesterol** 0mg, **Carbs** 22g, **Total sugars** 4g (added 0g), **Protein** 2g, **Fiber** 7g, **Sodium** 8mg, **Potassium** 582mg.

BONUS Beta-carotene from winter squash safeguards cells from cancer by encouraging them to communicate. When cells stop talking to each other, they can grow out of control and form tumors. Beta-carotene keeps the conversation flowing.

How to prep butternut squash

1. Cut squash in between neck and bulbous bottom.

2. Cut off stem and base ends.

3. Cut bulb in half. Use spoon to remove seeds and membranes.

4. Use a sharp knife or peeler to remove skin from bulbs halves and neck.

▲ **Carnival**
A cross between sweet dumpling and acorn, this speckled specimen has a green shell right after harvest that turns cream, green and orange as it sits.

◄ **Delicata**
This is the only winter squash that does not have a hard shell. Harvested in the fall and treated as a winter squash, delicata is actually a summer squash. The thin skins are edible when cooked.

◄ **Pumpkin**
Culinary pumpkins are generally smaller than decorative pumpkins and have sweet, dense flesh.

▲ **Acorn**
When cut open, the very hard dark green shell of this scalloped squash yields golden-yellow flesh that is somewhat fibrous but turns soft and nutty-tasting when cooked.

▲ **Hubbard**
Likely the largest squash at the market. The thick, hard shell ranges in color from dark green to bluish gray. The dense orange flesh has a fine grain and sweet flavor.

▲ **Butternut**
The flesh of this squash has a gorgeous golden hue and a firm, smooth texture that holds up well when cut into chunks and stirred into risotto. It also makes a sweet and velvety soup.

▼ **Spaghetti**
When cooked, the pale yellow flesh of this squash turns into firm, toothsome strands that approximate its namesake.

◄ **Kabocha**
Also called Japanese pumpkin, this small squash has dark green or deep orange skin. The bright orange flesh tastes like a cross between pumpkin and sweet potato.

CREAMY RYE & BUTTERNUT SQUASH SOUP

ACTIVE: 30 MIN **TOTAL:** 1 HR 5 MIN

This velvety soup is a lighter take on a traditional squash and rye bread soup from the Valle d'Aosta region of Italy, usually made rich with milk and cheese. This variation gets its richness from the creamy starches released by the bread and squash. If you like caraway, use seeded rye bread.

 1½ pounds butternut, kabocha *or* hubbard squash
   2 tablespoons extra-virgin olive oil
   2 cloves garlic, minced
   ¼ teaspoon crushed red pepper
   6 cups water
   1 teaspoon kosher *or* sea salt
   5 cups 1-inch pieces stale crustless rye bread *(see Tip, page 344)*
   2 tablespoons finely chopped fresh parsley

1. Peel and seed squash. Cut into enough 1-inch pieces to make about 4½ cups.

2. Heat oil in a large saucepan or pot over medium heat. Add garlic and crushed red pepper; cook, stirring, until fragrant, about 1 minute. Add the squash and stir to coat with the oil. Add water and salt. Bring to a boil. Reduce heat and simmer, partially covered, until the squash is tender, 15 to 20 minutes.

3. Mash about half the squash against the side of the pot to create a thick broth. Stir in bread; return to a simmer and cook, stirring occasionally, until the bread is beginning to break apart, 5 to 15 minutes (cooking time depends on how stale and/or dense your bread is).

4. Remove the soup from the heat, cover and let stand for 15 minutes. Stir in parsley and serve.

SERVES 6: 1⅓ CUPS EACH

Calories 172, **Fat** 6g (sat 1g), **Cholesterol** 0mg, **Carbs** 27g, **Total sugars** 3g (added 1g), **Protein** 4g, **Fiber** 5g, **Sodium** 426mg, **Potassium** 289mg.
Nutrition bonus: Vitamin A (169% daily value), Vitamin C (22% dv).

WINTER GREENS SALAD WITH SQUASH & CRANBERRY VINAIGRETTE

ACTIVE: 30 MIN **TOTAL:** 30 MIN
TO MAKE AHEAD: Steam squash (Step 1) and let stand at room temperature up to 3 hours; refrigerate vinaigrette (Step 2) up to 1 day.

The steamed squash in this salad has a tender, yielding texture and a mild, almost nutty taste. Add in some nutritious bitter greens and a sweet-sour cranberry vinaigrette and you have liftoff.

1 small kabocha squash *or*
   3 delicata squash, halved and
   seeded
½ cup walnut oil *or* extra-virgin
   olive oil
⅓ cup white balsamic vinegar *or*
   white-wine vinegar
1 small shallot, minced
1 medium clove garlic, minced
1 teaspoon Dijon mustard
1 teaspoon honey
½ teaspoon kosher salt
   Ground pepper to taste
½ cup dried cranberries
10 cups torn frisée
10 cups thinly sliced escarole
½ cup coarsely chopped walnuts,
   toasted

1. If using kabocha, cut lengthwise into quarters, then cut each quarter crosswise into 6 slices. For delicata, cut each half crosswise into 6 slices. (No need to peel either type of squash—the skin is edible.) Bring 1 inch of water to a boil in a large pot fitted with a steamer basket. Add the squash to the basket, cover and cook until just tender when pierced with a knife, 8 to 10 minutes. Carefully remove the steamer basket from the pot and transfer the squash to a large plate to cool.

2. Meanwhile, whisk oil, vinegar, shallot, garlic, mustard, honey, salt and pepper in a large bowl until well combined. Add cranberries; set aside for at least 10 minutes to let the cranberries soften.

3. When ready to serve, arrange the squash slices on a large platter. Drizzle with 2 tablespoons of the vinaigrette. Add frisée and escarole to the remaining vinaigrette; toss to coat. Transfer the greens to the platter and top with walnuts.

SERVES 12: ABOUT 1⅓ CUPS EACH

Calories 185, **Fat** 13g (sat 1g), **Cholesterol** 0mg, **Carbs** 18g, **Total sugars** 8g (added 4g), **Protein** 3g, **Fiber** 6g, **Sodium** 73mg, **Potassium** 520mg.
Nutrition bonus: Vitamin A (133% daily value), Folate (35% dv), Vitamin C (24% dv).

CHILI-BROWN SUGAR DELICATA SQUASH WITH PEARS

ACTIVE: 20 MIN **TOTAL:** 35 MIN

Pears and delicata squash are both in season in the fall—and make a happy match. To make this vegetarian, omit the bacon and toss the squash and pears with the brown sugar and chili powder during the last 5 minutes of roasting.

  1 pound delicata squash (about 1 large)
  2 medium ripe but firm pears, sliced
  2 teaspoons extra-virgin olive oil
  ¼ teaspoon salt
  ¼ teaspoon ground pepper
  2 slices bacon
  2 tablespoons water
  1 tablespoon light brown sugar
  1 teaspoon chili powder

1. Preheat oven to 425°F.

2. Cut squash in half lengthwise; scoop out the seeds. Cut crosswise into ¼-inch slices. Toss in a large bowl with pears, oil, salt and pepper. Spread on a large baking sheet.

3. Roast the squash and pears until just tender, stirring once or twice, 20 to 25 minutes.

4. Meanwhile, cook bacon in a large nonstick skillet over medium heat until crisp, 4 to 6 minutes. Transfer to a paper towel-lined plate.

5. Discard all but 2 teaspoons fat from the pan. Over medium heat, stir in water, brown sugar and chili powder. Add the squash and pears; toss to coat. Crumble the bacon on top.

SERVES 4: ABOUT ¾ CUP EACH

Calories 138, **Fat** 4g (sat 1g), **Cholesterol** 3mg, **Carbs** 26g, **Total sugars** 13g (added 2g), **Protein** 2g, **Fiber** 6g, **Sodium** 216mg, **Potassium** 413mg.
Nutrition bonus: Vitamin A (220% daily value), Vitamin C (31% dv).

WINTER SQUASH & CHICKEN TZIMMES

ACTIVE: 45 MIN **TOTAL:** 2 HRS 25 MIN

Tzimmes (pronounced "tsim-iss") can also be made with brisket and is often served during the Jewish New Year. This fairly sweet dish is said to offer wishes for a sweet year ahead.

- 9 cups cubed peeled butternut, buttercup *or* hubbard squash (1-inch cubes)
- 1 cup small pitted prunes
- 3 cloves garlic, minced
- 2 medium shallots, thinly sliced and separated into rings
- 1 teaspoon ground cinnamon
- 1 teaspoon dried oregano
- 1 teaspoon dried thyme
- 1 teaspoon salt, divided
- ½ teaspoon ground pepper
- 8 skinless, bone-in chicken thighs (about 3½ pounds), trimmed
- 1 cup reduced-sodium chicken broth *or* vegetable broth
- 1 teaspoon freshly grated orange zest
- ¼ cup orange juice

1. Preheat oven to 350°F.

2. Mix squash, prunes, garlic, shallots, cinnamon, oregano, thyme, ½ teaspoon salt and pepper in a large bowl. Transfer to a 9-by-13-inch baking dish. Sprinkle chicken with the remaining ½ teaspoon salt and place on top of the vegetables. Mix broth, orange zest and juice in a small bowl and pour over the chicken. Cover the baking dish with foil.

3. Bake for 40 minutes. Uncover and continue baking until the vegetables are tender and the chicken is cooked through, basting often, about 1 hour more.

SERVES 8

Calories 346, **Fat** 11g (sat 3g), **Cholesterol** 100mg, **Carbs** 33g, **Total sugars** 4g (added 0g), **Protein** 31g, **Fiber** 5g, **Sodium** 451mg, **Potassium** 960mg.
Nutrition bonus: Vitamin A (345% daily value), Vitamin C (65% dv), Potassium (27% dv), Magnesium & Zinc (22% dv), Iron (20% dv).

SPAGHETTI SQUASH LASAGNA WITH BROCCOLINI

ACTIVE: 30 MIN **TOTAL:** 40 MIN

This low-carb lasagna bakes right in the squash shells for a fun presentation. Serve with a big Caesar salad and some warm and crusty whole-grain bread.

1 2½- to 3-pound spaghetti squash, halved lengthwise and seeded
1 tablespoon extra-virgin olive oil
1 bunch Broccolini, chopped
4 cloves garlic, minced
¼ teaspoon crushed red pepper (optional)

2 tablespoons water
1 cup shredded part-skim mozzarella cheese, divided
¼ cup shredded Parmesan cheese, divided
¾ teaspoon Italian seasoning
½ teaspoon salt
¼ teaspoon ground pepper

1. Position racks in upper and lower thirds of oven; preheat to 450°F.

2. Place squash cut-side down in a microwave-safe dish; add 2 tablespoons water. Microwave, uncovered, on High until the flesh is tender, about 10 minutes. *(Alternatively, place squash halves cut-side down on a rimmed baking sheet. Bake in a 400°F oven until the squash is tender, 40 to 50 minutes.)*

3. Meanwhile, heat oil in a large skillet over medium heat. Add broccolini, garlic and red pepper (if using); cook, stirring frequently, for 2 minutes. Add water and cook, stirring, until the broccolini is tender, 3 to 5 minutes more. Transfer to a large bowl.

4. Use a fork to scrape the squash from the shells into the bowl. Place the shells in a broiler-safe baking pan or on a baking sheet. Stir ¾ cup mozzarella, 2 tablespoons Parmesan, Italian seasoning, salt and pepper into the squash mixture. Divide it between the shells; top with the remaining ¼ cup mozzarella and 2 tablespoons Parmesan.

5. Bake on the lower rack for 10 minutes. Move to the upper rack, turn the broiler to high and broil, watching carefully, until the cheese starts to brown, about 2 minutes.

SERVES 4: ½ STUFFED SQUASH HALF EACH

Calories 194, **Fat** 11g (sat 5g), **Cholesterol** 20mg, **Carbs** 13g, **Total sugars** 4g (added 0g), **Protein** 12g, **Fiber** 2g, **Sodium** 587mg, **Potassium** 334mg.
Nutrition bonus: Vitamin C (79% daily value), Calcium (33% dv), Vitamin A (23% dv).

Toasting Pumpkin Seeds

To harvest seeds from a pumpkin, scoop out the inside of the pumpkin. Separate the seeds from the flesh as well as you can, then place the seeds in a bowl of water. Use your hands to swish the seeds around to loosen any remaining flesh or strings. The seeds will float, so you can remove them with a spoon or your fingers. Drain the seeds on a dry dish towel or a plate lined with paper towels; pat dry with paper towels. Toss seeds with oil and spread on a parchment-lined baking sheet. Roast in a 350°F oven until golden, about 20 minutes.

ROASTED STUFFED PUMPKIN

ACTIVE: 50 MIN **TOTAL:** 3 HRS

This roast pumpkin with mushroom-and-bread stuffing is a beautiful vegetarian entrée for entertaining. Use a small pumpkin if you can find one, but a winter squash like kabocha or buttercup also works.

- 1 4- to 5-pound pumpkin *or* round winter squash
- ¾ teaspoon kosher salt, divided
- 1 teaspoon ground pepper, divided
- 6 cups whole-wheat bread, torn into ½-inch pieces
- 1 tablespoon canola oil *or* grapeseed oil
- 1 large onion, chopped
- 2 stalks celery, chopped
- 1 pound cremini mushrooms, sliced
- 2 cloves garlic, very finely chopped
- 2 teaspoons chopped fresh thyme *or* ¾ teaspoon dried
- 1 teaspoon chopped fresh sage *or* ½ teaspoon dried
   Pinch of cayenne pepper (optional)
- 3 large eggs, lightly beaten
- ½ cup low-fat milk
- ½ cup freshly grated Parmigiano-Reggiano cheese

1. Place rack in center of oven; preheat to 350°F. Line a rimmed baking sheet with parchment paper.

2. Using a sharp knife and working at a slight angle, cut a 5- to 6-inch diameter cap off the top of the pumpkin (or squash)—just like a jack-o'-lantern. (If necessary, cut a small slice off the bottom so it rests flat.) Using a metal spoon, remove the seeds and strings from the cap and the inside. Season the inside with ½ teaspoon each salt and pepper. Place the pumpkin (or squash) on the prepared baking sheet.

3. Place bread in a bowl. Heat 1 tablespoon oil in a large skillet over medium heat. Add onion and celery. Cook, stirring, until just beginning to brown, 3 to 5 minutes. Reduce the heat to medium-low, add mushrooms and season with ¼ teaspoon each salt and pepper. Cook, stirring occasionally, until the mushrooms are tender, 6 to 8 minutes. Add garlic and cook until fragrant, about 45 seconds. Transfer the vegetables to the bowl with the bread. Stir in thyme, sage, cayenne (if using) and the remaining ¼ teaspoon pepper. Add eggs, milk and cheese and stir to combine. Fill the pumpkin (or squash) with the mixture, pushing it down if necessary so it fits inside. (If you have extra stuffing, place it in a small baking dish, cover with foil and bake during the last

4. Bake for 1½ hours. Remove the cap and use a spoon to fluff up the stuffing so it comes up higher than the top of the pumpkin (or squash). Return to the oven (without the cap) and continue baking until it is tender enough to be pierced easily with the tip of a knife (check in several spots to be sure it's done) and an instant-read thermometer inserted in the center of the stuffing registers at least 160°F, 30 to 45 minutes more. Let rest for 10 minutes. Carefully transfer to a warmed serving plate.

SERVES 6

Calories 303, **Fat** 9g (sat 3g), **Cholesterol** 100mg, **Carbs** 43g, **Total sugars** 13g (added 2g), **Protein** 17g, **Fiber** 6g, **Sodium** 499mg, **Potassium** 1,375mg.
Nutrition bonus: Vitamin A (392% daily value), Potassium & Vitamin C (39% dv), Folate (26% dv), Calcium (24% dv) Iron & Magnesium (22% dv), Zinc (21% dv).

Sweet Potatoes

Although they are called "potatoes," sweet potatoes are not in the potato family at all but are a type of morning glory—a tropical vine whose tuberous roots can be white, yellow, orange, red, purple or brown.

There is much confusion about the difference between sweet potatoes and yams, but the truth is actually pretty clear-cut. They are not even related. A true yam is a starchy tropical vegetable that takes 8 to 11 months of warm weather to reach maturity. They are rarely found here, and when they are, they are likely to have been imported from the Caribbean.

The two types of sweet potato most commonly found in the market are a yellow-flesh potato with thin, light brown skin and an orange-flesh variety with deep pink-orange skin. Several decades ago the yellow-flesh variety was the only type that was widely available. When producers introduced the orange-flesh variety, it was labeled with an Anglicized version of the African word *nyami*—a vegetable similar to sweet potatoes—in order to distinguish it from the yellow-flesh type.

Orange-flesh potatoes tend to be denser, sweeter and more moist than the yellow-flesh variety, which are drier, milder in flavor and a bit more fibrous. No matter which type you prefer, sweet potatoes are one of the most nutrient-dense vegetables in the world. Both can be fried, roasted, boiled, steamed, mashed, baked whole or in a gratin.

The natural sweetness of sweet potatoes can be heightened with ingredients like molasses, maple syrup, honey, coconut milk and orange juice and zest—or with sweet spices, such as cinnamon, cloves and nutmeg. Or it can be tempered with earthy, aromatic and pungent spices, such as cumin, coriander, fennel and ground chile.

Sweet potatoes are available year-round but are best quality in fall and early winter.

Best in fall to early winter

AT THE MARKET

🖙 Choose sweet potatoes that have smooth skin and are firm and free of soft spots, cracks or bruises.

IN YOUR KITCHEN

🖙 Store whole unpeeled sweet potatoes—loose, not in plastic bags—in a cool (50°F to 60°F), dry place with good air circulation up to 1 month. Do not refrigerate; they will dry out and develop an unpleasant flavor from the intense cold.

🖙 Scrub sweet potatoes under cool running water with a vegetable brush. If desired, peel with a vegetable peeler.

COOKING BASICS

BAKE Prick sweet potatoes with a fork in several places. Place in a baking dish and bake in a 425°F oven until tender all the way to the center, about 1 hour. Cool 5 minutes. With a sharp knife, make a cross cut in the middle of potato. Push in and up at each end to open. Season lightly with salt, pepper and ½ teaspoon butter each.

MASH Cut peeled sweet potatoes into cubes. Bring a pot of water to a boil. Add the sweet potatoes. Cover and cook until very soft, 25 to 30 minutes. Add butter, salt and pepper. Mash with a potato masher.

MICROWAVE Prick sweet potatoes with a fork in several places. Microwave on High until tender all the way to the center, 12 to 15 minutes. Cool for 5 minutes. With a sharp knife, make a cross cut in the middle of potato. Push in and up at each end to open. Season lightly with salt and pepper and, if desired, top with plain yogurt.

ROAST (WEDGES) Coat a 9-by-13-inch baking dish with cooking spray. Arrange 3 large quartered sweet potatoes in the dish. Combine ¼ cup water, 3 tablespoons reduced-sodium soy sauce, 2 tablespoons each brown sugar and mirin (or sweet sherry) and 1 tablespoon each sesame oil and minced garlic in a small bowl. Pour over the sweet potatoes. Cover tightly with foil and roast in a 400°F oven until nearly tender, 35 to 45 minutes. Transfer to a plate to cool. Remove the foil and baste the sweet potatoes with sauce. Continue roasting, uncovered, until fully tender, 10 to 15 minutes longer. Spoon the glaze over the sweet potatoes and sprinkle with 1 tablespoon toasted sesame seeds. Serves 4.

SHRED Whisk 2 tablespoons canola oil, 1 tablespoon lime juice, 1½ teaspoons sesame oil and ½ teaspoon salt in a large bowl. Add 3 cups each coarsely grated, peeled sweet potato (about 1 large) and thinly shredded napa cabbage, 4 thinly sliced scallions and 1 teaspoon finely minced serrano or jalapeño chile with seeds (optional). Toss to combine. Serves 6.

NUTRITION

🖙 **1 medium baked sweet potato (with skin): Calories** 103, **Fat** 0g (sat 0g), **Cholesterol** 0mg, **Carbs** 24g, **Total sugars** 7g (added 0g), **Protein** 2g, **Fiber** 4g, **Sodium** 41mg, **Potassium** 542mg.

BONUS These spuds help fight fatigue. Jammed with slowly digested complex carbohydrates for sustained energy, each medium sweet potato also offers up four times your daily vitamin A to help build hemoglobin, needed to deliver energizing oxygen to cells throughout your body.

Roasted Sweet Potato Wedges
(see Cooking Basics, opposite)

MAPLE-LIME ROASTED SWEET POTATOES

ACTIVE: 15 MIN **TOTAL:** 1 HR

Sweet potatoes are eaten all over the world. This recipe offers a melting pot of traditions, using lime as you might find in a Caribbean dish to balance the sweetness of the sweet potatoes and real New England maple syrup.

- 2 tablespoons pure maple syrup *(see Tip)*
- 2 tablespoons dark brown sugar
- 2 tablespoons unsalted butter, melted
- 2 tablespoons sunflower oil
- 1 teaspoon salt
- ½ teaspoon ground cinnamon
  Pinch of cayenne pepper
- 4 pounds sweet potatoes, peeled and cut into 1-inch pieces
  Zest of 3 limes

1. Preheat oven to 350°F.

2. Combine maple syrup, brown sugar, butter, oil, salt, cinnamon and cayenne in a large bowl. Add sweet potatoes and toss until thoroughly coated. Transfer to a large rimmed baking sheet. Roast, stirring every 15 minutes, until tender, 45 minutes to 1 hour. Sprinkle lime zest over the sweet potatoes and gently stir to distribute.

SERVES 12: ABOUT ⅔ CUP EACH

Calories 138, **Fat** 4g (sat 2g), **Cholesterol** 5mg, **Carbs** 24g, **Total sugars** 11g (added 5g), **Protein** 2g, **Fiber** 3g, **Sodium** 228mg, **Potassium** 452mg.
Nutrition bonus: Vitamin A (355% daily value), Vitamin C (34% dv).

Pure Maple Syrup

There is no substitute for the flavor of real maple syrup. And, sweet news—it has health benefits too. Pure maple syrup contains polyphenols, antioxidants that quell inflammation, according to studies done by the University of Rhode Island. (Inflammation is linked to a slew of health conditions, from cancer to arthritis.) Grades of maple syrup were revised in 2014 to include only four types of Grade A—no Grade B. They are golden, amber, dark and very dark. Darker grades have the most robust flavor and the highest levels of antioxidants. Of course, it's still sugar, so enjoy in moderation.

Crème Fraîche

Sour cream and crème fraîche are similar in that both consist of cream that has been thickened with the addition of live cultures. Sour cream has a fat content of about 20%. Crème fraîche has a fat content of about 30%. It is a thinner but richer version of sour cream.

TWO-TONED MASHED POTATOES

ACTIVE: 20 MIN **TOTAL:** 35 MIN
TO MAKE AHEAD: Prepare sauce (Step 2) and vegetables (Steps 1 & 3) and refrigerate separately up to 1 day. Reheat vegetables, covered, in the microwave or a double boiler before continuing with Step 4.

Roughly smash Yukon Gold and sweet potatoes together with leeks and you get a beautiful mottled white-and-orange take on mashed potatoes. The crème fraîche topping offers a tangy counterpoint.

- 1 tablespoon buttermilk plus ⅔ cup, divided
- 2 tablespoons crème fraîche *or sour cream (see Tip)*
- ½ teaspoon onion powder *or granulated onion*
  Pinch of salt plus ¾ teaspoon, divided
- 1½ pounds Yukon Gold potatoes, cut into 1-inch chunks
- 1½ pounds sweet potatoes, peeled and cut into 1-inch chunks
- 1 small leek, halved lengthwise and thinly sliced, white and light green parts only
- 2 tablespoons butter, cut into 4 pieces
- ¼ teaspoon ground pepper
- 2 tablespoons minced fresh chives

1. Bring a large pot of water to a boil.

2. Combine 1 tablespoon buttermilk, crème fraîche (or sour cream), onion powder (or granulated onion) and pinch of salt. Cover and refrigerate while you cook the vegetables.

3. Add potatoes, sweet potatoes and leek to the boiling water and return to a boil. Reduce heat to maintain a vigorous simmer and cook until tender enough to pierce with a knife, 12 to 15 minutes. Drain and return the vegetables to the pan (off the heat).

4. Add the remaining ⅔ cup buttermilk, the remaining ¾ teaspoon salt, butter and pepper to the pan; coarsely mash with a potato masher. Serve topped with the sauce and chives.

SERVES 12: ½ CUP EACH

Calories 117, **Fat** 3g (sat 1g), **Cholesterol** 6mg, **Carbs** 21g, **Total sugars** 4g (added 0g), **Protein** 2g, **Fiber** 2g, **Sodium** 190mg, **Potassium** 318mg.
Nutrition bonus: Vitamin A (144% daily value).

SWEET POTATO PIE WITH CREAM CHEESE SWIRL

ACTIVE: 30 MIN **TOTAL:** 4½ HRS
TO MAKE AHEAD: Loosely cover and refrigerate to 1 day. Let stand at room temperature for 30 minutes before serving; blot any moisture on the top as needed.

This creamy sweet potato pie is seasoned like a pumpkin pie with plenty of cinnamon and nutmeg and gets nice ginger flavor from the gingersnap crust. For the best results, roast sweet potatoes in the oven; in a pinch, microwave them instead (see page 442).

Neufchâtel

Neufchâtel, a type of reduced-fat cream cheese, is a luscious way to add richness and creaminess to a dish without contributing excess fat and calories. Neufchâtel has about one-third less fat than regular cream cheese.

2 medium-large sweet potatoes
6 ounces crisp gingersnap cookies (26-28 small cookies)
2 tablespoons canola oil
¾ cup packed light brown sugar
¾ cup nonfat vanilla Greek yogurt, divided
2 large eggs
1 large egg yolk
¾ teaspoon ground cinnamon
¼ teaspoon ground nutmeg
¼ cup (2 ounces) reduced-fat cream cheese (Neufchâtel) (see Tip)
2 tablespoons confectioners' sugar
¼ teaspoon ground ginger

1. Preheat oven to 400°F.

2. Tightly wrap sweet potatoes in foil and place on a baking sheet. Roast until very tender, about 1¼ hours. Carefully unwrap and set aside to cool.

3. Reduce oven temperature to 350°F.

4. Process gingersnaps in a food processor until finely ground. Transfer to a bowl, add oil and stir until well combined. Using a spoon, spread and pat the crumbs into the bottom and up the sides of a 9-inch pie pan. Bake until just barely beginning to darken, about 10 minutes.

5. Clean and dry the food processor workbowl. Peel the sweet potatoes and transfer flesh to the food processor. Puree until smooth. Measure out 1½ cups (if you have extra puree, reserve it for another use). Return the 1½ cups puree to the food processor. Add brown sugar, ½ cup yogurt, eggs, egg yolk, cinnamon and nutmeg; pulse just until combined. Spread filling in warm crust.

6. Clean and dry the workbowl again. Add the remaining ¼ cup yogurt, cream cheese, confectioners' sugar and ginger; puree until smooth, stopping to scrape down the sides once or twice. Dollop tablespoonfuls of the cream cheese mixture onto the filling, spacing them evenly. Draw the tip of a wooden skewer or a thin knife through the cream cheese mixture and sweet potato filling repeatedly to create a swirled design.

7. Bake the pie until firm to the touch and starting to puff around the edges, 45 to 50 minutes. Let cool completely on a wire rack, at least 2 hours.

SERVES 10

Calories 249, **Fat** 7g (sat 2g), **Cholesterol** 60mg, **Carbs** 41g, **Total sugars** 25g (added 21g), **Protein** 5g, **Fiber** 2g, **Sodium** 144mg, **Potassium** 220mg.
Nutrition bonus: Vitamin A (157% daily value).

Tomatillos

In describing the tomatillo, it is helpful to reference the characteristics of a few other fruits. Also called the Mexican husk tomato because it looks like a small green tomato that grows encased in a delicate, papery shell, the tomatillo has a refreshingly tart and astringent flavor—a bit like a cross between a lemon and an apple.

Although tomatillo means "little tomato" in Spanish, it is not a tomato—even if both are members of the large and varied nightshade family that also includes peppers, potatoes and eggplant. The Chinese-lantern-like tomatillo is actually the berry of a hardy and highly adaptive plant that can be grown in tropical, semitropical or even cool climates. It just doesn't like frost. Tomatillos can range in size from that of a cherry tomato to a plum.

While tomatillos are not usually eaten solo, they lend tangy flavor to sauces and salsas, soups, stews, chili, tacos and enchiladas. They can be eaten raw or cooked—usually roasted or grilled. They are most commonly known as the key ingredient in Mexican salsa verde—a sprightly green sauce made from tomatillos, chiles, cilantro and onions. Cooking tomatillos intensifies their flavor. Grilling gives them a touch of smokiness, while roasting produces an earthy, nutty flavor.

Not surprisingly, tomatillos pair well with fiery chiles. Their tart pungency is mellowed by the richness of cheese or eggs. Spoon salsa verde over fried eggs or on grilled fish, beef, pork and chicken.

Tomatillos are intermittently available throughout the year but are best in late summer.

Best in late summer

AT THE MARKET

↘ Choose tomatillos that feel dry and firm to the touch and that have tightly fitting light brown husks. Avoid those that feel soft, have signs of mold or very loose husks. 'Toma Verde' is the most common variety.

↘ Some varieties of tomatillo turn yellow when ripe; others remain green. The best indicator of ripeness is a husk that has turned light brown. Green husks indicate that the tomatillo is not yet ready to eat.

IN YOUR KITCHEN

↘ Store tomatillos, husks intact, in an open paper bag in the refrigerator up to 3 weeks or at room temperature up to 1 week.

↘ Remove the papery husk by pulling it upward toward the stem. The fruit is covered with a sticky substance. Hold the fruit under cool running water, rubbing slightly, to rinse it off. Slice or dice as desired.

COOKING BASICS

FRESH GREEN SALSA Coarsely chop 1 pound tomatillos and hot chiles to taste (2 jalapeños or 4 serranos, seeded, if desired). In a food processor or blender process tomatillos, chiles, ¼ cup roughly chopped fresh cilantro and ½ cup water to make a coarse puree. Transfer to a serving bowl. Stir in ⅓ cup finely chopped white onion and ½ teaspoon salt. Makes 1 cup.

GRILLED TOMATILLO-CHIPOTLE SALSA Oil a grill rack. Arrange 2 pounds tomatillos, stem-end down, over medium heat. Grill, turning once, until blackened on both sides and slightly deflated, 15 to 25 minutes total, depending on size. Let cool 10 minutes. Mash 4 finely chopped cloves garlic with 1¼ teaspoons salt on a cutting board with a fork to form a paste. Transfer grilled tomatillos to a food processor or blender. Pulse to a very coarse puree. Add garlic paste and 1 to 3 teaspoons chipotle chile powder. Pulse once or twice to combine. Makes 2 cups.

NUTRITION

↘ **½ cup chopped raw tomatillos:** **Calories** 21, **Fat** 1g (sat 0g), **Cholesterol** 0mg, **Carbs** 4g, **Total sugars** 3g (added 0g), **Protein** 1g, **Fiber** 1g, **Sodium** 1mg, **Potassium** 177mg.

BONUS Tomatillos contain potent anti-inflammatory substances that block the action of COX-1 and COX-2, enzymes that cause pain and inflammation. One study found certain tomatillo compounds to be as powerful at halting these pain-inducing enzymes as aspirin or ibuprofen.

Grilled Tomatillo-Chipotle Salsa
(see Cooking Basics, opposite)

SPICY TOMATILLO QUINOA

ACTIVE: 10 MINUTES **TOTAL:** 40 MINUTES

In this easy side dish, tomatillos work double duty. Some are pureed to flavor the cooking liquid for the quinoa, while others are chopped and stirred in raw for color and texture.

  6 medium tomatillos (about 8 ounces), husked and rinsed, divided
¾-1 cup low-sodium chicken *or* vegetable broth
  ¾ cup coarsely chopped fresh cilantro, divided
  ½ cup coarsely chopped onion
  1 medium jalapeño, halved and seeded, if desired
  1 clove garlic
  1 cup red *or* white quinoa
  ½ teaspoon sugar
  ½ teaspoon salt
  1 cup corn, fresh *or* frozen (thawed)

1. Cut 4 tomatillos in half and puree in a food processor (or blender) with ¾ cup broth, ½ cup cilantro, onion, jalapeño and garlic until mostly smooth. Add enough of the remaining broth to equal 2 cups total.

2. Combine the tomatillo mixture, quinoa, sugar and salt in a large saucepan. Bring to a boil. Reduce heat, cover and simmer until the liquid is absorbed, 15 to 20 minutes. Let stand, covered, for 10 minutes.

3. Chop the remaining 2 tomatillos. Stir into the quinoa along with corn and the remaining ¼ cup cilantro.

SERVES 6: ABOUT ⅔ CUP EACH

Calories 149, **Fat** 3g (sat 0g), **Cholesterol** 0mg, **Carbs** 27g, **Total sugars** 5g (added 0g), **Protein** 6g, **Fiber** 3g, **Sodium** 210mg, **Potassium** 379mg.

FRESH TOMATILLO SALAD

ACTIVE: 20 MIN **TOTAL:** 50 MIN

This super-fresh salad spiked with crushed red pepper is a riot of tastes and textures—tart tomatillos, sweet and juicy ripe tomatoes and cooling and crunchy jicama. It makes an excellent side dish to a grilled steak.

- 12 medium tomatillos (about 1 pound)
- ½ medium jicama (about 12 ounces)
- ⅓ cup chopped fresh cilantro
- ¼ cup extra-virgin olive oil
- 2 tablespoons fresh lime juice
- ½ teaspoon crushed red pepper, or to taste
- 2 medium tomatoes, cut into thin wedges
- 1 teaspoon salt
-   Ground pepper to taste

1. Peel off and discard papery husks from tomatillos. Rinse away the sticky residue from the skin under warm water. Halve the tomatillos, then thinly slice and place in a large bowl.

2. Peel jicama, cut into quarters and thinly slice. Cut the slices into matchsticks. Add to the bowl.

3. Combine cilantro, oil, lime juice and crushed red pepper in a small bowl and stir to blend. Drizzle the dressing over the tomatillos and jicama. Add tomatoes and toss to coat. Season with salt and pepper. Let marinate at room temperature for 30 minutes to 1 hour before serving.

SERVES 8: ABOUT 1 CUP EACH

Calories 117, **Fat** 8g (sat 1g), **Cholesterol** 0mg, **Carbs** 13g, **Total sugars** 5g (added 0g), **Protein** 1g, **Fiber** 4g, **Sodium** 296mg, **Potassium** 361mg.
Nutrition bonus: Vitamin C (62% daily value).

OVEN-FRIED GREEN TOMATILLOS

ACTIVE: 35 MIN **TOTAL:** 35 MIN

This healthful twist on the crispy Southern favorite—fried green tomatoes—can be either a dunkable appetizer or a decadent burger topping.

Canola *or* olive oil cooking spray
1 pound tomatillos (about 12 medium), husked, rinsed and cut into ½-inch-thick slices
¼ teaspoon salt
¼ teaspoon ground pepper
¼ cup white whole-wheat *or* all-purpose flour
1 teaspoon garlic powder
1 teaspoon Creole *or* Cajun seasoning
2 large eggs
1¼ cups panko breadcrumbs
¼ cup ketchup
¼ cup low-fat mayonnaise

1. Position a rack in lower third of oven; preheat to 425°F. Coat a large baking sheet with cooking spray.

2. Sprinkle tomatillos with salt and pepper. Combine flour, garlic powder and Creole (or Cajun) seasoning in a shallow dish. Lightly beat eggs in another dish. Put breadcrumbs in a third dish. Dredge the tomatillos in the flour mixture, dip in the egg and then coat both sides with breadcrumbs. Place on the prepared baking sheet and generously coat with cooking spray.

3. Bake the tomatillos, turning once, until golden brown, 10 to 12 minutes.

4. Meanwhile, combine ketchup and mayonnaise in a small bowl. Serve the tomatillos with the dipping sauce.

SERVES 6: 4-5 TOMATILLO SLICES & 1½ TBSP. SAUCE EACH

Calories 128, **Fat** 3g (sat 1g), **Cholesterol** 23mg, **Carbs** 22g, **Total sugars** 6g (added 2g), **Protein** 3g, **Fiber** 2g, **Sodium** 350mg, **Potassium** 253mg.
Nutrition bonus: Vitamin C (15% daily value).

Lean Ground Pork

Depending on the supermarket, it might be hard to find a lean option for ground pork, but it's easy to grind your own in a food processor. Choose a lean cut, such as loin or tenderloin, and trim any excess fat. Cut into pieces and then pulse in a food processor until uniformly ground (being careful not to overprocess, turning the meat into mush). Or ask a butcher to grind it for you. Using lean pork instead of regular ground pork reduces up to 164 calories and 5 grams of saturated fat per 3 ounces of cooked meat.

TOMATILLO & PORK CHILI

ACTIVE: 40 MIN **TOTAL:** 1½ HRS
TO MAKE AHEAD: Refrigerate up to 3 days or freeze up to 3 months.

Whole-grain bulgur boosts the volume and fiber in this smoky pork chili. We like to simmer chili for close to an hour to develop the best flavor, but if you're in a hurry, reduce the liquid by half and simmer for 20 to 25 minutes.

3 tablespoons extra-virgin olive oil *or* canola oil
1 pound lean ground pork *(see Tip)*
1 large onion, chopped
4 cloves garlic, minced
1 pound tomatillos, husks removed, chopped (about 3 cups)
2 medium poblano peppers, chopped (about 1 cup)
½ cup bulgur
2 tablespoons minced chipotle chiles in adobo sauce *(see Tip, page 45)*

3 tablespoons dried oregano
2 teaspoons ground cumin
½ teaspoon salt
1 14-ounce can no-salt-added diced tomatoes *(see Tip, page 131)*
1 15-ounce can hominy *(see Tip, page 424)*, rinsed
1 15-ounce can no-salt-added pinto beans, rinsed
4 cups reduced-sodium chicken broth
Sliced radishes

1. Heat oil in a large pot over medium-high heat. Add pork, onion and garlic. Cook, stirring and breaking up the meat with a wooden spoon, until it is no longer pink, 3 to 5 minutes. Add tomatillos and poblanos and cook, stirring occasionally, until they are starting to soften, 5 to 7 minutes. Add bulgur, chipotles, oregano, cumin and salt. Cook, stirring, until aromatic, 30 seconds to 1 minute. Stir in tomatoes, hominy and beans. Add broth. Bring to a boil.

2. Reduce heat to a simmer, partially cover the pot and cook, stirring occasionally, until the liquid is reduced and thickened, about 50 minutes. Garnish with sliced radishes.

SERVES 6: ABOUT 1½ CUPS EACH

Calories 348, **Fat** 13g (sat 3g), **Cholesterol** 44mg, **Carbs** 37g, **Total sugars** 8g (added 0g), **Protein** 24g, **Fiber** 10g, **Sodium** 812mg, **Potassium** 901mg.
Nutrition bonus: Vitamin C (64% daily value), Potassium (26% dv), Iron (23% dv), Magnesium (21% dv).

◄ *Heirloom*

◄ *Beefsteak/Slicing*

▲ *Plum tomato (aka Roma)*

Tomatoes

Texas singer-songwriter Guy Clark famously opines that there are only two things that money can't buy—"that's true love and homegrown tomatoes." "Plant 'em in the spring, eat 'em in the summer," he sings. "All winter without 'em's a culinary bummer." A sun-ripened tomato plucked from the vine right when it is ready to eat has no equal.

Tomatoes weren't always so revered. Although cultivated by the Aztecs and Incas as early as 700 A.D., when the tomato made its way to Europe in the 16th century, it was highly suspect. Because tomatoes are part of the nightshade family—which includes some plants that can be poisonous, such as belladonna—they were believed to be unfit for human consumption.

It was the invention of pizza in Naples in the late 1880s that garnered favor for the fruit all over Europe. Word traveled across the Atlantic, and by the early 20th century, there were more than 150 named varieties as breeders endeavored to create meatier, juicier fruits. Many of these heirloom varieties are still available through online or mail-order sources and seed-saving exchanges.

Tomatoes are generally classified into three categories, depending on their primary culinary use: paste or plum tomatoes (cooking), cherry (salad) and beefsteak (slicing). Within those categories, tomatoes are a riot of sizes, shapes and colors, including red, pink, purple, orange, yellow—even green stripe.

Tomatoes grow best in a temperature range between 65°F and 75°F. They do fine in warmer weather as well but require more water to keep from wilting. They are at peak season in summer—when there are both early- and late-season varieties.

◄ *Cherry tomato*

◄ *Pear tomato*

Best in summer

AT THE MARKET

➤ Choose tomatoes that are firm (but not hard), fragrant and that have rich, saturated color. The flesh should give slightly to gentle pressure. They should feel heavy for their size and should be free of blemishes or cracks.

IN YOUR KITCHEN

➤ Store tomatoes in a cool place out of direct sunlight for up to 4 days, depending on level of ripeness. Do not refrigerate.

➤ Rinse tomatoes under cool running water. On large slicing tomatoes, cut out the stem and core with a small paring knife.

➤ To seed a tomato, cut it in half crosswise and scoop out the seeds with your finger while gently squeezing each half.

COOKING BASICS

BAKE Cut 4 medium ripe tomatoes in half horizontally. Divide ¼ cup grated Parmesan cheese, 2 teaspoons chopped fresh oregano and ¼ teaspoon salt among the halves. Season to taste with ground pepper. Drizzle each half with ½ teaspoon olive oil. Bake in a 450°F oven until the tomatoes are tender, about 15 minutes. Serves 4.

CAPRESE SALAD Cut 4 medium ripe tomatoes into wedges (using 2 yellow and 2 red adds contrast). Place in a large bowl and toss with ¾ cup diced fresh mozzarella cheese, 2 tablespoons chopped fresh basil, ¼ teaspoon salt and pepper to taste. Serves 4.

OVEN-DRIED (ROMAS) Cut 4 pounds of roma tomatoes in half lengthwise. Season with ¾ teaspoon salt; let stand 20 minutes. Arrange on a foil-lined rimmed baking pan. Bake in a 250°F oven until mostly dry, about 4 hours. Use immediately or store in a tightly sealed container in the refrigerator for up to 1 week.

NUTRITION

➤ **1 cup cherry tomatoes: Calories** 27, **Fat** 0g (sat 0g), **Cholesterol** 0mg, **Carbs** 6g, **Total sugars** 4g (added 0g), **Protein** 1g, **Fiber** 2g, **Sodium** 7mg, **Potassium** 353mg.

BONUS These nightshades pack lycopene, a beta-carotene relative that shields your skin from the sun's damaging UV rays. For the most lycopene, eat your tomatoes cooked. Heating releases extra lycopene from the plant's cells, making it even easier to absorb.

Grow Your Own

Although tomato seeds can be sown directly into the soil, most gardeners get a jump-start on the season by buying tomato seedlings at a nursery. Plant seedlings in fertile, well-drained soil in a sunny spot 2 weeks after the average last-frost date in your area. For small bush tomatoes, plant 1½ to 2 feet apart. Plant large varieties 3 to 4 feet apart. Stake or cage plants soon after planting (to avoid damaging the roots later) to provide support and keep the fruit off the ground. Remove any suckers—side branches that form at the joints where leaves join stems—and pinch them out just beyond the first two leaves that develop. Water consistently. Tomatoes are ready to harvest when they have reached the mature size for their variety and have good color.

HEIRLOOM TOMATO SALAD WITH FRIED CAPERS

ACTIVE: 25 MIN **TOTAL:** 25 MIN
TO MAKE AHEAD: Refrigerate vinaigrette (Step 1) up to 5 days. Bring to room temperature and whisk before using.

There's really nothing quite like the natural fruity sweetness of vine-ripened tomatoes, so it's tempting to serve them unadorned (or eat them out of hand like an apple). But pairing them with the salty crunch of fried capers and a mustardy vinaigrette creates a flavor sensation all its own. Solution: Pick enough tomatoes to eat them both ways. (Photo: page 4.)

 2 tablespoons red-wine vinegar
 1 tablespoon Dijon mustard
 3 tablespoons chopped fresh dill *or* tarragon
 ½ teaspoon ground pepper, plus more to taste
 ¼ teaspoon salt
 5 tablespoons extra-virgin olive oil, divided
 3 tablespoons capers, rinsed *(see Tip, page 236)*
2½ pounds heirloom tomatoes, sliced
 1 pint cherry tomatoes, mixed colors, halved

1. Whisk vinegar, mustard, tarragon (or dill), ½ teaspoon pepper and salt in a small bowl. Gradually whisk in 4 tablespoons oil and continue whisking until well combined.

2. Pat capers dry thoroughly. Heat the remaining 1 tablespoon oil over medium heat. Add the capers and cook, stirring occasionally, until light brown, about 3 minutes. Remove with a slotted spoon and drain on a paper towel.

3. Arrange tomato slices and cherry tomatoes on a platter. Drizzle with the vinaigrette and top with the fried capers. Season with pepper.

SERVES 8: 1 CUP EACH

Calories 103, **Fat** 8g (sat 1g), **Cholesterol** 0mg, **Carbs** 7g, **Total sugars** 5g (added 0g), **Protein** 2g, **Fiber** 2g, **Sodium** 140mg, **Potassium** 439mg.
Nutrition bonus: Vitamin C (41% daily value), Vitamin A (30% dv).

SUMMER TOMATO, ONION & CUCUMBER SALAD

ACTIVE: 20 MIN **TOTAL:** 50 MIN (INCLUDING 30 MIN MARINATING TIME)
TO MAKE AHEAD: Prepare through Step 2 up to 1 hour ahead.

This is the simplest salad possible and is best enjoyed at the height of summer, when tomatoes and cucumbers are fresh from the garden. If you like tangy flavors, use white vinegar instead of rice vinegar, which has more subtle flavor.

- 3 tablespoons rice vinegar
- 1 tablespoon canola oil
- 1 teaspoon honey
- ½ teaspoon salt
- ½ teaspoon ground pepper, or more to taste
- 2 medium cucumbers
- 4 medium tomatoes, cut into ½-inch wedges
- 1 Vidalia *or* other sweet onion, halved and very thinly sliced
- 2 tablespoons coarsely chopped fresh herbs, such as flat-leaf parsley, chives *and/or* tarragon

1. Whisk vinegar, oil, honey, salt and pepper in a large shallow bowl.

2. Remove alternating stripes of peel from the cucumbers. Slice the cucumbers into thin rounds. Add the cucumber slices, tomatoes and onion to the dressing; gently toss to combine. Let stand at room temperature for at least 30 minutes and up to 1 hour.

3. Just before serving, add herbs and toss again.

SERVES 6: ABOUT 1½ CUPS EACH

Calories 66, **Fat** 3g (sat 0g), **Cholesterol** 0mg, **Carbs** 10g, **Total sugars** 7g (added 1g),
Protein 2g, **Fiber** 2g, **Sodium** 204mg, **Potassium** 361mg.
Nutrition bonus: Vitamin C (29% daily value).

Cutting fresh basil into thin slivers is easy using a technique the French call "chiffonade," which literally means "made of rags." Stack fresh basil leaves, then roll into a cigar-shape. Using a sharp knife (to avoid crushing and bruising the basil), slice the roll into narrow ribbons.

PANZANELLA

ACTIVE: 20 MIN **TOTAL:** 25 MIN

This classic Italian bread salad, full of bright acidity and the sweetness of basil, is one of the finest ways to enjoy summer tomatoes. Bring out your best olive oil and vinegar.

  2 **pounds ripe tomatoes**
  ¼ **cup finely chopped red onion**
  ¼ **cup chopped flat-leaf parsley**
  3 **tablespoons finely slivered fresh basil** *(see Tip)*
  4 **cups torn bite-size pieces stale crusty white bread** *(see Tip, page 344)*
  ¼ **cup extra-virgin olive oil**
  3 **tablespoons red-wine vinegar** *or* **sherry vinegar**
  ½ **teaspoon kosher** *or* **sea salt**
  ¼ **teaspoon ground pepper**

1. Cut large tomatoes into wedges or chunks; cut any cherry tomatoes into halves or quarters. Combine in a large bowl with onion, parsley and basil. Add bread.

2. Whisk oil, vinegar, salt and pepper in a small bowl. Pour it over the salad and gently toss to coat the bread well. Let stand about 5 minutes before serving.

SERVES 6: ABOUT 1⅓ CUPS EACH

Calories 192, **Fat** 11g (sat 2g), **Cholesterol** 0mg, **Carbs** 21g, **Total sugars** 6g (added 1g), **Protein** 4g, **Fiber** 3g, **Sodium** 242mg, **Potassium** 423mg.
Nutrition bonus: Vitamin C (41% daily value), Vitamin A (31% dv).

Farro

Farro, also called emmer wheat, is an ancient grain with a satisfyingly toothsome texture and nutty taste. It was cultivated by the early Egyptians and became a staple of Roman soldiers during their occupation of that country. Although over time it was replaced by higher-yield types of wheat, it experienced a renaissance in popularity in Italy and became trendy in the U.S. in the 1990s. It's wonderful in baked goods and soups. Look for it with other whole grains in well-stocked supermarkets.

BACON, TOMATO & FARRO SALAD

ACTIVE: 30 MIN **TOTAL:** 30 MIN

High-fiber, whole-grain farro cooks in about 15 minutes. Here we combine it with smoky bacon, sweet cherry tomatoes and fresh basil for a summery side dish or light lunch.

    1 cup farro (*see Tip*) or quick-cooking barley
    2 slices center-cut bacon
    1 medium shallot, chopped
    2 tablespoons white-wine vinegar
    ¼ teaspoon salt
    ¼ teaspoon ground pepper
    1 pint cherry tomatoes, quartered
    ¼ cup chopped fresh basil

1. Place farro (or barley) in a medium saucepan; add enough water to cover by 2 inches. Bring to a boil. Cover, reduce heat and simmer until tender, 15 to 20 minutes for farro (about 10 minutes for barley). Drain and transfer to a large bowl.

2. Meanwhile, cook bacon in a nonstick skillet over medium heat until crisp. Drain on a paper towel-lined plate; leave the fat in the pan. Add shallot to the pan and cook, stirring, for 1 minute. Stir in vinegar, salt and pepper. Remove from heat.

3. Crumble or chop the bacon. Add to the bowl along with tomatoes, basil and the warm vinaigrette; gently stir to combine. Serve warm or at room temperature.

SERVES 6: ABOUT ¾ CUP EACH

Calories 134, **Fat** 2g (sat 0g), **Cholesterol** 2mg, **Carbs** 26g, **Total sugars** 3g (added 0g), **Protein** 5g, **Fiber** 3g, **Sodium** 136mg, **Potassium** 147mg.

BLENDER GAZPACHO

ACTIVE: 20 MIN **TOTAL:** 2 HRS 20 MIN
TO MAKE AHEAD: Prepare through Step 1. Refrigerate up to 2 days. Finish with Steps 2-3 just before serving.

This easy gazpacho is heavenly on a hot day. Just puree everything in a blender and top with a drizzle of excellent olive oil.

GAZPACHO

- 4 large tomatoes (about 2 pounds), cored and quartered
- 2 slices country white bread, crust removed if desired, torn into pieces
- 1 English cucumber, cut into chunks
- 1 medium green bell pepper, seeded and cut into chunks
- 1 large clove garlic, halved

- 2 tablespoons extra-virgin olive oil
- 2 tablespoons red-wine vinegar
- ¾ teaspoon salt
- ½ teaspoon ground pepper

CROUTONS

- 3 slices country white bread
- 1 clove garlic, halved
- 2 tablespoons extra-virgin olive oil
- ¼ teaspoon ground pepper
- ⅛ teaspoon salt
- ⅛ teaspoon dried thyme

1. To prepare gazpacho: Working in two batches, puree tomatoes, bread, cucumber, bell pepper, garlic, oil, vinegar, salt and pepper in a blender until smooth. Transfer to a large bowl, cover and refrigerate until chilled, at least 2 hours and up to 2 days.

2. To prepare croutons: Rub both sides of each slice of bread with garlic, then cut the bread into ½-inch cubes.

3. Heat oil in a large skillet over medium heat. Add the bread and cook, stirring often, until crispy. Sprinkle with pepper, salt and thyme. Serve the gazpacho garnished with the croutons.

SERVES 6: ABOUT 1 CUP EACH

Calories 220, **Fat** 11g (sat 1g), **Cholesterol** 0mg, **Carbs** 26g, **Total sugars** 8g (added 2g), **Protein** 5g, **Fiber** 4g, **Sodium** 518mg, **Potassium** 499mg.
Nutrition bonus: Vitamin C (65% daily value), Vitamin A (28% dv).

Canned-Tomato Variation

No fresh tomatoes? Drain two 14-ounce cans of fire-roasted tomatoes. Roast the jalapeño in a small dry skillet over medium heat, turning occasionally, until soft and blackened in spots, 10 to 15 minutes. Pulse the drained tomatoes, jalapeño and garlic in a food processor until chunky.

FIRE-ROASTED SALSA

ACTIVE: 20 MIN **TOTAL:** 20 MIN
TO MAKE AHEAD: Refrigerate up to 5 days or freeze up to 3 months.

Charring fresh tomatoes and jalapeños on the grill gives this chunky pureed salsa fire-roasted flavor. Charring works just as well under the broiler, and the salsa also tastes delicious made with canned fire-roasted tomatoes.

2 large ripe tomatoes *(see Tip)*
1 large jalapeño pepper
2 small cloves garlic, chopped
½-1 teaspoon salt

1. Preheat grill to high (or preheat broiler).

2. Grill tomatoes and jalapeño, turning frequently, until charred, 10 minutes for the tomatoes, about 5 minutes for the jalapeño. (To broil, place on a baking sheet and broil about 4 inches from the heat, turning once or twice, until charred, 8 to 10 minutes total.)

3. When cool enough to handle, core the tomatoes and remove the stem from the jalapeño. Place in a food processor along with garlic; pulse to form a chunky mixture. Season with salt to taste.

MAKES: ABOUT 2 CUPS (¼-CUP SERVING)

Calories 10, **Fat** 0g (sat 0g), **Cholesterol** 0mg, **Carbs** 2g, **Total sugars** 1g (added 0g), **Protein** 0g, **Fiber** 1g, **Sodium** 148mg, **Potassium** 115mg.

ROASTED CHERRY TOMATO & SAGE SAUCE

ACTIVE: 15 MIN **TOTAL:** 30 MIN
TO MAKE AHEAD: Refrigerate up to 3 days; reheat before using.

There are endless ways to use this sage-flecked roasted cherry tomato sauce. For starters, serve with baked or grilled fish, spread it on a panini or simply toss it with whole-wheat pasta.

  2 pints cherry tomatoes
  1 medium onion, thinly sliced
  4 cloves garlic, minced
¼ cup chopped fresh sage
  3 tablespoons extra-virgin olive oil, divided
  1 tablespoon red-wine vinegar
½ teaspoon salt
¼ teaspoon ground pepper

1. Preheat oven to 450°F.

2. Combine tomatoes, onion, garlic, sage, 1 tablespoon oil, vinegar, salt and pepper in a 9-by-13-inch metal pan. Roast, stirring once halfway through, until the tomatoes and onion are tender, 15 to 20 minutes.

3. Lightly mash the tomatoes to release their juices. Stir in the remaining 2 tablespoons oil. Serve warm.

MAKES: ABOUT 3 CUPS (½-CUP SERVING)

Calories 93, **Fat** 7g (sat 1g), **Cholesterol** 0mg, **Carbs** 7g, **Total sugars** 3g (added 0g), **Protein** 1g, **Fiber** 2g, **Sodium** 200mg, **Potassium** 278mg.
Nutrition bonus: Vitamin C (26% daily value).

GARDEN TOMATO SAUCE

ACTIVE: 30 MIN **TOTAL:** 2¼ HRS
TO MAKE AHEAD: Refrigerate up to 3 days or freeze up to 6 months.

If you have a bumper crop of tomatoes or just want to buy them in season and put them up for another day, canning is not your only option—try freezing them. Just remove the cores and freeze them whole. Then turn your frozen tomatoes into a garden-fresh sauce any time of the year. For pizza sauce: In Step 2, cook until thickened to about the consistency of pizza sauce, 1½ to 2 hours. Remove from the heat, transfer to a blender, add 2 tablespoons tomato paste and blend until smooth.

5 pounds cored whole tomatoes, fresh *or* frozen

3 tablespoons extra-virgin olive oil

2 medium onions, chopped

4 cloves garlic, minced

¾ teaspoon dried basil *or* 1 tablespoon chopped fresh

¾ teaspoon dried thyme *or* 1 tablespoon chopped fresh

¾ teaspoon dried oregano *or* 1 tablespoon chopped fresh

1¾ teaspoons salt

½ teaspoon ground pepper

1-2 teaspoons sugar (optional)

1. If using fresh tomatoes, bring a large pot of water to a boil. Make a small X in the bottom of each tomato and plunge into the boiling water until the skins are slightly loosened, 30 seconds to 2 minutes. Transfer to a bowl of ice water for 1 minute. Peel with a paring knife, starting at the X. If using frozen tomatoes, run each under warm water and peel or rub off the skin. Thaw in the refrigerator or defrost in the microwave until mostly thawed. Chop the tomatoes, reserving any juice.

2. Heat oil in a large pot over medium heat. Add onions and cook, stirring, until beginning to brown, about 4 to 6 minutes. Add garlic and cook, stirring, for 1 minute. Add the tomatoes (and any juice), basil, thyme, oregano, salt, pepper and sugar (if using). Bring to a boil. Reduce heat to maintain a simmer and cook until thickened to desired consistency, stirring occasionally, 1 to 1½ hours. Taste and season with additional salt, pepper and/or sugar.

MAKES: ABOUT 6 CUPS (½-CUP SERVING)

Calories 72, **Fat** 4g (sat 1g), **Cholesterol** 0mg, **Carbs** 9g, **Total sugars** 5g (added 0g), **Protein** 2g, **Fiber** 2g, **Sodium** 349mg, **Potassium** 442mg.
Nutrition bonus: Vitamin C (42% daily value), Vitamin A (29% dv).

Sweetening the Deal

Adding a little bit of sugar to tomato sauce balances and rounds out the natural acidity of the tomatoes. Start by adding 1 teaspoon of sugar. Let it dissolve thoroughly, then taste the sauce and add more if necessary. If you like sharper flavor, skip the sugar.

Turnips & Rutabagas

Gnarly turnips and rutabagas are not glamorous vegetables, but proper treatment brings out their best—the sweet, earthy goodness that is the calling card of these unassuming roots.

Turnips are often confused with rutabagas—and vice versa. Both are root vegetables that reside in the brassica family—but there are some differences.

Turnips usually have skin that is white or white with purple, and white flesh. Rutabagas—also called Swedes or yellow turnips—are a cross between turnip and cabbage. They are typically harvested when they are larger than turnips. Rutabagas usually have yellow skin tinged with purple, and yellow flesh. Both vegetables have sweet and peppery flavor—although rutabagas tend to be a little sweeter. They can be used interchangeably in most recipes and are delicious braised, roasted, mashed, steamed, grilled or gratinéed. Roasting intensifies the natural sugars of these roots and turns the exterior golden brown. They are wonderful mashed together or with potatoes and/or carrots—or stirred into soups.

Lightly steam baby turnips, drizzle with walnut oil and season with salt. Shred young turnips and/or rutabagas and toss with a little olive oil, lemon juice, salt, pepper and fresh dill for a refreshing salad. Look at farmers' markets for diminutive "hakurei" or "salad turnips" with thin, delicate skin that does not need peeling. The mild peppery flavor of both turnips and rutabagas complements the rich flavor of sharp cheeses, such as Gruyère, or aged Gouda or Cheddar.

Turnips and rutabagas are cool-weather crops. The two seasons for turnips are spring and fall. Rutabagas take longer to mature, so they are in season only in fall.

Best in spring and fall

AT THE MARKET

🐖 Look for small to medium turnips and rutabagas that feel heavy for their size. (Large roots tend to be woody and pithy.) Avoid turnips and rutabagas that show signs of shriveling or that have soft spots or cuts. Rutabagas are often waxed.

🐖 Any greens that are still attached to turnips should look fresh, not wilted. (Turnip greens are edible and can be sautéed or braised similar to other dark leafy greens.)

IN YOUR KITCHEN

🐖 If turnips have greens attached, cut them off and store separately from the roots if you intend to eat them. Store greens, unwashed, in a plastic bag in the refrigerator up to 4 days.

🐖 Store the roots in a plastic bag in the refrigerator up to 2 weeks.

🐖 Scrub turnips and rutabagas with a vegetable brush under cool running water. Cut off stem and root ends. Place on a flat surface. Using a small sharp knife, remove peel. (Baby turnips and salad turnips do not need peeling.)

🐖 Rinse turnip greens in cool water to remove sand and grit. Dry thoroughly. Slice or chop as desired.

COOKING BASICS

MASH Cut 1½ pounds trimmed and peeled rutabaga or turnips into small chunks. Place in a pot and cover with water. Add 2 cloves peeled garlic. Bring to a boil. Reduce heat to medium-low, cover, and simmer until vegetables are fork-tender, 12 to 15 minutes. Drain and return the vegetables to the pan. Place over low heat and toss for about 1 minute to dry slightly. Mash with 2 to 4 tablespoons nonfat milk to achieve desired consistency. Stir in ½ teaspoon chopped fresh thyme, ½ teaspoon salt and pepper to taste. Serves 6.

ROAST In a large bowl stir together 2 tablespoons olive oil, 1 clove minced garlic and ½ teaspoon each sweet paprika, ground cumin and salt. Cut 2 trimmed and peeled medium turnips and 2 trimmed and peeled medium rutabagas into 1-inch chunks. Toss with the spiced oil mixture. Spread in a single layer on a large rimmed baking sheet. Roast in a 425°F oven, stirring once or twice, until tender, 45 to 50 minutes. Serves 6.

NUTRITION

🐖 **1 cup cooked cubed turnip:**
Calories 34 **Fat** 0g (sat 0g), **Cholesterol** 0mg, **Carbs** 8g, **Total sugars** 5g (added 0g), **Protein** 1g, **Fiber** 3g, **Sodium** 25mg, **Potassium** 276mg.

BONUS Cup for cup, the humble turnip (and its tops) contains more cancer-quashing glucosinolates than cabbage, kale, broccoli and cauliflower. Because boiling cruciferous vegetables, like turnips and rutabagas, can cause up to 59 percent of their glucosinolates to leach out into cooking water, opt for steaming, microwaving and roasting.

How to prep a turnip or rutabaga

1. Cut off the stem.

2. Cut off the root end.

3. Place on a flat surface. Using a small sharp knife, cut from top to bottom to remove the peel *(opposite)*.

SPRING TURNIP FRITTATA

ACTIVE: 50 MIN **TOTAL:** 1 HR 10 MIN

Here we pair turnips with broccoli rabe, which has a similar flavor to turnip greens. If you are able to find turnip greens, by all means use those instead.

8 ounces broccoli rabe (about ½ bunch) *or* Broccolini, trimmed

2 teaspoons minced garlic

½ teaspoon salt, divided

2 tablespoons extra-virgin olive oil, divided

3½ cups shredded peeled turnips (about 2 medium; *see Tip*)

½ cup chopped onion

8 large eggs

2 large egg whites

¼ cup low-fat milk

½ cup shredded fontina *or* Cheddar cheese

1. Preheat oven to 425°F.

2. Bring a large pot of water to a boil. Add broccoli rabe (or Broccolini) and cook until very tender, 5 to 7 minutes. Drain well. Transfer to a large bowl and toss with garlic and ¼ teaspoon salt. Set aside.

3. Heat 1 tablespoon oil in a large nonstick ovenproof skillet over medium heat. Add turnips, onion and the remaining ¼ teaspoon salt. Spread the mixture into an even layer; cook, without stirring, for 2 minutes. Then stir and scrape up any browned bits. Pat into an even layer and continue cooking, without stirring, for 2 minutes more. Stir and spread out again; cook until mostly golden brown, 2 to 4 minutes more. Transfer to a plate. Wash and dry the pan.

4. Whisk eggs, egg whites and milk in a medium bowl. Heat the remaining 1 tablespoon oil in the pan over medium heat. Add the egg mixture and cook until beginning to set, about 1 minute. Remove from heat. Top with the turnip mixture and cheese, then the broccoli rabe (or Broccolini).

5. Transfer the pan to the oven. Bake until set, about 15 minutes. Let stand 5 minutes. Run a flexible rubber spatula along the edges, then underneath, until you can slide the frittata onto a cutting board. Cut into wedges.

SERVES 6

Calories 212, **Fat** 14g (sat 5g), **Cholesterol** 259mg, **Carbs** 7g, **Total sugars** 4g (added 0g), **Protein** 14g, **Fiber** 1g, **Sodium** 422mg, **Potassium** 232mg.
Nutrition bonus: Vitamin C (74% daily value), Vitamin A (58% dv).

Safe Shredding

To prevent nicking your fingers on the sharp holes of a box grater while shredding round root vegetables, such as turnips and rutabaga, shred about half the vegetable, then use a clean dish towel to grip the remaining half (and protect your fingers) as you shred. Or use the shredding blade on your food processor and let the machine do the work for you.

MISO-BUTTER BRAISED TURNIPS

ACTIVE: 45 MIN **TOTAL:** 45 MIN

Slowly braising turnips gives them a sweet flavor and velvety texture. The addition of turnip greens (which are sometimes sold separately in bunches) adds a peppery bite. For a mellower flavor, use spinach.

- 6 medium turnips (about 2 pounds) plus 5 cups chopped turnip greens *or* spinach, divided
- 2 tablespoons butter, divided
- ¼ teaspoon salt
- 1 cup reduced-sodium chicken broth, plus more if needed
- 1 teaspoon sugar
- 4 teaspoons white miso *(see Tip, page 32)*

1. Peel turnips and cut into 1-inch wedges. Melt 1 tablespoon butter in a large skillet over medium-high heat. Add the turnips and salt and cook, stirring occasionally, until browned in spots and beginning to soften, 7 to 9 minutes.

2. Add 1 cup broth and sugar; reduce heat to maintain a simmer. Cook, stirring frequently, until the turnips are tender and the liquid is almost completely evaporated, 15 to 20 minutes. (Add up to ½ cup more broth if the pan is dry before the turnips are tender.)

3. Meanwhile, mash miso with the remaining 1 tablespoon butter in a small bowl until combined.

4. When the turnips are tender, stir in the turnip greens (or spinach), cover and cook, stirring occasionally, until wilted, 2 to 3 minutes. Remove the pan from the heat. Add the miso-butter and gently stir until the turnips are well coated.

SERVES 6: ABOUT ¾ CUP EACH

Calories 85, **Fat** 4g (sat 3g), **Cholesterol** 10mg, **Carbs** 11g, **Total sugars** 6g (added 1g), **Protein** 2g, **Fiber** 4g, **Sodium** 365mg, **Potassium** 367mg.
Nutrition bonus: Vitamin A (55% daily value), Vitamin C (44% dv).

COUSCOUS WITH RUTABAGA & BEEF STEW

ACTIVE: 40 MIN **TOTAL:** 40 MIN

In this riff on a North African tradition, couscous is the base for beef and rutabaga stew made with an intoxicating blend of spices. Garnish with fresh parsley or cilantro and serve with sliced cucumber.

1 pound sirloin *or* strip steak, trimmed and cut into 1-inch cubes

½ teaspoon salt, divided

½ teaspoon ground pepper

2 tablespoons extra-virgin olive oil, divided

1 pound rutabaga (½ medium), cut into ½-inch cubes

1 medium onion, chopped

2 tablespoons tomato paste

½ teaspoon ground cinnamon

½ teaspoon ground turmeric

½ teaspoon ground coriander

⅛ teaspoon cayenne pepper (optional)

2 tablespoons all-purpose flour

3 cups reduced-sodium beef broth

1 cup water

⅔ cup whole-wheat couscous

1. Sprinkle steak with ¼ teaspoon salt and pepper. Heat 1 tablespoon oil in a large saucepan over medium heat. Add the steak and cook, stirring frequently, until no longer pink on the outside, about 4 minutes. Transfer to a plate.

2. Add the remaining 1 tablespoon oil to the pan over medium heat. Add rutabaga, onion, tomato paste, cinnamon, turmeric, coriander, cayenne (if using) and the remaining ¼ teaspoon salt; cook, stirring occasionally, until the onion begins to soften, about 4 minutes. Add flour and cook, stirring, 1 minute more. Add broth and bring to a boil over medium-high heat, scraping up any browned bits. Cook, stirring occasionally, until the rutabaga is tender, 10 to 14 minutes.

3. Meanwhile, bring water to a boil in a small saucepan over medium-high heat. Add couscous, cover and remove from heat. Let stand for 5 minutes.

4. When the rutabaga is tender, return the steak and any accumulated juice to the pan. Reduce heat to medium and cook the steak through, about 2 minutes more.

5. To serve, fluff the couscous with a fork and divide among 4 shallow bowls. Top with equal portions of the stew.

SERVES 4: 1½ CUPS STEW & ½ CUP COUSCOUS EACH

Calories 391, **Fat** 12g (sat 3g), **Cholesterol** 63mg, **Carbs** 41g, **Total sugars** 8g (added 0g), **Protein** 30g, **Fiber** 7g, **Sodium** 746mg, **Potassium** 813mg.
Nutrition bonus: Vitamin C (47% daily value), Zinc (30% dv), Potassium (23% dv).

Shao Hsing

Shao Hsing (or Shaoxing) is a seasoned rice wine. It is available in most Asian specialty markets and some larger supermarkets in the Asian section. If unavailable, dry sherry is an acceptable substitute.

PORK & TURNIP MISO RAMEN

ACTIVE: 35 MIN **TOTAL:** 35 MIN
EQUIPMENT: Vegetable spiralizer

Ramen gets a healthy makeover when you use a spiralizer to make noodles from turnips. We swap noodles made from mild turnips for ramen noodles, but other vegetables, such as zucchini and yellow squash, could also stand in for this Asian-inspired recipe. Serve with sriracha hot sauce for a kick.

1½ pounds purple-top turnips, peeled
2 teaspoons peanut oil
6 scallions, sliced into 1-inch pieces
1 tablespoon minced fresh ginger
1 large clove garlic, minced
8 ounces pork tenderloin, cut into 1-inch pieces
3 cups low-sodium chicken broth
3 cups water
2 tablespoons white miso *(see Tip, page 32)*
1 tablespoon reduced-sodium soy sauce
1 tablespoon Shao Hsing rice wine *(see Tip) or* dry sherry
6 ounces mixed mushrooms, sliced, and/or enoki mushrooms (about 3 cups)
6 cups baby spinach

1. Using a spiral vegetable slicer *(see Tip, page 272)* or a julienne vegetable peeler, cut turnips into long, thin strands. You should have about 10 cups of turnip "noodles."

2. Heat oil in a large pot over medium heat. Add scallions, ginger and garlic and cook, stirring, until fragrant, about 30 seconds. Add pork and cook, stirring, until starting to brown, about 1 minute. Add broth, water, miso, soy sauce and rice wine (or sherry); bring to a boil. Stir in the noodles, mushrooms and spinach. Cook, gently stirring to submerge the vegetables in the broth, until the noodles are just tender, about 3 minutes.

SERVES 5: ABOUT 2 CUPS

Calories 160, **Fat** 4g (sat 1g), **Cholesterol** 29mg, **Carbs** 15g, **Total sugars** 6g (added 0g), **Protein** 16g, **Fiber** 4g, **Sodium** 447mg, **Potassium** 889mg.
Nutrition bonus: Vitamin A (71% daily value), Vitamin C (63% dv), Folate (26% dv), Potassium (25% dv).

Watercress

In the wild, watercress, a vivid green plant with delicate round leaves, grows along running waterways. It is one of the oldest leafy greens consumed by humans, harvested from locations where there was a natural water source. The flavor—fresh and pungent with peppery heat—surely drew foragers to the streams again and again.

Because it is aquatic or semiaquatic, this member of the mustard family has adapted well to hydroponic cultivation, but it has a very short shelf life once picked. (Hydroponic watercress has a much milder flavor than field-grown watercress.)

Although it is usually served raw in salads or as an herbal accent, Chinese cooks stir-fry it. Given its pungency, watercress pairs well with mild flavors and creamy textures. Watercress soup, a potage of French origin, is a silky green puree of watercress and cooked potatoes with stock and a little cream. Watercress sandwiches—thinly sliced bread spread with a thin layer of butter and watercress—are a staple of English teatime. Watercress adds color and flavor to eggs—tuck it into an omelet just before serving to preserve its crisp texture.

If you come across beautiful green cress growing along a stream on a Sunday hike, a caveat: Aquatic plants are highly susceptible to contamination from the water in which they grow—which might be polluted with chemical runoff or animal waste. Buy watercress from a reputable vendor at a farmers' market or from the supermarket and leave the wild stuff in its native state.

Watercress is available throughout the year—depending on the method of cultivation—but is technically a cool-weather green. Gardeners who grow it harvest in spring and again in fall.

Best in spring and fall

AT THE MARKET

🔖 Watercress is sold both in bunches and plastic bags. Choose watercress that has crisp green leaves with no yellowing. If the bunch is bound with a rubber band or twist tie, check the stems to see that there is no sliminess.

🔖 Although there are several different varieties of watercress—some with round dime-size leaves and others that are spikier and more pointed—they can be used interchangeably.

IN YOUR KITCHEN

🔖 Remove the rubber band or twist tie from a bunch of watercress. Place the root end in a jar of water. Cover lightly with plastic wrap and refrigerate up to 3 days.

🔖 Trim oversize and woody stems. Rinse watercress in cool water to remove soil. Spin dry in a salad spinner or thoroughly pat dry with paper towels.

COOKING BASICS

SANDWICH Spread 2 slices of roggenbrot (German wholemeal rye bread, also called "fitness bread") with 2 tablespoons reduced-fat cream cheese. Layer 1 slice with watercress. Top with other slice. Cut in half. Serves 2.

SAUTÉ Heat 2 teaspoons olive oil in a large nonstick skillet over medium heat. Cook 1 clove minced garlic in hot oil until fragrant, about 1 minute. Add 8 ounces trimmed watercress to pan. Cook, stirring often, until wilted, 1 to 2 minutes. Season with ⅛ teaspoon salt and Champagne or white-wine vinegar and pepper to taste. Serves 2.

SIMPLE SALAD Whisk 2 tablespoons olive oil, 1 tablespoon white wine vinegar, ¼ teaspoon salt and pepper to taste in a large bowl. Add 4 cups watercress leaves and ½ of a small red onion, thinly sliced. Toss with vinaigrette and serve immediately. Serves 2.

NUTRITION

🔖 **1 cup chopped raw watercress:** Calories 4, **Fat** 0g (sat 0g), **Cholesterol** 0mg, **Carbs** 0g, **Total sugars** 0g (added 0g), **Protein** 1g, **Fiber** 0g, **Sodium** 14mg, **Potassium** 112mg.

BONUS Watercress contains chlorophyll, the pigment that gives plants their green tint. Chlorophyll is also believed to prevent cancer by binding to cancer-causing compounds in your gut and whisking them out of your body. Other top chlorophyll veggies include spinach, green beans and arugula.

WATERCRESS SALAD WITH SESAME-GARLIC DRESSING

ACTIVE: 35 MIN **TOTAL:** 35 MIN

Watercress stands up to the bold flavors of radicchio and a fish-sauce-spiked dressing in this spring salad. Consider shaking up some extra dressing to toss with your salads throughout the week.

- 4 large eggs
- 4 cups trimmed watercress *or* arugula (about 4 ounces)
- 2 cups torn radicchio (1-inch pieces)
- 1 small avocado, cut into bite-size pieces
- 1 cup sliced radishes
- ½ cup thinly sliced spring onions *or* scallions

- 2 tablespoons fresh lime juice
- 1 tablespoon fish sauce
- 1 tablespoon packed brown sugar
- 2 teaspoons minced fresh jalapeño
- 2 teaspoons minced garlic
- 2 teaspoons toasted sesame oil
- 2 teaspoons toasted sesame seeds (*see Tip*) (optional)

1. To hard-boil eggs, place in a small saucepan and cover with 1 inch of water. Bring to a simmer over medium-high heat. Reduce heat to low and cook at the barest simmer for 10 minutes. Remove from the heat, pour out hot water and cover the eggs with ice-cold water. Let stand until cool enough to handle before peeling. Cut into quarters.

2. Combine watercress (or arugula), radicchio, avocado, radishes and onions (or scallions) in a salad bowl. Add the eggs. Combine lime juice, fish sauce, brown sugar, jalapeño, garlic and oil in a jar; cover and shake to combine. Pour the dressing over the salad and gently toss to combine. Garnish with toasted sesame seeds, if desired.

SERVES 5: 1½ CUPS EACH

Calories 169, **Fat** 12g (sat 2g), **Cholesterol** 149mg, **Carbs** 11g, **Total sugars** 4g (added 3g), **Protein** 8g, **Fiber** 4g, **Sodium** 324mg, **Potassium** 487mg.
Nutrition bonus: Vitamin C (42% daily value), Vitamin A (25% dv).

Toasting Sesame Seeds

To toast sesame seeds, heat a small dry skillet over low heat. Add seeds and stir constantly, until golden and fragrant, about 2 minutes. Transfer to a small bowl and let cool.

WATERCRESS WITH RICE WINE-OYSTER SAUCE

ACTIVE: 25 MIN **TOTAL:** 25 MIN
TO MAKE AHEAD: Refrigerate the sauce (Step 1) up to 1 week.

If watercress is young and tender, stir-fry the whole stems. If stem ends are woody and tough, discard them. Use a salad spinner so the watercress is dry to the touch, or the stir-fry will become a braise.

RICE WINE-OYSTER SAUCE

   1 tablespoon Shao Hsing rice wine *(see Tip, page 482)* or dry sherry

   2 teaspoons oyster-flavor sauce *or* vegetarian oyster sauce

   ¼ teaspoon sugar

   ⅛ teaspoon salt

WATERCRESS STIR-FRY

   2 tablespoons canola oil

   2 medium cloves garlic, smashed

  24 cups watercress (14 ounces *or* about 6 bunches) *or* 16 cups spinach, tough stems trimmed

   1 teaspoon toasted sesame oil

1. To prepare the sauce: Whisk rice wine, oyster sauce, sugar and salt in a small bowl.

2. To prepare the watercress: Heat a 14-inch flat-bottom wok or large skillet over high heat until a bead of water vaporizes within 1 to 2 seconds of contact. Swirl canola oil into the pan, add garlic and stir-fry for 10 seconds. Add watercress and stir-fry until it just begins to wilt, about 1 minute. (The wok will become very full as the watercress is added; stir constantly to avoid scorching the greens.) Stir the sauce and swirl it into the pan; stir-fry until the watercress is just tender but still bright green, 1 to 2 minutes. Stir in sesame oil. Remove the garlic. Serve immediately.

SERVES 4: ABOUT ½ CUP EACH

Calories 104, **Fat** 8g (sat 1g), **Cholesterol** 0mg, **Carbs** 4g, **Total sugars** 1g (added 1g), **Protein** 5g, **Fiber** 1g, **Sodium** 285mg, **Potassium** 674mg.
Nutrition bonus: Vitamin C (146% daily value), Vitamin A (130% dv), Calcium (25% dv).

ORANGE, WATERCRESS & TUNA SALAD

ACTIVE: 35 MIN **TOTAL:** 35 MIN

This vibrant salad contrasts flavor, texture and color—velvety tuna steak is matched with crisp, peppery watercress and the floral tart-sweetness of blood oranges and aniseed. Blood oranges make the dish especially pretty—if you can't find them, use any oranges that look good.

3 medium oranges	Pinch of cayenne pepper
1 tablespoon canola oil	1-1¼ pounds tuna steaks (about
1 tablespoon rice vinegar	1 inch thick), cut into
1 teaspoon minced crystallized	4 portions *(see Tip)*
ginger *or* fresh ginger	¼ teaspoon ground pepper
½ teaspoon ground coriander	1 cup loosely packed tiny
½ teaspoon aniseed, chopped *or*	watercress sprigs *or* leaves
crushed, divided	(¾-1 inch long)
½ teaspoon kosher salt, divided	

1. Peel oranges with a sharp knife, removing all peel and white pith. Working over a medium bowl, cut the segments from the surrounding membranes and let them drop into the bowl. Squeeze the peels and membranes over the bowl to extract all the juice before discarding them. Gently stir in oil, vinegar, ginger, coriander, ¼ teaspoon aniseed, ¼ teaspoon salt and cayenne. Set aside.

2. Position oven rack 5 to 6 inches from the broiler; preheat to high. Cover a broiler pan with foil.

3. Season tuna with the remaining ¼ teaspoon each aniseed, salt and pepper. Place on the prepared pan. Broil about 2 minutes per side for medium-rare, 4 minutes per side for medium or to desired doneness.

4. Stir watercress into the orange mixture. Slice the tuna, divide among 4 plates and top with equal portions of the salad. Serve immediately.

SERVES 4

Calories 208, **Fat** 4g (sat 0g), **Cholesterol** 44mg, **Carbs** 13g, **Total sugars** 10g (added 0g), **Protein** 29g, **Fiber** 3g, **Sodium** 195mg, **Potassium** 712mg.
Nutrition bonus: Vitamin C (93% daily value), Vitamin B$_{12}$ (39% dv), Potassium (20% dv).

Sustainable Tuna

While the issues around tuna are complex, a good rule of thumb is that most U.S.-caught tuna, including Hawaiian, is considered a good or best choice for the environment because it is sustainably fished. Look for tuna that has been caught with a pole—"troll," "pole" or "hook & line" caught. If the method of catch is not on the label, ask your fishmonger how it was caught and tell him you want to know in the future. Avoid all bluefin and any species of imported longline tuna. For more information, visit *seafoodwatch.org*.

WATERCRESS & CITRUS TABBOULEH

ACTIVE: 45 MIN **TOTAL:** 1¼ HRS (INCLUDING 30 MINUTES CHILLING TIME)

This twist on the classic Middle Eastern bulgur, tomato and parsley salad is a refreshing combination of sweet and juicy citrus, peppery watercress and cool, crunchy cucumber.

Segmenting Citrus

To "suprême" citrus fruits (most often oranges or grapefruit) is to separate them into segments free of pith, membranes and seeds. To do this, cut a thin slice off the top and bottom of the fruit. Place on a flat surface. Slice off the peel from top to bottom, curving slightly as you cut to follow the curve of the fruit. Holding the fruit over a bowl, use a small sharp knife to cut between the membrane and each segment, letting the segments drop into the bowl. Do not add the juice from segmenting to the tabbouleh—it will make the salad too wet.

VINAIGRETTE

- 2 tablespoons minced shallot
- 2 tablespoons champagne vinegar
- 1 tablespoon finely grated orange zest
- 2 tablespoons freshly squeezed orange juice
- 2 tablespoons freshly squeezed grapefruit juice
- 3 tablespoons extra-virgin olive oil
- 1 teaspoon salt
  Ground pepper to taste

SALAD

- ¾ cup bulgur
- 1½ teaspoons extra-virgin olive oil
- 1½ cups boiling water
- 4 cups coarsely chopped watercress
- 3 medium oranges, segmented (*see Tip*) and roughly chopped
- 2 medium ruby-red grapefruit, segmented (*see Tip*) and roughly chopped
- 1 English cucumber, peeled and diced
- ¾ cup chopped fresh mint
- ½ cup sliced scallions

1. To prepare vinaigrette: Combine shallot, vinegar, orange zest, orange juice and grapefruit juice in a small bowl. Let stand 30 minutes. Whisking constantly, slowly drizzle in 3 tablespoons oil until the mixture thickens. Season with salt and pepper.

2. To prepare salad: Combine bulgur and oil in a large bowl. Pour in boiling water, cover and let stand until tender, 15 to 20 minutes. Drain in a strainer, pressing on the bulgur with the back of a large spoon to extract as much liquid as possible. Return to the bowl, fluff with a fork and let cool to room temperature.

3. Add watercress, oranges, grapefruit, cucumber, mint and scallions to the bulgur. Drizzle with the vinaigrette and stir gently to combine. Cover and chill for 30 minutes, then serve immediately.

SERVES 6: 1¼ CUPS EACH

Calories 225, **Fat** 9g (sat 1g), **Cholesterol** 0mg, **Carbs** 36g, **Total sugars** 13g (added 0g), **Protein** 5g, **Fiber** 7g, **Sodium** 408mg, **Potassium** 561mg.
Nutrition bonus: Vitamin C (135% daily value), Vitamin A (50% dv).

Yuca

First things first: Yuca ("YOO-ka") is not related to yucca ("YUK-ka"), an ornamental plant that is part of the Agave family—and only in North America will you see the vegetable labeled as yuca. Elsewhere in the English-speaking world it is cassava or manioc.

This starchy, rock-hard root is most familiar to Americans in its processed form—tapioca—in a bowl of milky and sweet pudding, with its toothsome and gelatinous little beads, or in the chewy and glutinous balls in bubble tea.

But south of the equator—in its native South America, as well as in the Philippines, the Caribbean, Southeast Asia and Africa—yuca is given a savory spin. The flesh, which is as firm and white as a coconut when raw, is usually boiled, fried or roasted. Cooked, it becomes buttery and translucent, with a definitive stickiness. It has a starchy, mild sweetness that readily absorbs other flavors.

In Brazil, it is pureed and used as an ingredient in a creamy sauce served with shrimp. In Puerto Rico, yuca is mashed and combined with broth, garlic, olive oil and pork cracklings or bacon in a dish called *mofongo*. In Venezuela and Colombia, crisp, fluffy yuca fries are served with fiery hot sauce. Cuban cooks top plain boiled yuca with a sauce of olive oil, sour orange juice and garlic.

Yuca is available all year but may be difficult to find. Look for it in well-stocked supermarkets and in Latin markets.

A word of reassurance: Yuca can contain varying amounts of naturally occurring cyanide. The varieties that make it to market in this country—almost exclusively products of Costa Rica and the Dominican Republic—have extremely low levels and cooking eliminates it.

Available year-round

AT THE MARKET

➤ Choose yuca that is rock-hard, with no soft spots, cracks, bald spots or mold. Yuca begins to dry out as soon as it's harvested, so the roots are almost always coated in wax to seal in moisture. If you are not following a recipe that calls for a specific amount, buy more yuca than you think you will need; about one-quarter to one-third of the original weight will be lost in trimming and peeling.

IN YOUR KITCHEN

➤ Store yuca in a cool, dry place for up to 5 days.

➤ Yuca should be peeled all the way below the pinkish layer of flesh underneath the rough, bark-like skin. Cut the root in 3-inch sections so this layer is easier to see, then cut each piece in half lengthwise. Use a small sharp paring knife to get under the pink layer and remove it and the brown skin. Cut out any remaining pink spots or dark streaks running through the root, a sign that the yuca is past its prime.

➤ A fibrous core or spindle runs through the center of each root. This core is most visible and easiest to remove after the yuca has been boiled.

COOKING BASICS

BOIL Trim and peel 3 pounds yuca and cut into 3-inch-long pieces. (You should have about 2 pounds trimmed yuca.) Place in a large saucepan and add 3 quarts water. Bring to a boil over high heat. Reduce heat to medium. Cook until desired tenderness (25 minutes for fork-tender, 40 minutes for very tender). Drain. Working quickly, cut out the fibrous core from each piece; discard the cores. Toss the yuca with 2 tablespoons olive oil, ½ teaspoon salt and pepper to taste. Mash or leave whole; serve immediately. (Yuca begins to congeal if it is allowed to cool.) Serves 6.

ROAST (OVEN FRIES) Follow directions for boiling 2 pounds yuca to a fork-tender texture *(see above)* and remove the cores. Cool to room temperature. Cut into matchsticks. Toss with 2 tablespoons olive oil, 1 teaspoon salt and pepper to taste. Arrange on a parchment-lined baking sheet. Roast in a 450°F oven, turning once, until browned and crisp, 20 to 25 minutes. Serves 6.

NUTRITION

➤ **½ cup cooked yuca: Calories** 165, **Fat** 0g (sat 0g), **Cholesterol** 0mg, **Carbs** 39g, **Total sugars** 2g (added 0g), **Protein** 2g, **Fiber** 2g, **Sodium** 14mg, **Potassium** 279mg.

BONUS This root provides manganese, a nutrient your body needs to properly metabolize carbohydrates, fats and proteins. Eat ½ cup of cooked yuca and you'll rack up 20 percent of your daily dose.

YUCA-SCALLION MOFONGO

ACTIVE: 45 MIN **TOTAL:** 45 MIN

In the Caribbean, these dumpling-like balls are made with plantains—but in Puerto Rico, yuca becomes the base. The root is cooked and mashed to a dough-like consistency with scallions, bacon, chicken broth and garlic, then formed into balls. Serve as a side dish to braised, grilled or roasted meat.

- 2 medium yuca (about 2 pounds)
- 2 tablespoons extra-virgin olive oil plus 1 teaspoon, divided
- ½ cup thinly sliced scallions
- 4 small cloves garlic, minced
- ½ teaspoon kosher salt
- 4 slices bacon, cooked and crumbled
- ¾ cup low-sodium chicken broth
- ¼ cup chopped fresh cilantro

1. Remove the thick peel from each yuca with a paring knife, then cut crosswise into 3-inch pieces. Quarter each piece lengthwise. Place in a medium saucepan and add enough water to cover by 1 inch. Bring to a boil. Reduce heat, cover and simmer until nearly tender, 20 to 25 minutes. Drain and pat dry. Remove the thin woody cores. Chop the yuca into ¾-inch pieces.

2. Heat 2 tablespoons oil in a large nonstick skillet over medium heat. Add the yuca and cook, stirring occasionally, until very tender, about 10 minutes. Stir in scallions. Cook for 1 minute more. Transfer to a bowl.

3. Using the side of a chef's knife or a mortar and pestle, smash garlic with salt and the remaining 1 teaspoon oil to make a paste. Stir the garlic paste and bacon into the yuca mixture, then add broth and mash the mixture with a potato masher to the consistency of chunky mashed potatoes.

4. To serve, use an ice cream scoop to shape the yuca mixture into 2-inch balls (about ⅓ cup each) and sprinkle with cilantro.

SERVES 6: 2 BALLS EACH

Calories 208, **Fat** 7g (sat 1g), **Cholesterol** 5mg, **Carbs** 33g, **Total sugars** 2g (added 0g), **Protein** 4g, **Fiber** 2g, **Sodium** 188mg, **Potassium** 309mg.
Nutrition bonus: Vitamin C (32% daily value).

LEMON-GARLIC YUCA MASHERS WITH CILANTRO PESTO

ACTIVE: 45 MIN **TOTAL:** 1¼ HRS

A swirl of Spanish-inspired pesto made with Marcona almonds and Manchego cheese gives this creamy side fabulous flavor and eye-catching color. Use the leftover pesto to flavor steamed or roasted vegetables.

1 medium yuca (about 1 pound)
1 pound Yukon Gold potatoes, peeled and cut into 2-inch chunks
5 small cloves garlic, divided
2 cups packed fresh cilantro leaves
¼ cup Marcona almonds *(see Tip)*, toasted and chopped
¼ cup grated Manchego cheese
5 tablespoons extra-virgin olive oil, divided
1 teaspoon lemon zest
1 tablespoon lemon juice
1 cup low-sodium chicken broth, heated
¾ teaspoon salt
½ teaspoon ground pepper

1. Remove the thick peel from yuca with a paring knife, then cut the yuca crosswise into 3-inch pieces. Place in a large saucepan and add enough water to cover by 1 inch. Bring to a boil. Reduce heat, cover and simmer until the yuca is falling apart, 50 minutes to 1 hour. After the yuca has cooked for 35 minutes, place potatoes and 4 garlic cloves in a medium saucepan. Add enough water to cover by 1 inch. Bring to a boil. Reduce heat, cover and simmer until the potatoes are tender, about 15 minutes.

2. Meanwhile, place the remaining garlic clove, cilantro, almonds, cheese, 3 tablespoons oil and lemon juice in a food processor. Pulse a few times, then process until pureed, scraping down the sides occasionally.

3. Drain the yuca; transfer to a cutting board. Remove the thin woody cores. Using a potato masher, mash the yuca in a large bowl. Drain the potatoes and garlic, add to the yuca and mash to the consistency of mashed potatoes.

4. Add the remaining 2 tablespoons oil, lemon zest, broth, salt and pepper. Using a rubber spatula, gently fold everything together. Add ¼ cup of the pesto and fold into the yuca mixture.

SERVES 8: ½ CUP EACH

Calories 167, **Fat** 7g (sat 1g), **Cholesterol** 1mg, **Carbs** 24g, **Total sugars** 1g (added 0g), **Protein** 3g, **Fiber** 2g, **Sodium** 256mg, **Potassium** 315mg.
Nutrition bonus: Vitamin C (20% daily value).

Marcona Almonds

Superbly crisp and buttery-tasting Marcona almonds have recently become more popular and more available. These Spanish almonds are a little flatter than ordinary almonds, with richer flavor.

Always skinned, most Marcona almonds have already been sautéed in oil and lightly salted when you get them. Find them in specialty stores or online at *tienda.com*.

Resources

HOW WE TEST & ANALYZE RECIPES

At EatingWell *we aim to create recipes that work perfectly and taste absolutely delicious. They also adhere to guidelines for healthful eating. To that end, we perfect through rigorous testing each recipe we publish—and then provide accurate nutritional information so you can make informed decisions about what you eat. Here's how we do it:*

HOW WE TEST RECIPES

❧ Recipes are tested on average seven times each by multiple testers—both home cooks and culinary school graduates.

❧ We test on both gas and electric stoves.

❧ We use a variety of tools and techniques.

❧ Testers shop major supermarkets to research availability of ingredients.

❧ Testers measure active and total time to prepare each recipe.

❧ "Active" time includes prep time (the time it takes to chop, dice, puree, mix, combine, etc., before cooking begins), but it also includes the time spent tending something on the stovetop, in the oven or on the grill—and getting it to the table. If you can't walk away from it, we consider it active minutes.

❧ "Total" includes both active and inactive minutes and indicates the entire amount of time required for each recipe, start to finish.

❧ "To Make Ahead" gives storage instructions to help you plan. If particular "Equipment" is needed, we tell you that at the top of the recipe too.

HOW WE ANALYZE RECIPES

❧ All recipes are analyzed for nutrition content by a registered dietitian.

❧ We analyze for calories, total fat, saturated (sat) fat, cholesterol, carbohydrate, total sugars, added sugars, protein, fiber, sodium and potassium using The Food Processor® SQL Nutrition Analysis Software from ESHA Research, Salem, Oregon.

❧ Garnishes and optional ingredients are not included in analyses.

❧ When a recipe gives a measurement range of an ingredient, we analyze the first amount.

❧ When alternative ingredients are listed, we analyze the first one suggested.

❧ We do not include trimmings or marinade not absorbed in analyses.

❧ Recipes are tested and analyzed with iodized table salt unless otherwise indicated.

❧ We estimate that rinsing with water reduces the sodium in canned foods by 35%. (Readers on sodium-restricted diets can reduce or eliminate the salt in a recipe.)

❧ To help people eat in accordance with the USDA's Dietary Guidelines, *EatingWell*'s suggested portions generally are based upon standard serving sizes. For example, suggested servings for meat, poultry and fish are generally 3 to 4 ounces, cooked. A recommended portion of a starch-based side dish, such as rice or potatoes, is generally ½ cup. Vegetable side dishes are a minimum of ½ cup.

❧ When a recipe provides 20 percent or more of the Daily Value (dv) of a nutrient, it is listed as a nutrition bonus. These values are FDA benchmarks for adults eating 2,000 calories a day.

For more on our nutritional-analysis process, visit eatingwell.com/go/ guidelines.

HOW TO FOLLOW AN *EATINGWELL* RECIPE

Once we're sure the recipe works well, it's up to you to follow the recipe. It's important to keep in mind a few simple guidelines and tips for how to read our recipes.

HOW TO READ AN INGREDIENT LIST

The comma matters. When we call for ingredients, pay attention to where the comma is because it can have a significant effect on what we're calling for. Here are some examples:

➤ "1 pound chicken, trimmed" means we are calling for 1 pound purchased chicken and then you trim it.

➤ "1 cup pecans, chopped" means we are calling for 1 cup of pecans and then you chop them. "1 cup chopped pecans," on the other hand, means you should chop your pecans and then measure out 1 cup of the chopped nuts.

➤ "1 cup frozen raspberries, thawed" means we are calling for 1 cup of frozen raspberries and then you thaw them. One cup thawed frozen raspberries, on the other hand, means that you thaw and then measure your berries.

➤ "1 cup sifted flour" means sift the flour first and then measure it. Alternately, "1 cup flour, sifted" means first measure your flour and then sift it.

Market quantities versus measures. We aim to make shopping as easy as possible, so we usually call for market quantities of ingredients rather than measures.

➤ For example, a market quantity would be 1 small onion, while a measure would be ¾ cup diced onion. When we call for a measure it is typically because we think that using the specified amount of the ingredient is important to the outcome of the recipe.

TIPS FOR MEASURING

Measuring accurately when cooking and baking is one of the best ways to guarantee successful results in the kitchen. In the EatingWell Test Kitchen, we use four types of standard U.S. measuring tools:

DRY MEASURING CUPS Metal or plastic measuring cups, usually sold in a set, that are available in ¼-, ⅓-, ½-, ¾- and 1-cup sizes. Dry ingredients, such as flour and grains, should be measured in dry measuring cups.

LIQUID MEASURING CUPS Clear glass or plastic cups with pour spouts that are available in 1-, 2-, 4- and 8-cup sizes that have measurements marked on the side of the cup. When measuring liquids, place a clear liquid measuring cup on a level surface. Pour in the liquid, then verify the measure by looking at it from eye level, not from above.

MEASURING SPOONS Small spoons in ¼-, ½-, 1-teaspoon and 1-tablespoon sizes designed to measure small quantities of dry or liquid ingredients. When a teaspoon or tablespoon measure is called for in a recipe, we don't mean the regular silverware spoons you eat with.

KITCHEN SCALE Although it is not necessary to have a kitchen scale to make our recipes, a small digital scale that can measure up to at least 5 pounds is a handy tool to have in the kitchen to ensure accuracy.

INGREDIENTS

FLOUR We use the "spoon and level" method to measure flours. To properly measure flour this way, use a spoon to lightly scoop flour from its container into a measuring cup. (There's no need to stir up the flour before you scoop it into the cup.) Use a knife or other straight edge to level the flour with the top of the cup. If the measuring cup is dipped directly into the container—a common mistake—the flour will be packed into the cup and result in extra flour being added to the recipe, yielding tough, dense baked goods.

GRANULATED SUGAR Granulated sugar should be spooned into the measuring cup. Use a knife or other straight edge to level the sugar with the top of the cup.

BROWN SUGAR Brown sugar should be firmly packed into the measuring cup and leveled by pressing it with your hand or a spoon.

CONFECTIONERS' SUGAR Confectioners' sugar should be measured in the same way as granulated sugar or flour, unless the recipe calls for it to be "packed"—in those recipes, it should be packed as you would brown sugar.

KNIFE SKILLS

How you cut ingredients is important; it helps distribute the ingredient throughout the dish (mincing or finely chopping garlic, for example), ensure that ingredients cook at the same time (like cutting carrots and potatoes into 1-inch dice) or improve texture (a thinly sliced piece of smoked salmon, for example, is more tempting on your bagel than a fat chunk). Pay attention to, but don't stress about, these terms. Your common sense will go a long way in helping as you cook.

MINCE & FINELY CHOP "Mincing" is the finest chop of all, less than ⅛ inch, achieved by cutting, then rocking the knife back and forth across the ingredients, while rotating the blade around on the cutting board. "Finely chop" is a little larger than mince.

CHOP & COARSELY CHOP You want to wind up with about a ½- to 1-inch piece when you chop, a bit larger when you "coarsely chop." The idea of chopping (unlike dicing) is that the ingredients don't have to be uniform in shape.

DICE & CUBE You're aiming for uniformity of size here. Most recipes that call for a "dice" or "cube" will indicate the preferred size for cooking in the time allotted (e.g., "cut into 1-inch cubes"). Ignore these measurements and you will alter the cooking time.

SLICE & THINLY SLICE "Slice" is a judgment call, but if you insist on a general rule, think of a slice no thinner than ¼ inch. "Thinly slice," however, means you will want to cut the food as thinly as possible. This will vary by ingredient: You can slice an apple to near-transparent thinness, which is hard to do with steak.

SLICE DIAGONALLY Also known as slicing "on the bias," this is just like slicing, but instead of making a perpendicular cut you cut on an angle. It's an attractive way to cut long vegetables, such as scallions, celery and zucchini. To slice diagonally, hold the knife at a 45-degree angle to the vegetable and then cut it.

CUT INTO JULIENNE Also known as matchstick cut: Food is cut into long thin strips. To get a matchstick, first slice the vegetable and then trim the edges to get even rectangles (about 1 to 2 inches long). Then stack the rectangles and slice lengthwise into matchsticks.

HEATING & COOKING

We try to use terms that are as clear as possible in recipes. But, of course, how you interpret those words can have an impact on how a dish turns out. Here are some of the words we use and what we mean.

SIMMER This is low steady cooking in which the liquid in the pan should be steaming and gently bubbling. Usually you can maintain a simmer over low or medium-low heat, depending on your stove. Often we instruct you to bring something to a boil and then reduce to a simmer. When you do this you will probably need to bring it to a boil over higher heat and then reduce the heat.

BRAISE, STEW These two terms (you can use them interchangeably) are a subset of "simmer" and involve cooking something in liquid over low heat. Braising is often used for tough cuts of meat, as in pot roast.

SAUTÉ Usually in a skillet over relatively high heat, sautéing is a quick method of cooking food in a little bit of fat. The food is stirred or moved around occasionally.

STIR-FRY A high-heat method of searing meats, poultry, fish and vegetables, usually associated with Asian cooking. You must use oil for stir-frying; otherwise, the high temperature will cause the natural sugars to burn and foods to stick to the pan—even a nonstick one.

STEAM Food is cooked by steam rather than by direct contact with a pan or a liquid. Usually we steam using a steamer basket. To steam, you need a pot large enough to hold both the steamer basket and 1 inch of water with plenty of airflow all around the basket. The food should not sit in the water. Check the water level from time to time to make sure the pan isn't dry.

ROAST Whether at a high or low heat, roasting involves a steady, even, dry heat that cooks from the outside in. Air (and thus heat) should circulate freely around whatever's being roasted; the oven rack should be placed in the center of the oven unless otherwise stated in the recipe.

BROIL This is an indoor cousin of grilling and sears food with high, direct heat. A broiler should always be preheated for at least 5 minutes; food should be placed so that it (not the broiler pan) is 4 to 6 inches from the heat source. Foods blotted dry broil with less mess.

FREEZING FOR FRESHNESS

Freezing vegetables is one of the easiest ways to preserve the abundance. Follow this easy guide to enjoy the harvest throughout the year.

VEGETABLE PREP

☞ The best vegetables to freeze are fresh from the field and at their peak ripeness. Trim and wash vegetables under cold water. Peel if necessary. Cut to desired size, if necessary (for example, carrots can be left whole or dice them for an easy addition to soup).

☞ Blanch vegetables before freezing. It stops ripening, helps get rid of dirt and bacteria, brightens color, slows nutrient loss and softens the vegetables so they are easier to pack. To blanch vegetables: Bring a large pot of water to a boil (use at least 1 gallon of water per pound of vegetables). Add the vegetables to the water. Once the water returns to a boil, cook the vegetables 1 to 3 minutes. Remove the vegetables from the boiling water with a slotted spoon and transfer immediately to a bowl of ice water until completely chilled. Drain well.

☞ Tomatoes and tomatillos do not need to be blanched before freezing. Just wash, peel (if desired) and remove the core.

CHOOSING CONTAINERS

☞ Frozen food develops off-flavors when in contact with air. Choose moistureproof and vaporproof containers—glass jars, freezer bags or other plastic containers designed for storing frozen foods. If using plastic bags, remove as much air as possible before sealing. A vacuum sealer is also useful for removing air and preserving quality.

PACKING

☞ There are two kinds of packing: solid-pack and loose-pack. To solid-pack vegetables, place the prepared produce in the desired container and freeze. Solid-packing conserves space and is useful when planning to use large batches of frozen vegetables at one time. To loose-pack, freeze one layer of vegetables on a baking sheet. Once the produce is frozen, transfer it to the storage container. Loose-packing takes up more space, but it is easier to remove just the amount desired, such as a handful of peas or corn kernels.

☞ Leave 1 inch of head space (open space at the top of the freezer container) when solid-packing produce, as food expands as it freezes. When loose-packing frozen foods, headspace is not necessary as the foods are already frozen. Wipe all container edges before sealing because moisture or food on the sealing edges of the container will prevent proper sealing. Label each container with the name and date packaged. Most produce will keep for 8 to 12 months.

FREEZING FRESH HERBS

☞ Tender herbs, such as basil, chives, cilantro, dill, mint and parsley, are best suited to freezing. Blanching them first helps capture their fresh flavor. Drop into boiling water for several seconds, then with a slotted spoon or tongs, transfer to a bowl of ice water to chill for several seconds more. Blot dry with paper towels. Spread a single layer of the blanched herbs on a wax paper-lined baking sheet, cover loosely with plastic and freeze until solid, about 1 hour. Transfer to plastic freezer bags. Freeze blanched herbs up to 4 months.

THE 'DIRTY DOZEN' & THE 'CLEAN FIFTEEN'

The Environmental Working Group—a nonprofit, nonpartisan organization that conducts research on human health and the environment—compiles the *Shopper's Guide to Pesticides in Produce*™ and updates it regularly. Its Dirty Dozen singles out fruits and vegetables that contain a higher pesticide load than other produce. These foods tested positive for a number of different pesticide residues—some as many as 15. In 2015, that list included apples, peaches, nectarines, strawberries, grapes, celery, spinach, sweet peppers, cucumbers, cherry tomatoes, imported snap peas and potatoes.

Conversely, the Clean Fifteen is a list of produce least likely to hold pesticide residues. In 2015, those fruits and vegetables included avocados, sweet corn, pineapples, cabbage, frozen peas, onions, asparagus, mangoes, papayas, kiwi, eggplant, grapefruit, cantaloupe, cauliflower and sweet potatoes. Relatively few pesticides were detected on these foods and tests found low total concentrations when they were present.

For more information, visit *ewg.org*.

RECIInde... RECIPE INDEX

Page numbers in *italics* refer to photos.

A

Aioli, Herbed Chipotle, Spicy Jicama & Red Onion Shoestrings with, 272, *273*
Aioli, Roasted Pepper, Beer-Battered Onion Rings with, 341
almonds
    Grape & Fennel Salad, 247
    Green Salad with Peaches, Feta & Mint Vinaigrette, *296*, 297
    Lemon-Garlic Yuca Mashers with Cilantro Pesto, 496, *497*
    Sole with Garlic-Almond-Caper Sauce, 259
    White Gazpacho, 226
anchovies
    anchovy-garlic vinaigrette (cooking basics salad), 190
    Artichokes, Cauliflower, Potato & Escarole Salad, 18–19
    Asparagus & Baby Kale Caesar Salad, *34*, 35
    crispy fried, 321
    mustard greens salad (cooking basics), 320
    Orecchiette with Broccoli Rabe, 108, *109*
    Potato-Leek Bisque, 348
    Roasted Vegetable Antipasto, *116*, 117
Antipasto, Roasted Vegetable, *116*, 117
apples
    Carrot-Orange Juice, 138, *139*
    Green Smoothie, 278, *279*
    Jicama-Apple Slaw, 271
    Maple-Bacon Roasted Apples & Celeriac, *174*, 175
    varieties for cooking, 167
    Warm Potato Salad with Bacon-Mustard Dressing, *390*, 391
applesauce, *in* Coconut-Carrot Morning Glory Muffins, 146, *147*
artichokes
    about, 12–14
    Artichoke & Parmesan Stuffed Mushrooms, 311
    Artichokes, Cauliflower, Potato & Escarole Salad, 18–19
    Artichokes with Lemon & Dill, 16, *17*
    interaction with wine, 16
arugula
    about, 21–22
    Arugula Pesto (cooking basics), 22, *23*
    arugula salad (cooking basics), 22
    Broccoli & Tortellini Salad with Arugula Pesto, 92, *93*
    Dandelion Salad with Goat Cheese & Tomato Dressing (option), 302, *303*
    Green Salad with Peaches, Feta & Mint Vinaigrette, *296*, 297
    Pear & Arugula Salad with Candied Walnuts, *24*, 25
    Simple Green Salad with Citronette, 192, *193*
    Watercress Salad with Sesame-Garlic Dressing (option), 487
    Wild Mushroom Pizza with Arugula & Pecorino, 26, *27*

Asiago cheese
    Arugula Pesto (cooking basics), 22, *23*
    Shaved Zucchini-Fennel Salad, 418
asparagus
    about, 28–30
    Asparagus & Baby Kale Caesar Salad, *34*, 35
    Asparagus & Mushroom Risotto, 316
    Asparagus-Goat Cheese Soufflés, 36, *37*
    Panko-Crusted Asparagus Spears, 32, *33*
    Penne alla Primavera, 57
    Roasted Garlic & Asparagus Salad, 258
avocados
    about, 38–40
    Chipotle-Cheddar Broiled Avocado Halves, *44*, 45
    creamy avocado dressing (cooking basics), 40
    Jason Mraz's Guacamole, 42, *43*
    Jicama-Apple Slaw, 271
    Pineapple & Avocado Salad (cooking basics), 40
    Pink Grapefruit & Avocado Salad, 46, *47*
    Super-Green Edamame Salad, 52, *53*
    Watercress Salad with Sesame-Garlic Dressing, 487

B

Baba Ghanoush, Grilled Eggplant &, 237
baby bella mushrooms. *See* cremini mushrooms
bacon. *See also* pancetta
    Bacon, Tomato & Farro Salad, 468
    Bacon Chard Quesadillas, 183
    center-cut bacon, 391
    Chili-Brown Sugar Delicata Squash with Pears, 434
    Dandelion Salad with Goat Cheese & Tomato Dressing, 302, *303*
    in healthful diet, 118
    Kale Salad with Bacon-Blue Cheese Vinaigrette, 283
    Maple-Bacon Roasted Apples & Celeriac, *174*, 175
    Sautéed Brussels Sprouts with Bacon & Onions, 118
    Sautéed Mushrooms with Caramelized Shallots, *309*, 310
    Scrambled Eggs with Ramps & Bacon, 345
    Spinach & Warm Mushroom Salad, 410, *411*
    Summer Corn & Scallop Pasta, 218
    Warm Potato Salad with Bacon-Mustard Dressing, *390*, 391
    Yuca-Scallion Mofongo, 495
bananas, *in* Green Smoothie, 278, *279*
barley, *in* Bacon, Tomato & Farro Salad (option), 468
Basic Green Soup, 186, *187*
basil
    Bacon, Tomato & Farro Salad, 468
    Caprese Salad (cooking basics), 462
    to chiffonade, 466
    Mediterranean Cauliflower Pizza, 156, *157*
    Paprika & Red Pepper Soup with Pistachios, 377
    Penne alla Primavera, 57
    Summer Corn & Scallop Pasta, 218

Bavarian Leek & Cabbage Soup, 130
beans, dry or canned
    Bacon Chard Quesadillas, 183
    Braised Greens & Cannellini Bean Panini, 208, *209*
    Celery & Parmesan Minestrone, 166, *167*
    to cook dry beans, 52
    Fava Bean Puree with Chicory, 200, *201*
    Ribollita Soup, 284, *285*
    sodium in canned beans, 183
    Super-Green Edamame Salad, 52, *53*
    Tomatillo & Pork Chili, 458, *459*
beans, fresh. *See* shell beans; snap beans
beef
    Borscht with Beef, 78, *79*
    Chimichurri Grilled Steak Salad, *300*, 301
    Couscous with Rutabaga & Beef Stew, 481
    Harissa-Rubbed Steak & Carrot Salad, 145
    Korean Steak & Mushroom Tacos with Kimchi, 317
    Moroccan-Style Stuffed Peppers, 381
    South Texas Steak Fajitas, *378*, 379
Beer-Battered Onion Rings with Roasted Pepper Aioli, 341
beets
    about, 71–72, *73*, 74
    Borscht with Beef, 78, *79*
    Pickled Beets, 74, *75*
    Roasted Beet Salad, *76*, 77
Belgian endive, *191*
    Artichokes, Cauliflower, Potato & Escarole Salad, 18–19
    Braised Endive, *194*, 195
    Kale Salad with Bacon-Blue Cheese Vinaigrette, 283
bell peppers
    about, *370*, 371–72
    Blender Gazpacho, 469
    Chimichurri Grilled Steak Salad, *300*, 301
    Moroccan-Style Stuffed Peppers, 381
    Paprika & Red Pepper Soup with Pistachios, 377
    Seafood Gumbo, 332–33
    Sicilian Pepper Salad, *374*, 375
    Summer Corn & Scallop Pasta, 218
    Super-Green Edamame Salad, 52, *53*
Bison & Squash Stew, Mexican, 424–25, *425*
black beans, *in* Bacon Chard Quesadillas, 183
Black-Eyed Peas & Okra, 54, *55*
Blender Gazpacho, 469
blue cheese, *in* Kale Salad with Bacon-Blue Cheese Vinaigrette, 283
Blue Cheese Dressing, Slivered Celery Salad with, 163
bok choy
    about, 80–82, *83*
    Roasted Baby Bok Choy, 84, *85*
    Tuna & Bok Choy Packets, 87
    Velvet Chicken with Baby Bok Choy, 86
Borscht with Beef, 78, *79*
Boston lettuce
    Peas & Lettuce, 362, *363*
    Pink Grapefruit & Avocado Salad, 46, *47*

Simple Green Salad with Citronette, 192, *193*
Braised Endive, *194,* 195
Braised Greens & Cannellini Bean Panini, 208, *209*
bratwurst, *in* Bavarian Leek & Cabbage Soup, 130
Bread Casserole, Roasted Garlic & Leek, 344
breadcrumbs, to make and store, 18, 240
broccoli, Broccolini, Chinese Broccoli
    about, 89–90, *91*
    Broccoli, Cauliflower & Romanesco Gratin, 159
    Broccoli & Tortellini Salad with Arugula
      Pesto, 92, *93*
    Broccoli-Cheddar-Chicken Chowder, 96, *97*
    Green Curry Soup, 412
    Mediterranean Roasted Broccoli &
      Tomatoes, *94,* 95
    Spaghetti Squash Lasagna with
      Broccolini, 436, *437*
    Spring Turnip Frittata, *478,* 479
    Stir-Fried Chinese Broccoli, 98, *99*
broccoli rabe
    about, 100–102
    Broccoli Rabe with Olives & Garlic, 104, *107*
    Crushed Red Potatoes with Winter
      Greens, *206,* 207
    Grilled Broccoli Rabe (cooking basics), 102, *103*
    Orecchiette with Broccoli Rabe, 108, *109*
    Spring Turnip Frittata, *478,* 479
    Stir-Fried Chinese Broccoli (option), 98, *99*
    Vietnamese-Flavored Broccoli Rabe, 105
Brussels sprouts
    about, 110–12
    Garlic Roasted Salmon & Brussels Sprouts, 119
    Roasted Vegetable Antipasto, *116,* 117
    Sautéed Brussels Sprouts with Bacon &
      Onions, 118
    Shaved Brussels Sprouts Salad with Lemon-Chile
      Vinaigrette & Toasted Hazelnuts, 114, *115*
bulgur
    Tomatillo & Pork Chili, 458, *459*
    Watercress & Citrus Tabbouleh, 490, *491*
buttercup squash
    Winter Salad with Roasted Squash &
      Pomegranate Vinaigrette, 198, *199*
    Winter Squash & Chicken Tzimmes, 435
Buttermilk Ranch Dressing (cooking basics), 294
butternut squash, *429*
    Creamy Rye & Butternut Squash Soup, 430, *431*
    to prep, 428
    Winter Salad with Roasted Squash &
      Pomegranate Vinaigrette, 198, *199*
    Winter Squash & Chicken Tzimmes, 435

C

cabbage
    about, 120–22, *123*
    Bavarian Leek & Cabbage Soup, 130
    Borscht with Beef, 78, *79*
    Chinese Chicken Salad with Citrus-Miso
      Dressing, *128,* 129
    Coleslaw (cooking basics), 122
    Mexican Bison & Squash Stew, 424–25, *425*
    Ribollita Soup, 284, *285*
    Roasted Cabbage with Chive-Mustard
      Vinaigrette, 124, *125*
    shredded sweet potatoes and cabbage (cooking
      basics), 442
    Simple Sauerkraut, 126–27
    Vegetarian Stuffed Cabbage, 131–32, *133*
Caesar Salad, Asparagus & Baby Kale, *34,* 35

cannellini beans
    Braised Greens & Cannellini Bean
      Panini, 208, *209*
    Celery & Parmesan Minestrone, 166, *167*
    Ribollita Soup, 284, *285*
capers
    Heirloom Tomato Salad with Fried
      Capers, *4,* 463
    Mediterranean Roasted Broccoli &
      Tomatoes, *94,* 95
    Mediterranean Sautéed Shrimp & Fennel, 251
    Radish Canapés with Creamy Dill
      Spread, 402, *403*
    Roasted Fennel with Olive Tapenade, Feta &
      Mint, 250
    Roasted Vegetable Antipasto, *116,* 117
    salt-packed, 236
    Sicilian Eggplant Caponata, 236
    Sole with Garlic-Almond-Caper Sauce, 259
Caponata, Sicilian Eggplant, 236
Caprese Salad (cooking basics), 462
Caramelized Onions, Romaine Wedges with
    Sardines &, 298, *299*
caramelized onions (cooking basics), 336
Caramelized Shallots, Sautéed Mushrooms
    with, *309,* 310
carrots
    about, 135–36
    Bavarian Leek & Cabbage Soup, 130
    Borscht with Beef, 78, *79*
    Carrot-Orange Juice, 138, *139*
    Celery & Parmesan Minestrone, 166, *167*
    Cider & Honey Kohlrabi Slaw with
      Radicchio, 289
    Coconut-Carrot Morning Glory
      Muffins, 146, *147*
    Coleslaw (cooking basics), 122
    Crunchy Confetti Tuna Salad, *164,* 165
    Harissa-Rubbed Steak & Carrot Salad, 145
    Korean Steak & Mushroom Tacos with
      Kimchi, 317
    Mexican Pickled Carrots, 140–41
    Pear & Celery Root Slaw, 172, *173*
    Penne alla Primavera, 57
    Pomegranate Molasses-Glazed Carrots with
      Pistachios, 137
    Quinoa Mushroom Soup, *314,* 315
    Ribollita Soup, 284, *285*
    Roasted Rainbow Carrots with Sage Brown
      Butter, *143,* 144
    Roasted Vegetable Antipasto, *116,* 117
cauliflower
    about, 149–50
    Artichokes, Cauliflower, Potato & Escarole
      Salad, 18–19
    Broccoli, Cauliflower & Romanesco Gratin, 159
    Cauliflower Steaks with Chimichurri, 152, *153*
    Dill-Havarti Mashed Cauliflower, *154,* 155
    Mediterranean Cauliflower Pizza, 156, *157*
    Roasted Cauliflower Salad with Walnuts, *8,* 158
Caviar, Twice-Baked Potatoes with Horseradish
    &, 394, *395*
celery
    about, 160–62
    Artichokes, Cauliflower, Potato & Escarole
      Salad, 18–19
    Bavarian Leek & Cabbage Soup, 130
    Borscht with Beef, 78, *79*
    Broccoli-Cheddar-Chicken Chowder, 96, *97*
    Celery & Parmesan Minestrone, 166, *167*
    Crunchy Confetti Tuna Salad, *164,* 165

Double Celery Soup, 176, *177*
Grape & Fennel Salad, 247
Mama's Potato Salad, 389
Quinoa Mushroom Soup, *314,* 315
to remove strings, 163
Ribollita Soup, 284, *285*
Roasted Stuffed Pumpkin, 438–39
Seafood Gumbo, 332–33
Sicilian Eggplant Caponata, 236
Slivered Celery Salad with Blue Cheese
    Dressing, 163
celery root
    about, 168–71
    Double Celery Soup, 176, *177*
    Maple-Bacon Roasted Apples &
      Celeriac, *174,* 175
    Parsnip-Celery Root Pancakes with
      Pancetta, 354, *355*
    Pear & Celery Root Slaw, 172, *173*
chard
    about, 179–80, *181*
    Bacon Chard Quesadillas, 183
    Basic Green Soup, 186, *187*
    Bavarian Leek & Cabbage Soup, 130
    Chard & Chorizo Frittata, *184,* 185
    Chard with Green Olives, Currants & Goat
      Cheese, 182
    Ribollita Soup, 284, *285*
chayote, *in* Mexican Bison & Squash Stew, 424–
    25, *425*
Cheddar cheese
    Broccoli, Cauliflower & Romanesco Gratin, 159
    Broccoli-Cheddar-Chicken Chowder, 96, *97*
    Cheesy Potato Casserole, 393
    Chipotle-Cheddar Broiled Avocado
      Halves, *44,* 45
    Creamed Spinach Casserole, 413
    Dill-Havarti Mashed Cauliflower
      (option), *154,* 155
    Peas & Ham Pasta Salad, 367
    Roasted Corn Cheese Dip, 216, *217*
    Spring Turnip Frittata, *478,* 479
cheese
    Asiago cheese
      Arugula Pesto (cooking basics), 22, *23*
      Shaved Zucchini-Fennel Salad, 418
    blue cheese
      Kale Salad with Bacon-Blue Cheese
        Vinaigrette, 283
      Slivered Celery Salad with Blue Cheese
        Dressing, 163
    Cheddar cheese
      Broccoli, Cauliflower & Romanesco
        Gratin, 159
      Broccoli-Cheddar-Chicken Chowder, 96, *97*
      Cheesy Potato Casserole, 393
      Chipotle-Cheddar Broiled Avocado
        Halves, *44,* 45
      Creamed Spinach Casserole, 413
      Dill-Havarti Mashed Cauliflower
        (option), *154,* 155
      Peas & Ham Pasta Salad, 367
      Roasted Corn Cheese Dip, 216, *217*
      Spring Turnip Frittata, *478,* 479
    cheesy cream sauce variations, 67
    cottage cheese, *in* Creamed Spinach
      Casserole, 413
    cream cheese (Neufchâtel)
      Curried Onion Dip, 340
      fat content, 446

Radish Canapés with Creamy Dill Spread, 402, *403*
Roasted Corn Cheese Dip, 216, *217*
Sweet Potato Pie with Cream Cheese Swirl, 448–49

feta
Citrus Salad with Olives and Radicchio, 196
Green Salad with Peaches, Feta & Mint Vinaigrette, *296*, 297
Indian-Style Mustard Greens & Kale with Toasted Naan, 322, *323*
Mediterranean Sautéed Shrimp & Fennel, 251
Persian Cucumber Salad with Lentils & Sprouts, 228, *229*
Roasted Fennel with Olive Tapenade, Feta & Mint, 250

fontina
Mini Onion Gratins, 342, *343*
Spring Turnip Frittata, *478*, *479*
Wild Mushroom & Polenta Casserole, 312, *313*

goat cheese
Asparagus-Goat Cheese Soufflés, 36, *37*
Chard with Green Olives, Currants & Goat Cheese, 182
Dandelion Salad with Goat Cheese & Tomato Dressing, 302, *303*
Goat Cheese Mashed Potatoes, 392
Green Salad with Peaches, Feta & Mint Vinaigrette (option), *296*, 297
Grilled Eggplant & Baba Ghanoush, 237
Pea, Pancetta & Tarragon Crostini, *360*, 361
Radish Canapés with Creamy Dill Spread, 402, *403*

Gruyère
Broccoli, Cauliflower & Romanesco Gratin, 159
Roasted Garlic & Leek Bread Casserole, 344

Havarti, *in* Dill-Havarti Mashed Cauliflower, *154*, 155

Manchego
Asparagus-Goat Cheese Soufflés (option), 36, *37*
Citrus Salad with Olives and Radicchio, 196
Lemon-Garlic Yuca Mashers with Cilantro Pesto, 496, *497*
Shaved Zucchini-Fennel Salad, 418

Mexican blend, *in* Chiles Rellenos with Chicken, 380

mozzarella
Eggplant Parmesan, 240–41
Mediterranean Cauliflower Pizza, 156, *157*
Spaghetti Squash Lasagna with Broccolini, 436, *437*
Wild Mushroom Pizza with Arugula & Pecorino, 26, *27*

paneer, *in* Indian-Style Mustard Greens & Kale with Toasted Naan, 322, *323*

Parmesan and Parmigiano-Reggiano
Artichoke & Parmesan Stuffed Mushrooms, 311
Asparagus & Baby Kale Caesar Salad, *34*, 35
Asparagus & Mushroom Risotto, 316
Broccoli & Tortellini Salad with Arugula Pesto, 92, *93*
Celery & Parmesan Minestrone, 166, *167*
Chard & Chorizo Frittata, *184*, 185
Dandelion Salad with Goat Cheese & Tomato Dressing, 302, *303*
Eggplant Parmesan, 240–41
Fennel Gratin, 248, *249*
mustard greens salad (cooking basics), 320

Pasta with Braised Radicchio, 197
Penne alla Primavera, 57
Roasted Stuffed Pumpkin, 438–39
Sausage-&-Quinoa-Stuffed Zucchini, 421
Spaghetti Squash Lasagna with Broccolini, 436, *437*
Spicy Jicama & Red Onion Shoestrings with Herbed Chipotle Aioli, 272, *273*
Wild Mushroom & Polenta Casserole, 312, *313*

Pecorino
Broccoli & Tortellini Salad with Arugula Pesto, 92, *93*
Wild Mushroom Pizza with Arugula & Pecorino, 26, *27*

pepper Jack, *in* Bacon Chard Quesadillas, 183
raclette, *in* Roasted Garlic & Leek Bread Casserole, 344
Taleggio, *in* Wild Mushroom & Polenta Casserole, 312, *313*
Cheesy Potato Casserole, 393
Chermoula, Green, Marinated Eggplant with, *238*, 239

chicken
Broccoli-Cheddar-Chicken Chowder, 96, *97*
Chiles Rellenos with Chicken, 380
Chinese Chicken Salad with Citrus-Miso Dressing, *128*, 129
Garlic Chicken, 260, *261*
Grilled Chicken Thighs with Cucumber-Mint Salad, 231
to skin chicken legs, 260
Slow-Cooker Chicken Stock, 130
Velvet Chicken with Baby Bok Choy, 86
Winter Squash & Chicken Tzimmes, 435

chickpeas, *in* Celery & Parmesan Minestrone, 166, *167*

chicories
about, 189–90, *191*
Artichokes, Cauliflower, Potato & Escarole Salad, 18–19
Braised Endive, *194*, 195
chicory salad (cooking basics), 190
Cider & Honey Kohlrabi Slaw with Radicchio, 289
Citrus Salad with Olives and Radicchio, 196
Crushed Red Potatoes with Winter Greens, *206*, 207
Fava Bean Puree with Chicory, 200, *201*
Kale Salad with Bacon-Blue Cheese Vinaigrette, 283
Pasta with Braised Radicchio, 197
Simple Green Salad with Citronette, 192, *193*
Spinach & Warm Mushroom Salad, 410, *411*
Spring Salad with Peas & Frizzled Shallots, 346, *347*
Watercress Salad with Sesame-Garlic Dressing, 487
Winter Greens Salad with Squash & Cranberry Vinaigrette, *432*, 433
Winter Salad with Roasted Squash & Pomegranate Vinaigrette, 198, *199*

chiles. *See* chipotles; hot peppers
Chiles Rellenos with Chicken, 380
Chili, Tomatillo & Pork, 458, *459*
Chili-Brown Sugar Delicata Squash with Pears, 434
Chimichurri Grilled Steak Salad, *300*, 301
Chinese Broccoli, Stir-Fried, 98, *99*
Chinese Chicken Salad with Citrus-Miso Dressing, *128*, 129

chipotles
about, 45

Chipotle-Cheddar Broiled Avocado Halves, *44*, 45
Grilled Tomatillo-Chipotle Salsa (cooking basics), 452, *453*
Tomatillo & Pork Chili, 458, *459*
Chips, Kale, *280*, 281

chives
Broccoli, Cauliflower & Romanesco Gratin, 159
Garlic Chicken, 260, *261*
Roasted Cabbage with Chive-Mustard Vinaigrette, 124, *125*
Roasted Garlic & Asparagus Salad, 258
Super-Green Edamame Salad, 52, *53*

chorizo
Chard & Chorizo Frittata, *184*, 185
Lima Beans with Chorizo, 56
Spanish chorizo, about, 185
Cider & Honey Kohlrabi Slaw with Radicchio, 289

cilantro
creamy avocado dressing (cooking basics), 40
Fresh Green Salsa (cooking basics), 452
Fresh Tomatillo Salad, 456
Green Curry Soup, 412
Jason Mraz's Guacamole, 42, *43*
Jicama-Apple Slaw, 271
Lemon-Garlic Yuca Mashers with Cilantro Pesto, 496, *497*
Marinated Eggplant with Green Chermoula, *238*, 239
Mexican Bison & Squash Stew, 424–25, *425*
Paprika & Red Pepper Soup with Pistachios, 377
Pork & Shrimp Stuffed Eggplant, *235*, 242–43
Potatoes with Green Tahini Sauce, 386, *387*
South Texas Steak Fajitas, *378*, 379
Spicy Tomatillo Quinoa, *454*, 455
Sweet Corn Salad, *214*, 215
Yuca-Scallion Mofongo, 495
Citronette, Simple Green Salad with, 192, *193*
Citrus Salad with Olives and Radicchio, 196
Citrus Tabbouleh, Watercress &, 490, *491*
Citrus-Miso Dressing, Chinese Chicken Salad with, *128*, 129

clementines, *in* Chinese Chicken Salad with Citrus-Miso Dressing, *128*, 129

coconut milk, *in* Pork & Shrimp Stuffed Eggplant, *235*, 242–43
Coconut-Carrot Morning Glory Muffins, 146, *147*

cod, *in* Tuna & Bok Choy Packets (option), 87
Coleslaw (cooking basics), 122

collard greens
about, 202–4
Braised Greens & Cannellini Bean Panini, 208, *209*
Crushed Red Potatoes with Winter Greens, *206*, 207
substitutes for, 207

condiments. *See* dips, spreads, condiments; pickled vegetables

corn. *See also* hominy
about, 211–12
Chiles Rellenos with Chicken, 380
Grilled Corn (cooking basics), 212, *213*
Kohlrabi-Corn Fritters with Herbed Yogurt Sauce, 290, *291*
Roasted Corn Cheese Dip, 216, *217*
Spicy Tomatillo Quinoa, *454*, 455
Summer Corn & Scallop Pasta, 218
Sweet Corn Ice Cream, 219
Sweet Corn Salad, *214*, 215
Three Sisters Succotash, 64

cottage cheese, *in* Creamed Spinach Casserole, 413
Couscous with Rutabaga & Beef Stew, 481

crabmeat, *in* Seafood Gumbo, 332–33
cranberries, dried
    Kale Salad with Bacon-Blue Cheese
        Vinaigrette, 283
    Winter Greens Salad with Squash & Cranberry
        Vinaigrette, *432,* 433
cream cheese (Neufchâtel)
    Curried Onion Dip, 340
    fat content, 446
    Radish Canapés with Creamy Dill
        Spread, 402, *403*
    Roasted Corn Cheese Dip, 216, *217*
    Sweet Potato Pie with Cream Cheese Swirl, 448–
        49
creamed kale (cooking basics), 276
Creamed Spinach Casserole, 413
Creamy Dill Spread, Radish Canapés with, 402, *403*
Creamy Parsnips & Pears, 353
Creamy Rye & Butternut Squash Soup, 430, *431*
cremini mushrooms (baby bella), 305
    Artichoke & Parmesan Stuffed Mushrooms, 311
    Mushroom Pâté, 307
    Penne alla Primavera, 57
    Roasted Stuffed Pumpkin, 438–39
    Vegetarian Stuffed Cabbage, 131–32, *133*
Crispy Potatoes with Spicy Tomato Sauce, 388
Crostini, Pea, Pancetta & Tarragon, *360,* 361
crowder peas, *in* Sunny-Side Beans, 68, *69*
Crunchy Confetti Tuna Salad, *164,* 165
Crushed Red Potatoes with Winter
        Greens, *206, 207*
cucumbers
    about, *220–21,* 220–22
    Blender Gazpacho, 469
    Cucumber & Radish Tzatziki, 224, *225*
    Dill Pickles, 227
    Grilled Chicken Thighs with Cucumber-Mint
        Salad, 231
    Persian Cucumber Salad with Lentils &
        Sprouts, 228, *229*
    Quick Cucumber Kimchi, 230
    Rosemary-Infused Cucumber Lemonade, 223
    Summer Tomato, Onion & Cucumber
        Salad, *464,* 465
    Watercress & Citrus Tabbouleh, 490, *491*
    White Gazpacho, 226
curly endive, *191*
    Fava Bean Puree with Chicory (option), 200, *201*
    Winter Salad with Roasted Squash &
        Pomegranate Vinaigrette, 198, *199*
currants
    Chard with Green Olives, Currants & Goat
        Cheese, 182
    Kale Salad with Bacon-Blue Cheese
        Vinaigrette, 283
    Moroccan-Style Stuffed Peppers, 381
    Sicilian Pepper Salad, 374, *375*
    Vegetarian Stuffed Cabbage, 131–32, *133*
Curried Onion Dip, 340

D
Dandelion Salad with Goat Cheese & Tomato
        Dressing, 302, *303*
delicata squash, *429*
    Chili-Brown Sugar Delicata Squash with
        Pears, 434
    Winter Greens Salad with Squash & Cranberry
        Vinaigrette, *432,* 433
desserts
    Sweet Corn Ice Cream, 219
    Sweet Potato Pie with Cream Cheese Swirl, 448

dill
    Artichokes with Lemon & Dill, 16, *17*
    Borscht with Beef, 78, *79*
    Dill Pickles, 227
    Radish Canapés with Creamy Dill
        Spread, 402, *403*
    Roasted Beet Salad, *76, 77*
    Roasted Cauliflower Salad with Walnuts, *8,* 158
Dill-Havarti Mashed Cauliflower, *154,* 155
dips, spreads, condiments. *See also* pickled
        vegetables; salsas and sauces
    Beer-Battered Onion Rings with Roasted Pepper
        Aioli, 341
    Crispy Potatoes with Spicy Tomato Sauce, 388
    Cucumber & Radish Tzatziki, 224, *225*
    Curried Onion Dip, 340
    gochujang, about, 317
    gomasio, about, 129
    Grilled Eggplant & Baba Ghanoush, 237
    Mushroom Pâté, 307
    Radish Canapés with Creamy Dill
        Spread, 402, *403*
    Roasted Corn Cheese Dip, 216, *217*
    sesame-miso sauce, *for* Panko-Crusted Asparagus
        Spears, 32, *33*
    Shallot, Tarragon & Lemon Vinegar, 349
Double Celery Soup, 176, *177*
dressings. *See* salads and dressings
drinks
    Carrot-Orange Juice, 138, *139*
    DIY juicing, 138
    Green Smoothie, 278, *279*
    Rosemary-Infused Cucumber Lemonade, 223

E
Edamame Salad, Super-Green, 52, *53*
eggplant
    about, *232–33,* 233–34
    Eggplant Parmesan, 240–41
    Grilled Eggplant & Baba Ghanoush, 237
    Japanese eggplant, about, 239
    Marinated Eggplant with Green
        Chermoula, *238,* 239
    Pork & Shrimp Stuffed Eggplant, *235,* 242–43
    Sicilian Eggplant Caponata, 236
eggs
    Asparagus-Goat Cheese Soufflés, 36, *37*
    to bring to room temperature, 68
    Chard & Chorizo Frittata, *184,* 185
    to hard-boil, 367
    Mama's Potato Salad, 389
    Peas & Ham Pasta Salad, 367
    safety, 35
    Scrambled Eggs with Ramps & Bacon, 345
    Spring Salad with Peas & Frizzled
        Shallots, 346, *347*
    Spring Turnip Frittata, *478,* 479
    Stir-Fried Mustard Greens with Eggs &
        Garlic, 321
    Sunny-Side Beans, 68, *69*
    Watercress Salad with Sesame-Garlic
        Dressing, 487
endive. *See* Belgian endive; curly endive
English peas, *357*
    Pea, Pancetta & Tarragon Crostini, *360,* 361
    Peas & Ham Pasta Salad, 367
    Peas & Lettuce, 362, *363*
    Penne alla Primavera, 57
    to prep, 358
    Spring Salad with Peas & Frizzled
        Shallots, 346, *347*

escarole, *191*
    Artichokes, Cauliflower, Potato & Escarole
        Salad, 18–19
    Citrus Salad with Olives and Radicchio, 196
    Crushed Red Potatoes with Winter
        Greens, *206,* 207
    Winter Greens Salad with Squash & Cranberry
        Vinaigrette, *432,* 433

F
Fajitas, South Texas Steak, *378, 379*
Farro Salad, Bacon, Tomato &, 468
fava beans, *48*
    Fava Bean Puree with Chicory, 200, *201*
    Penne alla Primavera, 57
    to shell, 50, *51*
fennel
    about, 245–46
    Fennel Gratin, 248, *249*
    Grape & Fennel Salad, 247
    Mediterranean Sautéed Shrimp & Fennel, 251
    Roasted Fennel with Olive Tapenade, Feta &
        Mint, 250
    Roasted Vegetable Antipasto, *116,* 117
    Seared Salmon with Sugar Snap-Fennel
        Slaw, 368, *369*
    Shaved Zucchini-Fennel Salad, 418
feta cheese
    Citrus Salad with Olives and Radicchio, 196
    Green Salad with Peaches, Feta & Mint
        Vinaigrette, *296,* 297
    Indian-Style Mustard Greens & Kale with
        Toasted Naan, 322, *323*
    Mediterranean Sautéed Shrimp & Fennel, 251
    Persian Cucumber Salad with Lentils &
        Sprouts, 228, *229*
    Roasted Fennel with Olive Tapenade, Feta &
        Mint, 250
Fire-Roasted Salsa, 470
fish. *See also* anchovies; shellfish
    canned tuna, safe and sustainable choices, 165
    Crunchy Confetti Tuna Salad, *164,* 165
    fresh tuna, sustainable choices, 489
    Garlic Roasted Salmon & Brussels Sprouts, 119
    Orange, Watercress & Tuna Salad, 489
    Romaine Wedges with Sardines & Caramelized
        Onions, *298,* 299
    salmon, sustainable choices, 368
    sardines, nutritional benefits, 298
    Seared Salmon with Sugar Snap-Fennel
        Slaw, 368, *369*
    sole, sustainable choices, 259
    Sole with Garlic-Almond-Caper Sauce, 259
    Tuna & Bok Choy Packets, 87
Fish Sauce with Chiles (cooking basics), 372, *373*
flounder, *in* Sole with Garlic-Almond-Caper Sauce
        (option), 259
fontina cheese
    Mini Onion Gratins, 342, *343*
    Spring Turnip Frittata, *478,* 479
    Wild Mushroom & Polenta Casserole, 312, *313*
freezing guidelines, 499
fresh beans. *See* shell beans; snap beans
Fresh Green Salsa (cooking basics), 452
Fresh Tomatillo Salad, 456
frisée, *191*
    Artichokes, Cauliflower, Potato & Escarole
        Salad, 18–19
    Simple Green Salad with Citronette, 192, *193*
    Spring Salad with Peas & Frizzled
        Shallots, 346, *347*

Winter Greens Salad with Squash & Cranberry Vinaigrette, *432, 433*
Winter Salad with Roasted Squash & Pomegranate Vinaigrette, 198, *199*
Frittata, Chard & Chorizo, *184, 185*
Frittata, Spring Turnip, *478, 479*
Fritters, Kohlrabi-Corn, with Herbed Yogurt Sauce, 290, *291*
Fusilli with Yellow Squash & Grape Tomatoes, *422, 423*

G
Garden Tomato Sauce (and pizza sauce variation), 472, *473*
garlic
about, 252–54, *255*
Broccoli Rabe with Olives & Garlic, 104, *107*
Crispy Potatoes with Spicy Tomato Sauce, 388
Garlic Bread (cooking basics), 254
Garlic Chicken, 260, *261*
garlic paste, to make, 254
Garlic Roasted Salmon & Brussels Sprouts, 119
Garlic Scape Pesto, *256, 257*
Garlic Stir-Fried Snow Peas & Pea Greens, *364, 365*
Garlic-Dijon Vinaigrette (cooking basics), 294
Lemon-Garlic Yuca Mashers with Cilantro Pesto, 496, *497*
Massaged Kale Salad with Roasted Garlic Dressing, 282
Ribollita Soup, 284, *285*
Roasted Beet Salad, *76, 77*
Roasted Garlic & Asparagus Salad, 258
Roasted Garlic & Leek Bread Casserole, 344
scapes, about, *255, 257*
Sole with Garlic-Almond-Caper Sauce, 259
Stir-Fried Mustard Greens with Eggs & Garlic, 321
Gazpacho, Blender, 469
Gazpacho, White, 226
ginger, to peel, 98
gluten-free recipes. *See* special-interest index, page 513
goat cheese
aged goat cheese, about, 36
Asparagus-Goat Cheese Soufflés, 36, *37*
Chard with Green Olives, Currants & Goat Cheese, 182
Dandelion Salad with Goat Cheese & Tomato Dressing, 302, *303*
Goat Cheese Mashed Potatoes, 392
Green Salad with Peaches, Feta & Mint Vinaigrette (option), *296*, 297
Grilled Eggplant & Baba Ghanoush, 237
Pea, Pancetta & Tarragon Crostini, *360,* 361
Radish Canapés with Creamy Dill Spread, 402, *403*
gomasio, *for* Chinese Chicken Salad with Citrus-Miso Dressing, *128,* 129
Grape & Fennel Salad, 247
grapefruit
Citrus Salad with Olives and Radicchio, 196
Pink Grapefruit & Avocado Salad, 46, *47*
to segment, 490
Watercress & Citrus Tabbouleh, 490, *491*
grapes, *in* White Gazpacho, 226
Gratins, Mini Onion, 342, *343*
Green Bean & Tommy-Toe Salad, 62, *63*
green beans. *See* snap beans
Green Chermoula, Marinated Eggplant with, *238,* 239

Green Curry Soup, 412
Green Salad with Citronette, Simple, 192, *193*
Green Salad with Peaches, Feta & Mint Vinaigrette, *296,* 297
Green Smoothie, 278, *279*
Green Tahini Sauce, Potatoes with, *386, 387*
Green Tomatillos, Oven-Fried, 457
greens. *See* chicories; lettuces and salad greens; *specific types*
Greens, Braised, & Cannellini Bean Panini, 208, *209*
Greens, Winter, Crushed Red Potatoes with, *206,* 207
Greens Salad, Winter, with Squash & Cranberry Vinaigrette, *432, 433*
grill rack, to oil, 301
Grilled Broccoli Rabe (cooking basics), 102, *103*
Grilled Chicken Thighs with Cucumber-Mint Salad, 231
Grilled Corn (cooking basics), 212, *213*
Grilled Eggplant & Baba Ghanoush, 237
Grilled Okra & Hot Peppers, *328,* 329
Grilled Steak Salad, Chimichurri, *300,* 301
Grilled Tomatillo-Chipotle Salsa (cooking basics), 452, *453*
Gruyère cheese
Broccoli, Cauliflower & Romanesco Gratin, 159
Roasted Garlic & Leek Bread Casserole, 344
Guacamole, Jason Mraz's, 42, *43*

H
ham and prosciutto
Pasta with Braised Radicchio, 197
Peas & Ham Pasta Salad, 367
Roasted Jerusalem Artichokes with Crispy Prosciutto & Walnuts (cooking basics), 264, *265*
Seafood Gumbo, 332–33
Harissa-Rubbed Steak & Carrot Salad, 145
Havarti cheese, *in* Dill-Havarti Mashed Cauliflower, *154,* 155
hazelnuts, *in* Shaved Brussels Sprouts Salad with Lemon-Chile Vinaigrette & Toasted Hazelnuts, *114, 115*
heart-healthy recipes. *See* special-interest index, page 514
Heirloom Tomato Salad with Fried Capers, *4,* 463
Hoisin-Sesame Dressing (cooking basics), 294
Homemade Hot Sauce, 376
homemade pumpkin pie spice, 420
hominy
about, 424
Mexican Bison & Squash Stew, 424–25, *425*
Tomatillo & Pork Chili, 458, *459*
honeydew melon, *in* White Gazpacho, 226
Horseradish & Caviar, Twice-Baked Potatoes with, 394, *395*
hot peppers. *See also* chipotles
about, *370–71, 371–72*
capsaicin in, 371, 376
Chiles Rellenos with Chicken, 380
Fish Sauce with Chiles (cooking basics), 372, *373*
Grilled Okra & Hot Peppers, *328,* 329
health benefits, 322
Homemade Hot Sauce, 376
Paprika & Red Pepper Soup with Pistachios, 377
South Texas Steak Fajitas, *378,* 379
Spicy Jicama & Red Onion Shoestrings with Herbed Chipotle Aioli, 272, *273*
Hot Sauce, Homemade, 376

hubbard squash, *429*
Creamy Rye & Butternut Squash Soup (option), 430, *431*
Winter Squash & Chicken Tzimmes, 435

I
Ice Cream, Sweet Corn, 219
Indian-Style Mustard Greens & Kale with Toasted Naan, 322, *323*
Indian-Style Sautéed Okra, 330, *331*

J
Jack cheese, *in* Bacon Chard Quesadillas, 183
Jason Mraz's Guacamole, 42, *43*
Jerusalem artichokes
about, 263–64
Jerusalem Artichoke-Potato Soup with Crispy Croutons, 266, *267*
Roasted Jerusalem Artichokes with Crispy Prosciutto & Walnuts (cooking basics), 264, *265*
jicama
about, 269–70
Fresh Tomatillo Salad, 456
Jicama-Apple Slaw, 271
Spicy Jicama & Red Onion Shoestrings with Herbed Chipotle Aioli, 272, *273*
Juice, Carrot-Orange, 138, *139*

K
kabocha squash, *429*
Creamy Rye & Butternut Squash Soup (option), 430, *431*
Winter Greens Salad with Squash & Cranberry Vinaigrette, *432, 433*
kale
about, 275–76, *277*
Asparagus & Baby Kale Caesar Salad, *34,* 35
Bavarian Leek & Cabbage Soup, 130
Braised Greens & Cannellini Bean Panini, 208, *209*
creamed kale (cooking basics), 276
Green Smoothie, 278, *279*
Indian-Style Mustard Greens & Kale with Toasted Naan, 322, *323*
Kale Chips, 280, *281*
Kale Salad with Bacon-Blue Cheese Vinaigrette, 283
Massaged Kale Salad with Roasted Garlic Dressing, 282
massaging, 282
Ribollita Soup, 284, *285*
kielbasa, *in* Bavarian Leek & Cabbage Soup, 130
Kimchi, Korean Steak & Mushroom Tacos with, 317
Kimchi, Quick Cucumber, 230
kohlrabi
about, 286–88
Cider & Honey Kohlrabi Slaw with Radicchio, 289
Kohlrabi-Corn Fritters with Herbed Yogurt Sauce, 290, *291*
Korean Steak & Mushroom Tacos with Kimchi, 317

L
leeks, *337*
Bavarian Leek & Cabbage Soup, 130
Braised Greens & Cannellini Bean Panini, 208, *209*
Jerusalem Artichoke-Potato Soup with Crispy Croutons, 266, *267*

Potato-Leek Bisque, 348
Ribollita Soup, 284, *285*
Roasted Garlic & Leek Bread Casserole, 344
Roasted Radishes & Leeks with Thyme, *404,* 405
Scrambled Eggs with Ramps & Bacon, 345
Two-Toned Mashed Potatoes, 448, *449*
Lemon & Dill, Artichokes with, 16, *17*
Lemon Vinegar, Shallot, Tarragon &, 349
Lemonade, Rosemary-Infused Cucumber, 223
Lemon-Chile Vinaigrette & Toasted Hazelnuts,
   Shaved Brussels Sprouts Salad with, 114, *115*
Lemon-Garlic Yuca Mashers with Cilantro
   Pesto, 496, *497*
Lentils & Sprouts, Persian Cucumber Salad
   with, 228, *229*
lettuces and salad greens. *See also* arugula;
   chicories; watercress
   about, 292–94, *295*
   Chimichurri Grilled Steak Salad, *300,* 301
   Crunchy Confetti Tuna Salad, *164,* 165
   Dandelion Salad with Goat Cheese & Tomato
     Dressing, 302, *303*
   Green Salad with Peaches, Feta & Mint
     Vinaigrette, *296,* 297
   Peas & Lettuce, 362, *363*
   Pink Grapefruit & Avocado Salad, 46, *47*
   Romaine Wedges with Sardines & Caramelized
     Onions, 298, *299*
   Simple Green Salad with Citronette, 192, *193*
   Spring Salad with Peas & Frizzled
     Shallots, 346, *347*
lima beans, 48
   Lima Beans with Chorizo, 56
   Penne alla Primavera, 57
   Sunny-Side Beans, 68, *69*
   varieties, 56

M

mahi-mahi, *in* Tuna & Bok Choy Packets
   (option), 87
Mama's Potato Salad, 389
Manchego cheese
   Asparagus-Goat Cheese Soufflés (option), 36, *37*
   Citrus Salad with Olives and Radicchio, 196
   Lemon-Garlic Yuca Mashers with Cilantro
     Pesto, 496, *497*
   Shaved Zucchini-Fennel Salad, 418
Maple-Bacon Roasted Apples & Celeriac, *174,* 175
Maple-Lime Roasted Sweet Potatoes, *444,* 445
Marcona almonds, *in* Lemon-Garlic Yuca Mashers
   with Cilantro Pesto, 496, *497*
Marinated Eggplant with Green
   Chermoula, *238,* 239
Mashed Cauliflower, Dill-Havarti, *154,* 155
Mashed Potatoes, Goat Cheese, 392
Mashed Potatoes, Two-Toned, 448, *449*
Mashers, Lemon-Garlic Yuca, with Cilantro
   Pesto, 496, *497*
Massaged Kale Salad with Roasted Garlic
   Dressing, 282
meats. *See* bacon; beef; chicken; pork and pork
   products
Mediterranean Cauliflower Pizza, 156, *157*
Mediterranean Roasted Broccoli &
   Tomatoes, *94,* 95
Mediterranean Sautéed Shrimp & Fennel, 251
Mexican Bison & Squash Stew, 424–25, *425*
Mexican cheese blend, *in* Chiles Rellenos with
   Chicken, 380
Mexican Pickled Carrots, 140–41
Minestrone, Celery & Parmesan, 166, *167*

Mini Onion Gratins, 342, *343*
mint
   Chinese Chicken Salad with Citrus-Miso
     Dressing, *128,* 129
   Green Salad with Peaches, Feta & Mint
     Vinaigrette, *296,* 297
   Grilled Chicken Thighs with Cucumber-Mint
     Salad, 231
   Moroccan-Style Stuffed Peppers, 381
   Penne alla Primavera, 57
   Roasted Fennel with Olive Tapenade, Feta &
     Mint, 250
   Watercress & Citrus Tabbouleh, 490, *491*
miso
   about, 32
   Chinese Chicken Salad with Citrus-Miso
     Dressing, *128,* 129
   Miso-Butter Braised Turnips, 480
   Panko-Crusted Asparagus Spears, 32, *33*
   Pork & Turnip Miso Ramen, 482, *483*
Mofongo, Yuca-Scallion, 495
morels, *in* Penne alla Primavera, 57
Morning Glory Muffins, Coconut-Carrot, 146, *147*
Moroccan-Style Stuffed Peppers, 381
mozzarella cheese
   Eggplant Parmesan, 240–41
   Mediterranean Cauliflower Pizza, 156, *157*
   Spaghetti Squash Lasagna with
     Broccolini, 436, *437*
   Wild Mushroom Pizza with Arugula &
     Pecorino, 26, *27*
Muffins, Coconut-Carrot Morning Glory, 146, *147*
mushrooms
   about, *304–5,* 305–6
   Artichoke & Parmesan Stuffed Mushrooms, 311
   Asparagus & Mushroom Risotto, 316
   Borscht with Beef, 78, *79*
   Green Curry Soup, 412
   Korean Steak & Mushroom Tacos with
     Kimchi, 317
   Mushroom Pâté, 307
   Peas & Ham Pasta Salad, 367
   Penne alla Primavera, 57
   Pork & Turnip Miso Ramen, 482, *483*
   Quinoa Mushroom Soup, *314,* 315
   Roasted Stuffed Pumpkin, 438–39
   Sautéed Mushrooms with Caramelized
     Shallots, *309,* 310
   Spinach & Warm Mushroom Salad, 410, *411*
   Vegetarian Stuffed Cabbage, 131–32, *133*
   Wild Mushroom & Polenta Casserole, 312, *313*
   Wild Mushroom Pizza with Arugula &
     Pecorino, 26, *27*
mustard greens
   about, 319–20
   Crushed Red Potatoes with Winter
     Greens, *206,* 207
   Indian-Style Mustard Greens & Kale with
     Toasted Naan, 322, *323*
   Stir-Fried Mustard Greens with Eggs &
     Garlic, 321

N

Neufchâtel cheese. *See* cream cheese
Not-Your-Grandma's Green Bean Casserole, 66, *67*
nuts
   almonds
     Grape & Fennel Salad, 247
     Green Salad with Peaches, Feta & Mint
       Vinaigrette, *296,* 297
     Lemon-Garlic Yuca Mashers with Cilantro
       Pesto, 496, *497*

Sole with Garlic-Almond-Caper Sauce, 259
   White Gazpacho, 226
hazelnuts, *for* Shaved Brussels Sprouts Salad
   with Lemon-Chile Vinaigrette & Toasted
   Hazelnuts, 114, *115*
pecans, *in* Zucchini Bread Pancakes, 420
pine nuts
   Arugula Pesto (cooking basics), 22, *23*
   Broccoli & Tortellini Salad with Arugula
     Pesto, 92, *93*
   Sicilian Pepper Salad, 374, *375*
   Vegetarian Stuffed Cabbage, 131–32, *133*
pistachios
   Paprika & Red Pepper Soup with
     Pistachios, 377
   Pomegranate Molasses-Glazed Carrots with
     Pistachios, 137
   Winter Salad with Roasted Squash &
     Pomegranate Vinaigrette, 198, *199*
to toast, 92
walnuts
   Mushroom Pâté, 307
   Pear & Arugula Salad with Candied
     Walnuts, 24, *25*
   Roasted Beet Salad, *76,* 77
   Roasted Cauliflower Salad with
     Walnuts, 8, *158*
   Roasted Garlic & Asparagus Salad, 258
   Roasted Jerusalem Artichokes with Crispy
     Prosciutto & Walnuts (cooking
     basics), 264, *265*
   Winter Greens Salad with Squash &
     Cranberry Vinaigrette, *432,* 433
   Winter Salad with Roasted Squash &
     Pomegranate Vinaigrette, 198, *199*

O

oats, *in* Coconut-Carrot Morning Glory
   Muffins, 146, *147*
okra
   about, 324–26
   Black-Eyed Peas & Okra, 54, *55*
   Grilled Okra & Hot Peppers, *328,* 329
   Indian-Style Sautéed Okra, 330, *331*
   Seafood Gumbo, 332–33
   Stewed Okra (cooking basics), 326, *327*
olives
   Broccoli Rabe with Olives & Garlic, 104, *107*
   Chard with Green Olives, Currants & Goat
     Cheese, 182
   Citrus Salad with Olives and Radicchio, 196
   Mediterranean Cauliflower Pizza, 156, *157*
   Mediterranean Roasted Broccoli &
     Tomatoes, *94,* 95
   Potato-Leek Bisque, 348
   Roasted Fennel with Olive Tapenade, Feta &
     Mint, 250
   Sicilian Eggplant Caponata, 236
onions. *See also* chives; leeks; scallions; shallots
   about, 334–36, *337–39*
   availability of sweet onions, 341
   Basic Green Soup, 186, *187*
   Beer-Battered Onion Rings with Roasted Pepper
     Aioli, 341
   to caramelize (cooking basics), 336
   Curried Onion Dip, 340
   Mini Onion Gratins, 342, *343*
   Romaine Wedges with Sardines & Caramelized
     Onions, 298, *299*
   Sautéed Brussels Sprouts with Bacon
     Onions, 118
   Sicilian Eggplant Caponata, 236

Spicy Jicama & Red Onion Shoestrings with Herbed Chipotle Aioli, 272, *273*
Summer Tomato, Onion & Cucumber Salad, *464,* 465
oranges, orange juice, orange zest
Carrot-Orange Juice, 138, *139*
Chinese Chicken Salad with Citrus-Miso Dressing, *128,* 129
Citrus Salad with Olives and Radicchio, 196
Green Smoothie, 278, *279*
Jicama-Apple Slaw, 271
Mexican Bison & Squash Stew, 424–25, *425*
Orange, Watercress & Tuna Salad, 489
to segment oranges, 490
Simple Green Salad with Citronette, 192, *193*
Watercress & Citrus Tabbouleh, 490, *491*
Winter Squash & Chicken Tzimmes, 435
Orecchiette with Broccoli Rabe, 108, *109*
Oven-Fried Green Tomatillos, 457

P
Pancakes, Parsnip-Celery Root, with Pancetta, 354, *355*
Pancakes, Zucchini Bread, 420
pancetta
Parsnip-Celery Root Pancakes with Pancetta, 354, *355*
Pea, Pancetta & Tarragon Crostini, *360,* 361
paneer cheese, *in* Indian-Style Mustard Greens & Kale with Toasted Naan, 322, *323*
Panini, Braised Greens & Cannellini Bean, 208, *209*
Panko-Crusted Asparagus Spears, 32, *33*
Panzanella, *466, 467*
Paprika & Red Pepper Soup with Pistachios, 377
Parmesan and Parmigiano-Reggiano cheese
about, 316
Artichoke & Parmesan Stuffed Mushrooms, 311
Asparagus & Baby Kale Caesar Salad, *34,* 35
Asparagus & Mushroom Risotto, 316
Broccoli & Tortellini Salad with Arugula Pesto, 92, *93*
Celery & Parmesan Minestrone, 166, *167*
Chard & Chorizo Frittata, *184,* 185
Dandelion Salad with Goat Cheese & Tomato Dressing, 302, *303*
Eggplant Parmesan, 240–41
Fennel Gratin, 248, *249*
mustard greens salad (cooking basics), 320
Pasta with Braised Radicchio, 197
Penne alla Primavera, 57
Roasted Stuffed Pumpkin, 438–39
Sausage-&-Quinoa-Stuffed Zucchini, 421
Spaghetti Squash Lasagna with Broccolini, 436, *437*
Spicy Jicama & Red Onion Shoestrings with Herbed Chipotle Aioli, 272, *273*
Wild Mushroom & Polenta Casserole, 312, *313*
parsley
Asparagus & Mushroom Risotto, 316
Caprese Salad (cooking basics), 462
Chimichurri Grilled Steak Salad, *300,* 301
Citrus Salad with Olives and Radicchio, 196
Marinated Eggplant with Green Chermoula, *238,* 239
Panzanella, *466, 467*
Penne alla Primavera, 57
Roasted Fennel with Olive Tapenade, Feta & Mint, 250
parsnips
about, 351–52
Creamy Parsnips & Pears, 353

Parsnip-Celery Root Pancakes with Pancetta, 354, *355*
pasta
Dandelion Salad with Goat Cheese & Tomato Dressing, 302, *303*
Fusilli with Yellow Squash & Grape Tomatoes, *422,* 423
Orecchiette with Broccoli Rabe, 108, *109*
Pasta with Braised Radicchio, 197
Peas & Ham Pasta Salad, 367
Penne alla Primavera, 57
shapes and sauces, 108
Summer Corn & Scallop Pasta, 218
Pâté, Mushroom, 307
pattypan squash, *in* Mexican Bison & Squash Stew, 424–25, *425*
Pea Greens, Garlic Stir-Fried Snow Peas &, *364,* 365
Peaches, Feta & Mint Vinaigrette, Green Salad with, *296,* 297
pears
Chili-Brown Sugar Delicata Squash with Pears, 434
Creamy Parsnips & Pears, 353
Green Smoothie, 278, *279*
Pear & Arugula Salad with Candied Walnuts, *24,* 25
Pear & Celery Root Slaw, 172, *173*
to ripen and store, 353
peas
about, *356–57, 356–58*
Chinese Chicken Salad with Citrus-Miso Dressing, *128,* 129
Garlic Stir-Fried Snow Peas & Pea Greens, *364,* 365
Pea, Pancetta & Tarragon Crostini, *360,* 361
Peas & Ham Pasta Salad, 367
Peas & Lettuce, 362, *363*
Penne alla Primavera, 57
Seared Salmon with Sugar Snap-Fennel Slaw, 368, *369*
Snap Pea & Cherry Tomato Stir-Fry, 366
Spring Salad with Peas & Frizzled Shallots, 346, *347*
pecans, *in* Zucchini Bread Pancakes, 420
Pecorino cheese
Broccoli & Tortellini Salad with Arugula Pesto, 92, *93*
Wild Mushroom Pizza with Arugula & Pecorino, 26, *27*
Penne alla Primavera, 57
pepper Jack cheese, *in* Bacon Chard Quesadillas, 183
pepperoni, *in* Chard & Chorizo Frittata (option), *184,* 185
peppers, hot. *See* chipotles; hot peppers
peppers, sweet. *See* bell peppers
Persian Cucumber Salad with Lentils & Sprouts, 228, *229*
pesto
Arugula Pesto (cooking basics), 22, *23*
Broccoli & Tortellini Salad with Arugula Pesto, 92, *93*
Garlic Scape Pesto, 256, *257*
Lemon-Garlic Yuca Mashers with Cilantro Pesto, 496, *497*
pickled vegetables
canning equipment, 140
Dill Pickles, 227
Mexican Pickled Carrots, 140–41
Pickled Beets, 74, *75*
pickling spice blends, 227
Quick Cucumber Kimchi, 230

Simple Sauerkraut, 126–27
Pie, Sweet Potato, with Cream Cheese Swirl, 446–47
pine nuts
Arugula Pesto (cooking basics), 22, *23*
Broccoli & Tortellini Salad with Arugula Pesto, 92, *93*
Sicilian Pepper Salad, 374, *375*
Vegetarian Stuffed Cabbage, 131–32, *133*
Pineapple & Avocado Salad (cooking basics), 40
pink beans, *in* Super-Green Edamame Salad, 52, *53*
Pink Grapefruit & Avocado Salad, 46, *47*
pinto beans
Super-Green Edamame Salad, 52, *53*
Tomatillo & Pork Chili, 458, *459*
pistachios
Paprika & Red Pepper Soup with Pistachios, 377
Pomegranate Molasses-Glazed Carrots with Pistachios, 137
Winter Salad with Roasted Squash & Pomegranate Vinaigrette, 198, *199*
Pizza, Mediterranean Cauliflower, 156, *157*
Pizza, Wild Mushroom, with Arugula & Pecorino, 26, *27*
pizza sauce (Garden Tomato Sauce variation), 472
Polenta Casserole, Wild Mushroom &, 312, *313*
pomegranates and pomegranate molasses
Pink Grapefruit & Avocado Salad, 46, *47*
Pomegranate Molasses-Glazed Carrots with Pistachios, 137
to seed, 198
Winter Salad with Roasted Squash & Pomegranate Vinaigrette, 198, *199*
pork and pork products. *See also* bacon
Bavarian Leek & Cabbage Soup, 130
Chard & Chorizo Frittata, *184,* 185
ground pork, about, 458
Lima Beans with Chorizo, 56
Parsnip-Celery Root Pancakes with Pancetta, 354, *355*
Pasta with Braised Radicchio, 197
Pea, Pancetta & Tarragon Crostini, *360,* 361
Peas & Ham Pasta Salad, 367
Pork & Shrimp Stuffed Eggplant, *235, 242–43*
Pork & Turnip Miso Ramen, 482, *483*
Roasted Jerusalem Artichokes with Crispy Prosciutto & Walnuts (cooking basics), 264, *265*
Seafood Gumbo, 332–33
Spanish chorizo, about, 185
Tomatillo & Pork Chili, 458, *459*
potatoes
about, 382–83, *385*
Artichokes, Cauliflower, Potato & Escarole Salad, 18–19
Bavarian Leek & Cabbage Soup, 130
Broccoli-Cheddar-Chicken Chowder, 96, *97*
Chard & Chorizo Frittata, *184,* 185
Cheesy Potato Casserole, 393
Crispy Potatoes with Spicy Tomato Sauce, 388
Crushed Red Potatoes with Winter Greens, *206,* 207
Double Celery Soup, 176, *177*
Fava Bean Puree with Chicory, 200, *201*
Goat Cheese Mashed Potatoes, 392
Jerusalem Artichoke-Potato Soup with Crispy Croutons, 266, *267*
Kale Salad with Bacon-Blue Cheese Vinaigrette, 283
Lemon-Garlic Yuca Mashers with Cilantro Pesto, 496, *497*
Mama's Potato Salad, 389
Potatoes with Green Tahini Sauce, 386, *387*

Potato-Leek Bisque, 348
Ribollita Soup, 284, *285*
for salad, 389
Twice-Baked Potatoes with Horseradish &
Caviar, 394, *395*
Two-Toned Mashed Potatoes, 448, *449*
Warm Potato Salad with Bacon-Mustard
Dressing, *390,* 391
Primavera, Penne alla, 57
prosciutto
Pasta with Braised Radicchio, 197
Roasted Jerusalem Artichokes with
Crispy Prosciutto & Walnuts (cooking
basics), 264, *265*
prunes, *in* Winter Squash & Chicken
Tzimmes, 435
Pumpkin, Roasted Stuffed, 438–39
pumpkin pie spice, homemade, 420

Q
Quesadillas, Bacon Chard, 183
Quick Cucumber Kimchi, 230
quinoa
about, 421
Quinoa Mushroom Soup, *314,* 315
Sausage-&-Quinoa-Stuffed Zucchini, 421
Spicy Tomatillo Quinoa, *454,* 455

R
raclette cheese, *in* Roasted Garlic & Leek Bread
Casserole, 344
radicchio, *191*
Artichokes, Cauliflower, Potato & Escarole
Salad, 18–19
Cider & Honey Kohlrabi Slaw with
Radicchio, 289
Citrus Salad with Olives and Radicchio, 196
Pasta with Braised Radicchio, 197
Simple Green Salad with Citronette, 192, *193*
Spinach & Warm Mushroom Salad, 410, *411*
Watercress Salad with Sesame-Garlic
Dressing, 487
Winter Salad with Roasted Squash &
Pomegranate Vinaigrette, 198, *199*
radishes
about, 397–98
Crunchy Confetti Tuna Salad, *164,* 165
Cucumber & Radish Tzatziki, 224, *225*
Persian Cucumber Salad with Lentils &
Sprouts, 228, *229*
Radish Canapés with Creamy Dill
Spread, *402,* 403
Roasted Radishes & Leeks with Thyme, *404,* 405
Spring Radish Salad, 399, *401*
Watercress Salad with Sesame-Garlic
Dressing, 487
raisins, *in* Coconut-Carrot Morning Glory
Muffins, 146, *147*
Ramen, Pork & Turnip Miso, 482, *483*
Ramps & Bacon, Scrambled Eggs with, 345
recipes, how to follow, 500–501
Ribollita Soup, 284, *285*
rice
Asparagus & Mushroom Risotto, 316
Moroccan-Style Stuffed Peppers, 381
Pork & Shrimp Stuffed Eggplant, *235,* 242–43
Vegetarian Stuffed Cabbage, 131–32, *133*
Rice Wine-Oyster Sauce, Watercress with, 488
Risotto, Asparagus & Mushroom, 316
Roasted Baby Bok Choy, 84, *85*
Roasted Beet Salad, *76,* 77

Roasted Cabbage with Chive-Mustard
Vinaigrette, 124, *125*
Roasted Cauliflower Salad with Walnuts, *8,* 158
Roasted Cherry Tomato & Sage Sauce, 471
Roasted Corn Cheese Dip, 216, *217*
Roasted Fennel with Olive Tapenade, Feta &
Mint, 250
Roasted Garlic & Asparagus Salad, 258
Roasted Garlic & Leek Bread Casserole, 344
Roasted Pepper Aioli, Beer-Battered Onion Rings
with, 341
Roasted Radishes & Leeks with Thyme, *404,* 405
Roasted Rainbow Carrots with Sage Brown
Butter, *143,* 144
Roasted Stuffed Pumpkin, 438–39
Roasted Sweet Potato Wedges (cooking
basics), *442,* 443
Roasted Sweet Potatoes, Maple-Lime, *444,* 445
Roasted Vegetable Antipasto, *116,* 117
romaine lettuce, *295*
Chimichurri Grilled Steak Salad, *300,* 301
Romaine Wedges with Sardines & Caramelized
Onions, 298, *299*
Simple Green Salad with Citronette, 192, *193*
Romanesco Gratin, Broccoli, Cauliflower &, 159
Rosemary-Infused Cucumber Lemonade, 223
rutabagas. *See* turnips and rutabagas
Rye & Butternut Squash Soup, Creamy, 430, *431*

S
Sage Brown Butter, Roasted Rainbow Carrots
with, *143,* 144
Sage Sauce, Roasted Cherry Tomato &, 471
salad greens. *See* arugula; chicories; lettuces and
salad greens; watercress
salads and dressings
Artichokes, Cauliflower, Potato & Escarole
Salad, 18–19
arugula salad (cooking basics), 22
Asparagus & Baby Kale Caesar Salad, *34,* 35
Bacon, Tomato & Farro Salad, 468
Broccoli & Tortellini Salad with Arugula
Pesto, 92, *93*
Buttermilk Ranch Dressing (cooking basics), 294
Caprese Salad (cooking basics), 462
chicory salad (cooking basics), 190
Chimichurri Grilled Steak Salad, *300,* 301
Chinese Chicken Salad with Citrus-Miso
Dressing, *128,* 129
Cider & Honey Kohlrabi Slaw with
Radicchio, 289
Citrus Salad with Olives and Radicchio, 196
Coleslaw (cooking basics), 122
creamy avocado dressing (cooking basics), 40
Crunchy Confetti Tuna Salad, *164,* 165
Dandelion Salad with Goat Cheese & Tomato
Dressing, 302, *303*
Fresh Tomatillo Salad, 456
Garlic-Dijon Vinaigrette (cooking basics), 294
Grape & Fennel Salad, 247
Green Bean & Tommy-Toe Salad, 62, *63*
Green Salad with Peaches, Feta & Mint
Vinaigrette, *296,* 297
Grilled Chicken Thighs with Cucumber-Mint
Salad, 231
Harissa-Rubbed Steak & Carrot Salad, 145
Heirloom Tomato Salad with Fried
Capers, *4,* 463
Hoisin-Sesame Dressing (cooking basics), 294
Jicama-Apple Slaw, 271

Kale Salad with Bacon-Blue Cheese
Vinaigrette, 283
Mama's Potato Salad, 389
Massaged Kale Salad with Roasted Garlic
Dressing, 282
mustard greens salad (cooking basics), 320
Panzanella, *466, 467*
Pear & Arugula Salad with Candied
Walnuts, *24,* 25
Pear & Celery Root Slaw, 172, *173*
Peas & Ham Pasta Salad, 367
Persian Cucumber Salad with Lentils &
Sprouts, 228, *229*
Pineapple & Avocado Salad (cooking basics), 40
Pink Grapefruit & Avocado Salad, *46, 47*
Roasted Beet Salad, *76, 77*
Roasted Garlic & Asparagus Salad, 258
Romaine Wedges with Sardines & Caramelized
Onions, 298, *299*
Seared Salmon with Sugar Snap-Fennel
Slaw, 368, *369*
Shaved Brussels Sprouts Salad with Lemon-Chile
Vinaigrette & Toasted Hazelnuts, 114, *115*
Shaved Zucchini-Fennel Salad, 418
shredded sweet potatoes and cabbage (cooking
basics), 442
Sicilian Pepper Salad, 374, *375*
Simple Green Salad with Citronette, 192, *193*
simple watercress salad (cooking basics), 486
Slivered Celery Salad with Blue Cheese
Dressing, 163
Spinach & Warm Mushroom Salad, 410, *411*
Spring Radish Salad, 399, *401*
Spring Salad with Peas & Frizzled
Shallots, 346, *347*
Summer Tomato, Onion & Cucumber
Salad, *464,* 465
Super-Green Edamame Salad, 52, *53*
Sweet Corn Salad, *214,* 215
Warm Potato Salad with Bacon-Mustard
Dressing, *390,* 391
Watercress & Citrus Tabbouleh, 490, *491*
Winter Greens Salad with Squash & Cranberry
Vinaigrette, *432, 433*
Winter Salad with Roasted Squash &
Pomegranate Vinaigrette, 198, *199*
salmon
Garlic Roasted Salmon & Brussels Sprouts, 119
Seared Salmon with Sugar Snap-Fennel
Slaw, 368, *369*
sustainable choices, 368
Tuna & Bok Choy Packets (option), 87
salsas and sauces. *See also* dips, spreads, condiments
Arugula Pesto (cooking basics), 22, *23*
Fire-Roasted Salsa, 470
Fresh Green Salsa (cooking basics), 452
Garden Tomato Sauce (and pizza sauce
variation), *472, 473*
Garlic Scape Pesto, *256,* 257
Grilled Tomatillo-Chipotle Salsa (cooking
basics), *452, 453*
Homemade Hot Sauce, 376
Roasted Cherry Tomato & Sage Sauce, 471
Sardines & Caramelized Onions, Romaine Wedges
with, 298, *299*
Sauerkraut, Simple, 126–27
sausages
Bavarian Leek & Cabbage Soup, 130
Chard & Chorizo Frittata, *184,* 185
Lima Beans with Chorizo, 56
Sausage-&-Quinoa-Stuffed Zucchini, 421
Spanish chorizo, about, 185

Sautéed Brussels Sprouts with Bacon & Onions, 118
Sautéed Mushrooms with Caramelized
    Shallots, *309, 310*
scallions, *337*
    Chard & Chorizo Frittata, *184, 185*
    Chiles Rellenos with Chicken, 380
    Grape & Fennel Salad, 247
    Green Curry Soup, 412
    Penne alla Primavera, 57
    Pork & Shrimp Stuffed Eggplant, *235, 242–43*
    Pork & Turnip Miso Ramen, *482, 483*
    Seafood Gumbo, 332–33
    shredded sweet potatoes and cabbage (cooking
        basics), 442
    Slivered Celery Salad with Blue Cheese
        Dressing, 163
    Velvet Chicken with Baby Bok Choy, 86
    Watercress & Citrus Tabbouleh, *490, 491*
    Watercress Salad with Sesame-Garlic
        Dressing, 487
    Yuca-Scallion Mofongo, 495
Scallop Pasta, Summer Corn &, 218
Scrambled Eggs with Ramps & Bacon, 345
seafood. *See* anchovies; fish; shellfish
Seafood Gumbo, 332–33
Seared Salmon with Sugar Snap-Fennel
    Slaw, *368, 369*
sesame seeds
    Chinese Chicken Salad with Citrus-Miso
        Dressing, *128, 129*
    gomasio, about, 128
    Hoisin-Sesame Dressing (cooking basics), 294
    Panko-Crusted Asparagus Spears, *32, 33*
    Roasted Sweet Potato Wedges (cooking
        basics), *442, 443*
    Snap Pea & Cherry Tomato Stir-Fry, 366
    Spicy Stir-Fried String Beans, 65
    to toast, 487
    Watercress Salad with Sesame-Garlic
        Dressing, 487
shallots, *339*
    Braised Greens & Cannellini Bean
        Panini, *208, 209*
    Double Celery Soup, *176, 177*
    Sautéed Mushrooms with Caramelized
        Shallots, *309, 310*
    Shallot, Tarragon & Lemon Vinegar, 349
    Spring Salad with Peas & Frizzled
        Shallots, *346, 347*
    Winter Squash & Chicken Tzimmes, 435
Shaved Brussels Sprouts Salad with Lemon-Chile
    Vinaigrette & Toasted Hazelnuts, *114, 115*
shell beans
    about, *48–49, 49–50*
    Black-Eyed Peas & Okra, *54, 55*
    lima bean varieties, 56
    Lima Beans with Chorizo, 56
    Penne alla Primavera, 57
    Sunny-Side Beans, *68, 69*
    Super-Green Edamame Salad, *52, 53*
shellfish
    Mediterranean Sautéed Shrimp & Fennel, 251
    Pork & Shrimp Stuffed Eggplant, *235, 242–43*
    scallops, to buy, 218
    Seafood Gumbo, 332–33
    shrimp sizes and sustainable choices, 249
    Summer Corn & Scallop Pasta, 218
shiitake mushrooms, *304*
    Asparagus & Mushroom Risotto, 316
    Green Curry Soup, 412
    Korean Steak & Mushroom Tacos with
        Kimchi, 317

shredded sweet potatoes and cabbage (cooking
    basics), 442
shrimp
    Mediterranean Sautéed Shrimp & Fennel, 251
    Pork & Shrimp Stuffed Eggplant, *235, 242–43*
    Seafood Gumbo, 332–33
    sizes and sustainable choices, 249
Sicilian Eggplant Caponata, 236
Sicilian Pepper Salad, *374, 375*
Simple Green Salad with Citronette, *192, 193*
Simple Sauerkraut, 126–27
simple watercress salad (cooking basics), 486
slaw
    Cider & Honey Kohlrabi Slaw with
        Radicchio, 289
    Coleslaw (cooking basics), 122
    Jicama-Apple Slaw, 271
    Pear & Celery Root Slaw, *172, 173*
    Seared Salmon with Sugar Snap-Fennel
        Slaw, *368, 369*
    shredded sweet potatoes and cabbage (cooking
        basics), 442
Slivered Celery Salad with Blue Cheese
    Dressing, 163
Slow-Cooker Chicken Stock, 130
Smoothie, Green, *278, 279*
snap beans
    about, 58–60
    Green Bean & Tommy-Toe Salad, *62, 63*
    Green Curry Soup, 412
    Not-Your-Grandma's Green Bean
        Casserole, *66, 67*
    Spicy Stir-Fried String Beans, 65
    String Beans & Summer Squash, 419
    Sunny-Side Beans, *68, 69*
    Three Sisters Succotash, 64
Snap Pea & Cherry Tomato Stir-Fry, 366
snap peas. *See* sugar snap peas
Snow Peas & Pea Greens, Garlic Stir-Fried, *364, 365*
Sole with Garlic-Almond-Caper Sauce, 259
Soufflés, Asparagus-Goat Cheese, *36, 37*
soups and stews
    Basic Green Soup, 186, *187*
    Bavarian Leek & Cabbage Soup, 130
    Blender Gazpacho, 469
    Borscht with Beef, *78, 79*
    Celery & Parmesan Minestrone, *166, 167*
    Couscous with Rutabaga & Beef Stew, 481
    Creamy Rye & Butternut Squash Soup, *430, 431*
    Double Celery Soup, *176, 177*
    Green Curry Soup, 412
    Jerusalem Artichoke-Potato Soup with Crispy
        Croutons, *266, 267*
    Mexican Bison & Squash Stew, *424–25, 425*
    "no-chicken" broth, about, 226
    Paprika & Red Pepper Soup with Pistachios, 377
    Potato-Leek Bisque, 348
    Quinoa Mushroom Soup, *314,* 315
    Ribollita Soup, *284, 285*
    Seafood Gumbo, 332–33
    Tomatillo & Pork Chili, *458, 459*
    White Gazpacho, 226
sour cream
    Bavarian Leek & Cabbage Soup, 130
    Borscht with Beef, *78, 79*
    Curried Onion Dip, 340
    Summer Corn & Scallop Pasta, 218
    Twice-Baked Potatoes with Horseradish &
        Caviar, *394, 395*
South Texas Steak Fajitas, *378, 379*
Spaghetti Squash Lasagna with Broccolini, *436, 437*

Spicy Jicama & Red Onion Shoestrings with Herbed
    Chipotle Aioli, *272, 273*
Spicy Stir-Fried String Beans, 65
Spicy Tomatillo Quinoa, *454, 455*
Spicy Tomato Sauce, Crispy Potatoes with, 388
spinach
    about, 407–8, *409*
    Basic Green Soup, 186, *187*
    Creamed Spinach Casserole, 413
    Dandelion Salad with Goat Cheese & Tomato
        Dressing, *302, 303*
    Green Curry Soup, 412
    Miso-Butter Braised Turnips, 480
    Pork & Turnip Miso Ramen, *482, 483*
    Simple Green Salad with Citronette, *192, 193*
    Spinach & Warm Mushroom Salad, *410, 411*
    Super-Green Edamame Salad, *52, 53*
spring onions, *in* Watercress Salad with Sesame-
    Garlic Dressing, 487
Spring Radish Salad, *399, 401*
Spring Salad with Peas & Frizzled Shallots, *346, 347*
Spring Turnip Frittata, *478, 479*
Sprouts, Persian Cucumber Salad with Lentils
    &, *228, 229*
squash. *See* summer squash; winter squash
Stewed Okra (cooking basics), *326, 327*
Stir-Fried Chinese Broccoli, *98, 99*
Stir-Fried Mustard Greens with Eggs & Garlic, 321
string beans. *See* snap beans
String Beans & Summer Squash, 419
stuffed vegetables
    Artichoke & Parmesan Stuffed Mushrooms, 311
    Chiles Rellenos with Chicken, 380
    Moroccan-Style Stuffed Peppers, 381
    Pork & Shrimp Stuffed Eggplant, *235, 242–43*
    Roasted Stuffed Pumpkin, 438–39
    Sausage-&-Quinoa-Stuffed Zucchini, 421
    Spaghetti Squash Lasagna with
        Broccolini, *436, 437*
    Twice-Baked Potatoes with Horseradish &
        Caviar, *394, 395*
    Vegetarian Stuffed Cabbage, *131–32, 133*
Succotash, Three Sisters, 64
sugar snap peas, *356*
    Chinese Chicken Salad with Citrus-Miso
        Dressing, *128, 129*
    Garlic Stir-Fried Snow Peas & Pea Greens
        (option), *364,* 365
    Seared Salmon with Sugar Snap-Fennel
        Slaw, *368, 369*
    Snap Pea & Cherry Tomato Stir-Fry, 366
    Summer Corn & Scallop Pasta, 218
summer squash
    about, 414–16, *417*
    Fusilli with Yellow Squash & Grape
        Tomatoes, *422,* 423
    Mexican Bison & Squash Stew, *424–25, 425*
    Ribollita Soup, *284, 285*
    Sausage-&-Quinoa-Stuffed Zucchini, 421
    Shaved Zucchini-Fennel Salad, 418
    String Beans & Summer Squash, 419
    Three Sisters Succotash, 64
    Zucchini Bread Pancakes, 420
Summer Tomato, Onion & Cucumber
    Salad, *464, 465*
sun-dried tomatoes, *in* Mediterranean Cauliflower
    Pizza, *156, 157*
sunflower seeds, *in* Cider & Honey Kohlrabi Slaw
    with Radicchio, 289
Sunny-Side Beans, *68, 69*
Super-Green Edamame Salad, *52, 53*

Sweet Corn Ice Cream, 219
Sweet Corn Salad, *214, 215*
sweet peppers. *See* bell peppers
sweet potatoes
about, 440–42
Maple-Lime Roasted Sweet Potatoes, *444,* 445
Roasted Sweet Potato Wedges (cooking basics), 442, *443*
shredded sweet potatoes and cabbage (cooking basics), 442
Sweet Potato Pie with Cream Cheese Swirl, 448–49
Two-Toned Mashed Potatoes, 448, *449*

T
Tabbouleh, Watercress & Citrus, 490, *491*
Tacos, Korean Steak & Mushroom, with Kimchi, 317
tahini
about, 158, 386
Grilled Eggplant & Baba Ghanoush, 237
Potatoes with Green Tahini Sauce, 386, *387*
Roasted Cauliflower Salad with Walnuts, *8,* 158
Taleggio cheese, *in* Wild Mushroom & Polenta Casserole, 312, *313*
Tapenade, Olive, Feta & Mint, Roasted Fennel with, 248
Three Sisters Succotash, 64
tomatillos
about, 451–52
Fresh Green Salsa (cooking basics), 452
Fresh Tomatillo Salad, 456
Grilled Tomatillo-Chipotle Salsa (cooking basics), 452, *453*
Oven-Fried Green Tomatillos, 457
Spicy Tomatillo Quinoa, *454,* 455
Tomatillo & Pork Chili, 458, *459*
tomatoes, canned
Celery & Parmesan Minestrone, 166, *167*
Crispy Potatoes with Spicy Tomato Sauce, 388
Eggplant Parmesan, 240–41
Fire-Roasted Salsa (canned-tomato variation), 470
Mediterranean Sautéed Shrimp & Fennel, 251
Ribollita Soup, 284, *285*
Seafood Gumbo, 332–33
sodium in, 131
Tomatillo & Pork Chili, 458, *459*
Vegetarian Stuffed Cabbage, 131–32, *133*
tomatoes, dried
Mediterranean Cauliflower Pizza, 156, *157*
to oven-dry romas (cooking basics), 462
tomatoes, fresh
about, *460–61,* 461–62
Bacon, Tomato & Farro Salad, 468
Blender Gazpacho, 469
Caprese Salad (cooking basics), 462
Carrot-Orange Juice, 138, *139*
Dandelion Salad with Goat Cheese & Tomato Dressing, 302, *303*
Fire-Roasted Salsa, 470
Fresh Tomatillo Salad, 456
Fusilli with Yellow Squash & Grape Tomatoes, *422,* 423
Garden Tomato Sauce (and pizza sauce variation), 472, *473*
Green Bean & Tommy-Toe Salad, 62, *63*
Heirloom Tomato Salad with Fried Capers, *4,* 463
Homemade Hot Sauce, 376
Mediterranean Roasted Broccoli & Tomatoes, *94,* 95
Mexican Bison & Squash Stew, 424–25, *425*

Orecchiette with Broccoli Rabe, 108, *109*
oven-dried romas (cooking basics), 462
Panzanella, 466, *467*
Roasted Cherry Tomato & Sage Sauce, 471
Romaine Wedges with Sardines & Caramelized Onions, 298, *299*
Sausage-&-Quinoa-Stuffed Zucchini, 421
Sicilian Eggplant Caponata, 236
Snap Pea & Cherry Tomato Stir-Fry, 366
Summer Tomato, Onion & Cucumber Salad, *464,* 465
Sweet Corn Salad, *214,* 215
Tortellini Salad, Broccoli &, with Arugula Pesto, 92, *93*
tuna, canned, *in* Crunchy Confetti Tuna Salad, *164,* 165
tuna, fresh
Orange, Watercress & Tuna Salad, 489
sustainable choices, 489
Tuna & Bok Choy Packets, 87
turkey sausage, *in* Sausage-&-Quinoa-Stuffed Zucchini, 421
turnips and rutabagas
about, 475–76
Couscous with Rutabaga & Beef Stew, 481
Miso-Butter Braised Turnips, 480
Pork & Turnip Miso Ramen, 482, *483*
to shred, 479
Spring Turnip Frittata, *478,* 479
Twice-Baked Potatoes with Horseradish & Caviar, 394, *395*
Two-Toned Mashed Potatoes, 448, *449*
Tzatziki, Cucumber & Radish, 224, *225*
Tzimmes, Winter Squash & Chicken, 435

V
vegan recipes. *See* special-interest index, page 514
vegetarian recipes. *See* index, special-interest page 514
Vegetarian Stuffed Cabbage, 131–32, *133*
Velvet Chicken with Baby Bok Choy, 86
Vietnamese-Flavored Broccoli Rabe, 105
Vinegar, Shallot, Tarragon & Lemon, 349

W
walnuts
Mushroom Pâté, 307
Pear & Arugula Salad with Candied Walnuts, *24,* 25
Roasted Beet Salad, *76,* 77
Roasted Cauliflower Salad with Walnuts, *8,* 158
Roasted Garlic & Asparagus Salad, 258
Roasted Jerusalem Artichokes with Crispy Prosciutto & Walnuts (cooking basics), 264, *265*
Winter Greens Salad with Squash & Cranberry Vinaigrette, *432,* 433
Winter Salad with Roasted Squash & Pomegranate Vinaigrette, 198, *199*
Warm Potato Salad with Bacon-Mustard Dressing, *390,* 391
watercress
about, 485–86
Green Salad with Peaches, Feta & Mint Vinaigrette, *296,* 297
Orange, Watercress & Tuna Salad, 489
Simple Green Salad with Citronette, 192, *193*
simple watercress salad (cooking basics), 486
Watercress & Citrus Tabbouleh, 490, *491*
Watercress Salad with Sesame-Garlic Dressing, 487

Watercress with Rice Wine-Oyster Sauce, 488
White Gazpacho, 226
Wild Mushroom & Polenta Casserole, 312, *313*
Wild Mushroom Pizza with Arugula & Pecorino, 26, *27*
Winter Greens, Crushed Red Potatoes with, *206,* 207
Winter Greens Salad with Squash & Cranberry Vinaigrette, *432,* 433
Winter Salad with Roasted Squash & Pomegranate Vinaigrette, 198, *199*
winter squash
about, 427–28, *429*
Chili-Brown Sugar Delicata Squash with Pears, 434
Creamy Rye & Butternut Squash Soup, 430, *431*
Roasted Stuffed Pumpkin, 438–39
Spaghetti Squash Lasagna with Broccolini, 436, *437*
Winter Greens Salad with Squash & Cranberry Vinaigrette, *432,* 433
Winter Salad with Roasted Squash & Pomegranate Vinaigrette, 198, *199*
Winter Squash & Chicken Tzimmes, 435

Y
Yellow Squash & Grape Tomatoes, Fusilli with, *422,* 423
yellow wax beans. *See* snap beans
yogurt
Cheesy Potato Casserole, 393
Chiles Rellenos with Chicken, 380
creamy avocado dressing (cooking basics), 40
Cucumber & Radish Tzatziki, 224, *225*
Kohlrabi-Corn Fritters with Herbed Yogurt Sauce, 290, *291*
Romaine Wedges with Sardines & Caramelized Onions, 298, *299*
Slivered Celery Salad with Blue Cheese Dressing, 163
Sweet Potato Pie with Cream Cheese Swirl, 448–49
yuca
about, 493–94
Lemon-Garlic Yuca Mashers with Cilantro Pesto, 496, *497*
Yuca-Scallion Mofongo, 495

Z
zucchini, *417*
Ribollita Soup, 284, *285*
Sausage-&-Quinoa-Stuffed Zucchini, 421
Shaved Zucchini-Fennel Salad, 418
Three Sisters Succotash, 64
Zucchini Bread Pancakes, 420

SPECIAL-INTEREST INDEXES

GLUTEN-FREE

Does not include wheat, barely and rye or any ingredient that contains or is derived from one of these ingredients (e.g., triticale, spelt, kamut, farina, wheat bran, durum flour, enriched flour and semolina). Recipes including oats or ingredients derived from oats (e.g., oat bran) are also excluded, as contamination during growing or processing of oats is common. Check the labels of processed foods to make sure they don't contain hidden sources of gluten.

Artichokes with Lemon & Dill, 16, *17*
Arugula Pesto (cooking basics), 22, *23*
Asparagus & Baby Kale Caesar Salad, *34,* 35
Asparagus & Mushroom Risotto, 316
Basic Green Soup, 186, *187*
Black-Eyed Peas & Okra, 54, *55*
Borscht with Beef, 78, *79*
Broccoli Rabe with Olives & Garlic, 104, *107*
Carrot-Orange Juice, 138, *139*
Cauliflower Steaks with Chimichurri, 152, *153*
Chard & Chorizo Frittata, *184,* 185
Chard with Green Olives, Currants & Goat Cheese, 182
Chili-Brown Sugar Delicata Squash with Pears, 434
Chimichurri Grilled Steak Salad, *300,* 301
Chinese Chicken Salad with Citrus-Miso Dressing, *128,* 129
Chipotle-Cheddar Broiled Avocado Halves, *44,* 45
Cider & Honey Kohlrabi Slaw with Radicchio, 289
Citrus Salad with Olives and Radicchio, 196
creamy avocado dressing (cooking basics), 40
Creamy Parsnips & Pears, 353
Crispy Potatoes with Spicy Tomato Sauce, 388
Crunchy Confetti Tuna Salad, *166,* 167
Crushed Red Potatoes with Winter Greens, *206,* 207
Cucumber & Radish Tzatziki, 224, *225*
Curried Onion Dip, 340
Dill-Havarti Mashed Cauliflower, *154,* 155
Dill Pickles, 227
Double Celery Soup, 176, *177*
Fava Bean Puree with Chicory, 200, *201*
Fire-Roasted Salsa, 470
Fish Sauce with Chiles (cooking basics), 372, *373*
Fresh Tomatillo Salad, 456
Garden Tomato Sauce, 472, *473*
Garlic Roasted Salmon & Brussels Sprouts, 119
Garlic Scape Pesto, *256,* 257
Garlic Stir-Fried Snow Peas & Pea Greens, *364,* 365
Goat Cheese Mashed Potatoes
Grape & Fennel Salad, 247
Green Bean & Tommy-Toe Salad, 62, *63*
Green Curry Soup, 412
Green Salad with Peaches, Feta & Mint Vinaigrette, *296,* 297
Green Smoothie, 278, *279*
Grilled Broccoli Rabe (cooking basics), 102, *103*
Grilled Chicken Thighs with Cucumber-Mint Salad, 231

Grilled Corn (cooking basics), 212, *213*
Grilled Eggplant & Baba Ghanoush, 237
Grilled Okra & Hot Peppers, *328, 329*
Grilled Tomatillo-Chipotle Salsa (cooking basics), 452, *453*
Harissa-Rubbed Steak & Carrot Salad, 145
Heirloom Tomato Salad with Fried Capers, *4, 463*
Homemade Hot Sauce, 376
Indian-Style Sautéed Okra, 330, *331*
Jason Mraz's Guacamole, 42, *43*
Jicama-Apple Slaw, 271
Kale Chips, *280,* 281
Kale Salad with Bacon-Blue Cheese Vinaigrette, 283
Korean Steak & Mushroom Tacos with Kimchi, 317
Lemon-Garlic Yuca Mashers with Cilantro Pesto, 496, *497*
Lima Beans with Chorizo, 56
Mama's Potato Salad, 389
Maple-Bacon Roasted Apples & Celeriac, *174,* 175
Maple-Lime Roasted Sweet Potatoes, *444,* 445
Marinated Eggplant with Green Chermoula, *238, 239*
Massaged Kale Salad with Roasted Garlic Dressing, 282
Mediterranean Cauliflower Pizza, 156, *157*
Mediterranean Roasted Broccoli & Tomatoes, *94,* 95
Mediterranean Sautéed Shrimp & Fennel, 251
Mexican Bison & Squash Stew, 424–25, *425*
Mexican Pickled Carrots, 140–41
Miso-Butter Braised Turnips, 480
Moroccan-Style Stuffed Peppers, 381
Mushroom Pâté, 307
Orange, Watercress & Tuna Salad, 489
Paprika & Red Pepper Soup with Pistachios, 377
Pear & Arugula Salad with Candied Walnuts, *24,* 25
Pear & Celery Root Slaw, 172, *173*
Peas & Lettuce, 362, *363*
Persian Cucumber Salad with Lentils & Sprouts, 228, *229*
Pickled Beets, 74, *75*
Pineapple & Avocado Salad (cooking basics), 40
Pink Grapefruit & Avocado Salad, 46, *47*
Pomegranate Molasses-Glazed Carrots with Pistachios, 137
Pork & Shrimp Stuffed Eggplant, *235,* 242–43
Pork & Turnip Miso Ramen, 482, *483*
Potatoes with Green Tahini Sauce, 386, *387*
Quick Cucumber Kimchi, 230
Quinoa Mushroom Soup, *314,* 315
Ribollita Soup, 284, *285*
Roasted Baby Bok Choy, 84, *85*
Roasted Beet Salad, *76,* 77
Roasted Cabbage with Chive-Mustard Vinaigrette, 124, *125*
Roasted Cauliflower Salad with Walnuts, *8,* 158
Roasted Cherry Tomato & Sage Sauce, 471
Roasted Corn Cheese Dip, 216, *217*
Roasted Fennel with Olive Tapenade, Feta & Mint, 250

Roasted Garlic & Asparagus Salad, 258
Roasted Radishes & Leeks with Thyme, *404, 405*
Roasted Rainbow Carrots with Sage Brown Butter, *143,* 144
Roasted Vegetable Antipasto, *116,* 117
Romaine Wedges with Sardines & Caramelized Onions, 298, *299*
Rosemary-Infused Cucumber Lemonade, 223
Sausage-&-Quinoa-Stuffed Zucchini, 421
Sautéed Brussels Sprouts with Bacon & Onions, 118
Sautéed Mushrooms with Caramelized Shallots, *309,* 310
Scrambled Eggs with Ramps & Bacon, 345
Seared Salmon with Sugar Snap-Fennel Slaw, 368, *369*
Shallot, Tarragon & Lemon Vinegar, 349
Shaved Brussels Sprouts Salad with Lemon-Chile Vinaigrette & Toasted Hazelnuts, 114, *115*
Shaved Zucchini-Fennel Salad, 418
Sicilian Eggplant Caponata, 236
Sicilian Pepper Salad, 374, *375*
Simple Green Salad with Citronette, 192, *193*
Simple Sauerkraut, 126–27
Slivered Celery Salad with Blue Cheese Dressing, 173
Snap Pea & Cherry Tomato Stir-Fry, 366
Spaghetti Squash Lasagna with Broccolini, 436, *437*
Spicy Stir-Fried String Beans, 65
Spicy Tomatillo Quinoa, *454,* 455
Spinach & Warm Mushroom Salad, 410, *411*
Spring Radish Salad, 399, *401*
Spring Salad with Peas & Frizzled Shallots, 346, *347*
Spring Turnip Frittata, *478,* 479
Stewed Okra (cooking basics), 326, *327*
Stir-Fried Chinese Broccoli, 98, *99*
Stir-Fried Mustard Greens with Eggs & Garlic, 321
String Beans & Summer Squash, 419
Summer Tomato, Onion & Cucumber Salad, *464,* 465
Sunny-Side Beans, 68, *69*
Super-Green Edamame Salad, 52, *53*
Sweet Corn Ice Cream, 219
Sweet Corn Salad, *214,* 215
Three Sisters Succotash, 64
Tuna & Bok Choy Packets, 87
Twice-Baked Potatoes with Horseradish & Caviar, 394, *395*
Two-Toned Mashed Potatoes, 446, *447*
Vegetarian Stuffed Cabbage, 131–32, *133*
Velvet Chicken with Baby Bok Choy, 86
Vietnamese-Flavored Broccoli Rabe, 105
Warm Potato Salad with Bacon-Mustard Dressing, *390,* 391
Watercress Salad with Sesame-Garlic Dressing, 487
Watercress with Rice Wine-Oyster Sauce, 488
Wild Mushroom & Polenta Casserole, 312, *313*
Winter Greens Salad with Squash & Cranberry Vinaigrette, *432,* 433
Winter Salad with Roasted Squash & Pomegranate Vinaigrette, 198, *199*
Winter Squash & Chicken Tzimmes, 435

HEART-HEALTHY

Recipes included in this list meet thresholds for saturated fat and sodium based on the guidelines for the American Heart Association (AHA) Heart-Check program and general recommendations for reduced saturated fat (≤ 7% of total calories) and reduced sodium (≤1,500 mg/day).

Artichokes, Cauliflower, Potato & Escarole Salad, 18–19
Artichokes with Lemon & Dill, 16, *17*
Bacon, Tomato & Farro Salad, 468
Braised Endive, *194*, 195
Carrot-Orange Juice, 138, *139*
Chili-Brown Sugar Delicata Squash with Pears, 434
Cider & Honey Kohlrabi Slaw with Radicchio, 289
Creamy Parsnips & Pears, 353
Crushed Red Potatoes with Winter Greens, *206*, 207
Cucumber & Radish Tzatziki, 224, *225*
Dill Pickles, 227
Fusilli with Yellow Squash & Grape Tomatoes, *422*, 423
Garlic Roasted Salmon & Brussels Sprouts, 119
Garlic Stir-Fried Snow Peas & Pea Greens, *364*, 365
Grape & Fennel Salad, 247
Green Smoothie, 278, *279*
Grilled Broccoli Rabe (cooking basics), 102, *103*
Grilled Corn (cooking basics), 212, *213*
Heirloom Tomato Salad with Fried Capers, *4*, 463
Kale Chips, *280*, 281
Lima Beans with Chorizo, 56
Maple-Lime Roasted Sweet Potatoes, *444*, 445
Massaged Kale Salad with Roasted Garlic Dressing, 282
Mexican Pickled Carrots, 140–41
Moroccan-Style Stuffed Peppers, 381
Orange, Watercress & Tuna Salad, 489
Panzanella, 466, *467*
Pear & Arugula Salad with Candied Walnuts, *24*, 25
Pear & Celery Root Slaw, 172, *173*
Peas & Lettuce, 362, *363*
Penne alla Primavera, 57
Pickled Beets, 74, *75*
Pineapple & Avocado Salad (cooking basics), 40
Pink Grapefruit & Avocado Salad, 46, *47*
Pomegranate Molasses-Glazed Carrots with Pistachios, 137
Pork & Turnip Miso Ramen, 482, *483*
Potatoes with Green Tahini Sauce, 386, *387*
Quick Cucumber Kimchi, 230
Radish Canapés with Creamy Dill Spread, 402, *403*
Roasted Baby Bok Choy, 84, *85*
Roasted Beet Salad, *76*, 77
Roasted Cauliflower Salad with Walnuts, *8*, 158
Roasted Cherry Tomato & Sage Sauce, 471
Roasted Garlic & Asparagus Salad, 258
Sautéed Mushrooms with Caramelized Shallots, *309*, 310
Seared Salmon with Sugar Snap-Fennel Slaw, 368, *369*
Shaved Brussels Sprouts Salad with Lemon-Chile Vinaigrette & Toasted Hazelnuts, 114, *115*
Sicilian Pepper Salad, 374, *375*
Simple Green Salad with Citronette, 192, *193*
Spicy Jicama & Red Onion Shoestrings with Herbed Chipotle Aioli, 272, *273*
Spicy Tomatillo Quinoa, 454, 455

Spring Radish Salad, 399, *401*
Stewed Okra (cooking basics), 326, *327*
String Beans & Summer Squash, 419
Summer Tomato, Onion & Cucumber Salad, *464*, 465
Sweet Corn Ice Cream, 219
Sweet Corn Salad, *214*, 215
Sweet Potato Pie with Cream Cheese Swirl, 448–49
Tuna & Bok Choy Packets, 87
Two-Toned Mashed Potatoes, 446, *447*
Velvet Chicken with Baby Bok Choy, 86
Winter Greens Salad with Squash & Cranberry Vinaigrette, *432*, 433
Winter Salad with Roasted Squash & Pomegranate Vinaigrette, *198*, 199
Winter Squash & Chicken Tzimmes, 435
Yuca-Scallion Mofongo, 495

VEGETARIAN & VEGAN

*Meatless (e.g., no meat, poultry or seafood) or includes meatless options and contains no ingredients derived from these meat-based products (e.g., gelatin, animal-based broths, fish or oyster sauce). These recipes may still include eggs, egg products, butter and milk or other dairy-containing products. *Recipes marked with an asterisk are also vegan, based on their omission of all animal-based products (e.g., meat, poultry, fish, milk and eggs) and ingredients from animal sources (i.e., butter, lard, gelatin, fish or oyster sauce, animal-based broths, etc.). Check the label of ingredients to make sure they do not contain any hidden sources of animal products.*

Artichoke & Parmesan Stuffed Mushrooms, 311
*Artichokes with Lemon & Dill, 16, *17*
Arugula Pesto (cooking basics), 22, *23*
Asparagus & Mushroom Risotto, 316
Asparagus-Goat Cheese Soufflés, 36, *37*
*Basic Green Soup, 186, *187*
Beer-Battered Onion Rings with Roasted Pepper Aioli, 341
*Blender Gazpacho, 469
*Braised Greens & Cannellini Bean Panini, 208, *209*
Broccoli & Tortellini Salad with Arugula Pesto, 92, *93*
Broccoli, Cauliflower & Romanesco Gratin, 159
*Broccoli Rabe with Olives & Garlic, 104, *107*
*Carrot-Orange Juice, 138, *139*
*Cauliflower Steaks with Chimichurri, 152, *153*
Chard with Green Olives, Currants & Goat Cheese, 182
Cheesy Potato Casserole, 393
Chipotle-Cheddar Broiled Avocado Halves, *44*, 45
Cider & Honey Kohlrabi Slaw with Radicchio, 289
Citrus Salad with Olives and Radicchio, 196
Coconut-Carrot Morning Glory Muffins, 146, *147*
Creamed Spinach Casserole, 413
creamy avocado dressing (cooking basics), 40
Creamy Parsnips & Pears, 353
*Creamy Rye & Butternut Squash Soup, 430, *431*
*Crispy Potatoes with Spicy Tomato Sauce, 388
Crushed Red Potatoes with Winter Greens, *206*, 207
Cucumber & Radish Tzatziki, 224, **225**
Curried Onion Dip, 340
*Dill Pickles, 227
Dill-Havarti Mashed Cauliflower, *154*, 155

Eggplant Parmesan, 240–41
*Fava Bean Puree with Chicory, 200, *201*
*Fire-Roasted Salsa, 470
*Fresh Tomatillo Salad, 456
*Fusilli with Yellow Squash & Grape Tomatoes, *422*, 423
*Garden Tomato Sauce, 472, *473*
*Garlic Scape Pesto, 256, *257*
*Garlic Stir-Fried Snow Peas & Pea Greens, *364*, 365
Goat Cheese Mashed Potatoes, 392
*Grape & Fennel Salad, 247
*Green Bean & Tommy-Toe Salad, 62, *63*
*Green Curry Soup, 412
Green Salad with Peaches, Feta & Mint Vinaigrette, *296*, 297
*Green Smoothie, 278, *279*
*Grilled Broccoli Rabe (cooking basics), 102, *103*
*Grilled Corn (cooking basics), 212, *213*
Grilled Eggplant & Baba Ghanoush, 237
*Grilled Okra & Hot Peppers, *328*, 329
*Grilled Tomatillo-Chipotle Salsa (cooking basics), 452, *453*
*Heirloom Tomato Salad with Fried Capers, *4*, 463
*Homemade Hot Sauce, 376
Indian-Style Mustard Greens & Kale with Toasted Naan, 322, *323*
*Indian-Style Sautéed Okra, 330, *331*
*Jason Mraz's Guacamole, 42, *43*
*Jicama-Apple Slaw, 271
*Kale Chips, *280*, 281
Kohlrabi-Corn Fritters with Herbed Yogurt Sauce, 290, *291*
Lemon-Garlic Yuca Mashers with Cilantro Pesto, 496, *497*
Mama's Potato Salad, 389
Maple-Lime Roasted Sweet Potatoes, *444*, 445
*Marinated Eggplant with Green Chermoula, *238*, 239
*Massaged Kale Salad with Roasted Garlic Dressing, 282
Mediterranean Cauliflower Pizza, 156, *157*
*Mediterranean Roasted Broccoli & Tomatoes, *94*, 95
*Mexican Pickled Carrots, 140–41
Mini Onion Gratins, 342, *343*
*Mushroom Pâté, 307
Not-Your-Grandma's Green Bean Casserole, 66, *67*
Oven-Fried Green Tomatillos, 457
Panko-Crusted Asparagus Spears, 32, *33*
*Panzanella, 466, *467*
Paprika & Red Pepper Soup with Pistachios, 377
*Pear & Arugula Salad with Candied Walnuts, *24*, 25
Pear & Celery Root Slaw, 172, *173*
*Peas & Lettuce, 362, *363*
Penne alla Primavera, 57
Persian Cucumber Salad with Lentils & Sprouts, 228, *229*
*Pickled Beets, 74, *75*
*Pineapple & Avocado Salad (cooking basics), 40
*Pink Grapefruit & Avocado Salad, 46, *47*
Pomegranate Molasses-Glazed Carrots with Pistachios, 137
*Potatoes with Green Tahini Sauce, 386, *387*
*Quinoa Mushroom Soup, *314*, 315
Radish Canapés with Creamy Dill Spread, 402, *403*
*Ribollita Soup, 284, *285*
*Roasted Baby Bok Choy, 84, *85*

*Roasted Beet Salad, *76, 77*
*Roasted Cabbage with Chive-Mustard
  Vinaigrette, 124, *125*
*Roasted Cauliflower Salad with Walnuts, *8,* 158
*Roasted Cherry Tomato & Sage Sauce, 471
Roasted Corn Cheese Dip, 216, *217*
Roasted Fennel with Olive Tapenade, Feta &
  Mint, 250
*Roasted Garlic & Asparagus Salad, 258
Roasted Garlic & Leek Bread Casserole, 344
Roasted Radishes & Leeks with Thyme, *404,* 405
Roasted Rainbow Carrots with Sage Brown
  Butter, *143,* 144
Roasted Stuffed Pumpkin, 438–39
*Roasted Sweet Potato Wedges (cooking
  basics), *442, 443*
*Roasted Vegetable Antipasto, *116,* 117
*Rosemary-Infused Cucumber Lemonade, 223
*Shallot, Tarragon & Lemon Vinegar, 349
Shaved Brussels Sprouts Salad with Lemon-Chile
  Vinaigrette & Toasted Hazelnuts, 114, *115*
Shaved Zucchini-Fennel Salad, 418
Sicilian Eggplant Caponata, 236
*Sicilian Pepper Salad, 374, *375*
*Simple Green Salad with Citronette, 192, *193*
*Simple Sauerkraut, 126–27
Slivered Celery Salad with Blue Cheese
  Dressing, 163
*Snap Pea & Cherry Tomato Stir-Fry, 366
Spaghetti Squash Lasagna with
  Broccolini, 436, *437*
Spicy Jicama & Red Onion Shoestrings with
  Herbed Chipotle Aioli, 272, *273*
*Spicy Stir-Fried String Beans, 65
*Spring Radish Salad, 399, *401*
Spring Salad with Peas & Frizzled
  Shallots, 346, *347*
Spring Turnip Frittata, *478,* 479
*Stewed Okra (cooking basics), 326, *327*
*Stir-Fried Chinese Broccoli, 98, *99*
Summer Tomato, Onion & Cucumber
  Salad, *464,* 465
Sunny-Side Beans, 68, *69*
*Super-Green Edamame Salad, 52, *53*
Sweet Corn Salad, *214,* 215
Sweet Potato Pie with Cream Cheese Swirl, 448–49
Three Sisters Succotash, 64
Two-Toned Mashed Potatoes, 446, *447*
*Vegetarian Stuffed Cabbage, 131–32, *133*
*Watercress & Citrus Tabbouleh, 490, *491*
*Watercress with Rice Wine-Oyster Sauce, 488
*White Gazpacho, 226
Wild Mushroom & Polenta Casserole, 312, *313*
Wild Mushroom Pizza with Arugula &
  Pecorino, 26, *27*
Winter Greens Salad with Squash & Cranberry
  Vinaigrette, *432,* 433
*Winter Salad with Roasted Squash & Pomegranate
  Vinaigrette, 198, *199*
Zucchini Bread Pancakes, 420

CONTRIBUTORS

CONTRIBUTORS

Our thanks to these fine food writers whose work was previously published in *EatingWell* magazine.

Bruce Aidells: Bavarian Leek & Cabbage Soup, 130; Fire-Roasted Salsa, 470; Mexican Bison & Squash Stew, 424; Pork & Shrimp Stuffed Eggplant, 242

Lidia Bastianich: Braised Greens & Cannellini Bean Panini, 208; Ribollita Soup, 284; Simple Green Salad with Citronette, 192

Mario Batali: Penne alla Primavera, 57

Jane Black: Fava Bean Puree with Chicory, 200; Orecchiette with Broccoli Rabe, 108

David Bonom: Asparagus & Mushroom Risotto, 316; Moroccan-Style Stuffed Peppers, 381

Danielle Centoni: Heirloom Tomato Salad with Fried Capers, 463

Mary Cleaver: Maple-Lime Roasted Sweet Potatoes, 445

Lyle Davis & Sylvia R. Tawse: Grilled Eggplant & Baba Ghanoush, 237; Sicilian Pepper Salad, 374; Sweet Corn Salad, 215

Dave DeWitt: South Texas Steak Fajitas, 379

Eula Mae Doré: Seafood Gumbo, 332

Naomi Duguid: Fish Sauce with Chiles, 372

Tyler Florence: Roasted Fennel with Olive Tapenade, Feta & Mint, 248

Darra Goldstein: Pineapple & Avocado Salad, 40

Joyce Goldstein: Artichokes, Cauliflower, Potato & Escarole Salad, 18; Green Salad with Peaches, Feta & Mint Vinaigrette, 297

Kathy Gunst: Garlic Scape Pesto, 257; Garlic Stir-Fried Snow Peas & Pea Greens, 365; Roasted Cabbage with Chive-Mustard Vinaigrette, 124; Roasted Garlic & Asparagus Salad, 258; Simple Sauerkraut, 126; Sole with Garlic-Almond-Caper Sauce, 259; Vegetarian Stuffed Cabbage, 131

Jessica B. Harris: Stewed Okra, 326

Giuliano Hazan: Fusilli with Yellow Squash & Grape Tomatoes, 423

Joyce Hendley: Borscht with Beef, 78

Emily Horton: Creamy Rye & Butternut Squash Soup, 430; Panzanella, 466; Roasted Garlic & Leek Bread Casserole, 344

Lia Huber: Two-Toned Mashed Potatoes, 448

Raghavan Iyer: Paprika & Red Pepper Soup with Pistachios, 377

Nancy Harmon Jenkins: Broccoli Rabe with Olives & Garlic, 104; Sicilian Eggplant Caponata, 236

Barbara Kafka: Peas & Lettuce, 362

Lori Longbotham: Orange, Watercress & Tuna Salad, 489; Pink Grapefruit & Avocado Salad, 46

Ronni Lundy: Green Bean & Tommy-Toe Salad, 62; Sunny-Side Beans, 68; Three Sisters Succotash, 64

Deborah Madison: Roasted Sweet Potato Wedges, 442

Ivy Manning: Quinoa Mushroom Soup, 315

April McGreger: Mexican Pickled Carrots, 140

Jason Mraz: Jason Mraz's Guacamole, 42

Michel Nischan: Sautéed Mushrooms with Caramelized Shallots, 310

Ellen Ecker Ogden: Dandelion Salad with Goat Cheese & Tomato Dressing, 302

Odessa Piper: Goat Cheese Mashed Potatoes, 392

Jamie Purviance: Quick Cucumber Kimchi, 230

Victoria Abbott Riccardi: Asparagus-Goat Cheese Soufflés, 36; Lima Beans with Chorizo, 56; Panko-Crusted Asparagus Spears, 32

Roberto Santibañez: Grilled Tomatillo-Chipotle Salsa, 452

Bill Scepansky: Broccoli, Cauliflower & Romanesco Gratin, 159; Winter Greens Salad with Squash & Cranberry Vinaigrette, 433

Bjorn Shen: Stir-Fried Mustard Greens with Eggs & Garlic, 321

Marie Simmons: Celery & Parmesan Minestrone, 166; Slivered Celery Salad with Blue Cheese Dressing, 163

Michael Solomonov: Marinated Eggplant with Green Chermoula, 239; Potatoes with Green Tahini Sauce, 386; Roasted Beet Salad, 77; Roasted Cauliflower Salad with Walnuts, 158

Romney Steele: Persian Cucumber Salad with Lentils & Sprouts, 228; Winter Salad with Roasted Squash & Pomegranate Vinaigrette, 198

Molly Stevens: Cauliflower Steaks with Chimichurri, 152; Mediterranean Cauliflower Pizza, 156

Anna Thomas: Basic Green Soup, 186; Green Curry Soup, 412

Alice Waters: Sautéed Brussels Sprouts with Bacon & Onions, 118

Katie Webster: Arugula Pesto, 22; Coconut-Carrot Morning Glory Muffins, 146; Kale Salad with Bacon-Blue Cheese Vinaigrette, 283; Romaine Wedges with Sardines & Caramelized Onions, 298; Super-Green Edamame Salad, 52

Bruce Weinstein & Mark Scarbrough: Winter Squash & Chicken Tzimmes, 435

Cathy Whims: Wild Mushroom & Polenta Casserole, 312; Wild Mushroom Pizza with Arugula & Pecorino, 26

Virginia Willis: Mama's Potato Salad, 389; Roasted Stuffed Pumpkin with Spiced Pumpkin Seeds, 438; Summer Tomato, Onion & Cucumber Salad, 465

Grace Young: Velvet Chicken with Baby Bok Choy, 86; Stir-Fried Chinese Broccoli, 98; Watercress Salad with Sesame-Garlic Dressing, 487; Watercress with Rice Wine-Oyster Sauce, 488